The Politics of
Multiculturalism

The Politics of Multiculturalism

Multicultural Governance in Comparative Perspective

Augie Fleras

THE POLITICS OF MULTICULTURALISM
Copyright © Augie Fleras, 2009.

First published in 2009 by PALGRAVE MACMILLAN® in the
United States - a division of St. Martin's Press LLC, 175 Fifth Avenue,
New York, NY 10010.

Where this book is distributed in the UK, Europe and the rest of
the world, this is by Palgrave Macmillan, a division of Macmillan
Publishers Limited, registered in England, company number 785998,
of Houndmills, Basingstoke, Hampshire RG21 6XS.

Palgrave Macmillan is the global academic imprint of the above
companies and has companies and representatives throughout the world.

Palgrave® and Macmillan® are registered trademarks in the United
States, the United Kingdom, Europe and other countries.

ISBN: 978–0–230–60454–4

Library of Congress Cataloging-in-Publication Data
Fleras, Augie, 1947–
    The politics of multiculturalism : multicultural governance
    in comparative perspective / Augie Fleras.
        p.   cm.
    Includes bibliographical references and index.
    ISBN-13: 978–0–230–60454–4 (alk. paper)
    ISBN-10: 0–230–60454–4 (alk. paper)
    1. Multiculturalism—Political aspects—Cross-cultural studies.
    2. Ethnicity—Political aspects—Cross-cultural studies.
    3. Comparative government.   I. Title.
    HM1271.F55 2009
    320.08—dc22   2008055637

Design by Integra Software Services

First edition: September 2009

10 9 8 7 6 5 4 3 2 1

Printed in the United States of America

Contents

Preface   vii

1 Multiculturalisms as Governance: Principles and Paradoxes,
   Policies and Perspectives   1
2 Theorizing Multicultural Governances: Making Society
   Safe from Difference, Safe for Difference   23
3 Managing Difference, Making a Difference:
   Multiculturalism as Inclusive Governance in Canada   55
4 Multiculturalisms in the United States: Multicultural
   Governances, American Style   89
5 Multiculturalisms "Down Under": Multicultural
   Governances across Australia   113
6 Contesting Governances in Aotearoa New Zealand:
   Monoculturalism, Biculturalism, Multiculturalism, and
   Binationalism   129
7 Dutch Multiculturalism: Unsettling Multicultural
   Governance in the Netherlands   147
8 Multiculturalism in Britain: Contesting Multiculturalisms,
   Evolving Governances   165
9 The Politics of Multicultural Politics: Transatlantic Divides,
   Intercontinental Discourses   187
10 Reconstitutionalizing Multiculturalism: Governance
   Pathways for the Twenty-first Century   203

Bibliography   225

Index   267

Preface

The optics are not looking good. From the Americas to the Antipodes by way of the European Union, a commitment to multiculturalism is undergoing a harrowing decline. Having outworn its welcome and apparently outlived its usefulness, multicultural models of governance are increasingly maligned as a good idea gone bad or, alternatively, a wretchedly defined project unfolding according to plan. Multiculturalism as governance may have originated as a political project to advance national interests by depoliticizing differences. At present, however, the politics of governance are shifting toward anti-multiculturalism, if only to abort the drift into divisiveness or threat of extremism. Even in the country that invented it, Canada, multiculturalism is sometimes criticized as mushiness or menace—little more than a bloated legacy from a cloyingly interventionist Trudeau era (Granastein 2007; Kay 2008). In short, a broadly based narrative crisis has emerged—often without much awareness of the complex histories of ambivalence and incoherence that informed multicultural projects—that criticizes multiculturalism as a failed experiment with a misplaced emphasis on differences over commonality, diversity over cohesion, and separation over solidarity (Lentin and Titley 2009).

But before interring the corpse of multiculturalism, a few questions are in order. If multiculturalism has outlived its usefulness, why was it so useful in the first place? If multiculturalism is dying, what is it dying of—rejection? flaws? indifference? backlash? expediency? misinformation? improper definition? If multiculturalism is not working, who says so, why, on what grounds, and upon whose standards of success or failure (Lentin and Titley 2009; Reitz 2009)? Or to paraphrase Hurriyet Babican (2006) has multiculturalism failed society or has society failed multicultural principles?Is multiculturalism floundering because of increasingly politicized diversity, or because the interplay of global terrorism with the politicization of faith-based minority groups fosters an antimulticulturalism (Kymlicka 2005; Hage 2006; Parekh 2008)? Is it unfairly scapegoated because of a mistaken tendency to conflate multiculturalism with the sins of immigration or the costs of integration failures, in addition to links with emotionally charged debates over cultural relativism, international human rights, racism, accommodation, belonging, and citizenship (Siddiqui 2007)? And if not the principles and practices of multiculturalism for the governance of diversity and living together with difference, what then? It is within this interrogative context of challenge and opportunity that *The Politics of Multiculturalism* justifies its excursion into the undertheorized realm of multicultural governance along comparative lines.

In the "security-conscious" post-9/11 and 7/7 era, the politics of multiculturalism is contesting the legitimacy and logic of multicultural governance, with some saying yes, others insisting on no, and still others confused or indifferent. For some, a commitment to multiculturalism constitutes an unmitigated recipe for disaster; for others, a blueprint for success; and for yet others, a two-edged phenomenon with costs and/or benefits depending on context or criteria. In looking to navigate around these tricky shoals of the good versus the bad by way of the in-between, *The Politics of Multiculturalism* employs a comparative perspective to analyze and assess the multicultural management of diversity and difference in Canada and the United States, Australia and New Zealand, and Britain and the Netherlands (also Panossian et al. 2007; Koenig and de Guchteneire 2007). Attention is focused on how and why a shift toward multiculturalism as governance evolved—then devolved—in many of the jurisdictions under study. Particular attention focuses on explaining the popularity and persistence of multiculturalism as a long-term investment in some jurisdictions but not in others. In addressing these controversies, the book grapples with a central dilemma regarding the future of multiculturalism: What can be done to realign patterns of multicultural governance in ways that promote the *social* (redistribution) with the *cultural* (recognition) without imperiling the *national* (integration) (also Asari et al. 2008)?

The book's main line of argument unfolds as follows: In contrast to assimilationist or separatist templates of the past, an inclusive multicultural governance appears better positioned to achieve social cohesion and economic integration, secure positive identities and meaningful citizenship, and avoid ethnic strife (also Koenig 1999). This assertion—that an inclusive multicultural governance can enhance cooperative coexistence—reinforces the centrality of core topics in this book, including (1) the relation of multiculturalism to a multicultural governance; (2) conceptual gaps between multicultural ideals (what it purports to do) and governance realities (what it really does); (3) how debates over difference are playing politics with the principles and practice of multiculturalism; (4) the rationale behind political/state responses to minority claims-making activities for respecting difference and removing disadvantage (Triandafyllidou et al. 2006); and (5) the prospects and pitfalls of implementing a multicultural governance. Admittedly, ensuing debates over the pros and cons of multiculturalism rarely yield a consensus about preferred models of multi-cultural governance (Choudhry 2007; Kunz and Sykes 2008). Nevertheless, a dearth of consensus in sorting through the yeas and the nays and the maybes is not entirely detrimental. Such open-endedness not only provides the catalyst for this comparative study of multicultural governance; it also secures "wiggle room" for exploring alternative governance frameworks by realigning critically informed responses with contested realities.

Aimed at scholars as well as the nonspecialists, *The Politics of Multiculturalism* strives to be scholarly without being impenetrable, descriptive without abandoning analysis and comparison. The objective of this book is twofold: (1) to establish a blueprint for analyzing the politics of multi-cultural governance along cross-national contexts and (2) to formulate a theoretical framework for conceptualizing the politics of multiculturalism in establishing an inclusive governance. Three important caveats prevail as well. First, this book addresses the politics of multiculturally man-aging immigrant (or ethnic) difference in those wealthy societies where constitutional primacy reflects the political norms of liberal democracy and individual rights (also Modood 2007). A commitment to multicultur-alism endorses varying governance initiatives in these domains, ranging from immigration settlement to antiracist initiatives, from accommo-dating collective rights claims to challenging the internal organization and cultural neutrality of state institutions, from moves for advanc-ing gender and sexual orientation equality to fostering a framework for what Leeuwen (2008) calls everyday multiculturalism, including those affective-dynamic aspects involving the daily rhythms of social life. To the extent this book embraces a macro orientation (the "big picture") rather than a micro orientation ("street-level multiculturalism"), emphasis is drawn toward Multiculturalism with a capital *M* rather than a lower-case multiculturalism.

Second, *The Politics of Multiculturalism* addresses the concerns of migrants and minorities rather than the exclusionary politics of nation-hood (McGarry and O'Leary 2007). With its focus on institutional inclu-siveness, the multicultural governance of immigrants and descendants of immigrants prevails over the sovereignty politics of national minorities or indigenous peoples. The rationale for this distinction is readily defended: With the exception of New Zealand, where multicultural discourses are inextricably conjoined with debates over biculturalism, the politics of "isms" reflects foundationally different discursive frameworks (Maaka and Fleras 2005). In conceding that different kinds of difference pose fun-damentally diverse challenges and responses, in effect reinforcing those governance frameworks that acknowledge different ways of acknowledging difference and diversity, this book explores the politics of multiculturalism at the level of migrants and minorities. Attention is directed at multiculturalism as governance that responds to the demands of ethnic, linguistic, religious, and cultural differences, and does so in ways that foster inclusiveness, difference, and equity without bankrupting national interests (also Choudhry 2008).

Third, the book avoids the trap of collapsing multiculturalism into the singular (Kymlicka 2004/2007). Rather than a single doctrine or achieved state of affairs, the opposite is true: Neither a unitary multiculturalism model that applies cross-nationally nor a universal experience of multicultural governance is known to exist (Sandercock 2003; Nye 2007). In acknowledging the folly of a one-size-fits-all model applicable to all places and times (Rex and Singh 2004), despite the possibility of recurrent themes, references to multiculturalism as governance are shown to vary accordingly: To one side are official versions (such as Canada and Australia) that openly abide by multicultural principles, policies, and programs for living together with difference. To the other side are those de facto multiculturalisms (including the United States and New Zealand) whose underlying logic must be inferred from the varied programs and local initiatives that are multicultural in everything but name. As well, there are the quasi-official multiculturalisms in Britain and the Netherlands, where an explicit commitment to multicultural principles and practices can be discerned, but without statutory basis or constitutional recognition to anchor or authorize it. In all cases, references to multiculturalism can subsume a wide variety of messy processes and conflicting politics that rarely comply with the normative ideals of political theory or official policy. Finally, policies and programs may unwittingly promote multiculturalism without being labeled as such, especially with the drift toward civic integration as preferred governance model in a growing number of European societies.

In that multicultural discourses are not cut from the same discursive cloth, but historically conditioned and situationally specific, this book is comparative rather than evaluative (Bousetta and Jacobs 2006). In terms of organization, the first two chapters establish a framework for analyzing multiculturalism as an instrument of multicultural governance. Chapter 1 deconstructs the concept of multiculturalisms as governance with respect to principles, policies, paradoxes, and perspectives. Different models of multiculturalism are explored, in the process exposing the gap between multicultural rhetorics (what it says it's doing) and multicultural realities (what it's really doing) in advancing an inclusive governance (Berman 2007; Panossian et al. 2007). Chapter 2 theorizes multicultural governances in terms of assumptions, objectives, and outcomes. The role of multiculturalism in depoliticizing difference is shown to be critical in constructing patterns of multicultural governance that makes society safe from difference, safe for difference Chapter 2.

The last two chapters focus on discussing in an analytic and critical way the multiculturalism in a multicultural governance. The chapters revolve around a seeming paradox: In a relatively short period of time, governments in Europe and the Antipodes have deliberately discarded multiculturalism from policy vocabularies and national discourses (IMISCOE 2006). Canada, by contrast, continues to vigorously embrace a robust multiculturalism, in effect prompting inquiries into its popularity and persistence. By comparatively analyzing governance patterns, the book addresses what works, what doesn't, and why. To be sure, constructing a definitive model of multicultural governance is not a primary goal; nor is the articulation of principles and vocabulary for implementation and enforcement (Robinson 2007). Nonetheless, even if the focus is explanatory rather than evaluative or prescriptive, there is much of value that can be gleaned by improving the design of multicultural governances for doing what is workable, necessary, and fair (Hagan 2006).

In between these introductory and concluding chapters, the book explores the politics of multiculturalism in classic immigrant countries like Canada, the United States, Australia, and New Zealand, in addition to so-called historically complete societies, the Netherlands and Britain (see Castles and Miller 2003). Each of the countries under study is shown to have evolved diverse multicultural discourses, agendas, and programs, with Canada and Australia demonstrating strong multicultural orientations, in contrast to the more moderate expressions of multicultural governance in New Zealand, the United States, the Netherlands, and the United Kingdom (Banting and Kymlicka 2006; Banting 2008) . With the possible exception of Canada, however, each has also revamped its governance agenda along the lines of integration, cohesion, and citizenship, without abandoning a commitment to inclusiveness (but see Kunz and Sykes 2008; Libin 2009). Last, all of the substantive chapters discuss how and why the multiculturalism is—or is not—experiencing an identity crisis (what is it) and a crisis of confidence (what should it be doing). Insofar as these crises may prove opportunistic in consolidating the principles of an inclusive multicultural governance, in part by making society safe from difference, safe for difference, *The Politics of Multiculturalism* is unmistakably optimistic in tone and outlook.

I

Multiculturalisms as Governance: Principles and Paradoxes, Policies and Perspectives

Introduction: A Contested Domain

Of the conceptual tripwires and cultural landmines strewn across the Western landscape in recent years, few have triggered as much vitriol or controversy as multiculturalism (Possner 1997; Day 2000; Gilroy 2004). Timing in particular has played politics with a modernist project that many regard as passé for the post-9/11 (and 7/7 in London) realities of the twenty-first century. Multiculturalism as a popular and political discourse may have originated in an era of optimism and reform but is badly listing at present because of concerns over security or instability (Rex and Singh 2004; also Gregg 2006). What started out as a society-building idea with noble intentions has morphed into a flashpoint for tension. On one side are advocates who continue to worship at the altar of multiculturalism; on another side are those who recoil at the very prospect of foisting on an unsuspecting public even more insecurity and insincerity; on yet another side are growing concerns over its role in eroding a sense of belonging that ensures minority attachment and loyalty; and on still another side are critics who sneer at something so irrelevant or counterproductive (see Ley 2005; Pearce 2006).

To say we inhabit a multicultural world is surely an assertion—and a provocation—of understated proportions (Kymlicka 2007d; Moghaddam 2008). Until recently, the new world order (which had replaced the difference-aversive old world order of conformity and homogeneity) pivoted around diversity discourses, including immigrant-driven demographic changes, an emergent politics of difference, an adherence to multiculturalism as blueprint for cooperative coexistence, and the codification of multicultural principles into a inclusive governance. But the moral panics of the post-9/11 epoch have contested the status and role of multiculturalism, with assessments ranging from apoplectic hostility to puzzled perplexity. Against this backdrop of vilification or vexation, questions abound:

- Can multiculturalism provide a bulwark against the sense of alienation and exclusion that may motivate disaffected second-generation immigrant youth into antisocial activities?
- Is multiculturalism a move toward a meaningful alternative? Or, as an assimilation in slow motion, is it a cynical ploy to paper over contradictions behind a façade of well-intentioned platitudes?
- How potent is multiculturalism as an instrument of change? Does it promise more than it can deliver (metaphorically speaking, a sheep hiding in wolf's clothing) or, alternatively, is it more of a threat than it's willing to say (that is, a metaphorical wolf camouflaged in sheep clothing) (Fleras 2007)?
- Is multiculturalism accountable for a host of integration failures (Jakubowicz 2007; Siddiqui 2007; also Biles and Spoonley 2007)? Or does scapegoating multiculturalism give it more (dis)credit than it deserves (Terkessidis 2007).
- To what extent has deference to those multiculturalisms that failed to lay down the law or to draw the line resulted in the emergence of parallel communities or illiberal practices? Of particular concern is a multicultural paradox: that the very act of defining people as 'minorities' to defend their rights may well have the perverse effect of not only segregating them from the mainstream but also creating more communal tension and less integration (Abbas 2005).
- Which dimension of multiculturalism should prevail: the cultural (who decides what counts as difference, what differences count?), the social (ensuring equal treatment and treatment as equals), or the national (making society safe from difference, safe for difference)?
- Is the widespread rejection of multiculturalism as governance a case of mistaken semantics or a substantive transformation in defining a living together with differences?

The conclusion bears closer scrutiny: Multiculturalism as a governance discourse is subject to doubts, disagreements, and debates (Grillo 2007). Just as diversity politics and the politics of difference rarely evoke any semblance of consensus or consistency, so too are references to multiculturalism racked with internal inconsistencies over objectives, premises, process, and outcomes. Responses will vary depending on (a) the frame of reference (official multiculturalism versus popular multiculturalism), (b) the distinction between the general (multiculturalism as the informal, the interpersonal, the contextual) and the specific (Multiculturalism as the formal, the official, the principled), (c) the level of analysis (micro versus macro), (d) a proposed model of multiculturalism (mosaic or arboreal or orbit or tossed salad or kaleidoscope), and (e) the contribution of minorities in achieving this vision (positive or negative). Contributing to the varying responses is the discursive disconnect between the ideal and the real: What does multiculturalism say it's doing, and is this consistent with what it's really doing, what people think it's doing or should do, and what realistically it can do under the circumstances? In that multiculturalism can mean everything, yet nothing because of the reality gap, its status as a "solution" in search of a "problem" is solidified.

Contradictions abound in such a contested domain: On the one hand, multiculturalism may inadvertently encourage the very divisiveness it hoped to avoid; on the other, it may unwittingly end up reinforcing the very assimilation it hoped to discourage. To one side, multiculturalism espouses modernism by advancing a multicultural governance in which everyone is treated equally (i.e., the same) regardless of race or ethnicity because everyone is equal before the law (Dustin 2007). To the other, it appears to be antimodern (or postmodern) in privileging difference over sameness, particularly in contexts where people must be treated *as equals* ("differently") to ensure inclusion and equality. In rejecting the notion of multicultural governance as an unbending mosaic of paint-by-number cultural tiles, postmodernism envisions society as the interplay of multiple identities, hybridic cultures, and conflicting poses (Modood 2007). It remains to be seen if a postmodern multicultural governance can address the ever-changing terrain of identity politics and contested ethnicities.

This chapter focuses on conceptualizing multiculturalism as a principled—official or state—response to the governance of diversity and difference. It emphasizes the theorizing of an official multiculturalism with respect to principles, policies, models, and perspectives, in the process exposing multiculturalism's uncanny knack of *rarely meaning what it says, rarely saying what it means.* The chapter begins by looking at the characteristics and contradictions that inform the contested domain of multiculturalism. It addresses debates over its contemporary relevance, especially in societies that are rapidly changing and increasingly interconnected because of globalization, postmodernism, and the human rights agenda. Different models of multiculturalism as governance are discussed as well, including conservative, liberal, and plural models, each of which ideally purports to be distinctive because of foundationally diverse assumptions and projections. Exploring different models of multiculturalism provides a conceptual framework for analyzing multicultural governance in democratic societies. The chapter concludes by surveying the more common criticisms of official multiculturalism, thus acknowledging what many already know: that living together differently and equitably is a complex and paradoxical challenge that rarely yields consensus or contentment. In that an official multiculturalism represents a principled response to this paradox, attention must focus on what's really going on and why.

Theorizing (Official) Multiculturalism

The multiculturalism paradox: Not meaning what it says, not saying what it means

The dearth of consensus over multiculturalism as governance—what, why, and how—makes it abundantly clear: a theorizing of official multiculturalism has proven an enigmatic and elusive exercise, in large part because multiculturalism, by definition, encourages a range of opinions outside of mainstream discourses (Willett 1998). For some, multiculturalism is about conditions of racial and ethnic diversity because of immigration, including support for cultural differences; for others, it consists of policies and programs for managing this diversity such as removing hostility and discriminatory barriers; and for yet others, a remaking of the public sphere to advance a vision of a tolerant, equitable and inclusive society (Fleras 2002; Forbes 2009). Like postmodernism, multiculturalism appears aversive to normative theorizing, preferring instead to be defined by what it isn't. In doing so, it seeks to interrogate (or deconstruct) dominant systems of meaning, hegemonic versions of knowledge and truth, and absolutist claims to moral authority. Political and philosophical debates over multiculturalism are so fractured—ranging from questions of how to balance collective rights with individual freedoms, to debates over establishing a framework for equality between groups without sacrificing individual rights within groups—as to short-circuit any possible consensus. Such a spectrum of perspectives and applications may provide ample grist for discussion and debate; nevertheless, it complicates the prospect of theorizing an official (or state) multiculturalism (Willet 1998).

Any theorizing of multiculturalism must begin by acknowledging different levels of meaning, namely, multiculturalism as *empirical fact*; multiculturalism as *ideology*; multiculturalism as *policy* and *program*;

multiculturalism as *practice*; and multicultural as *counterhegemony* (Fleras 2002).

- Few have difficulty in equating multiculturalism with an empirical reality. The world we inhabit is demographically diverse because of global migration patterns that show few signs of diminishing in the foreseeable future. In a multicultural society, people with diverse ethnic backgrounds must live, work, and interact with each together by learning to tolerate and accept those who are ethnically different.
- Much more contentious are notions of multiculturalism as ideology (or philosophy), including a set of ideas and normative ideals for balancing minority rights with national interests and the public good. As many have noted, the term *multicultural* constitutes an adjective referring to ethnocultural diversity; the term *multiculturalism* represents a normative response to this fact, together with a belief in the righteousness of respecting cultural differences and promoting social equality as a positive basis for society building and living together.
- Another level of theorizing is embodied by multiculturalism as policy and program. Governments (or states) around the world have capitalized on the principles of multiculturalism (however they may be defined) to construct official frameworks for advancing the social and the cultural without imperiling the national. Whereas an everyday or lived multiculturalism entails the mixing and merging (hybridizing) of cultural forms, an official multiculturalism (as state policy) often endorses a mosaic of fixed identities and identifiable ethnicities (Huijsers 2004).
- Multiculturalism as practice constitutes a fourth semantic level. In acknowledging the convergence of policy and philosophy at a grounded level, multiculturalism as practice involves its application by politicians, minorities, and institutions across a broad range of activities.
- As counterhegemony, multiculturalism as critique challenges the Eurocentrism that underpins the racialized foundational principles of a liberal constitutional order (Shohat and Stam 1994), thus providing the ideological infrastructure for multicultural social movements. Particularly in the United States, multiculturalism is often associated with identity politics rooted in the experiences of blacks, gays, women and other marginalized groups whose realities are structured by discourses of victimization (Hjort 1999; also McDonald and Quell 2008). However, since the book addresses the multiculturalisms in a multicultural governance rather than multiculturalism in general, the concept of counter-hegemony will receive less attention.

Official multiculturalism, multiculturalism as governance

An official multiculturalism is clearly consistent with a policy domain. In contrast to ideological multiculturalism with its focus on idealizing governance patterns (Gagnon and Iacovino 2007), a state-based multiculturalism is concerned with putting these principles into policy. To be sure, the link between philosophical ideals and official policy is often fraught with ambiguity; after all, what sounds good in theory may prove neither implementable nor workable. As policy, moreover, multiculturalism often represents an aspirational discourse for establishing idealistic standards of cooperative coexistence. Nevertheless, as a normative vision for governing diversity and difference, in addition to those policies and programs for achieving this political ideal, a commitment to multiculturalism advocates the once unthinkable: the promotion of an inclusive governance around the legitimacy of difference as different yet equal. A policy framework establishes the full and equal participation of minorities through removal of discriminatory barriers, while creation of cultural space confirms a minority right to be treated equally (the same) as a matter of course, yet to be treated as equals (differently) when circumstances dictate.

Inasmuch as multiculturalism pushes society to constructively engage differences without collapsing into anarchy in the process, its constitutional status as governance is widely acknowledged. And yet, except as criticism over its potential or shortcomings, both real and perceived, the theorizing of multiculturalism as governance is often overlooked (but see Rex and Singh 2004; Kymlicka 2008). One reason lies in applying a relatively new concept (governance) to multiculturalism. Another reason reflects the elusiveness of multiculturalism as a single comprehensive or theorizable reality. Rather than a finished product or singular project, multiculturalism as governance constitutes a multipronged response to circumstances and challenges that differ over time and across space (Hall 2000; Nye 2007). In acknowledging multiculturalism as context dependent instead of a universal formula (contextual rather than categorical), questions arise over the commensurability of multiculturalisms for discussion or application along comparative lines. Yet commensurate or not, consensus or not, approve or disapprove, all democratically diverse societies must address the challenges of constructing an inclusive governance for living together. They also confront an inescapable multicultural conundrum: managing difference by making society safe *from* diversity politics and the politics of difference while making society safe *for* diversity and difference (Schlesinger 1992).

In striving for a multiculturally informed governance, one question looms larger than others: how to construct a cohesive yet prosperous society without undermining either its interconnectedness or the integrity of its constituent parts (May 2004). Nowhere is the challenge more contested than in immigrant societies—those that regulate the intake of immigrants, see immigrants as a society-building asset, expect immigrants to take out citizenship, and endorse programs like multiculturalism or employment equity (affirmative action) for improving newcomer integration (Ucarer 1997; Fleras 2009). The inextricable link between immigration and multiculturalism underscores their centrality for governance building. Three multicultural building blocks can be discerned in constructing an immigrant-driven governance: (a) rejecting the idea of the state as the exclusive domain of a dominant group; (b) replacing exclusionary governance with a commitment to accommodation; and (c) acknowledging the importance of difference to state building (see Kymlicka 2004/2007).

No less critical in theorizing multiculturalism is its status as a tool of control and containment. Put bluntly the multiculturalism in a multicultural governance is primarily a political instrument to achieve political goals in a politically acceptable manner (Peter 1978; Ahmed 2000). In that it's all about "ruling elites" controlling "unruly ethnics," the fundamental logic underlying an official multiculturalism is patently pragmatic, with national and vested interests prevailing over ancilliary concerns (Bader 2007a). Because an official multiculturalism is primarily a hegemonic discourse in defense of dominant ideology, it constitutes a clever branding strategy for conflict resolution and impression management—all in defense of a racialized status quo. As observers of the Canadian scene have noted (Mackey 1998; Bannerji 2000; Thobani 2007), multiculturalism originated in response to the crisis of legitimacy over consent and consensus, in effect helping to reinvent Canada by recasting its national identity as a tolerant and inclusive liberal democracy that differs from its colonial past and its American neighbor (also Kim 2004).

Of particular relevance to this hegemonic project is the "cooling out" of troublesome constituents. In masking white supremacist order while muting the deeply entrenched conflicts of race and power, the inception of multiculturalism as governance fostered the illusions of change and inclusiveness, without substantially disrupting racialized patterns of power and privilege (Thobani 2007). To be sure, a state multiculturalism is not only about containment and control. National and vested interests are counterbalanced by a commitment to social equality and cultural recognition, although, paradoxically, the attainment of these commitments may consolidate patterns of control. Nevertheless, insofar as multiculturalism reflects, reinforces, and advances both state and vested interests, the conclusion is inescapable: multiculturalism as governance involves an exercise in depoliticizing difference by co-opting diversity into the realm of the acceptable and non-threatening (also Lentin and Titley 2008).

An exercise in political hegemony? An enlightened program for living together with differences? A euphemism for tolerance and reasonable accommodation? A scapegoat for the sins of society? A solution in search of a problem (or vice versa!)? A pragmatic investment in doing what is workable, necessary, and fair? Answers to these questions not only foster more questions, but also capture the contradictions in theorizing multiculturalism as governance, including the following conceptual tensions:

- If official multiculturalism is a solution, what is the problem? If the problem is multiculturalism, what is the solution?
- Is multiculturalism about creating a governance in which diversities can live together by minimizing differences while emphasizing commonalities? Or is multiculturalism concerned with creating a governance in which differences are taken seriously as a basis for cooperative coexistence?
- In addressing the problem of inequality and exclusion, should multiculturalism focus on culture-conscious pluralism (differences) or culture-blind participation (similarities)? Does equality arise from ignoring differences and treating everyone the same (equally) regardless of differences or, alternatively, by recognizing differences and treating people differently when required (as equals) (UNDP 2004)?
- Is multiculturalism about difference (culture) or disadvantage (equality)? About recognition (culture) or redistribution (equality) Does multiculturalism celebrate differences in hopes of removing disadvantage? Or does it emphasize the removal of discriminatory barriers as a precondition to respecting differences? Is multiculturalism a travesty when it focuses on culture rather than on social justice and citizenship rights (Barry 2001; Ramadan 2008)? Or is it too much to ask of multiculturalism to address those inequities of power and privilege that are so deeply embedded in the design and dynamics of a racialized and gendered society (and institutions) that many are unaware of the systemic biases that advantage some, marginalize others (Wallis and Fleras 2009)?
- Is multiculturalism primarily a theory of political inclusion and equal citizenship when it privileges the politics of culture over socioeconomic integration (Bloemraad 2007). Conversely, is it a discourse about socioeconomic integration by enhancing the participation of those whose cultural differences disadvantage them?

- Is multiculturalism a paternalistic top-down solution to the problem of minorities and difference? Or should it be framed as the political outcome of ongoing power struggles and collective negotiations that are reshaping the public spheres and civil societies around contested notions of citizenship, nationality, and identity (Modood and Werbner 1997).

- What are the behavioral assumptions behind multiculturalism? Do assumptions about human behaviour and inter-group dynamics contribute to or detract from the working of multiculturalism (Reitz 2009)?

- Is multiculturalism about society-in-difference or difference-in-society? Does a multiculturalism endorse a particular vision of the good society by asking how much difference can be incorporated without disturbing the status quo? Or does multiculturalism prioritize the legitimacy and desirability of cultural difference and redesign the good society accordingly (Sandercock 2003)?

- As a visionary framework for intergroup relations, does multiculturalism hinder or help minority integration? How much accommodation is required of those being integrated compared to those who are accommodating, who decides, and on what grounds(Jedwab 2005)?

- Does an official multiculturalism contribute to or detract from society building (Reitz 2009)? Does multiculturalism intensify the risk of ethnic conflict by encouraging difference at the expense of national unity? Or do multicultural policies establish a framework for cooperative coexistence by depoliticizing the threat of ethnicity?

- Should the study of multicultural governance entail a macro political process and/or the micropolitics of peoples' lived experiences in diverse contexts? Can multicultural models articulated by academics and politicians be reconciled with the everyday subjective experiences that foster hybridity and multiple identities, including those street-level transformations arising from serendipitous encounters in neighborhoods and workplaces (Levine-Rasky 2006)?

- Is multiculturalism a plural ideology of governance that advocates mutual coexistence of distinct ethnocultural communities in a single society, without which individual rights could not be expressed (Taylor 1992; Kymlicka 1995; Gagnon and Iacovino 2007)? Is it about the right of individuals to affiliate with the culture of their choice, if they so choose?

- In that multiculturalism as an ongoing political project that simultaneously creates new forms of belonging to citizenship and country, while helping to sustain origins and diaspora, should the focus be on respecting individual rights to affiliation or group-based cultural and religious practices (Modood 2005; Squires 2008)?

- Does multiculturalism endorse the universality principle that what we have in common as rights-bearing individuals is more important for purposes of renewal and recognition than what insulates individuals into culturally distinct groups? Or does multiculturalism reject the universality of liberalism as the basis for belonging and entitlement by emphasizing the primacy of group-differentiated rights?
- Is multiculturalism about "us" or "them"? Is it about inclusion or exclusion? Should multiculturalism focus on addressing the concerns of minority women and men? Or should multiculturalism attend to changing mainstream mindsets and institutional structures in hopes of removing the prejudicial and discriminatory barriers that preclude minority integration (Sniderman and Hagendoorn 2007)?
- Can multiculturalism address the the deep differences of those faith-based immigrants who may profess a society-transcending commitment beyond that of the nation-state (Hage 2006)? Or is multiculturalism best restricted to the realm of a pretend pluralism by addressing relatively superficial differences of immigrants who are anxious to "get in"?
- Who decides on what is or is not acceptable under an official multiculturalism? In a governance that espouses multicultural principles, how do we reconcile the inconsistency between defending the minority's rights to protect their culture and prohibiting practices the state deems to be illiberal? Can intolerance be tolerated by a tolerant and liberal multiculturalism, especially if the intolerant prefer to disagree with the tolerance principle of agreeing to disagree?
- Is multiculturalism an end (*integrative multiculturalism*) or a means (*multicultural integration*)? Should integration be treated as a model of multiculturalism for constructing a society of many cultures through the integration of migrants and minorities (an *integrative model of multiculturalism*)? Or should multiculturalism be seen as one of several possible models for integrating difference on more equitable and culturally responsive grounds (a *multicultural model of integration*)?
- Is an official multiculturalism little more than a cagey political strategy of social control—a pragmatic strategy of difference containment by way of divide and rule (Bennett 1998)? Or should it be seen as an exercise in inclusiveness that challenges exclusion and inequality without unnecessarily disrupting the status quo?

- Is multiculturalism a radical policy departure (a "new wine in new bottles") or more of the same with fancier labels (old wine in new bottles)? Does multiculturalism involve a new normative framework for integrating minorities on more equitable grounds (Kymlicka 2005)? Or is multiculturalism little more than a glorified reference to hegemonic assimilation in slow motion (Hage 2006)?
- To what extent is multiculturalism more than it admits (a wolf masquerading in sheep's clothing) or less than it promises (a sheep trussed up in wolf's clothing)? Is it a program full of sound and fury, but signifying nothing, or is its revolutionary import yet to be played out (Fleras and Elliott 2007)? Can multiculturalism be held responsible for the London bombings of July 2005; the terrorist plot uncovered in Toronto in June 2006; race riots at Cronulla Beach in Sydney in December 2005; the murder of Theo van Gogh in the Netherlands; or the events of 9/11 in the United States? Or is it simply convenient to scapegoat multiculturalism for the failures of society to integrate migrants and minorities.
- Is multiculturalism wielded as an excuse to trample on individual rights? Will multiculturalism—in the name of tolerance and cultural freedom—condone cultural practices that compromise gender equity rights (Reitman 2005; Stein 2007)? Can a principled multiculturalism accommodate and respect different ways of life without violating individual rights or compromising common values (Cardozo 2005)?

However popular and successful official multiculturalism may be, staunch support has not congealed into consensus about definition, attributes, or applications (Hall 2000; Hesse 2000). Even in Canada, as Kymlicka (2004/2007) observes, confusion and uncertainty rule, since multiculturalism as policy has never been honestly explained to the general public. Such waffling is hardly surprising; after all, when a concept over conflicting visions of society infiltrates public debate, it loses what salience it once possessed (Soroka et al. 2006; Hill 2007). In that multiculturalism rarely means what it says or says what it really means, a disconnect divides multicultural ideals from multicultural realities.

The evidence is inescapable: championed yet maligned, idealized as well as demonized, an official multiculturalism has absorbed such a mélange of often conflicting social articulations and political objectives that many despair of any clarity or consensus (Caws 1994). Multiculturalism increasingly appears to resemble a blank screen on which individuals of vastly different political stripes can project their anxieties and aspirations. As a loaded term so full of multiple and contradictory meanings that its potential for misleading is virtually guaranteed, multiculturalism can serve as an amorphous label for a (dis)array of interventions and subventions (Hesse 2000; Uitermark et al 2005), resulting in yet more confusion and contestation at the expense of sensible debate or political direction (Modood 2007). Homi Bhabha (1998) concedes as much:

> Multiculturalism—a portmanteau term for anything from minority discourse to postmodernist critique, from gay and lesbian studies to chicano/a fiction—has become the most charged sign for describing the scattered social contingencies that characterize contemporary *Kulturkritik*. That multiculturalism has itself become a "floating signifier" whose enigma lies less in itself than in the discursive uses of it to mark social processes where differentiation and condensation seem to happen almost synchronically.

Clearly, then, references to an official multiculturalism connote an uncanny knack for meaning everything—yet nothing—depending, of course, on context or criteria (Fleras 2002). Hardly a consistent or comprehensive concept but sufficiently distinctive to justify its status as an "ism" (Modood 2007), multiculturalism evokes a preference for consensus but does so alongside a platform of criticism and reform, of hegemony yet resistance, of conformity yet difference, of control yet emancipation, of exclusion yet participation, of building bridges yet erecting walls, of belonging yet of exclusion. Ellie Vasta (1996:48) captures the dialectical tensions that inform the politics of multiculturalism when she explains:

> As public policy, multiculturalism is concerned with the management of cultural differences. It is this apparently innocuous objective that all the ambivalence of multiculturalism arises; it is simultaneously a discourse of pacification and emancipation; of control and participation; of the legitimation of the existing order and of innovation. Multiculturalism is part of a strategy of domination over minorities by the majority, but also points beyond this, to the possibility of new forms of social and cultural relations. As such, multiculturalism is a power relationship, and has something of the intrinsic ambivalence of power that Hegel demonstrated in his analysis of the master-slave relationship.

Because consensus about an official multiculturalism rarely prevails, disagreements persist. Multiculturalism is notoriously immune to definition by consensus, partly because definitions are context specific, partly because the concept is always changing, and partly because of a gap between rhetoric and reality. Such open-endedness has proven both perplexing and provocative. As multiculturalism can mean whatever the context allows—a kind of "floating signifier" in which meanings are absorbed or manipulated without much fear of contradiction or accountability

(Gunew 1999)—confusion results (Willett 1998). To complicate matters further, a diverse range of interpretations and implications eliminates the possibility of converging all multiculturalisms into a singular framework (Modood 2007; Nye 2007). For example, not all multiculturalisms are cut from the same discursive cloth as Canada's official multiculturalism (official as in policy, statute, constitution, and national identity). The fortuitous circumstances that ushered in Canadian Multiculturalism may make it difficult to export or duplicate (Kymlicka 2004/2007). That acknowledgement makes it doubly important to theorize different models of official multiculturalism in advancing the goals of multicultural governances.

Models of Multiculturalism as Governance

An official multiculturalism constitutes a late-twentieth-century experiment for rewriting the rules of pluralistic governance (Gagnon and Iacovino 2007). Designed to accommodate minority claims, in contrast to earlier eras that rejected ethnicity and ethnic politics as inherently destabilizing, multicultural policies arose in response to the ethnic political mobilization of the 1960s (Kymlicka 2008). By codifying responses to this challenge through policy, laws, and constitutional reform, the governance of diversity and difference shifted accordingly. Settler societies like Australia and Canada endorsed the principles of multiculturalism as a formal blueprint for managing difference by cooling out troublesome constituents (Fleras and Spoonley 1999; Pearson 2001). Other countries like Britain, the United States, the Netherlands, and New Zealand are multicultural by default or drift; that is, without an explicit formal policy but multicultural in all but name (Banting and Kymlicka 2006). As a result, concessions and practical fixes are established at national and local levels that amount to a de facto multiculturalism without actually saying so (Eckardt 2007; Phillips 2007).

Models of multiculturalism can be classified along three lines of governance—conservative, liberal, and plural. Each of these multicultural models differs in terms of defining the challenges of living together differently, underlying assumptions, proposed solutions and anticipated outcomes. Each can also be codified around governance patterns (including policies, laws, constitution, or practices) that describe and prescribe the relation of difference to society (or majority-minority relations) as grounds for living together (Bass 2008).

Conservative models of multiculturalism endorse the principles of a culture-blind governance. This "republican" view proposes equal treatment before the law for everyone regardless of who they are or what they look like. Everyone is entitled to full democratic rights and equal citizenship despite their differences, in effect paying homage to the principle that true equality results when everyone is treated the same without exception. No one should be denied or excluded because of culture or color, according to this line of multicultural reasoning; by the same token no one should be given special treatment because of difference. Differences are tolerable under a conservative multicultural model, but should neither hinder nor help in defining who gets what. To the extent that cultural differences are tolerated, support is conditional: they must comply with mainstream values, cannot be employed to justify reward or recognition, must not block the rights of others because such intolerance is intolerable in a tolerant democracy, cannot define the content of public space, and can persist so long as everyone "agrees to disagree" by being different in the same way.

To be sure, a conservative multiculturalism is not necessarily anti-difference. Instead of rejection per se, a different logic prevails despite its commitment to the superficialities of a pretend pluralism, a color-blind agenda, a one-size-fits-all mentality, and a neutral state that spurns any cultural, religious, or collective project beyond personal freedom, safety, and welfare (Sen 2006; Shabani 2007; also Kymlicka 2008). Individual and group attachment to cultural differences should be restricted to the private domain, thereby ensuring a strict impartiality in public domains for allocating valued resources or avoiding ethnic entanglements (Neill and Schwedler 2007). And because differences are superficial and/or irrelevant in defining who gets what (entitlements), no one's racial or ethnic origins should determine destiny. For a conservative model, then, multiculturalism consists of a belief that a governance of many cultures is possible (i.e., different people can cooperatively coexist under a single polity) *as long as cultural differences are dismissed for purposes of recognition or reward*. A gentler version of a conservative multiculturalism suggests the possibility of a society of many cultures *as long as people's differences do not get in the way of full participation and equal treatment*. In acknowledging that no one should be excluded (or included) because of race or ethnicity, France and (to a lesser extent) the United States are widely regarded as proponents of culture-blind multiculturalism. With many European countries recoiling from the multiculturalism in multicultural governances, conservative models are attracting increased attention, albeit under the label of integration.

Liberal models of multiculturalism are predicated on the principle of unity and equality within difference and diversity. With liberal multiculturalism, a society of many cultures is deemed to be possible provided that (1) the dominant culture is willing to move over and make space for difference, (2) minorities have a right to identify with the culture of their choice without incurring a penalty by foreclosing full and equal participation, and (3) minorities must be treated equally (the same) as a matter of routine regardless of their difference, but should be treated as equals (differently) precisely because of their difference when the situation arises. This model acknowledges a key paradox: Yes, everyone is entitled to identical (equal) treatment regardless of who or why. Yet, the application of identical treatment to unequal contexts may well have the perversely unintentional effect of perpetuating patterns of inequality by freezing the status quo. To overcome the tyranny of standardization at institutional levels (equal treatment), an equivalence of treatment (treatment as equals) endorses the salience of cultural differences. Group-customized temporary measures that address the specific needs of the historically disadvantaged may be introduced, including the institutionalization of difference in the public sphere with special provisions for language, education, and health care and the organization of representation along ethnic lines (Grillo 2007).

In short, a liberal multicultural model of governance concedes the need for people to be treated equally and as equals. Equal (the same) treatment reinforces our commonalities; treatment as equals (as equivalent) acknowledges the situational importance of difference. In acknowledging that equality and inclusion connote a commitment to both commonalities and differences (Modood 2008), difference must be taken into account, admittedly, within limits and without creating undue hardship for the institutions in questionwith respect to workforce and service delivery. Under a liberal multiculturalism these concessions are neither institutionalized nor racialized but intended primarily as a temporary measure for addressing the needs of the historically disadvantaged. Accordingly, then, a liberal multiculturalism endorses a governance (or society) of many cultures *as long as people are treated the same (equally) as a matter of course, yet treated similarly (as equals) by taking differences into account when necessary to ensure equality, belonging, and participation.* The logic of a liberal universalism prevails: since differences are only skin-deep, what we share as individuals is more important for purposes of recognition or reward than the group-specific differences that divide. Differences are permissible but must respect human rights, obey laws, and be grounded on the rights of individuals rather than group rights. To date, the multiculturalism in Canada's multicultural governance (and to a lesser extent, in Australia) conforms most closely to a culture-tolerant liberal model.

Plural models of multiculturalism endorse a robust commitment to cultural diversity because, frankly, difference matters. As anthropologists have long noted, humans have a fundamental need for cultural attachments—a need that is best secured in complex societies by publicly validating and protecting different cultures (also Taylor 1992; Kymlicka 1995). Even in societies based on the principle that citizenship entails individual rights, cultural identities are important in grounding human existence, so that each cultural group has the right to be a meaningful part of the civic whole (Modood 2008). Insofar as all cultures are fundamentally different yet of equal worth and value, differences must be taken seriously under this robust multiculturalism—despite their potential to reinforce the society-dismantling principles of collective autonomy, group rights, differential citizenship, institutionalization of differences, separate institutional development, hermetically sealed communities or ethnic enclaves, and recognition of minorities as legally constituted entities on the basis of which societal rewards are allocated (May 2004). Not only are diverse cultural practices immune to criticism because of the radical relativism of a plural multiculturalism, plural models also insist that group rights (including institutionalized subordination of women) may trump individual equality rights (Stein 2007). In other words, the primacy of multiple and coexisting groups and identities within a state-bounded territory takes precedence over the salience of liberal universalism as a basis for governance (Gagnon and Iacovino 2007).

Taking difference seriously is not without consequence. Inasmuch as cultural backgrounds are crucial in framing a person's identity in terms of who they are, all cultures must be treated with respect and dignity (Malik 2008). In going beyond a simple respect for difference, a plural multiculturalism concedes the centrality of recognizing and respecting group identities in constructing a sense of self worth within the public domain (Modood 2008.With a plural multiculturalism, society is organized around an ideology that legitimizes the existence and value of numerous cultural groups, each of which lives by its distinctive beliefs and traditional practices (Ben-Eliezer 2008). In contrast to conservative and liberal models of multiculturalism, which tend to blur, transcend, or crosscut differences, a plural multicultural model proposes to recognize, institutionalize, and empower difference—at times out of conviction or morality, but often from cowardice, political correctness, or indifference and default (see Choudhry 2008). This tendency toward a *coexistence without commingling* puts the onus on protecting collective rights and group differences.

A plural multiculturalism model can be defined accordingly: a governance of many cultures is possible *if differences are taken seriously by taking them into account as a basis for living together differently—up to and including the creation of parallel institutions, competing value orientations, and separate communities.* Both Britain and the Netherlands experimented with a pluralist model but have rejected it in favor of more conservative/liberal

Table 1.1 Models of "Official" Multiculturalism

Conservative "Culture-blind" Multiculturalism	Liberal "Culture-tolerant" Multiculturalism	Plural "Culture-conscious" Multiculturalism
A belief that a society of many cultures is possible but only if cultural differences are dismissed as immaterial for attainment of recognition or reward. True equality and full participation arise from treating everyone the same, (*equally*) regardless of their cultural differences, because, in a society that aspires to culture-blindness, everyone is equal before the law.	A belief that a society of many cultures is possible when cultural differences are tolerated but normally rejected as a framework for living together differently and equitably. Unless circumstances dictate otherwise, culturally diverse minorities are treated equally as a matter of course but treated *as equals* when necessary by taking their differences into account. In other words, difference blind as a general rule, difference conscious as the exception, thereby making society safe from difference, safe for difference.	A belief that a society of many cultures is possible but only if people's cultural differences are taken seriously, up to and including separate treatment, autonomous institutions, separate communities, or collective group rights. Under a culture-conscious multiculturalism, differences matter, so that society must be reconfigured accordingly to ensure that differences are made safe from society, safe for society.

models. It remains to be seen if any livable governance can be sustained under the radical relativism of a robust plural multiculturalism in which society is reduced to little more than a convenience of different but equal life-ways (Uitermark et al. 2005; Orwin 2007). Survival would be provocative at best; Darwinian at worst. Table 1.1 compares the different models of multiculturalism as governance in terms of the culture (recognition of diversities), social (redistribution of rewards) and the national (unity and identity).

Of course, other multicultural models prevail. For example, there is a distinction between "soft" multiculturalism, which espouses tolerance and discrimination-free equality, versus "hard" multiculturalism with its radically relativist notion that, in the absence of absolute standards of right or wrong, two conclusions follow: (1) no culture is superior to another and therefore cultural practices are beyond criticism and (2) cultural differences should be not just tolerated but promoted because of their centrality to human lives, even if they break the law or violate individual rights (West 2005). Or consider a critical multiculturalism that challenges the foundational principles of state (official) multiculturalism (see chapter 4). Whereas a liberal multiculturalism sets the terms of the agenda for minority participation, a critical multiculturalism espouses the legitimacy of different ways of thinking, being, and doing (Anthias 2007). Under a critical multiculturalism, Eurocentric universalism and liberalism are critiqued, with particular emphasis on challenging the system, privileging group rights over individual rights, providing a voice for the oppressed, and condemning the false universalism of the dominant sector as the normative standard (Goldberg 1994). While the validity and legitimacy of this and other multiculturalisms cannot be questioned, especially when contesting conventional multicultural governances, these discourses are technically beyond the scope of this book on official multiculturalisms and subsequently are excluded from further discussions except in Chapter 4.

In short, models of official multiculturalism span a spectrum of meanings, implications, and scenarios. Multiculturalism itself is loosely defined as a normative framework and political program that describes initiatives for "governancing" difference by (re)negotiating the terms of minority incorporation/integration into society along conservative, liberal, or plural lines. Admittedly, the distinctions involving conservative, liberal, and plural models of multiculturalism are more categorical (analytical) rather than contextual (lived), with the result that most jurisdictions embody an inconsistent package of multicultural dos and don'ts. Nevertheless, distinctions prevail. Both liberal and (to a lesser extent) conservative models tend to create conditions for securing the status quo by facilitating the more gentle integration of newcomers and minorities into the existing social and cultural framework. By contrast, plural models often promote the relative isolation of minority cultures, including the long-term maintenance of multiple and separate cultures, with each maintaining a degree of control over internal religious, political, and cultural affairs (McGarry and O'Leary 2007). But while competing models make it difficult to theorize an official multiculturalism, given the plethora of conflicting discourses and hidden agendas, there is no paucity of criticism and concern.

Critiquing Official Multiculturalisms: The Good, the Bad, and the Bogus

Multiculturalism was designed to create a progressive and inclusive society. Tolerance toward people's cultural identity would secure the basis for social equality and equal opportunity, while equity initiatives within public institutions sought to engineer a change in attitudes and practices to create a society comfortable with difference. And yet democratic governance in capitalist societies involves a contradictory relationship: the importation of migrant labor to one side, and a state commitment to security, order, and unity to the other side (Turner 2006). In that multiculturalism represents a political strategy to solve this political contradiction in a politically acceptable way, critiquing it exposes hidden agendas that paper over these paradoxes (Thobani 2007).

Reactions to multiculturalism as governance are varied. Recourse to multiculturalism has proven a boon to some, a detriment to others, a source of solace for a few, confusion for many, and testimony to indifference for the rest. Many have criticized official (or state) multiculturalism as a paternalistic sop for cooling out troublesome minorities as problem people. Others endorse it as a long-term investment for society building, in part by making society safe from difference, safe for difference. Yet others equate multiculturalism with progressive moves in advancing the politics of recognition and authenticity. Still others approach it as the political outcome of power struggles over competing agendas. Finally, there are those who acknowledge the double-edged propensity of multiculturalism as benefit or cost, depending on context, criteria, or consequences. Moreover, as demonstrated below, criticism is double edged because of confusion and uncertainty over what people think multiculturalism is doing versus what it really is doing.

Critics pounce on multiculturalism as governance regardless of what it does or doesn't do, partly because the paradoxes and ambiguities implicit within its many manifestations justify the criticism (Bannerji 2000; Cameron 2004). Many accuse multiculturalism of being too radical or too reactionary, of promoting too much or not enough change, of promising more than it can deliver or of delivering more than bargained for. And while multiculturalism may be embraced by many as a strength to be admired, others may dismiss it as a weakness to be condemned or exploited, as noted by Irshad Manji.

> As Westerners bow before multiculturalism, we anesthetize ourselves into believing that anything goes. We see our readiness to accommodate as a strength—even a form of cultural superiority ... Radical Muslims, on the other hand, see our inclusive instincts as a form of corruption that makes us soft and rudderless. They believe the weak deserve to be vanquished. Paradoxically, then, the more we accommodate to placate, the more their contempt for our "weakness" grows. And the ultimate paradox may be that in order to defend our diversity, we'll need to be less tolerant. (Manji 2005: A-19)

Critics on the Left have pounced on Multiculturalism as ineffective except as a mantra for politicians to trot out for publicity purposes. Multiculturalism is criticized as a colossal hoax perpetuated by vested interests to ensure minority co-optation through ideological indoctrination (false consciousness) (Thobani 1995). As a capitalist obfuscation to divide and distract the working classes, "multiculti-schism" ghettoizes minorities into occupational structures and residential arrangements, thereby concealing the prevailing distribution of power and wealth behind a smokescreen of well-oiled platitudes (Bannerji 2000; Dei 2000). A multicultural commitment to inclusion, equity, and justice is compromised by too much emphasis on culture at the expense of more fundamental categories of social analysis—class, race, or gender (Lentin and Titley 2008; also Forbes 2009). A custom-costume-cuisine multiculturalism is dismissed as little more than an opiate for the masses that dulls the sense and distracts from more pressing social issues pertaining to disparities in income and wealth (Ford 2005). Multiculturalism not only represents a polite and euphemistic way of masking unequal power relations and institutionalized racism, it also essentializes racial differences by representing them as equal differences (Kim 2004; Lentin and Titley 2008) In other words, an official multicultural discourse tends to frame diversity as 'add-on' to the existing system rather than being mainstreamed and integral to a changing society, thus reinforcing its weakness in promoting equality or intergroup relations (Anthias 2007).

Those on the Right repudiate multiculturalism as a costly drain of resources that runs the risk of eroding national unity, identity, and security (Bell 2004). At best, a careless use of multiculturalism can result in a tribalization of society along cultural lines; at worst, a misplaced multiculturalism reinforces the legitimacy of those identities that pose a threat by making society vulnerable to infiltration by terrorists. Or alternatively, multiculturalism is taken to task for repudiating liberal ideals of difference-blind state neutrality and equality before the law (Bader 2007b). In between are the moderates who are unsure of where to stand or what to believe. Official Multiculturalism may sound good in theory, but implementation may falter because of difficulties in balancing abstractions with reality. For example, while its intent may be to facilitate the integration of immigrants and secure their loyalty, multiculturalism may have a perverse effect of strengthening immigrants' attachment to their homeland by way of diasporic connections (Kurien 2006). Conversely, while multiculturalism may provide minorities with a platform for promoting distinctiveness, the very act of participation may have the paradoxical effect of co-opting them into the dominant culture (Pearson 2001). In promoting the creation and perpetuation of groups as enduring and bounded, a mosaic multiculturalism institutionalizes culture into essentialized and deterministic boxes, freezes cultural differences as timeless museum pieces, and reifies cultural communities as static silos rather than dynamic flows with complex and changeable identities (Pieterse 2007; Nagle 2008).

The conclusion seems inescapable: in its role as the self-appointed catalyst for social engineering, multiculturalism has attracted its share of criticism (Ley 2005). National shortcomings for some reason tend to polarize around the multicultural governance of diversity and difference (Siddiqui 2007), and sometimes deservedly so. Too often, multiculturalism is long on principle and promise, but has proven short on delivery except to convey an air of mutual indifference in which citizens share geographic and political space but little else (Ignatieff 2001). Much of what passes for multiculturalism involves partisan politics and electoral advantage rather than sound policies of inclusion and anti-racist programs . Support is often elite driven and reflects a political consensus, while "subterranean" discontents and resentments are rarely measured or acknowledged.

Nevertheless, criticism should be tempered somewhat, especially if multiculturalism is taken as a general principle with aspirational goals rather than a specific program with articulated goals and enforceable implementation. A sense of perspective is helpful—an official Multiculturalism appears to occupy a third space, one that hovers in between the positive (benefits) and the negative (costs). Both critics and supporters tend to gravitate toward extremist positions. Accordingly, those who stoutly defend multiculturalism at all costs are as ideological as those who disparage it for lacking any redeeming value whatsoever. In that there are many publics, with different expectations and needs, the impact of official Multiculturalism is neither all good nor all bad. Rather, it may be either good or bad depending on context, criteria, and consequences.

A sense of proportion is equally useful. Multiculturalism may be both good *and* bad simultaneously, both liberating yet marginalizing, unifying yet divisive, inclusive yet exclusive, with benefits yet costs. The benefits of multiculturalism cannot be discounted, thus reflecting the ability of the powerless to convert the very tools for controlling them into levers of resistance and change (Pearson 1994). However, recourse to official Multiculturalism can depoliticize the potency of difference by channeling it into the private or personal. Far from being a threat to the social order, multiculturalism as governance constitutes a discourse in defense of dominant ideology. Depending on where one stands on the political spectrum, this conclusion may prove cause for euphoria or consternation.

2

Theorizing Multicultural Governances: Making Society Safe from Difference, Safe for Difference

Introduction: Living Together with Difference

In a world awash with the politics of diversity and difference, the challenge of accommodating migrants and minorities ranks high on the global agenda (Shachar 2007). In acknowledging the importance of marrying social equality with cultural diversity to achieve inclusivness, governments have begun to revisit their public policies and governance rules. Relations between minorities and majorities have shifted accordingly, with realignment varying between countries and evolving over time (Watt 2006; Kymlicka 2007d). Conventional models of intergroup governance—including assimilation, segregration, and separation—are increasingly contested by those diversity politics that rejects the normative standard of a homogenizing governance and racialized state. Governance models are proposed instead that promote the prospect of living together with differences in ways that are workable, necessary, and fair.

The politics of governance is at the forefront of public debate over managing diversity and difference (EDG 2007). Originating from a number of sources, including globalization, immigration, decline of traditional moral consensus, consolidation of human rights agendas, and liberal emphasis on individual choice (Laviec 2005), the diversity politics of difference continues to contest and provoke. Proposals for the governance of this politicized difference pose a multicultural dilemma, particularly in light of the diversity-dampening agendas of the post-9/11 era (Parekh

2005). One governance question in particular prevails: How can newcomers be incorporated into a cohesive social whole without loss of national identity or erosion of minority rights? Or phrased alternatively, in a multicultural governance, is it possible to reconcile the diverse claims of constituent groups and individuals with the claims of the nation-state as a whole without losing a complex balancing act between two oppositional dynamics—the need for social cohesion with the rights of minorities to recognition and reward (McKnight 2005)? In that democracies can neither suppress difference nor dispense with unity, a pluralist governance framework is required for reconciling these seemingly conflicting tensions.

The management and accommodation of diversities and difference under a multicultural governance is accelerating to the forefront of global political agendas. In contrast to the past, when nation-states were dominated by a majority national group who co-opted the state for self-serving purposes, the present no longer condones an openly monocultural agenda. Most democratic societies (or nation-states) are confronted by diversity politics and the politics of difference, reflecting, in part, the interplay of demographics with minority political assertiveness and an emergent human rights agenda (Kymlicka 2007a; Tierney 2007). Ethnic heterogeneity rather than monocultural homogeneity typify the demographics of most societies, resulting in deep social cleavages because of religious prejudice, economic gaps, cultural differences, intergroup competition, and historical hatreds (Peleg 2007). And yet the notion of multiculturalism with its corresponding concept of accommodating those who do not share the dominant cultural ethos is not without consequences. Political and governance problems are created that have no parallel in history (Abbas 2005) Worse still, those programs, skills, and vocabulary that evolved for conducting the politics of culturally homogeneous states are of limited help or pose a debilitating handicap in reconciling the legitimate demands of unity and diversity.

Consider the following governance challenges: Nearly 40 percent of the world's nation-states contain five or more significant ethnic groups, including Nigeria, or the former USSR with over a hundred ethnic groups within their borders. The 200 million strong who live across Indonesia's 17 000 islands are divided into over 300 different ethnic groups and languages. In 30 percent of the world's states, the largest national group is not even a majority but constitutes a plurality that finds itself in competition with other minorities for control of valued resources. The potential for conflict is ever present under these circumstances, especially when one mainstream ethnic group dominates the society's political process, controls its social institutions, and wields political power to promote vested interests (Peleg 2007). Even a plurality of smaller ethnic groups is no guarantee of political tranquillity without an overarching visionary blueprint for smoothing over governance bumps.

In the wake of recent social transformations and the politicization of difference, cultural and religious minorities are challenging conventional notions of democratic governance (Koenig 1999; Shachar 2007). A commitment to cultural homogeneity, which was once envisaged as indispensable for national identity and social integration, is now sharply contested. Government policies and governance structures may have sought to centralize all power and authority, to privilege the dominant language and culture across all public institutions, and to render invisible the presence of minorities within the public domain (Kymlicka 2007c). But the politics of multiculturalism is now calling the shots. Instead of a homogeneous state and centralized governance structure—increasingly viewed as anachronistic in a postnational world of transnational identities, diasporic linkages, and human rights agendas—pressure is mounting to rethink the conventional.New governance arrangements are evolving that incorporate minority rights and identity claims without revoking the principles of social justice or the pursuit of national unity (Inglis 1996). To be sure, Western societies continue to impose patterns of governance that have the intent or effect of solidifying a business-as-usual mindset. Nevertheless, by repudiating the once-sacrosanct notion that conflated the state with the dominant group, governance models can no longer explicitly exclude, marginalize, or stigmatize without invoking a corresponding loss of legitimacy (Guibernau 2007).

To date, modern liberal democratic societies have capitalized on the principles of multiculturalism in advancing multicultural governance, in part through policies of recognition, in part through redistribution programs. Paradoxically, however, many of these same jurisdictions are embarking on a retreat from multiculturalism as a template for 21st century governance. A commitment to multiculturalism as governance no longer resonates with legitimacy and authority, although migrants and minorities continue to bank on its relevance and value in safeguarding their interests. This conflict of interest generates a fundamental contradiction: To one side, increasingly politicized minorities demand a redistribution of power and privilege, so that full and equal inclusion in society does not compromise their particularistic identities in the public domain (Koenig and de Guchteneire 2007). To the other side, central authorities retrench and resist in hopes of consolidating the center against the margins. In the hope of reconciling these conflicting interests without compromising a commitment to national unity or minority difference, a principled frame-work is evolving for constructing a viable community out of ethnically diverse populations. The challenge lies in balancing a liberal commitment to the individuality of autonomy, diversity, and equality with a society-building agenda of a common language, shared culture, and national iden-tity (Baubock 2005). But stumbling blocks are inevitable. In the absence of measurable values for operationalizing the concepts of "unity" and "diver-sity," questions abound with regard to "how much unity," "what kind of diversity," and "who says so, and why?"

Therein lies the quintessential paradox underpinning a multicultural governance: how *to create an inclusive and pluralistic governance for living together differently yet equally in ways that makes society safe from difference, yet safe for difference?*. What governance principles should guide inter-group relations in those multicultural societies that abide by the principles of multiculturalism? How can governance be achieved and sustained in those political contexts where power is distributed unevenly and sharply contested (Fox and Ward 2008)? In looking for answers and insights, this chapter explores the politics of the how, the what, and the why behind the principles and practices of multicultural governance. The chapter argues that the concept of multicultural governance remains largely undertheo-rized as an explanatory framework because of politics that conceal rather than reveal, confuse rather than enlighten, and marginalize rather than empower.It also argues that, notwithstanding a lack of conceptual clarity and operational difficulties, a multicultural governance remains the gover-nance of choice in coping with the diversity politics of difference. In terms of content and organization, the chapter begins by examining the distinc-tion between diversity and difference. This is followed by a look at those paradoxes that underscore the challenges of living together with diver-sity and difference. Particular attention is devoted to examining different governance models for managing diversity and difference, including geno-cide, assimilation, segregation, integration, and pluralism (Fleras 2009). The chapter concludes by analyzing the concept of multicultural gover-nance: first by comparing it with its alter ego, monocultural governance; second by deconstructing multicultural governance in terms of properties and promises.

Despite continued perception of diversities and difference as contrary to society building (Beissinger 2008), a commitment to an inclusive multi-cultural governance offers a workable alternative. The goal of inclusiveness under a multicultural governance becomes a matter of negotiation and compromise, thus addressing the aspirations and grievances of migrants and minorities, without neglecting mainstream interests and national goals in the process (see also Bogaards 2006). The challenge of recon-ciling diverse political claims of individuals and groups with the claims of the nation-state as a whole is shown to require a complex governance act between two countervailing demands – social cohesion on the one hand and inclusion of diversity and difference on the other hand (Reitz 2009).

Diversity Politics, the Politics of Difference

Diversity and difference, to all appearances, are alive and flourishing (Boli and Elliott 2008). In the community, school, media, and workplace, diversity is prized and practiced throughout the world. Ideologies promoting diversity and difference are widely embraced, while their institutionalization is expressed in official government policy and practice, in legislation and celebrations. Businesses routinely adopt recruitment, promotion, and retention initiatives that are designed to ensure a diverse and inclusive workforce through removal of discriminatory barriers. As Boli and Elliott (2008: 542) point out, academic journals seek out diverse editorial boards, companies want diverse boards of directors, broadcasters are casting about for diverse anchor teams, and organizations establish executive offices whose primary responsibility is the pursuit of ever-increasing inclusiveness. To be sure, critics of diversity are legion in arguing that a diversity commitment is not without its flaws. Such a commitment erodes integration and stability, generates conflict because of incompatible values, legitimates unacceptable practices and human rights violations, subordinates individuality to collective identities, distorts the principle of meritocracy (diversity trumps ability), and reflects a focus on the superficial ("pretend pluralism") instead of more pressing issues related to power and inequality (Lentin and Titley 2008). Nevertheless, a commitment to diversity continues to be valued and legitimized on moral grounds (people have a right to be different yet the same) and instrumental grounds (from enhancing creativity to bolstering the bottom line).

The first decade of the twenty-first century has made it abundantly clear that the management of diversity and difference can no longer be taken for granted or left to chance. The intersection of globalization and communication/transportation technologies has seen to that, as have transglobal migration flows and emergent human rights agendas (Fleras 2009). Diversity politics and the politics of difference are now a common if contested feature of the contemporary political landscape (Frederickson 1999). In a world of shifting boundaries, assertive minorities, and contested nationalities, how could it be otherwise? Few would assert that the growing politicization of diversity is irrelevant or temporary. To the contrary, the politics of difference is here to stay as well as to challenge and change in advancing a cooperative coexistence.

The onset of a new millennium has yielded yet another twist in difference debates. On one hand, diversity is increasingly politicized because of open competition for power, resources, and recognition; this is hardly surprising, since society building (or "nation-state building") often imposes a burden on migrants and minorities who chafe at the prospect of assimilating into a difference-aversive system (Kymlicka and Opalski 2001). On the other hand is mounting evidence of mainstream resistance and majority backlash. Countries once in the forefront of multicultural governance are rethinking the governance blueprint along more restrictive lines. With the backlash against multiculturalism as national narrative and public discourse firmly established, what increasingly prevails is a neomonocultural commitment to those core values, shared identities, and singular citizenship that constitute "nationhood" (Joppke 2004). The interplay of difference politics with political backlash secures what might be called "a multicultural governance but without the multiculturalism." That is, an explicit rejection of multiculturalism as governance, in exchange for a commitment to integration models, without actually discarding those pluralistic principles and practices that are deeply entrenched in society, persists at local and regional levels rather than nationally or formally, and reflect outcomes that are multicultural in all but name.

In challenging the prevailing distribution of power and resources, the diversity politics of difference has profoundly altered the concept of what society is for. Responses to difference-based politics tend to be confused or hostile, with reactions varying (a) from difference as superficial and irrelevant, to difference as fundamental and worthy of recognition, (b) from difference as a threat and challenge, to difference as an opportunity and asset, (c) from difference as disempowering with potential to deny or exclude, to difference as a source of recognition and reward, and (d) from difference as contrary to society building, to difference as constitutive of an inclusive society. Such polarities in opinion should come as no surprise. Difference may be tolerated, even encouraged as a positive contribution to society. But its acceptance hinges on accepting a common institutional framework that often compresses differences into a one-size-fits-all sameness or, alternatively, dismisses them as reflective of an essentially universal humanity (Fish 1997). Not surprisingly, the centrality of power in driving the politics of difference is unmistakable. Those in positions of power can control the diversities agenda by defining what differences count, what counts as difference (Johnston 1994). The powerless, in turn, politicize their differences as tactical leverage in competing for scarce resources. Such a contested power brokering draws a multicultural society into a governance paradox: how to engage difference without either caricaturing or marginalizing it, while advancing the goals of justice and inclusiveness against a backdrop of national interests.

The conclusion is inescapable: approve or disapprove, like it or not, the diversification of societies is inevitable, with attendant implications for the governance of diversity and difference. Admittedly, there is no magical formula for enhancing the prospects of living together with difference—even as pressure mounts to dislodge conventional governance models in a rapidly changing and increasingly diverse world. Nor is there much agreement about constructing a governance that takes differences seriously. Questions abound: What kind of differences are permissible? How much diversity and difference is acceptable? How much conformity is required? Where do we draw the line? Who decides and on what grounds? Answers to questions about the nature and scope of multicultural governance are continually contested, with little consensus. One conclusion seems certain, however. Minority women and men no longer condone a monocultural governance that marginalizes them as colorful orbits around a mainstream core. Preference, instead, leans toward a multicultural governance that posits difference *as* the mainstream. The mainstream, in turn, is under pressure to reposition itself as part of the multicultural kaleidoscope rather than the tacitly assumed center around which differences orbit. The politics of multicultural governance addresses the challenge of putting these seemingly contradictory proposals into transformative practice the politics of multicultural governance.

Diversity and difference in historical perspectives

In the post-9/11 era of borders, security, and homegrown terrorism, the inescapable seems inevitable. The paradigmatic expression of multicultural governance is inseparable from diversity politics and the politics of difference—with or without official approval. But while debates over the legitimacy and value of diversity and difference may appear to be of relatively recent origins, the intellectual roots are deep. Nineteenth-century European societies promulgated the ideal of a monocultural nation-state (Guibernau 2007). An ideology of nationalism transformed Europe's perception of the nation-to-the state relationship by embracing the nationalist principle that each autonomous nation was entitled to the status of sovereign state. To ensure a commonality, purity, and homogeneity of culture, history, identity, and language (Choudhry 2007), foreign elements had to be dispelled. Those who fell outside the parameters of the dominant group suffered accordingly. They were isolated and ignored, absorbed into dominant culture and society, forcibly expelled, or exterminated. Even as nation-states extolled the virtues of inclusiveness, an ambivalence toward difference prevailed: protection and promotion of the dominant culture as unique alongside a ruthless suppression of difference in promoting unity.

By contrast, much of the twentieth century was ostensibly consumed by two seemingly opposed and antinationalist governance trends: Marxism and liberalism. By refusing to take differences seriously, both Marxism (including communism and socialism) and liberal universalism asserted the universality of humankind. To one side of the ledger was a commitment to liberal universalism. With its connotation that differences are only skin deep, a liberal universalism proposed that, in defining who gets what, people's similarities as morally autonomous and free-wheeling individuals superseded their group-specific differences. To the extent they existed, differences were tolerable—even acceptable—but only if everyone differed in the same kind of way. This commitment to a "pretend pluralism" was cryptically captured by the prominent Latino scholar and activist, Arturo Madrid, who proclaimed, "Long live diversity as long as it conforms to my standards, to my mind set, to my view of life, to my sense of order."

To the other side of this political spectrum—but no less universalistic in tone and outcome—were Marxist models. A common human condition was espoused under various Marxist strands, one in which individual equality was secured through collective action and universal progress. Insofar as oppressions existed, they embodied a singular contradiction, namely, unequal class relations with a corresponding clash of interests. The ruling class did everything at its disposal to protect and promote power, wealth, and privilege; the working class was equally adamant in bringing about a more equitable distribution of valued resources. In that the ruling class (and working class as well) derived benefits from fomenting internal divisiveness, class relations logically preceded the salience of ethnicity. But notwithstanding obvious dissimilarities in defining an ideal society, both Marxists and liberalist ideologies concurred with a commitment to universality. True equality pivoted around treating everyone the same, regardless of their racial differences or ethnic backgrounds.

In a world partitioned by race and class, a commitment to universalism as governance proved an enlightened advance—even if denying the salience of diversity and difference badly miscalculated the human condition. But the emergence of a postmodernist sensibility has undermined the legitimacy of liberalism or Marxism as governance options. In contrast to the modernist embrace of the universal and the uniform as a basis for living together, the ethos of postmodernism endorses a framework that inverts the universal and the objective by extolling the distinctive and discursive as grounds for recognition, rewards, and relationships. Conventional notions of modernity and modernism—namely, order and rationality in addition to universality and hierarchy—are discredited largely because the realities of a fluid and fragmented world cannot be essentialized, pigeonholed, and hierarchically arranged (Dustin 2007). According to this line of thinking, there is no such thing as absolute truth or objective reality in a mind dependent world, only discourses about truth and reality, whose "truthfulness" or "realness" is socially constructed, context dependent, and power embedded. To the extent that this postmodernist turn has reinforced those multicultural discourses critical of modernism and modernity, the yardsticks have shifted accordingly, including (see West 1996) the following:

(a) Rejection of the centralized, monolithic, uniformity, and conformity in favor of decentralized, diversity, heterogeneity, and multiplicity; in a globalizing world both interconnected and differenced as well as changing and contested, the major stumbling block for living together is not difference but mindless conformity
(b) Rejection of the totalizing, the abstract, and the universal in favor of the customized, concrete, and specific
(c) Rejection of the rigid and doctrinaire in favor of the contingent, changing, and provisional
(d) Rejection of the so-called objective and absolute in favor of multiple "realities" as all surfaces, hybrids, and discourses

The emergence of postmodernist ideals and conditions of postmodernity is disrupting conventional notions of governance. The classic immigrant societies are particularly vulnerable to the disassembling process. Large-scale immigration into Canada, Australia, the United States, and, more recently, New Zealand has profoundly re-configured the once monocultural landscape of these settler societies. European societies are no less implicated by these challenges. The combination of guest workers, refugee/asylum seekers, and colonial subjects has culminated in governance politics that often says more about mainstream fears and insecurities than about minority needs and migrant realities. As a result, the interplay of politics with diversity is proving problematic. For some, the diversity of difference poses a threat at both personal and societal levels, with no redeeming value to speak of for society building. The status quo is preferred instead as the basis for recognition, relationships, and reward. Others are intuitively drawn to difference as something inherently valid in its own right as well as a resource for society at large. Still others are indifferent to the point that they couldn't care less, or they endorse difference as worthwhile and workable in its own right but fret over costs and consequences as potentially divisive, unduly provocative, and contrary to national interests.

Diversity and difference: Conceptualizing the contrasts

The politicization of diversity and the politics of difference have catapulted to the forefront of governance debates (Lentin and Titley 2008).

Compare this with the past when references to diversity and difference were routinely disparaged either as irrelevant and inferior or, alternatively, as over-romanticized and misunderstood (Hall 2000). This transformation makes it doubly important to distinguish diversity from difference. For some, diversity is widely seen as a mixture of items characterized by differences and similarities . For others, diversity is perceived as a "thing" out there that evokes images of fixed and distinct cultures persisting in states of separate being. Individuals are subsequently slotted into these preexisting cultural categories without much option or choice. Such a static and essentialized notion is metaphorically conveyed by reference to a sticky multicultural mosaic, with its paint-by-number panorama of culturally discrete tiles, each of which is fastened into place by mainstream grout.

But reference to diversity as static and disembodied "thing" out there does a disservice. Much of value is lost by disembodying diversity from the realities of social dynamics, power relations, or political contexts. Promoting diversity as a condition of separate existence that privileges preexisting and essentialized categories tends to ignore history, power, and context (McLaren 1994). An undue emphasis on diversity as a series of dichotomies results in dualities that are pitted in opposition to each other (see Cooper 2004). Such a categorical (rather than contextual) approach to variety not only "flattens analysis" by diverting attention from internal group relations and power distributions that cut across all groups.Insistence on seeing diversity as categorical rather than contextual also subordinates one half of the pair to the other. This subordination invariably implies relationships of superiority and inferiority, with minority women and men permanently clamped into hermetically sealed categories at odds with mainstream society.<In other words, any understanding of diversity must transcend the categorical. A reading of diversity must go beyond the descriptive and essentialized by focusing on the fluid and situational, the contested and the changing. References should not dwell on the exotic ('food') or the esoteric ('costumes'), but acknowledge the dynamics of power within a broader context of inequality (Dei 2000).

Clearly the two concepts are not synonymous. If diversity is about categorization, then difference is about contextualization. Whereas diversity represents an empirical statement about its existence in society, difference invokes its politicization within the context of unequal power relations. If diversity describes heterogeneity, then difference as normative prescription capitalizes on this empirical reality to challenge, resist, and transform. If diversity tends toward the de-contextualized, the domain of difference consists of stratified relationships of power and inequality, reflecting the placement of individuals by those with the power to identify, name, and categorize differences into fluid and flexible groupings that are both contested and evolving (Dei 2000: 306; Fleras 2008a). Admittedly, the concepts of diversity and difference are interchangeably used at the governance level where references to diversity represent a managerial reading of differences that need to be harnessed, harmonized, controlled, and depoliticized (Ang and Saint Louis 2005). In that the logic behind official multiculturalism is based on taking the difference out of diversity, therein lies the source of confusion and conflict, especially when the politics of difference is downgraded to the level of diversity for policy purposes.

Let's rephrase the debate over diversity and difference with the help of the prominent American scholar Stanley Fish (1997). People are known to vary in their perception of diversity and difference. For some, difference is largely about diversity—for example, ethnic restaurants and brightly costumed weekend festivals. This "boutique" multiculturalism (or "pretend pluralism") does not take difference very seriously. Human differences are simply a superficial overlay over a fundamentally rational and common humanity. For others, however, there is a tacit approval of diverse cultural practices, even those at odds with mainstream norms and values. Yet support for the "strong" approach (again, Fish's terminology) comes with strings attached. Inasmuch as intolerant cultural traditions cannot apply in a society that espouses the principle of tolerance, conditions must apply. Diversity is deemed deviant and problematic when differences infringe on individual (or human) rights, break the law, or transgress core constitutional values. Still others, with a third view, go to the wall for difference. Insofar as all cultures are deemed to be of equal value and worth, it is impossible to evaluate or even criticize them. Differences are taken so seriously under a "really strong" multiculturalism that virtually "anything goes" for fear of compromising the larger principle. Yet such a situation may be more accurately described as a plural monoculturalism inasmuch as it relativizes the equivalence of all cultures in isolation from others (Sen 2006).

The pluralist dilemma is obvious: Too little commitment to diversity and difference can stifle and oppress, thereby making a mockery of any commitment to pluralism. Too much endorsement of it can dissolve and destroy. Too much privileging of cultural differences privileges identity (recognition)at the expense of redistribution (equality) (Yates 2001; Hollinger 2008). Too little attention to difference can have a marginalizing effect on those whose differences are disadvantaging. A major governance rift is subsequently exposed: those who believe in the fundamental sameness of humanity versus those who believe in its essential differences. If people are fundamentally alike, the former might argue,then paying attention to differences is relatively unimportant in defining who gets what.

If people are fundamentally different,then governance must take differences seriously by taking these differences into account as grounds for recognition and reward. In between are notions of differences as situationally important and deserving of respect and of recognition when necessary to ensure full partipation and equal citizenship.

In short, each of these difference discourses poses alternatives for living together differently. Consider the options: a boutique pluralism endorses a superficial reading of diversity ("multiculturalism lite," so to speak); an abstracted pluralism supports differences in principle rather than in practice; and a radical pluralism embraces the primacy of difference regardless of cost to others or society. Not surprisingly, countries with high levels of difference and diversity can respond accordingly. One pattern of governance is to accommodate as many diverse interests and demands as possible by institutionalizing exceptions as the rule (plural multicultural model). Another is to establish a common framework and uniform set of standards that apply to all members of society regardless of who they are (conservative multicultural model) (Hansen 2007). A third governance pattern falls in between these admittedly ideal model types. A liberal multicultural model simultaneously acknowledges the importance of treating everyone equally as a matter of course; it also acknowledges the salience of difference in defining who gets what when the situation arises.

Living Together Differently as a Governance Conundrum

At the core of a multicultural governance is a pluralistic commitment to living together with differences. This expression, "living together with differences," exudes reassurance if repeated often enough. But the concept itself is fraught with ambiguity and uncertainty. Living together with differences is relatively simple when minorities endorse mainstream beliefs such as "family values," a commitment to education and the work ethic, and a willingness to live and let live. A willingness to agree to disagree is simple enough when the differences are superficial, the folk are friendly, and choices are easy. "Shall we order Thai takeout tonight? How about a falafel? Anyone care for jerk chicken? Let's do the multicultural festival weekend." Dealing with difference gets more complex when mutually opposed values come into play. Culture clashes arise when (a) immigrant differences are so pronounced and provocative that they rattle mainstream composure or compassion, (b) customary immigrant practices are perceived as repugnant, contrary to core values, infringing on human rights, or threatening security, or (c) immigrant groups appear to despise the mainstream or reflect an indifference to all it has to offer.

In other words, references to "living together" and "differences" are neither intuitive nor self-explanatory. The following questions provide some insight into the complexities of living together differently under the aegis of a multicultural governance:

- Descriptive or Prescription? Is living together simply a descriptive term for coexistent diversities? Or should it refer to a normative ideal involving culturally diverse people who aspire to abide by certain principles?

- Liberal Universalism or Ethnic Particularism? How sustainable or desirable is a multicultural governance based on the seemingly benign concept of coexisting yet distinct cultures within a single nation-state? Or should such a plural governance be dismissed as paradoxical and replaced with a liberal governance that treats all individuals equally and as equals regardless of who they are or where they come from? In terms of ensuring equality without trampling on minority cultural differences, how should we balance the collective rights of minority groups with the individual rights of members of those groups?

- Cohesion or Chaos? Does promoting diversity and difference undermine living together? For some, endorsing difference either exacerbates the very divisions multiculturalismis designed to dampen (Choudry et al. 2007) or encourages those dangerous identities that may imperil a living together (for example, by tolerating extremism or ethnic enclaves). For others, those individuals who are confident in their cultural identity are likely to feel more welcome, with a corresponding commitment to society, thereby facilitating an inclusive governance (Berry 2006; Banting et al. 2007; Beissinger 2008).

- Commonality or Difference? How should multicultural governances respond to the differences in living together with differences? (1) Recognize, institutionalize, and empower differences; or (2) impose governance initiatives that blur, transcend, and crosscut differences; or (3) promote integration by depoliticizing both the politics of difference and a commitment to multiculturalism?

- Equality or As Equals? Should differences be ignored or incorporated as a basis for living together? Does true equality arise from treating everyone the same ("equally") as a matter of course regardless of difference? Or from treating people differently ("as equals") by taking their differences into account when the situation warrants it? Does the right to difference entail recognizing the legitimacy of specific minority cultures or acknowledging their right to occupy public space and participate in public affairs (Sandercock 2003)?

- Tolerance or Intolerance? Should illiberal differences be allowed in a society that espouses liberal-universalist principles? In a society that abides by the principles of liberal tolerance for living together differently, what cultural practices are acceptable and which are not? Who decides, on what grounds, and why? Should tolerance be offered to those who are intolerant of others because they prefer to disagree with the tolerance principle of agreeing to disagree, thus raising the perennially thorny question of whether a tolerant multicultural governance can tolerate those who are intolerant of tolerance?

- Unity or Diversity? If people are fundamentally the same, how much difference should be accommodated in designing a living together with differences? Conversely, if people are essentially different, how much similarity of treatment is required? Is it possible to reconcile the recognition of difference with that of universalism without imperiling national interests (Siapera 2006)? How much difference can be accommodated before the collapse of national unity and identity? Conversely, how much conformity is required before a society self-implodes?

- Recognition or Redistribution? Is a living together with differences an attainable goal and sustainable in the long run—even in societies that aspire to multicultural principles? Is it possible to balance the concerns of social justice with cultural diversity within a framework of national interests? How possible is it to respect and respond to difference without creating divisiveness or fostering potentially negative consequences such as reifying cultures or essentializing identities (Kunz and Sykes 2008)? How can we sort out the contradictory logic involved in demands for recognition and respect (which are predicated on difference) and demands for redistribution and inclusion (which are based on equality) (Siapera 2006)?

- Hierarchy or Egalitarian? How much hierarchy is necessary for living together differently? Can a multicultural governance be constructed that extends equitable status to all distinct cultural and religious groups, with no one group dominating? Or is it the case that a dominant group must dominate to ensure order and control for the benefit of all?

The unprecedented flow of international migrants and the politicization of more assertive minorities has made it abundantly clear: the concept of living together differently is proving far more complex and elusive than many had imagined. A fundamental paradox intrudes: Yes, the infusion of difference brings new rhythms, creativity, learning, and excitement (Leeuwen 2008); yet, the very same infusion may also erode social capital by fostering suspicion, distrust, uncertainty, and resentment (Putnam 2007). Exposure to cultural differences is known to unsettle people's dependence on those shared understanding that contribute to a sense of trust, security, and place—in part by undermining the self-evident character of common sense, in part by inserting uncertainties about what is normal and acceptable. But just as cultural strangeness can threaten psychological integrity when engaging difference through the daily rhythms of everyday social life, so too can it unsettle national unity.

Consider the possibility of public resentment when migrants and minorities insist on incorporating their cultural differences into the mainstream. Perceptions of growing minority entitlement and grievance not only encourage provocation and partition; they also put pressure on institutions to adjust and atone (rather than the reverse—as was once the case—wherein minorities adjusted to institutions and society). Encouraging difference may intensify outgroup hostilities by targetting migrants and minorities as objects of resentment and rejection (Sniderman and Hagendoorn 2007). In that living together with cultural differences can diminish or empower, as well as include or exclude, depending on the context or criteria, the politics of governance acknowledges a fine line between minimizing negatives and maximizing positives.

Finally, any theorizing of governance must acknowledge how societies differ in managing diversity-based difference (Parekh 1999). A broad range of governance strategies are required for managing difference because of societal variations, including societies (a) where large cultural minorities coexist alongside smaller or marginalized groups; (b) where differences as cultural markers run deeply for some, not others; (c) where some groups want to be left alone, but others prefer to be actively involved in reconstructing society; (d) where some minorities are territorially concentrated, while others are spatially dispersed; (e) where some constitute recent arrivals, whereas others are deeply rooted; and (f) where some members want protection of individual rights, while others seek entrenchment of their collective rights. No less important are governance strategies that acknowledge distinctions between indigenous peoples and national minorities (forcibly incorporated involuntary minorities who are looking to "get out") versus immigrant populations (voluntary migrants who want to "get in"). Refusal to acknowledge the range and import of these distinctions for assessment runs the risk of oversimplifying analysis or misdiagnosing policy projections. They also reinforce a multicultural paradox, namely, how to live together with difference without letting these differences get in the way of community and consensus. Therein lies the challenge of deconstructing the concept of multicultural governance.

Governing Difference: Historical Patterns, Conceptual Distinctions

Democracies historically capitalized on two governance options for managing diversity and difference (Soroka et al. 2006). The first is an assimilationist liberal governance (Peleg 2007; McGarry and O'Leary 2007). Under liberal assimilationism, difference was disparaged as an anathema to society building. Accordingly, it was ruthlessly suppressed or benignly discouraged through a homogenizing universalism whose laws and policies promoted cohesion and control rather than diversity and difference (Shabani 2007). This commitment to a monocultural governance was advanced through an imposed absorption that intertwined the fragments of diversity into the concepts of community and commonality. As a result of this exclusionary process, some were privileged, others disprivileged. The second option is an accommodationist governance. Increased diversity and its politicization into difference have upended traditional notions of society building, resulting in the acceptance of more inclusive multicultural governances. This multicultural agenda reflects a commitment to inclusiveness through programs and initiatives that interweave cultural differences with social equality in pursuing a fairer integration of migrants and minorities. Or, alternatively, a plural multicultural governance endorses the promotion and maintenance of multiple and separate cultures that coexist without commingling.

To date, political governance in Western democracies hovers between these governance frameworks. To one side of the governance debate is the principle of liberal universalism. According to liberal universalism, what we have in common as morally autonomous, rights-bearing, and freedom-yearning individuals is logically prior to and more important than differences because of group-based membership—at least for purposes of reward or recognition. A fundamental respect for the universality of individual equality rights compels governments to turn a blind eye to differences in ethnicity or religion in public institutions, while reinforcing the salience of citizenship as a civic attachment rather than an ethnic affiliation (Bloemraad 2007). True equality is attainable, in other words, but only if cultural differences are ignored when defining who gets what—in effect treating all individuals the same for purposes of entitlement. To the other side of the governance divide is the principle of ethnic particularlism. In contrast to a liberal indifference toward differences because of our commonality, a commitment to particularism emphasizes the specificity and salience of essentially different groups in shaping outcomes as varied as citizenship, belonging, recognition, and entitlements (Taylor 1992; Kymlicka 1998). Such a commitment also acknowledges that, because individuals may construct their sense of identity through such membership, true equality is contingent on taking differences seriously to circumvent the tyranny of universally imposed standards. However progressive, difference-sensitive concessions have rekindled new worries about stability and solidarity. Consider a central paradox of multicultural governance and the democratic state: Any functioning democracy depends on citizen attachment to the state; otherwise, the consequences include disenchantment or disloyalty or, worse, the specter of violence. Yet democratic states must foster allegiance and harmony without applying naked force or infringing on those civil liberties that, perversely, may embolden minorities to pursue identities and agendas at odds with state interests. Empowering those groups whose loyalties are partly outside the state may not dampen their discontent but, paradoxically, reinforce more yet isolation or challenge (Elkins and Sides 2007). Questions about governance proliferate: Can a multicultural governance curtail those behaviors or practices at odds with social cohesion and national identity while securing a sense of citizenship and belonging—even as people's identities become more diffuse or transglobal (Satzewich and Wong 2006)? If religious and ethnocultural minorities continue to play hardball, critics ask, what is to keep society from disintegrating? Is accommodating seemingly illiberal differences consistent with liberal principles of tolerance and neutrality? What should be done about groups that refuse to play the "agreeing to disagree" game, preferring instead to insist on the primacy of dogma ("disagreeing to agree to disagree") over debate ("agreeing to disagree")? Is it possible to operationalize the tension between difference and unity without falling into the trap of stifling conformity or unchecked chaos (Shabani 2007)?

Different models of governance with respect to difference and diversity can be discerned (Tiryakian 1994). These include expulsion or elimination of difference, that is, ethnic cleansing (Bosnia, Rwanda, Darfur); exclusion or denial of citizenship (South African apartheid); nonrecognition of diversity and difference but access to citizenship (France); recognition of minority cultures within the framework of dominant culture (Canada); and recognition of minority cultures but not as part of the national order (the Netherlands). Historically, five major models encapsulated the governance of difference and diversity, namely, *genocide, assimilation, segregation, integration,* and *pluralism* (Fleras 2009). In theory, each of the governance models contains its own set of assumptions about the status of difference and diversity in society—at least from the vantage point of central authorities—including a preferred relationship between dominant and subdominant groups, prescriptions for "managing" these relations, and proposed outcomes for society building. In reality, however, these ideal-typical models of intergroup relations are not strictly discrete. Some degree of overlap and duplication is inevitable in making these distinctions; after all, such is the nature of social reality that it cannot possibly be squeezed into static and exclusive categories. Moreover, while critical for analysis and assessment, definitions do run the risk of simplifying, essentializing, or rigidifying what in reality is complex, shifting, and contextual (Fleras 2008a). In other words, overlap is the rule rather than the exception because reality itself is contextual rather than categorical. Finally, these governance models are not always explicitly articulated or codified into law or policy. But frequently they are, and they often attain official status as policy, statute, or program.

Genocide as governance

Genocide represents the most extreme of governance models. Insofar as genocide openly rejects the legitimacy of diversity and difference as a basis for living together, it may arguably fall outside a multicultural frame of reference. Most definitions of genocide include the notion of deliberate and systematic mass killings of a despised domestic minority who live in a territory controlled by those who are often government-backed killers (Taras and Ganguly 2002). A state apparatus that openly condones violence against its own citizens furnishes the key criteria for demarcating genocide from related crimes against humanity (Rummel 2005). Others prefer a more expansive definition that includes the unintended yet genocidal consequences of seemingly well-intentioned policy initiatives (Deak 2002). Not surprisingly, the concept of genocide encompasses a broad range of actions, according to the UN-based convention of 1948, including the following five classes of harm: (1) members of a group are slaughtered with the intent of bringing about their disappearance as a people; (2) conditions are created that foster the dispersal of the group by destroying the essential foundations of community life, in the process pushing remnants of the population to an edge from which recovery is difficult; (3) intense psychological abuse or physical discomfort is inflicted, culminating in the dissolution of the group; (4) children are transferred from one group to another, thus bringing about the demise of the culture; and (5) births are prevented through involuntary sterilization, birth control, or abortion. Such a broad range of abusive activities complicates the quest for a working definition (Caplan 2005).

Contrary to public perception or media sensationalism, genocide as governance does not necessarily erupt because of primeval urges, tribal hatreds, or dormant hostilities. What may look like mindless and barbaric aggression is often a ruthless and orchestrated strategy to defend a sacred ideal: to destroy a group perceived as a threat to the ruling regime; to diminish those who are hated or envied; to transform the ideological basis of society; to eliminate foreign elements from society; to consolidate elite advantage; or to secure economic gain (Rummell 2005; also Koenigsberg 2004). Outside of local outbursts that may spiral out of control, genocide involves the manipulation of racialized differences by cynical elites who will stop at nothing to retain power, achieve advantage, secure political support, conceal economic difficulties, and distract from internal squabbles (Ignatieff 1995). Rather, the victims and victimizers fall into a gendered pattern, with young males often the perpetrators and victims, but women increasingly the targets for rape and infections (Caplan 2005). To be sure, not all genocides are blunt or direct. The process of genocide can encompass varying strategies, from those that explicitly seek to exterminate "troublesome minorities" to those well-intentioned initiatives that inadvertently have the effect (rather than intent) of eliminating the "other." Annihilation of this magnitude may be accomplished directly through military means or indirectly through the spread of disease, loss of livelihood, compulsory sterilization, or forced resocialization. In both cases, diversity and difference are callously expunged in constructing a monocultural governance.

Assimilation as governance

Assimilation as governance and policy model for multiethnic states connotes a one-way process of absorption (Inglis 1996). The assimilation concept was taken from biology (absorption through digestion) and reflects a largely naturalistic belief that social life could be better understood by drawing upon simplified analogies with the natural world (Jaret 1995). Used in this specific and organic sense, assimilation implies absorption by dissolving something into a substance of its own nature. In the more general and abstract sense, assimilation involves a process of similarity: to become more similar or to treat similarly (Brubaker 2004). Applied to the social world, assimilationism as a governance principle argues that a society cannot be cohesive or consensual without a common national culture and shared commitments (Parekh 2005). In that nation-states were initially aligned along nationalist lines with a centralist state that pursued an essentialized national identity, the outcome was a foregone conclusion. The dominant sector imposed its culture, authority, values, and institutions over subdominant sectors, with a corresponding abandonment of their cultural distinctiveness through exposure to conformity pressures (Inglis 1996). Migrants and minorities were expected to be absorbed into a monocultural mainstream to ensure moral and cultural uniformity (Ben-Eliezer 2008).

To be sure, assimilationist policies were rarely intended to transform minorities entirely. The complete absorption of everybody was neither easily attainable nor always desirable; after all, few majorities possessed either the resources or the political will to enforce wholesale absorption. Instead they endorsed a commitment to dominant-conformity (or Anglo-conformity in areas under British control). A dominant-conformity model required outward compliance with dominant values and practices. Select elements of a subdominant lifestyle were tolerated as long as they (1) were restricted to the private or personal realm, (2) did not challenge prevailing patterns of authority, (3) conformed to majority notions of decency, and (4) did not violate moral principles or the law. Simple enough in theory but when applied to the human condition, assimilation represents a complex and multidimensional process that unscrolls at a varying pace, sometimes deliberately but often unconsciously. It involves different intensities of absorption, ranges in scope from the cultural to the social, and entails varying degrees of conformity (Alba and Nee 2003; Bloemraad 2006). Even reference to the "new assimilation" rejects a return to the normative expectations, analytical models, or public policies associated with Anglo-conformity or Americanization (Brubaker 2004). Acknowledged instead under newer readings of assimilation is a much more nuanced yet complex world of hybrid and multiple identities, crosscutting connections, and transnational affiliations (Cheng 2005).

Assimilation emerged as an "enlightened" social policy for its time. Compared to alternatives such as forced separation or genocide, assimilation secured a working governance framework for managing indigenous peoples in settler societies in ways progressive and compassionate. But assimilation rarely prevails as an explicit policy principle. There is little inclination to openly support an assimilationist agenda that once dismissed group differences as inferior, irrelevant, or detrimental. Instead of a weakness to be denied or excluded as had been the case under assimilation, diversity and difference are now touted as a strength to be nurtured, especially as a gateway to global markets. Still, appearances can be deceiving. Although publicly scorned and officially rebuked as a model for managing diversity and difference, assimilation as governance continues to play a prominent role for leveraging migrants and minorities into the mainstream, reasserting core values, and excluding those who don't fit. As racialized minorities become increasingly involved in the mainstream, assimilation is proving the rule rather than the exception—in large part because of the often-unintended consequences of choices made by individuals who are looking to settle down, fit in, and move up. Finally, assimilation can also be inferred as the logic underlying all government actions. The logical consequences of even seemingly progressive initiatives to assist racialized minorities (for instance, employment equity initiatives) may have the effect of absorption into the "system" (Pearson 2001).

Segregation as governance

The differentialist concept of segregation (or separation) provides another governance model (Inglis 1996). Segregated (or plural) societies are segmented into relatively autonomous dominant and subdominant groups who live apart because of perceived incompatibilities and very real power relations. In cases of de jure segregation, the government deliberately keeps the races apart, thus stigmatizing the inferior by restricting them to second-class facilities. A de facto segregation results in the government tacitly condoning forced separation by not actively intervening to dismantle the social architecture of forced separation. To achieve these goals—that is, avoidance of conflict and maintenance of power relations through a process that sharply reduces group contact and interaction—segregation often involves a forced and physical isolation. Contact between the "races" is kept to an absolute minimum, except in contexts of obvious benefit to the controlling sector. What little interaction there is happens primarily in the marketplace ("selective incorporation"), where the dominant group exercises monopolistic control over the economy and distribution of wealth. Compliance in unequal contexts is rarely secured by value consensus or social norms. In the absence of any morally legitimate basis to govern, the dominant group must rely on physical threats to compel obedience. Yet segregation goes beyond a physical separation of unequal groups. Also implicated is a social relationship involving ideologies of domination (Jaret 1995). The dominant group defines itself as superior because of technological prowess, military might, and moral superiority. "Others" are dismissed as inferior or threatening to the society-building process.

Segregation as a policy model is usually imposed from above. Few cases of segregation have been as highly profiled as that of apartheid in South Africa, where a comprehensive set of segregationist laws and practices compartmentalized blacks and whites into separate groups at social, economic, and political levels. Canada's reserve system for the status of Aboriginal peoples may also be interpreted as segregation—at least in consequence if not intent—given the government's long-standing commitment to "no more Indians" as a solution to the so-called Indian problem. No less segregationist was the color bar that existed in both the United States and Canada (Horton and Horton 2004). Whites were segregated from blacks at institutional, occupational, interactional, and residential levels, in large part because of the power of the Ku Klux Klan that terrorized the American South and parts of Canada during the 1930s (Walker 1997; Backhouse 1999; Wallis and Fleras 2009).

As a model of governance, segregation can also be generated from "below" by groups who prefer to voluntarily separate from a society for lifestyle or strategic purposes. Voluntary separation is not the same as segregation or apartheid, despite similarities in appearance and structure. Racialized minorities, indigenous peoples, and religious groups may prefer to isolate themselves from the mainstream to preserve their independence and identity. For example, those peoples or nations who have been forcibly incorporated into someone else's political arrangement because of colonialism or conquest may want to "get out," as is the case with Canada's Aboriginal peoples who are exploring aboriginal models of self-determining autonomy as a blueprint for living together *separately* (Maaka and Fleras 2008).

Integration as governance

Integration represents a fourth model of governance. A commitment to integration emerged as a preferred governance model for managing difference after World War II when the contradiction of fighting for freedom over there clashed with the realities of oppression over here. The tilt toward integration reflected a growing disillusionment with assimilation as a workable model for living together, in large part because of international conventions that sought to protect human rights. Yet despite mounting popularity as a governance alternative in European countries and countries like Australia, the concept of integration is largely immune to rigorous analysis, resulting in a wildly disparate body of ideas and ideals (Parekh 2005; Frideres 2008). The concept remains poorly defined or undertheorized, with the result that terms like acculturation, accommodation, incorporation, and adaptation are randomly interspersed with integration. For example, in a publication by Parekh (2005), the preface describes integration as a two-way process, with both immigrants and the host society assuming a responsibility for mutual adjustments and dual rights and obligations toward each other. After all, immigrants cannot hope to integrate if members of the society don't accept them as equals or initiate programs of action to incorporate them (Laviec 2005). By contrast, the body of the paper refers to integration as a one-way process (Parekh 2005: 8). Even its popularity is suspect, since integration may be acquired by default, in large part by straddling an acceptable governance space among less attractive alternatives—segregation, assimilation, and multiculturalism.

Strictly speaking, the concept of integration stands in opposition to that of segregation. Segregation involves the forced separation of people who live apart from each other, socially and geographically. Integration, by contrast, refers to a process whereby individuals interact as equals at all institutional levels through removal of discriminatory barriers and those color bars that divided and demeaned (Jaret 1995). It entails a process by which immigrant newcomers achieve economic mobility and social inclusion in the larger society . . . a two-way process that involves changes on the part of both immigrants and members of the receiving community (Fix et al. 2008). A distinction between desegregation and integration is also useful. Desegregation entails removing physical or social barriers to achieve formal equality; by contrast, integration involves unifying disparate parts into a cooperative and functioning whole.

Two variations underlie integration as a governance alternative. First, integration as cultural governance represents a process of adjustment by which the dominant and subdominant sectors are brought together in a single comprehensive lifestyle, without either losing its distinctiveness. Whereas assimilation endorses a one-way process of absorption in which minority identities are collapsed into the mainstream, integration upholds a two-way system of synthesis that proposes full and equal participation without forgoing cultural identity as the price of admission. Another variant involves a process by which the dominant and the subdominant groups merge like different colors of paint in a bucket. The result of this "blending" process is a new cultural amalgam comprising constituent elements of this mixture. This fusion of the "modern" with the "traditional" into a relatively homogeneous entity is metaphorically captured by the concept of the melting pot, an image that is often invoked to describe and prescribe American race and ethnic relations.

Second, integration as a socioeconomic concept is a commitment to social policy implying that (1) no one should be excluded from society or treated unequally and (2) those included in society should be incorporated into society so that they become an integral and indistinguishable part (Parekh 2005). Under integration, society is held together not by a single national culture but by a common body of institutions and values that ensure uniformity and predictability. Thus while minorities can organize their private lives as they please, a willingness to commit is a precondition for equal treatment and attainment of success. Integration is defined subsequently in terms of loyalty, participation, and adaptation. Immigrants must express their loyalty to the country of settlement; they must participate in the social, political, and economic life of their chosen society; and they must internalize the basic values, institutions, and practices of society.

To date, several European countries have expressed enthusiasm for integration over multiculturalism as a preferred governance model. In reaction to perceptions that immigrants were pampered by rights without corresponding obligations, multicultural models of governance have shifted accordingly—from a plural approach to a more integrative model of multicultural governance (de Hart 2007). Of particular note in advancing an integrative agenda are citizenship tests, "civic integration" programs that obligate newcomers to enroll in language and values courses on (or before) arrival. To be sure, the concept of integration is poorly theorized and rarely problematized, and often glossed over as a default option occupying undefined conceptual space between the unfashionable (assimilation) or the problematic (multiculturalism). A lack of indicators for specifying the parameters of successful integration is no less worrying (but see Reitz and Banerjee [2007] who offer this Canadian list: a sense of belonging, trust in the other, identification with society at large, acquisition of citizenship, life satisfaction, a spirit of volunteerism, and exercise of voting rights). Nevertheless, in 2004 the European Council adopted a commitment to integration whose principles are paraphrased as follows (for a critique see Joppke 2007):

- Integration is a dynamic two-way process of mutual accommodation by immigrants and host country.
- Integration implies respect for the basic values of the European Union.
- Employment is a key part of the integration process for immigrants and host country.
- Basic knowledge of the host country's language, history, and institutions is indispensable to integration.
- Access to education is critical to the integration of immigrants.
- Immigrant integration requires full and nondiscriminatory access to institutions and public and private goods and services.
- Frequent encounters and creative interaction between immigrants and member-state citizens secures successful integration.
- Integration is predicated on guaranteeing the practice of diverse cultures and religions, provided these practices do not conflict with rights or laws.

- Immigrant participation in the democratic process is critical, especially in the formulation of programs and policies that impact on their lives.
- Integration is contingent on mainstreaming integration policies and measures in all relevant portfolios and levels of government and public services.
- Clear goals, indicators, and evaluation mechanisms must be in place to adjust immigration policies and evaluate progress.

As discussed in Chapter 3, this commitment to integration—with its focus on a two-way process of accommodation—resembles the principles of Canada's Multiculturalism Act of 1988. In doing so, it provides a reminder that, while helpful, the distinction between integration and multiculturalism is potentially misleading since the goals of both are neither mutually exclusive nor at cross-purposes (see Choudhry 2007: 612–613). Both are ultimately concerned with creating a more inclusive governance, one that enhances minority participation, belonging, and equality without foresaking either the legitimacy of difference or commitment to national unity. On balance, however, multiculturalism may lean more toward the "difference" in balancing difference-with-unity, whereas integration may emphasis the "unity" in a unity-within-difference equivalence.

Pluralism as governance

Finally, pluralism is an inclusive governance model that envisages the full incorporation of individuals and groups without losing their distinctiveness in the process. (Inglis 1996; Rex and Singh 2004; Kymlicka and Bashir 2008). A commitment to pluralism emerged as a reaction to assimilation and segregation. It sought to construct a kaleidoscope of associations and cultural identities that challenged the singularity of the nation-state, which historically was grounded in the attainment of a culturally and linguistically homogeneous population with a corresponding rejection of difference (Ben-Eliezer 2008). That this commitment to pluralism is routinely accepted and promoted (at least until recently) says a lot about the politics of difference in the twenty-first century.

Acceptance of difference as a basis for a more inclusive governance within a national framework is called pluralism (not to be confused with plural society). Pluralism as governance goes beyond a simple existence of racial or ethnic minorities in society. Instead it proposes a belief that a society of many cultures is possible, preferable, and desirable—provided, of course, certain safeguards are in place to balance unity with diversities and difference. Both color/culture-blind and color/culture-conscious variants of pluralism can be discerned, with some proposing to ignore differences as a basis for recognition and reward, while others acknowledge the need to take differences seriously by incorporating them into patterns of entitlement and recognition. For some, market forces should prevail in determining who gets what; for others, a degree of government intervention may be required to protect and promote minority needs, primarily by reaffirming individual rights, rectifying past injustices, reducing social inequities by removing discriminatory barriers, providing positive actions through employment equity programs, and ensuring protection of traditional language and culture. Reactions to these patterns vary: A commitment to pluralism provides minorities with the recognition that legitimizes their presence in society, while securing both full and equal participation. Yet this very commitment may prove a recipe for disaster by impeding socioeconomic mobility, creating silos of underclass minorities, and intensifying threats to national unity and political stability (see Bloemraad 2007).

Pluralism as governance can be expressed in diverse ways, including multiculturalism, biculturalism, and multinationalism. A commitment to pluralism transforms into multiculturalism (and biculturalism and multinationalism) when diversity and difference are recognized and incorporated as a legitimate component of social reality, government policy, and governance patterns. Multiculturalism tends to endorse the legitimacy of ethnic diversities as different yet equal by creating institutional space for migrants and minorities without fear of jeopardizing national unity (Ben-Rafael and Peres 2005). It provides a basis for organizing political governance on grounds other than the nationalism of nation-states (that is, that sovereign states should be ethnic nations, and vice versa (Lupul 2005) . Biculturalism resembles multiculturalism in many ways but is focused on the relationship between two major groups or peoples, each of which stands in a relationship of partnership with the other. For example, biculturalism describes the preferred framework for realigning the relationship between the indigenous Maori peoples and the non-Maori in New Zealand/Aotearoa (Fleras and Spoonley 1999; Fleras 2008b). Last, multimultinationalism implies the existence of multiple nations or peoples who see themselves as political communities—both autonomous ("sovereign") in their own right and sharing in the sovereignty of society (Asch 1997; Maaka and Fleras 2005). For example, Canada is increasingly described as a multinational coalition comprising Aboriginal peoples, the Québécois, and the English-speaking sectors, including immigrants and descendants of immigrants (Fleras 2009).

Conceptualizing Multicultural Governance

Defining governance

Reference to governance has progressed from relative obscurity to repetitive slogan in less than a decade(Chhotray and Stoker 2009). The concept emerged at the forefront of political debate in the late 1980s by representatives of different ideological convictions (Koenig 1999). Despite its popularity at conceptual and practical levels, uncertainties prevail: What are the characteristics of good governance? Are there universal principles of good governance? Can ethnically charged conflicts be defused by working within conventional governance channels? How can patterns of power under a governance regime be justified in terms of decision making and accountability (Institute of Governance 2007b)? Definitions are no less elusive, with the result that people literally talk past each other because of slippages in meanings (Rhodes 1996; Hyden et al. 2004). A useful working definition broadly defines governance as collective decision-making, that is, "... the rules of collective decision-making in settings where there is a plurality of actors or organisations and where no formal control system can dictate the terms of the relationship between these actors and organisations" (Chhotray and Stoker 2009:3). For our purposes, then, governance can be defined as *a framework for rules that establishes a principled relationship between ruler and ruled including a corresponding exchange of rights and obligations*. With governance, relations between people and central authorities are defined by way of rules, principles, and norms that prevent conflict and promote cohesion (Turton et al. 2007). Procedures and protocols are invoked that are both descriptive and prescriptive for creating consensus and control in order to meet a specific objective (Fox and Ward 2008), including the following attributes that point to how

- authority is divided;
- power is distributed;
- policies are formulated;
- valued resources are allocated;
- priorities and agendas are set;
- decisions are made;
- accountability is rendered;
- transparency in decision-making is assured
- implementation is secured;
- rules of the political game are respected.

Two governance dimensions prevail. One is a working relationship by which citizens articulate their interests, mediate their differences, and exercise their political and economic rights (Cheema and Rondinelli 2007). The other exemplifies the politics and policies employed by central authorities (or government as a shorthand) for governing citizens by allocating power among the constituent units. It should be noted that governance and government are not synonymous (Rhodes 1996). Reference to government entails the institutional expression of governance, namely, the specific forms of this relationship between ruler(s) and ruled by way of prescribed rules. In turn, government policies are best understood as a temporary expression of state ideology, representing the accommodation of plural interests and competing agendas within the broader framework of liberal capitalism.

Monocultural governance

One way of conceptualing a multicultural governance is by deconstructing its conceptual opposite, namely, a monocultural governance. Put simply, whereas multicultural governance is based on the principle of accommodating difference by acknowledging its legitimacy in defining who gets what, a monocultural governance is committed to suppressing it—either by decision or by default—thereby reflecting, reinforcing, and advancing the exclusiveness of a dominant culture, language, and identity (Panossian et al. 2007). A monocultural governance embraces the principles of assimilation and/or segregation, although certain variations of both integration and multiculturalism may prove monocultural in outcome if not necessarily by intent. By contrast, a multicultural governance upholds the pluralist principles as the foundational dogma, even if certain forms of assimilation and integration—and even segregation—may appear pluralist in all but name.

A commitment to monocultural governance is no stranger to Western societies. In keeping with nineteenth-century nationalist ideologies that sought to conflate the nation with a sovereign state, nation-states strove for the ideal of the culturally homogeneous society by rejecting any foreign elements as contrary to successful governance. Successful monocultural governance and national homogeneity had to be actively courted and constructed in advancing a centralized society, with a corresponding priority to suppress all differences in constructing an overarching national identity. On the assumption that each nation was entitled to its own sovereign state, with a corresponding right to protect its unity and identity, the ideology of monocultural nationalism embraced an inherent bias toward uniformity.

Emphasis focused on unifying an otherwise disparate population by generating a shared sense of national identity through cultural and linguistic homogenization (Guibernau 2007). Inasmuch as the state preferred a uniform and homogeneous citizenship, the concept of the unmarked and universal citizen was central to the national project (Sacks 1997; Scott 1998; Sturgess 1998). To the extent they were tolerated, cultural differences were dismissed as a kind of embellishment for adding a splash of color, restricted to the private sphere and beyond the reach of core liberal values or individual rights (Fukuyama 2007). In other words, the mononational state possessed and was possessed by a dominant national group who manipulated its hegemonic powers to control and contain. Those who didn't belong to the dominant national group were subject to expulsion, discrimination, and assimilation—or worse (Kymlicka 2004/2007).

Multicultural governance

Monoculturalism as governance was eventually discredited for different reasons. According to critics, it reflected a false view of human ideals, it was tainted by association with nationalism and war, and it was perceived as needlessly repressive of individuality and authenticity (Sacks 2007). In its place has emerged what might be called a multicultural governance. Admittedly, the concept of governance has been neither fully theorized nor fully applied to the challenges of living together multiculturally (Bader 2007b, but see Rex and Singh 2004; Panossian et al. 2007). Not surprisingly, the search continues for models of multicultural governance whose principles, structures, and values match the realities of the twenty-first century (Institute of Governance 2007b).

The challenge of a multicultural governance is propelled by a deceptively simple yet elusive objective, namely, the creation of a culturally diverse yet socially inclusive society without compromising national and vested interests in the process. Central authorities have responded differently to this challenge. Some endorse the separation of minorities into segregated enclaves as a basis for multicultural governance; others condone assimilation and integration as a guiding blueprint; and still others advocate an inclusiveness along pluralist and multicultural lines. For some, a person's cultural background is relatively unimportant in defining who gets what or who is who. For others, a person's culture frames his or her identity so that it becomes critical in acknowledging those dimensions that nourish a person's sense of well-being (Malik 2008). Regardless of the preference path, even the most democratically progressive societies confront a governance paradox for cooperative coexistence: how to reconcile the seemingly opposing dynamics of liberal universalism with ethnic particularism within a framework that balances the social (reward) with the cultural (recognition) without reneging on the national (unity). In that any response to these questions must unlock the secrets of living together with differences without collapsing into chaos or conformity, the challenge remains the same: to create a multicultural governance that is protective of national interests and majority entitlements yet supportive of the public good and protection of minority rights.

Of particular salience to multicultural governance is the status of diversity and difference. Historically, migrants and minorities tended to accept their subordinate status and social/geographical confinement as a matter of course. By contrast, contemporary governance patterns no longer dismiss diversity and difference as irrelevant or marginal; they are seen as legitimate and integral components of society—thanks in large part to the emergence of democratic ideals of equal status and rights; national identities that avoid the taint of intolerance; and minority demands for equal opportunity and treatment including removal of discrimination, and the right to contribute to society at large (Parekh 2005). A commitment to multicultural governance means the state should not explicitly identify with any particular ethnicity or religion but remain neutral and impartial when engaging its constituent individuals and communities. A multicultural model of governance endorses the notion that the state belongs to all its citizens, not just a single national group; the rights of all migrants and minorities to full and equal participation without forfeiting a right to ethnic identity; and recognition that all citizens have the same institutional access accorded to the national group (Kymlicka 2004/2007). Under a multicultural governance, then, difference and diversity are framed and promoted in ways that make it less threatening but more palatable to society and pivotal to society building (Banting and Kymlicka 2006).

The multicultural governance challenge is clearly before us: to construct policies and programs, including strategies, normative standards, and institutional arrangements for constructively engaging difference in ways that not only promote democracy, justice, and social peace, but also are respectful, reflective, and responsive to migrants and minorities (see also Banting et al. 2007; Panossian et al. 2007). In conceding an agenda that emphasizes a working collaboration rather than direct control (Tsasis 2008), a commitment to multicultural governance acknowledges the importance of going beyond benign government indifference (Gagnon and Iacovino 2007). What must transpire instead involves proactively managing difference by balancing competing claims and opposing value orientations. To advance national interests, a multicultural governance entails a two-pronged approach by (a) fostering positive relations between diverse communities (through tolerance and engagement) and (b) promoting active interventions by central authorities through removal of prejudice and discrimination, construction of shared values and commonalities across communities of difference, and the creation of commitment and consensus among diverse constituents. References to respecting differences are combined with acknowledging the importance of connections, commitments, community, consensus, and common areas of engagement across differences (Nye 2007). To be sure, the real and ideal do not always match. As Daniel Salee (2007) points out, when managing difference in a multicultural governance, the problem is not always the "soundness" of policy. Rather, the problem often involves failure to implement or enforce programs that sound good on paper.

To sum up: multicultural governance strives to comply with the principles of the Universal Declaration of Human Rights. Special attention is devoted to protecting all rights and freedoms regardless of race, ethnicity, or religion, including a minority's rights to their own language, culture, religion, and identity except where specific practices violate national law or contravene international standards. Multicultural governance also recognizes that a cooperative coexistence is possible, but only when power is shared rather than monopolized, devolved rather than centralized, and meaningful rather than perfunctory (Bogaards 2006). Advancing this agenda without compromising national interests and the public good remains a societal priority for the twenty-first century.

Adopting multiculturalism as a policy strategy represents an integral component in advancing an inclusive governance, albeit not in the sense that many might think. The politics of difference under a multicultural governance should not be framed as a problem to be solved. To the contrary: in a world that is increasingly diverse, rapidly changing, and more connected than ever, a commitment to conformity poses problems. In acknowledging the value and benefits of diversity and differences as solutions or assets, the multiculturalism in a multicultural governance points to a new way of thinking that balances commonality with difference, cohesion with ethnicity, and shared values with cultural relativism (see Lentin and Titley 2009). Nor should responses to the diversity paradox and the difference challenge be interpreted as final or solvable. Rather, the politics of an inclusive and multicultural governance should be framed as a journey to be traveled, a tension to be accommodated, an arrangement to be lived with, a sense of community to be nurtured, an opportunity to be seized, and an imperfect situation that can yield unanticipated outcomes (Fleras 2009; also Gwyn 1996). Chapters 3 through 8 will embark on this journey of discovery to demonstrate how the multiculturalism in a multicultural governance has proven an opportunity at times, a crisis at other times.

3

Managing Difference, Making a Difference: Multiculturalism as Inclusive Governance in Canada

Introduction: The Paradoxicality of Multiculturalism in Canada

Canada represents one of several democratic societies to have capitalized on multicultural principles as a principled (formal/official/rule-based) basis for multicultural governance. That it has managed to pull off the once seemingly impossible is quite astonishing—namely, to forge a working unity from its disparate parts without compromising its principles in the process (see Saul 2008). Multiculturalism emerged as part of a broader liberalization process for shoring up minority rights by abolishing inherited forms of inequality and capricious patterns of exclusion consistent with Canada's long-standing self-definition as a "white man's country" (Kymlicka 2007a). In redefining conventional patterns of governance, multiculturalism sought to establish a new political arrangement based on individual multicultural rights rather than on the tyranny of nationalistic (French-English) group attachments (Lupul 2005). In hopes of harmonizing competing ethnicities without losing control of the overall agenda, Canada's official Multiculturalism persists for similar reasons—the pursuit of political, ideological, and economic considerations involving state functions, private interests, and electoral survival. A commitment to multiculturalism is reaping dividends: Canada's reputation in spearheading the concept of multicultural governance has garnered rave reviews—as gleaned from high-flying personalities including Bono of U2, who claims the world "needs more Canadas," and the Aga Khan, who praised Canada as the world's most "successful pluralist society" (see Biles et al. 2005:25).

In advancing Canada's society-building interests while acknowledging a commitment to social justice and cultural identity, official Multiculturalism has emerged as the quintessential strategy of pluralistic governance. A normative framework is established to not only prescribe a proactive role in facilitating interethnic equity through removal of discriminatory barriers and prejudicial attitudes but also secure national interests by defusing potential intergroup conflicts (Goodey 2007; Ley 2007). In that narratives about Canada's national identity pivot around its much-ballyhooed status as a tolerant and inclusive society (Moosa 2007), Canadianness is increasingly informed by an embrace of multiculturalism. But theory is one thing, practice has proven another. When it comes to the multiculturalism in a multicultural governance, Canadians appear better at "talking the walk" rather than "walking the talk," in effect reinforcing the complexities and contradictions of operationalization, implementation, and enforcement. In other words, no matter how revered or vilified, an official Multiculturalism is inescapably prone to paradoxes that invariably generate oppositional tensions, including the following (also Belkhodja et al. 2006).

- To one side, Canadians believe that all citizens are equal before law; to the other side is the notion that the majority should reasonably accommodate minority rights (within limits and without imposing undue hardships on the host society), even when cultural practices clash with core mainstream values.
- A multicultural Canada is predisposed to accommodate diverse cultural practices, but how can it do so without compromising the commonalities that bind and unite (Cardozo 2005)?
- How does Canada's Multiculturalism balance collective rights with the rights of individuals within minority communities (Kymlicka 1995; Okin 1999; Stein 2007), and can it do so without rupturing a commitment to national unity and identity?
- Multiculturalism is about recognition and respect alongside integration and inclusion. It also constitutes a political act to achieve the political goals of preserving the prevailing distribution of power, privilege, and resources.
- Multiculturalism is about challenging and changing patterns of inequality, but it appears to have had minimal impact in dislodging a racialized status quo.
- Canada is widely regarded as the quintessential multicultural society in need of constant reinforcement and modification., However multiculturalism is so woven into the fabric of people's lives and Canadian society that its assumptions or hidden agendas are rarely questionned.

- Multiculturalism is explicitly about justice, participation, and inclusion for minorities and migrants; implicitly its about securing dominant interests and the prevailing status quo.
- Multiculturalism creates a long-term investment for living together with differences, although it also constitutes a stopgap measure for cooling out troublesome constituents.
- While Multiculturalism may reflect the sincerest intentions of creating a just and inclusive Canada, it can end up exerting the opposite effect by inadvertently fostering inequality, ethnic separatism, and intergroup friction (Berliner and Hull 2000; Kostash 2000).
- Critics of Multiculturalism often label it as a scapegoat for the failures of immigration and integration (Siddiqui 2007). Such accusations may be unfair; nevertheless, Multiculturalism can be justifiably criticized for glossing over structural barriers that deter full and equal inclusion, upholding a static and essentialized notion of culture, and paying insufficient attention to institutional designs that deny or exclude.

In short, a central paradox underpins the question of multicultural governance: how to establish a rules-based framework alongside a set of normative standards that can engage difference as different yet equal, without eroding the goals of unity, identity, and prosperity in the process? Or phrased alternatively, how to construct a multicultural governance that makes Canada safe "for" difference (maximizes benefits), yet safe "from" difference (minimizes costs) (see Schlesinger 1992; Samuel and Schachhuber 2000; Pearson 2001). The perils of balancing unity (commonality) with diversity are all too obvious. Too much difference and not enough unity may destabilize a governance to the point of dismemberment. Too little difference but too much unity can create a one-size-fits-all leviathan that stifles as it standardizes (Fish 1997). This paradox—multiculturalism as progressively inclusive yet potentially exclusionary—reinforces a widely held perception that Canada's official Multiculturalism suffers from a dearth of critical analysis with respect to what it says it is doing versus what it is really doing, and why (Dupont and Lemarchand 2001; Wood and Gilbert 2005).

In that Canada defines itself as the premier multicultural governance in terms of demographics, ideology, policies and programs, and outcomes, there is much to commend in taking a closer look at what works—how and why. This chapter addresses the principles, policies, and practices of Canada's official Multiculturalism as well as its politics and paradoxes in constructing an inclusive governance, one that engages the politics of difference without capitulating to chaos or abandoning a commitment to community, consensus, and cohesion. The chapter contends that, notwithstanding shifts in emphasis and narratives since its inception in 1971, an official Multiculturalism retains it core mission—a commitment to an inclusive governance where none are excluded (or rewarded) because of who they are or where they come from. The chapter also emphasizes Multiculturalism as official policy and program in terms of (a) its evolving political framework, (b) its implementation as practice at political, minority, and institutional levels, (c) promotion of a multicultural integration and integrative multiculturalism, (d) debates over reasonable accommodation, and (e) public opinion and critical reactions. Competing notions of multiculturalism in Canada are also addressed, namely Quebec's interculturalism project with its focus on an inclusive nation building. The chapter concludes, accordingly; that Canada's multicultural agenda may not be perfect in aspirational design or enforceable implemention. Nevertheless, with its pragmatic blend of checks and balances, it may constitute one of the least imperfect governance models for living together with differences.

Diversity and Difference in Canada

To say that Canada is a diverse society is clearly an understatement. Canada's diversity is reflected in the visibility of its demographics, the nature of its immigration program, and its patterns of immigration settlement. It is also reflected in the decisions of numerous migrants and minorities to preserve their ethnocultural distinctiveness. The following overview provides a look at diversity and difference in Canada based on 2006 Census data. This overview is disaggregated into visible minorities and immigrants, a Canada-wide picture, and breakdowns by province and urban areas. Also included are immigrant sources and flows for 2006.

- In the 2006 Census, over 200 ethnic origins (including Aboriginal) existed in Canada. In 1901, only 25 ethnic origins were reported. Canadian was the most frequently reported ethnic origin in 2006 with just over 10 million, either alone or in combination with other ethnic origins (comprising 32 percent of the total responses, down from 39 percent in 2001). Following behind Canadian were (both single and multiple origins) English (6.6 million), French, Scottish, Irish, German, Italian, Chinese, North American Indian, Ukrainian, and Dutch (1 million). The percentage of those reporting multiple origins continued to rise, from 35.8 percent in 1996 to 41.4 percent in 2006. A total of 5,068,100 persons claimed to belong to the category of visible minority (itself a contentious category; Fleras 2008a), thus accounting for 16.2 percent of Canada's population, up from 11.2 percent in 1996 and 4.1 percent in 1981. Canada's visible minority population increased by 27.1 percent between 2001 and 2006 compared to an increase of 5.4 percent for the total population. Fully 75 percent of all immigrants who arrived between 2001 and 2006 were visible minorities. South Asians surpassed Chinese as the largest visible minority group in 2006, with blacks as the third-largest minority. Most South Asians reported ancestral backgrounds from the Indian subcontinent, with East Indians the largest in number, followed by those from Pakistan and Sri Lanka. Over half of the black population reported Caribbean origins, followed closely by African origins. Next were those who identified with the British Isles, Canadian, and French origins.

- With 54.2 percent of Canada's visible minority population living in Ontario, visible minorities are 22 percent of Ontario's population. Twenty-five years ago, visible minorities accounted for 6.4 percent of Ontario's population.
- Nearly 96 percent of visible minorities lived in a Metropolitan census area, compared with 68.1 percent of the general population. If just the MTV areas—Montreal, Toronto, and Vancouver—are included, they are home to 75 percent of visible minorities. Markham, Ontario (just north of Toronto City), has the highest percentage of visible minorities at 65.4 percent of its population. Richmond BC follows closely behind with about 64 percent. By contrast, cities like Moncton, Trois Rivieres, and Saguenay reported statistically insignificant levels of visible minorities.
- Toronto remains the demographic diversity hub of Canada; 42.9 percent of Canada's visible minority population live in Toronto (as well, over 40 percent of all immigrants to Canada), while 42.9 percent of Toronto's population declare a visible minority status. Vancouver's visible minority population accounts for 41.7 percent of its total population; the figure for Montreal is 16.5 percent, with the vast majority living on the island rather than in the suburbs.
- The year 2006 was a fairly typical year for immigration with respect to overall numbers, source countries, and patterns of selection. A total of 251,639 immigrants arrived in Canada, with the majority arriving under the economic class (138,257), followed by the family class (70,508), refugee and protected persons class (32,492), and other (10,223). Plans for 2007 and 2008 are to admit between 240,000 and 265,000 new permanent residents (immigrants) (Citizenship and Immigration 2006). Also, 112,658 temporary work permits were

issued to foreign workers; 61,703 new study permits were granted to international students; 13,412 temporary resident permits were dispensed; 987,378 temporary visitor visas were issued; and Canadian citizenship was granted to 259,802 permanent residents who qualified to apply for citizenship after living in Canada for three years. Nearly 80 percent of immigrants to Canada reflect non-European and non-American sources, with India, China, Pakistan, and the Philippines ranking as the top four.

Putting Canada's Multiculturalism into Perspective

Canada is widely admired for its many qualities; two, however, appear foremost. First, people around the world marvel at Canada's ability to resist the pressures of absorption as the fifty-first state of the world's most powerful melting pot. Second, people are also astonished by Canada's resourcefulness in weaving a united society from the strands of diversity (Adams 2007). How do Canadians manage to keep a lid on those ethnic tensions that have fractured other societies into warring factions? Consider the relatively smooth transformation of once stodgy provincial capitals like Toronto and Vancouver into cosmopolitan complexes without experiencing paralyzing strife (Ibbitson 2005). To be sure, the potential for unraveling Canada's social fabric along ethnic lines is always present. But while other countries are groping for solutions to "accommodate difference," Canada is pursuing a promising, if unprecedented, quest for multicultural coexistence along principled lines (Adams 2007; Kymlicka 2007a). Or as Canada's governor-general, Michaëlle Jean, put it, Canada constitutes a multicultural role model in the art of living together with differences (cited in O'Neill 2008).

How does this assessment stand up to scrutiny? Any response must acknowledge a sense of perspective. First, compared with its historical past, Canada's engagement with diversity and difference has shown vast improvement. The country's racist history left much to be desired: Canada originated in the dispossession of Aboriginal peoples and their lands, while Canada-building was predicated on policies and practices that routinely exploited or excluded racialized minorities—including restrictions to Chinese and East Indian immigrants (Li 2003); the internment and dispossession of Japanese-Canadians during World War II (Sunahara 1981); the enslavement of blacks and their segregation from mainstream institutions until the 1950s (Walker 1997; Backhouse 1999); and the pervasive anti-Semitism of the 1920s and 1930s, which culminated in the rejection of Jewish émigrés from Nazi Germany (Penslar 2005). The extent to which this exclusion went beyond the perversions of a few misguided bigots but pervaded both institutional structures and government policies speaks volumes of the systemic embeddedness of white supremacist ideologies (Thobani 2007; Wallis and Fleras 2009; Hier et al. 2009).

Second, consider global comparisons. Compared with other societies that routinely violate human rights, with abuses ranging from ethnic cleansing and mass expulsion to forced exploitation and coercive assimilation, Canada possesses an enviable reputation as a paragon of virtue, tolerance, and compassion. The enshrinement of the 1960 Bill of Rights, the Human Rights Act of 1977, and the Charter of Rights and Freedoms that came into effect in 1985 has seen to that. And yet Canada's commitment to the protection and promotion of aboriginal rights is routinely criticized both domestically and internationally. Canada's rejection of a widely backed UN protocol to protect indigenous people's rights has done little to disabuse critics of this notion (Maaka and Fleras 2008). To add insult to injury, UN Human Rights Committees have rebuked Canada's treatment of vulnerable minorities, citing antiterrorist legislation that is too broad and imprecise, especially over the issuing of security certificates to arrest, detain, or expel immigrants without due process. Paradoxically, however, Canada's lofty status as a global pacesetter makes it vulnerable to criticism. Even the smallest of infractions, which would barely register a mention in many foreign countries, tend to be amplified in Canada because of its exacting standards (Levitt 1997). Not surprisingly, Canadians appear perplexed and angry when international bodies chastise Canada for relatively minor human rights violations, including its use of the label "visible minorities" (Fleras 2008a), while rogue regimes are rarely condemned.

Third, while Canada glitters by comparison with its past and with others, it also falls short of established benchmarks. Canadians are adept at "talking the walk" when articulating the ideals of tolerance, openness, and inclusiveness; they are less inclined to put these ideas into practice. Relations between racialized minorities and the rest of Canada tend to waver uneasily between grudging acceptance and thinly veiled racism, with the specter of public backlash ever present (Hier and Bolaria 2007). Discrimination and racism are not simply relics from the past, but are so deeply ingrained and structurally embedded that any chance of disappearing in the foreseeable future is nil to none (Razack 2004; Jiwani 2006; Thobani 2007). And while racism is no longer blatant, more subtle forms of racism exert an equally powerful negative impact. Anti-Semitism persists, albeit in different guises (Weinfeld 2005); white supremacist groups proliferate because of digital media and mobile technology; and racialized minorities continue to do poorly in socioeconomic terms despite a commitment to inclusiveness, justice, and participation (Galabuzi 2006; Henry and Tator 2006; Jimenez 2009). The fact that highly skilled immigrants find it difficult to secure appropriate employment exposes a gap between immigration ideals and multiculturalism realities (Pendakur 2005; Teelucksingh and Galabuzi 2005). Of particular dismay as Canada's most egregious human rights violation is the continued disengagement of Aboriginal peoples (Belanger 2008). In that Aboriginal communities remain politically repressed, economically depressed, and culturally oppressed, such an indictment reflects poorly on Canada's lavish reputation (Frideres and Gadacz 2008).

This admittedly selective overview paints a discordant picture of Canada's multicultural aspirations. From a distance, Canada looks idyllic; up close and the picture blurs, with little to boast about in the *mis*management of diversity and difference. That discord suggests the possibility of a *fourth* interpretation—that Canada is positioned somewhere in between the extremes of good and bad. Neither a paragon of virtue nor the fountainhead of all evils, Canada's record for managing difference probably falls somewhere in the middle. In comparison to the past or to other countries, Canada soars; when compared to the ideals that many Canadians espouse, Canada misses the mark. Initiatives for engaging diversity and difference are enlightened at times, yet callously expedient at other times, especially as Canadians strive to balance minority rights with national interests. Perhaps the best possible spin acknowledges a creative tension at the heart of Canada's multicultural governance, with difference (cultural) and equality (social) and unity (national) pulling in opposite directions. And nowhere are the paradoxes and promises more evident than in the emergence and evolution of Canada's official multiculturalism as an aspirational blueprint for multiculturally governing difference and diversity.

Official Multiculturalism: An Unfinished Policy-Project in Progress

That Canada is officially multicultural is stating the obvious. Yet the irony is improbable: from its inception in 1971 when it barely garnered a paragraph in Canada's national newspaper, official Multiculturalism has evolved to the point where it constitutes an inextricable component of Canada's national narrative. Having profoundly altered how Canadians think about themselves and their relationship to the world, four decades of official Multiculturalism have orchestrated a national consensus over the principle of living together without disassembling Canada in the process. The origins of Multiculturalism revolved around the pragmatism of inclusiveness—to make ethnicity irrelevant as a marker in Canadian society by rejecting the single minded nature of nationalism with its corresponding belief that one nation's culture is superior to others (Kruhlak 2003; Jacobs 2008). Ethnicity would no longer be used to rank Canadians or to exclude them because they lacked the status of the so-called founding nation groups (English and French). As a result, the inception of multiculturalism not only altered the conception of who legitimately was Canadian but also transformed the nature of power relations in Canada along the lines of justice, empowerment, and participation (Reitz 2009).

Multiculturalism also originated around the quest for Canada-building by establishing an inclusionary framework for intercultural relations (Kunz and Sykes 2008). It continues to persist for precisely the same reasons, namely, the inclusion of migrants and minorities by modifying the rules of integration (Kymlicka 2001). The goal of multiculturalism as governance has never wavered from its underlying rationale—the possibility of living together with differences without letting differences get in the way of the "living together." Only the means for achieving this goal have changed because of demographic upheavals and political developments, with ethnicity-based solutions giving way to equity-grounded reforms and, more recently, the promotion of civic belonging and participation. Three overlapping policy stages can be discerned in describing Multiculturalism as an evolving political framework: *ethnicity, equity, and civic multiculturalism*. An *integration* stage is an emergent possibility (Kunz and Sykes 2008).

Ethnicity multiculturalism (1970s)

A commitment to multiculturalism within a bilingual framework was articulated by the Liberal government in 1971 when the then prime minister Pierre Elliott Trudeau declared his government's intentions to embrace "multiculturalism within a bilingual framework." In the words of Trudeau, the linking of individual rights with equal status under multiculturalism would "strengthen the solidarity of the Canadian people by enabling all Canadians to participate fully and without discrimination in defining and building the nation's future." Four major principles secured this reconfiguring of Canada along multicultural lines:

- *Equality of status:* Canada does not have an official culture; all cultures are equal. Yes, Canada would continue to have laws, rules, conventions, and so forth, but it would not explicitly favor any particular culture, while consciously supporting an individual's freedom of choice (Forbes 2007).

- _Canadian identity:_ Diversity lies at the heart of Canadian identity.
- _Personal choice:_ Individuals have the right to identify with the cultural tradition of their choice.
- _Protection of individual rights:_ Everyone is entitled to freedom from discrimination through removal of discriminatory barriers and cultural jealousies.

To put these principles into practice—preservation, participation, and interaction—the government proposed initiatives to (1) help those cultural groups that demonstrated a commitment to develop, share, and contribute to Canada; (2) assist the members of all cultural groups to overcome cultural barriers to full participation in Canadian society; (3) promote creative encounters and exchanges among all Canadian cultural groups in advancing national unity; and (4) equip immigrants to acquire one of Canada's official languages to ensure full participation in Canadian society.

An ethnicity commitment to multiculturalism initially focused on the protection and promotion of Canada as an ethnic mosaic. Multicultural discourses were rooted in an almost essentialized understanding of ethnicity as primordial and immutable—rather than flexible, dynamic, and relational—with members locked into hermetically sealed groups. According to tabled documents, however, the government flatly rejected the principle of assisting any group to cut themselves off from the rest of Canada (Foote 2006). But a commitment to cultural preservation or celebrating diversity was not high on the multicultural agenda—at least not beyond an initial commitment when powerful ethnic lobbyists prevailed. If anything, the goals of an official Multiculturalism were twofold. The first was to eliminate discriminations rooted in cultural prejudices while improving minority and migrant participation and integration into a more inclusive Canada. This commitment was predicated on the assumption that migrants and minorities are more likely to emotionally embrace Canada— not less—if they cultivated a sense of shared identity and community pride (Adams 2008). The second was to create a new symbolic order: together with an official bilingualism (implemented in 1969), an official multiculturalism was designed to wean Canada away from its former essentialist conception of Britishness (and Frenchness), while differentiating Canada's multicultural mosaic from America's melting pot assimilationism (Dupont and Lemarchand 2001). Hegemonic interests prevailed as well. As Sunera Thobani points out, in addition to addressing the crisis of legitimacy created by Aboriginal, French, and minority protest, adoption of multiculturalism helped to stabilize notions of Canada as a white man's society by reinventing a national narrative that masked—and continues to mask—the racism and power intrinsic to Canada-building. She writes:

> Multiculturalist policies and its after-effects on popular culture eroded the salience of anti-racist politics and discourses; it disguised the persistence of white supremacy and power in the new constitution of whiteness as signifying "tolerance" Multiculturalism avoided recognition of the critical intersection of institutional power and interpersonal forms of racism, demanding only tolerance at the interpersonal level of interaction. Knowledge about the nature of racism, and the role it has historically played in Canadian nation-building, has thus been made peripheral. (Thobani 2007:160)

Equity multiculturalism (1980s)

The focus of official Multiculturalism underwent significant change by the early 1980s. Instead of emphasizing interethnicity as the multicultural core, the logic behind an equity Multiculturalism embraced the more pragmatic concerns of racialized immigrants. The often-different requirements of immigrants from so-called nonconventional sources proved more perplexing, since their visibility complicated the prospect of settling down, fitting in, and moving up (Fleras 2009). Migrant and minority concerns shifted accordingly: for new immigrants, the importance of dismantling racial barriers to opportunity superseded concerns over cultural preservation (McRoberts 1997). The earlier emphasis on ethnicity and identity as keys to integration was subsequently replaced by a commitment to the principles of equity, social justice, and institutional inclusiveness (Agocs and Boyd 1993; Donaldson 2004). Funding allocations shifted as well. Rather than simply doling out money to ethnocultural organizations or events as had been the case in the very early days of multiculturalism, authorities channeled multicultural spending into equity goals of antiracism, race relations, and removal of discriminatory barriers at institutional levels.

Subsequent developments consolidated the political profile of official multiculturalism. The Charter of Rights and Freedoms, which came into effect in 1985, constitutionally entrenched multiculturalism as a distinguishing feature of Canadian life. Section 27 read: "This Charter shall be interpreted in a manner consistent with the preservation and enhancement of the multicultural heritage of Canadians." Implications of Section 27 were two-edged: Emergence of multiculturalism as an interpretative tool at the highest levels of constitutional decision making may have reinforced its status as a fundamental characteristic of Canada. But as an interpretive clause, with little enforcement clout, multiculturalism constituted a weak, almost empty, norm (Eliadis 2007). The prominence of multiculturalism was further secured with passage of the Multiculturalism Act in 1988, in the process consolidating Canada's status as the world's first statutory multiculturalism. Passage of the act sought to respect cultures, promote participation, reduce discrimination, encourage ingroup bonding as a precondition for outgroup bridging, and accelerate institutional inclusiveness at the federal level by helping all Canadians overcome racialized barriers. Under the Act, all government departments and Crown corporations must annually disclose their specific initiatives to preserve and enhance Canada's multicultural heritage—a commitment honored more in the breach than in the observance.

* * *

Canadian Multiculturalism Act 1985 (assented to on July 21 1988): An Act for the Preservation and Enhancement of Multiculturalism in Canada

Preamble

* Whereas the Constitution of Canada provides that every individual is equal before and under the law and has the right to the equal protection and benefit of the law without discrimination and that everyone has the freedom of conscience, religion, thought, belief, opinion, expression, peaceful assembly and association and guarantees these rights equally to male and female persons;

* And whereas the Constitution of Canada recognizes the importance of preserving and enhancing the multicultural heritage of Canadians; . . .

* And whereas the Government of Canada recognizes the diversity of Canadians as regards race, national or ethnic origins, colour and religion as a fundamental characteristics of Canadian society and is committed to a policy of multiculturalism designed to preserve and enhance the multicultural heritage of Canadians while working to achieve the equality of all Canadians in the economic, social, cultural, and political life of Canada.

Multiculturalism Policy of Canada

It is hereby declared to be the policy of the Government of Canada to

    (a) recognize and promote the understanding that multiculturalism reflects the cultural and racial diversity of Canada and acknowledges the freedom of all members of Canadian society to preserve, enhance, and share their cultural heritage;

(b) to recognize and promote the understanding that multiculturalism is a fundamental characteristic of the Canadian heritage and identity and that it provides an invaluable source in the shaping of Canada's future;

(c) promote the full and equitable participation of individuals and communities of all origins in the continuing evolution and shaping of all aspects of Canadian society and assist in the elimination of any barrier to that participation;

(d) recognize the existence of communities whose members share a common origin and their historic contribution to Canadian society, and enhance their development;

(e) ensure that all individuals receive equal treatment and equal protection under the law, while respecting and valuing their diversity;

(f) encourage and assist the social, cultural, economic and political institutions of Canada to be both respectful and inclusive of Canada's multicultural character;

(g) promote the understanding and creativity that arise from the interaction between individuals and communities of different origins;

(h) foster the recognition and appreciation of the diverse cultures of Canadian society and promote the reflection and evolving expressions of these cultures;

(i) preserve and enhance the use of languages other than French or English while strengthening the status and use of the official languages of Canada; and

(j) advance multiculturalism throughout Canada in harmony with the national commitment to the official languages of Canada

*   *   *

Even a cursory reading of the Act makes it abundantly clear. As an inclusionary framework for living together differently, Multiculturalism endorses a commitment to integration over separation, interaction over isolation, and participation over withdrawal (Adams 2008). But commitment is not the same as enactment. With its broad set of ideals for living together differently rather than a blueprint with specific goals, measurable targets, and enforceable timetables, the Multiculturalism Act remains largely an aspirational document (Reitz and Banerjee 2007). Nevertheless, aspirational or not, the Act contributed to the Canada-building project associated with passage of the Official Languages Act in 1969, the Statement on Multiculturalism in 1971 and its enshrinement in the Constitution Act of 1982 and the inception of the Charter of Rights and Freedoms in 1985. Each of these initiatives converged in hopes of creating a distinctive and unified Canada, based on the principle that as self-defining agents all individuals should be able to participate fully and equally regardless of differences (Breton 2000).

Civic multiculturalism

Canada's Multiculturalism continues to acknowledge the importance of cultural identity. Its commitment to social equality is no less vibrant, including an emphasis on institutional inclusions to ensure minority access, representation, and equitable treatment at institutional levels. Equally evident is a more explicit commitment to national interests by equating multiculturalism with citizenship. In eschewing a Multiculturalism that was aimed only at minorities, the scope of a civic multiculturalism focused on "break[ing] down the ghettoization of multiculturalism," according to Hedy Frey, former minister for Multiculturalism (1997):

> As a national policy of inclusiveness, multiculturalism's activities aim to bring all Canadians closer together, to enhance equal opportunities, to encourage mutual respect among citizens of diverse backgrounds, to assist in integrating first-generation Canadians, to promote more harmonious intergroup relations, and to foster social cohesion and a shared sense of Canadian identity.

This shift was formalized in 1996 following the renewal of the Multiculturalism program. Three strategic goals prevailed: civic participation (full and equal involvement), social justice (equitable treatment), and identity (respect for people's differences in securing a belonging and attachment to Canada regardless of ethnic background). The renewed program prioritized the following proposals: (a) facilitate active participation of ethnic minorities, (b) support community initiatives to reduce ethnic conflict and hate crimes, (c) make public institutions respectful of, reflective upon, and responsive to difference, (d) foster more inclusive federal departments and agencies, and (e) increase public awareness of multiculturalism and cross-cultural understanding of difference. Finally to symbolically commemorate a commitment to Multiculturalism, the federal government announced that each June 27 would celebrate the diverse contributions of all Canadians to Canada.

The current Multiculturalism program continues along these inclusionary lines, namely, *social justice* (ensure fair and equitable treatment), *cultural identity* (foster a Canada in which all Canadians feel a sense of attachment and belonging regardless of their ethnocultural background), and *civic participation* (improve citizens' involvement in community and Canada). Priority objectives include a commitment to institutional change (inclusiveness through removal of discriminatory barriers), federal institutional change (integration of diversity into policies, programs, and services), combat against racism (removal of discriminatory barriers, antiracism programs, and cross-cultural understanding), and civic engagement (promotion of active and shared citizenship plus building capacity for minorities to participate in public decision making) (Annual Report, Canadian Heritage, 2005/2006). With its emphasis on fostering a sense of belonging, a civic engagement, an active involvement in community life, and a shared awareness of Canadian identity against the broader backdrop of Canada's national interests, the conclusion seems inescapable: all signs point to inclusive multiculturalism as the governance of choice for the twenty-first century.

To summarize: Canada's official Multiculturalism constitutes a complex and contested governance policy that has evolved over time in response to social and political changes (Seiler 2002). Despite shifts in emphasis— from ethnicity to equity to civic participation—an official multiculturalism has never waivered from its central mission: Canada-building through institutional inclusion and minority integration (Cardozo and Pendakur 2008: 27). In advancing the principle of inclusion through removal of discriminatory barriers and respect for cultural differences, an inclusive multiculturalism promotes a two-way process of mutual adjustment that bodes well for democratic governance. The following Table 3.1 compares and contrasts the different stages in the evolution of Canada's inclusive multiculturalism, keeping in mind the inevitability of simplification when comparing ideal-typical categories (Fleras 2009).

Table 3.1 Canada's inclusive multiculturalism: policy shifts

	Ethnicity multiculturalism (1970s)	Equity multiculturalism (1980s-early 1990s)	Civic multiculturalism (1995s–2000s)
Dimension	Cultural	Structural	Social
Focus	Respecting differences	Fostering equality	Living together
Mandate	Ethnicity	Race relations	Citizenship
Magnitude	Individual adjustment	Institutional accommodation	Full engagement
Problem	Prejudice	Racism/discrimination	Exclusion
Solution	Cultural sensitivity	Removing barriers	Inclusion
Outcomes	Cultural capital	Human capital	Social capital
Key Metaphor	"Mosaic"	"Level playing field"	"Belonging"

There are signs of yet anothershift in Canada's multicultural trajectory. A new multicultural agenda may be taking shape in reaction to post-9/11 security concerns, including the Toronto Terror Scare in June 2006 (when 18 males were apprehended on suspicion of fomenting terror). Its focus is broadly aimed at depoliticizing the multiculturalism in a multicultural governance by promoting integration for neutralizing the threat of ethnoreligious extremism (Annual Report 2008; Freeze 2008; Kunz and Sykes 2008). A speech by Jason Kenney, now Minister of Citizenship, Immigration, and Multiculturalism (2008; also Libin 2009) confirms a proposed shift in fine tuning Canada's multicultural program toward integration, social cohesion, and core liberal values:

> The key to building such a Canada, to maintaining our model of unity-in-diversity, is the successful integration of newcomers. And that should be the focus of today's multiculturalism. Integration that empowers newcomers by ensuring that they can speak one or both of our languages. Integration that opens the doors of economic opportunity by properly recognizing the skills, experiences, and education of new Canadians. Integration that ensures that new Canadians know, own, and identify our country's history, symbols, and institutions. And integration which results in new Canadians giving back to Canada, not just as consumers, workers, or taxpayers. But as active citizens, as volunteers, as members of our Armed Forces, police and emergency services . . .

To be sure, with its emphasis on inclusion, this commitment to an integrative multiculturalism is not altogether different from the civic phase. Nevertheless, a repositioning toward integration as governance mode reflects parallel developments in Europe and the Antipodes, including a shift from diversity and disadvantage to that of integration, youth-at-risk, intercultural understanding, and Canadian values (Annual Report 2009). The

Table 3.2 Proposed shift in Canadian multiculturalism. Integrative multiculturalism (2010s -)

Dimension	Societal
Focus	Integration
Mandate	Living Together
Magnitude	National (Comm)unity
Problem source	Segregation, Extremism
Solution	Shared Canadian Values
Outcome	Cohesiveness
Key metaphor	Citizenship

Table 3.2 speculates on what an integrative multiculturalism might look like when compared using the aforementioned criteria.

Interculturalism as Multicultural Governance in Quebec

Federal multiculturalism is not the only governance in Canada. With the possible exception of Newfoundland and Labrador, each of Canada's ten provinces has established formal policies, laws, advisory boards, or commitments that often overlap with federal commitments. Of these provincial multiculturalisms, few have attracted as much attention—or notoriety—as Quebec's multicultural governance model. Called interculturalism (or transculturalism), it arguably shares similarities with Canada's federal multiculturalism, yet also reflects differences in tone and emphasis (Gagnon and Iacovino 2007), with some arguing the case for fundamentally different governance priorities in integrating immigrants, while others dismiss any agenda differences as largely semantic (Gagnon 2008; Reitz 2009).

Quebec's commitment toward interculturalism as governance and minority integration was first articulated by the 1990 Policy Statement on Immigration and Integration. An interculturalism commitment reflects what might be metaphorically called an arboreal model of multiculturalism; that is, the tree trunk is unflinchingly French in language and culture, while minority cultures represent the branches grafted onto the trunk. According to the tree-trunk tenets of interculturalism, immigrants and their contributions are welcome. However, they must enter into a "moral contract" involving a reciprocal exchange of rights, duties, and obligations between newcomers and Quebec. They must also abide by the primacy of French as the language and culture of Quebec, observe prevailing cultural norms and rule of law, actively participate as citizens in Quebec's society, become involved in community dialogue and exchanges, and respect democratic principles and practices (Gagnon and Iacovino 2007). With interculturalism, in other words, limits are explicit—you can be Haitian but always a Haitian in Quebec with a corresponding commitment to its values, institutions, and norms as set out in laws and constitution. As of January 2009, future immigrants to Quebec will be required to sign a declaration promising to learn French and respect Quebec's shared values, including gender equity, separation of church and state, nonviolence, rule of law, democracy, and protection of individual rights and freedoms (Hamilton 2008).

Clearly, then, both federal multiculturalism and Quebec's interculturalism share a core theme: a common commitment to incorporate newcomers into the larger community by way of an inclusive governance (Nugent

2006; Salee 2007; Gagnon 2008). Two broad governance agendas prevail (Banting et al. 2007):

1) A difference agenda that seeks an inclusive citizenship by encouraging migrants and minorities to recognize, express, and share their cultural identities
2) An integrative agenda for incorporating migrants and minorities into the mainstream while strengthening the bonds of solidarity, community, and support

For some, the major difference lies in Quebec's willingness to be more explicit about what it expects of migrants and what they can expect in return, what constitutes the limits of acceptable behavior, and the unassailable primacy of French language and culture. For others, the governance models appear to reflect distinct society-building projects. Canada's multicultural governance model is aimed at constructing a universal citizenship based on nominal recognition of diversity and difference. In promoting the governance principle of unity within diversity, Canada's Multiculturalism resembles a planetary model, that is, minority cultures orbiting around a mainstream center. By contrast, Quebec's arboreal governance model aims at articulating a distinct political community whose cultural and language priorities supersede ethnic diversities. This governance establishes French as the language of intercultural communication; cultivates a pluralistic notion of society that is sensitive to minority rights; preserves the creative tension between minority and migrant difference and the continuity and predominance of the French culture; and emphasizes the centrality of integration and interaction to the interculturalism process (Bouchard-Taylor Commission 2008).

The logic behind federal and Quebec multicultural governance makes it difficult to mix or merge. According to the Bouchard-Taylor Commission on Reasonable Accommodation (2008), Quebec cannot possibly duplicate the federal multiculturalism policy. The paradoxicality of Quebec's majority/minority status—a majority in Quebec, but a minority in Canada and North America—generates a heightened defensiveness because of perceived threats to their identity and integrity as a French-speaking oasis in an ocean of English-speaking North Americans (Gagnon 2008). The paradox of reconciling a growing pluralism with preservation of a small cultural minority in North America undermines any move toward Canada's so-called laissez-faire multiculturalism. To do so would be tantamount to linguistic and cultural suicide. English Canada can afford a looser concept of multiculturalism as governance, concludes the Commission, because of fewer anxieties over English as a threatened language, less insecurities because they are a majority, and less rationale for protecting a founding nation since those who identify as British descent constitute only one-third of Canada's population. Yes, Quebec <u>can be a society that is pluralistic and open to outside contributions</u>, but <u>this pluralism can flourish only within the limitations imposed by Quebec's French character, its democratic values, and the need for intercommunity dialogue and exchanges</u> (Bouchard-Taylor Commmission 2008). Or as the commission concluded when acknowledging that Quebec and English-speaking Canada are playing by different rules:

> French-speaking Quebec is a minority culture and needs a strong identity to allay its anxieties and behave like a serene majority.

In other words, as the Bouchard-Taylor Commission implored, Quebecers should continue to support the interculturalism principles of pluralism, equality, and reciprocity. With its emphasis on immigrant integration around a common culture, a moral contract, and centrality of French, a commitment to interculturalism as governance provides Quebecers with the best chances for survival as irrevocably French yet unmistakenly cosmopolitan.

Putting Multicultural Policy Principles into Practice

The implementation of multicultural policy principles is central to any multicultural governance. In acknowledging the convergence of policy and philosophy at a grounded level, multiculturalism as practice involves its application and manipulation by political, institutional, and minority sectors for advancing vested interests, promoting hidden agendas, and securing public good. The practice of multiculturalism incorporates a range of activities, including its implementation by government programs; its manipulation by political sectors for electoral advantages; its inclusion within mainstream institutions; and its use by multicultural minorities for articulating both individual and collective interests. An examination of how multiculturalism works by watching it work reinforces its status in advancing an inclusive governance.

Political agendas

The governing apparatus of the Canadian state has long relied on multiculturalism to fulfill a variety of legitimating functions related to national unity, economic prosperity, and electoral survival (Fleras 2002). Multiculturalism originated in 1971 as part of an all-party agreement in Parliament, acquired constitutional recognition in 1982, and received royal assent with passage of the Multiculturalism Act in 1988. (To be sure, a commitment to multicultural principles of tolerance existed in Canada long before 1971; Bramadat and Seljak 2008). With British values losing their saliency as identity markers in Canada and elsewhere (see Jakubowicz 2005), Multiculturalism represented an ideological moral glue for bonding Canadians by bridging differences. A new national unity strategy evolved, based on a iconoclastic vision of Canada—not as a bicultural partnership between founding peoples, but as a multicultural mosaic of equality-seeking individuals (McRoberts 1997). It was hoped that an official multiculturalism would formulate a new founding myth of Canada as a land of opportunity and equality rather than a racialized colonial state. In addition to uniting all Canadians at a time of political turmoil without initiating any fundamental redistribution of power (Helly 1993; Mackey 1998; Bannerji 2000; Thobani 2007), Multiculturalism also sought to shore up electoral strength in urban Ontario, to counterbalance Western resentment over perceived favoritism toward the Québécois, to facilitate adoption of the Official Languages Act by alleviating mounting public pressure over official bilingualism (Gagnon 2008), to neutralize Quebec nationalism, and to preempt the encroachment of American cultural values by erecting a multicultural firewall.

Introduction of Multiculturalism is widely regarded as Canada's foremost contribution to intergroup harmony and global peace. Yet it reflected a degree of political opportunism rather than any long-term vision or clearly articulated theory (Wood and Gilbert 2005). Instead of a compassionate or courageous social experiment devised by well-meaning liberals, Multiculturalism originated primarily as a pragmatic response to ongoing political struggles; that is, *a political program to achieve political goals in a politically astute manner* (Peter 1978). With evolving immigration patterns, multiculturalism secured a long-term investment for transforming Canada into a cosmopolitan galaxy without experiencing major disruptions in the process. Containment and control informed an official Multiculturalism, in other words, while its primary objective dwelt on cooling out potentially troublesome constituents. That critics say it persists for the same reason—the control of "unruly ethnics by ruling elites"—makes it doubly important to concede the power of conflict management in fostering the illusion of change.

Also widely touted is the commercial potential of multiculturalism. The then prime minister Brian Mulroney promoted a business model of multiculturalism rooted in economic rationality and national interest in his "Multiculturalism Means Business" speech at a Toronto conference in 1986. <u>The commercial value of multiculturalism remains stronger than ever because of the demands of a global economy.</u> Diversity and the market are closely intertwined; after all, capitalizing on differences is good for the economy, especially when 40 percent of Canada's GDP is export based.

> The ethnocultural diversity of Canada's population is a major advantage when access to global markets is more important than ever to our economic prosperity. Protecting this advantage means that steps to eradicate racism are essential... Canada cannot afford to have any of its citizens marginalized. As a knowledge-based economy in an increasingly global marketplace, every mind matters. All Canadians must have the opportunity to develop and contribute to their full potential. (Canadian Heritage 2001)

Like staple products in the past, Multiculturalism continues to be promoted as a commodity for sale or export (Abu-Laban and Gabriel 2002; Abu-Laban 2003). By enhancing Canada's sales image and competitive edge in a global economy—particularly by cultivating and tapping into the lucrative Asian market (Hage 1998)—references to multiculturalism are touted as having the potential to harness lucrative trade contracts, to establish international linkages and mutually profitable points of contact, to attract members of the transnational elite, and to penetrate export markets (Multiculturalism/Secretary of State 1993; also Jupp 1986 for Australian equivalent). The promotion of multiculturalism as an ideology of racial harmony and ethnic coexistence reassures nervous investors and fidgety capital markets (Mitchell 1993). Perception of Canada as difference friendly transforms it into a desirable destination to work, live, study, and do business in. Its reputation for multicultural tolerance snares a competitive advantage in the global competition for foreign investment, tourism, and skilled immigrants (Kymlicka 2004). Moreover, as the globalization of capitalist market economies continues to expand, multiculturalism may well provide the networking for addressing the realities of a shifting and increasingly borderless world. In that multicultural priorities will continue to be driven by an economic agenda more interested in improving Canada's competitive advantage than in securing institutional inclusiveness, Multiculturalism indeed means business.

Minority agendas

Multicultural minorities are equally inclined to see multiculturalism as a resource for attaining practical goals. The needs of the minorities are basic: they as a group want to become established, expand economic opportunities for themselves and their children, eliminate discrimination and exploitation, and retain access to their cultural heritage without loss of citizenship rights—that is, to retain their identities and heritage without abandoning a primary sense of belonging to Canada. Multiculturalism is employed as a tool for meeting these needs by opening up opportunities through elimination of discriminatory barriers in employment, education, housing, and criminal justice. With multiculturalism, minority women and men are empowered with a platform for staking out their claims while articulating their demands alongside those of the mainstream. An otherwise powerless sector is empowered with the leverage to prod or provoke central policy structures by holding them accountable for failure to close the gaps between multicultural ideals and everyday results. Appeals to official Multiculturalism are thus calculated to extract public sympathy and global scrutiny—in the same way Canada's Aboriginal peoples have relied on international fora (such as the United Nations) in leveraging concessions from the federal government. For minorities, rather than separate homelands and autonomous states, the driving force behind multiculturalism is equality, not nationalism; participation, not ghettoization; integration, not isolation; and inclusion, not separation.

Institutional inclusiveness

Canada's historical track record for "doing multiculturalism" is not without blemish. Prejudice and discrimination reinforced a dismissive belief in difference as inimical to society building. Racialized immigrants were expected to integrate into the existing institutional framework, yet mainstream institutions routinely excluded minority women and men from the workplace or delivery of services (Henry and Tator 2006). With the inception of an official Multiculturalism, however, institutional responsiveness has improved markedly. Multicultural differences are no longer disparaged as a bothersome anomaly, with no redeeming value outside a personal or private context. Rather than being trivialized as a problem to solve or a challenge to surmount, difference is instead promoted as an integral and legitimate component of Canada's social fabric, with untapped potential for improving national wealth and international standing. Its promotion as an asset for improving the bottom line, enhancing workplace climate, or delivering social services is critical in putting multiculturalism to work at institutional levels.

Few contest the necessity for more multiculturally responsive institutions. Only the pace or scope of adjustments remain open to debate. Public and private institutions are increasingly anxious to enhance overall effectiveness by maximizing the talent and creativity they can contribute. For service organizations eager to improve delivery quality, a commitment to multiculturalism can reap institutional dividends by easing workplace tensions, generating creative synergies, and facilitating community access. For private companies, the inclusion of diversity is tantamount to money in the bank. Corporations increasingly rely on the language skills, cultural knowledge, life experiences, and international connections that diverse people bring to the workplace. Diversity connections can also provide the catalyst for internationalizing domestic businesses, thus improving competitive advantage in global markets.

A commitment to inclusiveness entails a rethinking and restructuring of "how we do things around here." It involves a process of adjustment (in design, values, operation, and outcomes) to make institutions more reasonably accommodate difference—both within the workplace (being more respectful and reflective of difference, and responsive to it) and outside (making service delivery more available, accessible, and appropriate). Yet efforts at putting multiculturalism to work have proven uneven. The commitment may be there, but it is easily undermined by the lack of political will or an adequate resource base for implementation, in effect leaving a slippage between rhetoric/theory and reality/practice. Resistance to institutional inclusiveness reflects the deep ambiguities that surface when attempting to simultaneously balance seemingly opposing models of inclusion, namely, culture-blind (equal treatment) versus culture-conscious (treatment as equals) (see also Lieberman 2006). This gap should come as no surprise. Institutions are complex, often baffling landscapes of domination, power, and control, invariably pervaded by prejudice, nepotism, patronage, and the "old boys' network." Moreover, moves to be inclusive are rarely simple or straightforward; rather, they routinely encounter individual resistance, structural barriers, and institutional inertia. Conventional views remain firmly entrenched as vested interests balk at discarding the tried and true. Newer visions are compelling but lack the critical mass to scuttle traditional ways of doing business. The interplay of these juxtapositions can prove disruptive as institutions are transformed into a "contested site" involving competing worldviews and opposing agendas.

Service-oriented institutions such as media, education, health, and policing are under particular pressure to move over and make institutional space (Fleras and Elliott 2007). Their mandate as agencies of socialization and social control expose them to greater demands for accountability and transparency in decision making. No one should be surprised by this. Both processes not only strike at the hub of social existence; they also influence the degree to which people are in harmony with their communities or alienated from them. Media and education furnish the "blueprint" for acceptable behavior; by contrast, police and health services control the limits of unacceptable behavior by enforcing the rules. Consider these developments in doing multiculturalism by capitalizing on inclusiveness initiatives (Fleras 2002):

1. Educational institutions have responded to the challenges of multiculturalism by realigning the schooling and education along inclusiveness lines. Different levels of multicultural education can be discerned in engaging difference and including enlightenment, enrichment, and empowerment. Antiracist education transcends the principles of multicultural education by acknowledging structural barriers that underpin inequality both in schools and in workplaces (Dei 2005).

2. The criminal justice system has also taken steps toward more inclusiveness. Both the courts and the prison system have modified procedures and structures to become more diversity friendly. Of particular note is the policing service, which has embraced the principles of inclusive community policing (power sharing, partnership, prevention, problem solving) alongside those of conventional police work (Cryderman et al. 1998).

3. Mainstream mass media have stepped up to the challenge of diversity by way of programming and coverage that bodes well for the representational basis of media minority relations. But while many media institutions have improved both the quality and quantity of minority representation on television or advertising, other media processes such as newscasting continue to treat Aboriginal peoples and racialized minorities as troublesome constituents who are problems or who create problems (Fleras and Kunz 2001).

4. Health services in Canada are equally cognizant of the need to provide a range of services (from prevention to treatment to rehabilitation) that are accessible, available, and appropriate for the health needs of Canada's increasingly diverse population. Particularly relevant is the challenge of constructing community-based and culturally responsive social work services and mental health supports for assisting often-traumatized immigrants and refugees (Fleras 2006; Cooke et al. 2007).

Mainstream institutions are under pressure to advance a more inclusive Canada. Some institutions have taken up the challenge in ways deemed workable, necessary, and fair. But not all institutions are gung ho about jumping aboard the inclusion bandwagon, resulting in gaps between multicultural ideals and multicultural practices. A focus group study by

Catalyst (2008) concluded as much. Despite Canada's much-lauded multiculturalism, including a commitment to respect, recognize, reflect, and respond, minorities believed they had to Canadianize—that is, shed their culture and lose their accent—if they entertained any hope for promotional success.

Nor is there much consensus regarding what constitutes inclusiveness. Consider the options: (1) should reform be directed at changing the institutional culture or revamping patterns of power? (2) should efforts aim at changing personal attitudes or reshaping institutional structures? (3) should programs and services be customized for particular cultural needs or should a one-size-fits-all approach prevail to ensure common standards? Responses vary: To one side is the belief that a Canada of many cultures is possible as long as people's cultural differences do not get in the way of full and equal participation in society. Cultural differences are deemed largely irrelevant under multiculturalism; after all, true equality and inclusion arises from treating everyone the same regardless of their differences. To the other side is a belief that a Canada of many cultures is possible, but only when treating people as equals by taking differences into account when necessary. Rather than ignoring differences, in other words, true equality and inclusion arises by incorporating them into public policy processes and outcomes. The politics of this paradox animates the dynamics of multiculturalism within a multicultural governance.

Reasonable accommodation as institutional inclusiveness

The politics of reasonable accommodation extend the debate over institutional inclusiveness. Canada's official multiculturalism is predicated on promoting inclusiveness, in a two-way process of integration ("you adjust, we adapt; we adjust, you adapt") through reasonable accommodation (within limits and without undue hardship). Yet there remains unnecessary confusion over the concept of reasonable accommodation in terms of what it is, what it does, and its relationship to multicultural governance in Canada. As explained by the deputy minister of Canadian Heritage in a briefing to the federal secretary of state for Multiculturalism, "There is now a sense of urgency to more clearly define and explain the principle of reasonable accommodation, as alarming shifts regarding the split between 'them' and 'us' may occur" (cited in Wente 2007).

In debating how far Canada should go in accommodating difference, responses vary. Just as the Canadian state expects faith- and ethnic-based minorities to accommodate reasonably into society, so too do minorities expect the state to reasonably accommodate them. The politics of mutual adjustment by way of reasonable accommodation raises questions: How much accommodation should be reciprocated; that is, what can "they" expect of "us" versus what should "we" expect of "them"? Should immigrants discard all outward signs of religiosity from hijabs to kirpans as part of the accommodation process, or does accommodation entail adoption of core Canadian values including a nominal separation of church and state, acceptance of religion primarily as a private matter, and respect for religious dissidents? Is this exercise in cultural bullying yet another example of privileging Eurocentric values in seeming opposition to Canada's official Multiculturalism? Are Canadians too accommodative of difference, thus compromising the integration of newcomers into Canada? Or is Canada so systemically racist that discriminatory barriers invariably coax immigrants into their own religious and cultural cocoons?

Despite the centrality of reasonable accommodation to Canada's inclusiveness debates (Abu-Laban and Abu-Laban 2007), Canadians tend to be confused or uncertain over references to "reasonable," "accommodation," "within limits," and "undue hardship." Questions abound: Is there a principled basis for defining reasonable accommodation with respect to institutional workplaces that are responsive, representative, and respectful, including services that are available, accessible, and appropriate? In creating *reasonable accommodation within limits and without undue hardship*, who decides, why, and on what grounds? Consider this response by a UN report (2006): While employees have a duty to accommodate, it is the claimant's responsibility to justify the reasonable, whereas institutions must assume the responsibility for justifying undue hardship and within limits.

Developments in the United States may untangle these conundra. The concept of reasonable accommodation sprang into prominence over religious-based discrimination in the employment sector (UN Report 2006). It was subsequently applied to the disability context, culminating in the 1990 Americans with Disabilities Act, which called on employers to reasonably accommodate qualified applicants or employees with disabilities. Under the ADA, reasonable accommodation consists of any institutional adjustment—from building design to job duties—that does not inflict undue hardship on the employer (Goren 2007). In determining whether an accommodation poses an undue hardship on the employer or service provider, the following factors are considered: (1) the nature and cost of the accommodation vis-à-vis institutional size, budget limitations, employee numbers, and types of facilities; and (2) the degree to which the accommodation could substantially alter the job requirement or the nature of the operation (Epilepsy Foundation 2007). To ensure reasonableness, an underlying proportionality test is implied, one that balances burdens with benefits for all persons affected by the proposed adjustment (UN Report 2006).

The situation is similar in Canada. The obligation to provide reasonable accommodation is enshrined within federal and provincial human rights legislation, in addition to judicial interpretation of the non-discrimination clause of the Charter of Rights and Freedoms (UN Report 2006). According to the Ontario Human Rights Code, institutions have a duty to abolish those practices and programs that may exert a discriminatory impact on minorities. Institutions also have an obligation to implement programs and procedures for balancing a person's religious or ethnic practices with a requirement, qualification, or practice (Task Force 2006). The Supreme Court, too, has ruled that refusal by institutions such as school boards to make reasonable accommodations violates the constitutional rights of Canadians, namely the religious freedom guaranteed by the Charter (Abu-Laban and Abu-Laban 2007). Finally, the Employment Equity Act of 1996 obligates employers to reasonably and proportionately accommodate persons from the designated groups. In deciding whether an accommodation would impose undue hardship, the factors of *health, safety, and cost* must be considered, ranging from disproportionate costs to operational disruptions (Bouchard-Taylor Commission 2008). As well, there are limits to inclusiveness under reasonable accommodation as a frame of reference. Interventions that violate the rights of individuals (especially accommodations that victimize the most vulnerable members of a group), break the law, or contravene core constitutional values are rejected as unreasonable.

A sense of perspective is helpful; reasonable accommodation entails a process of making institutions more inclusive by making them more reflective of, responsive to, and respectful of diversity. It consists of any modification to service delivery or employment context that secures equal opportunities (a level playing field) for qualified minority women and men, in part by treating minorities equally as a matter of course (the same), in part by treating them as equals when necessary (differently). Modifications include those pertaining to the application process to expand the applicant pool; accommodations on the job to take distinctive needs into account; and ongoing adjustments to ensure all workers enjoy equal benefits and privileges (Epilepsy Foundation 2007). Two dimensions prevail in fostering reasonable accommodation: (1) the reactive, to remove discriminatory barriers, and (2) the proactive, to take necessary positive measures (affirmative action or employment equity) to improve institutional access, representation, and equity in training, participation, rewards, and advancement (UN Report 2006). Failure to provide reasonable accommodation at reactive and proactive levels can be construed as discriminatory (European Union 2005). It can also be interpreted as violating the principles of multiculturalism in advancing an inclusive governance.

A Multicultural Model of Inclusive Governance/An Inclusive Model of Multicultural Governance

Canada's official Multiculturalism revolves around an inclusive society-building agenda. In conjunction with the Official Languages Act in 1969 and the Charter of Rights and Freedoms in 1985, multiculturalism represented the remaining piece of the puzzle for constructing a distinctive yet unified Canada (Gagnon and Iacovino 2007; Kymlicka 2008). In hoping to solve Canada's unity and identity problems, a commitment to multiculturalism challenged conventional political wisdom. Many had assumed that diversity and difference were incompatible with good governance, given the perceived difficulties of forging unity and fostering identity from a hodgepodge of ethnicities. But a multicultural governance was predicated on an entirely different principle, namely, that a society of many cultures was possible provided that people were accepted and included regardless of their racial or ethnic differences. Such a governance was possible provided an overarching vision and a normative framework for managing difference was in place. As a calculated gamble in the governance of an ethnically diverse Canada, official Multiculturalism parlayed a potential weakness into an unanticipated strength without sacrificing a commitment to social cohesion, national identity, and domestic peace.

Canada's Multiculturalism conforms most closely to a liberal model of multiculturalism. As noted earlier, a liberal multiculturalism aspires toward a multicultural governance that acknowledges the possibility of a Canada of many cultures as long as people's cultural differences don't get in the way of full citizenship and equal participation. Everyone is treated the same (equally), according to the universalism implicit in liberal Multiculturalism; after all, our commonalities as rights-bearing individuals outweigh any group-based differences—at least for purposes of recognition and reward. And yet Canada's liberal Multiculturalism also concedes the need to take differences into account to ensure that individuals are treated as equals when their differences prove disadvantaging—as long as the concessions are needs based and temporary.

Clearly then, Canada's liberal Multiculturalism operates at two levels: the micro (social and cultural) and the macro (national). First, it acknowledges the right of each individual to identify with the cultural tradition of his or her choice, as long as this ethnic affiliation does not interfere with the rights of others, violate the laws of the land, or infringe on core values or institutions. Under Canada's liberal Multiculturalism, everyone has the right to be treated equally (the same) irrespective of their ethnicity; everybody also has the right—when required—to be treated differently (as equals) because of their ethnicity. Cultural differences are thus transformed into a discourse about *social inequalities* by privileging primacy of institutional inclusiveness and removal of discriminatory barriers (Hesse 1997).

Second, an official multiculturalism is concerned with society-building governance. Multiculturalism as governance does not set out to celebrate ethnic differences per se or to promote cultural diversity except in the most innocuous manner. Nor does it condone the creation of segregated ethnic communities with parallel power bases and special collective rights. The objective of a society-building multiculturalism is national in scope, that is, to create an inclusive Canada in which differences are incorporated as legitimate and integral without undermining either the interconnectedness of the whole or the distinctiveness of the parts (Fleras 2009). Diversity and difference are endorsed, to be sure, but only to the extent that all differences are equivalent in status, subject to similar treatment, stripped of history or context, and consistent with Canada's self-proclaimed prerogative for defining the outer limits of acceptable differences. No voice shall predominate in creating a community of communities, according to an official discourse, except the voice that says no voices shall prevail in defining what counts as difference, what differences count (Johnston 1994). Containment by multiculturalism could not be more artfully articulated.

The ethos of Canada's Multiculturalism is unabashedly inclusionary (Kymlicka 2007a). This multicultural ethos reinforces a commitment to inclusiveness through promotion of social justice, identity, and civic participation. Emphasis is focused on fostering tolerance toward difference, protecting a culture of rights, reducing prejudice, removing discriminatory barriers, eliminating cultural ethnocentrism, enhancing equitable access to services, expanding institutional inclusion, improving creative intergroup encounters, and highlighting citizenship (also Duncan 2005). With Multiculturalism, Canada affirms the value and dignity of all citizens, including equality before the law and equal opportunity, regardless of origins or ethnicity. As the editors of the Spring 2006 issue of the journal *Canadian Diversity* put it:

> Canadian multiculturalism is fundamental to our belief that all citizens are equal. Multiculturalism ensures that all citizens can keep their identities, can take pride in their ancestry, and have a sense of belonging. Acceptance gives Canadians a feeling of security and self confidence, making them more open to, and accepting of, diverse cultures. The Canadian experience has shown that multiculturalism encourages racial and ethnic harmony

and cross-cultural understanding, and discourages ghettoization, hatred, discrimination, and violence. Through multiculturalism, Canada recognizes the potential of all Canadians, encouraging them to integrate into their society and take an active part in its social, cultural, economic, and political affairs.

To be sure, a commitment to inclusion and integration is not without limits and costs. An inclusive multiculturalism is concerned with integrating people into the framework of an existing Canada rather than in bringing about transformative social change. The disruptiveness of difference is depoliticized by the simple expedient of institutionalizing differences or privatizing them into the personal. Emphasis is on neutering these cultural differences by channeling potentially troublesome conflicts into relatively harmless avenues of identity or folklore. Differences are further depoliticized (or "neutered") by treating all differences as the same, by circumscribing the outer limit of permissible differences, while stripping culturally charged symbols from public places. Difference is endorsed, but only to the extent that all differences are equivalent in status, justified by need rather than by rights, subject to similar treatment, in compliance with laws and core values, consistent with Canada's self-proclaimed right to 'draw the line', and commensurate with the principles of liberal universalism (a belief that what we have in common as rights-bearing individuals is more important than what divides us through group membership). Far from being a threat to the social order, in other words, Canada's Multiculturalism constitutes a hegemonic discourse in defense of dominant ideology. Depending on where one stands on the political spectrum, this discursive framework is cause for concern or contentment.

Public Perceptions/Critical Reactions

Public perceptions

Despite Canada's much-lauded status as the quintessential multicultural governance, public perception varies. Some Canadians are vigorously supportive; others are in total rejection or denial; still others are indifferent; and yet others are plainly uninformed (see Cardozo and Musto 1997; Cameron 2004). For some, multiculturalism is at the root of many of Canada's problems; for others, multiculturalism is too often scapegoated for everything that goes wrong when minorities are involved (Siddiqui 2007). The majority appear to be caught somewhere in between, depending on their reading of multiculturalism and its contribution (or lack thereof) to Canadian society. Variables such as age, income, level of education, and place of residence are critical in gauging support, with higher levels of approval among the younger, more affluent, better educated, and urban (Anderssen and Valpy 2003). To the extent that many Canadians are unsure of what Canada's official Multiculturalism is trying to do, and why, the prospect of living differently together is compromised.

Public support for official Multiculturalism is also subject to diverse interpretations. Opinion polls are known to provide different answers depending on the kind of questions asked. Nevertheless, national surveys on Multiculturalism suggest a solid base of support, often in the 60 to 70 percent range (Angus Reid 1991; ACS/Environics 2002; Dasko 2005; Jedwab 2005; Berry 2006). Yet, support for Multiculturalism is not as transparent as the data would suggest.

- First, Canadians may be supportive of multiculturalism as principle or as a demographic fact, yet reject Multiculturalism as official policy or mistakenly conflate Multiculturalism with unpopular government programs like Employment Equity.
- Second, support is not the same as enthusiasm. Canadians appear to embrace multiculturalism as a reality to be tolerated rather than an ideal to be emulated or passion to be pursued.
- Third, support or rejection tends to be selective and inconsistent. Most Canadians support some aspect of multiculturalism, including providing a hand up for newcomers, but are conflicted over issues of reasonable accommodation (Collacott 2006) or unintended consequences, such as worries over fostering conditions that breed terrorism, discourage integration, or encourage ghettoization (Baubock 2005; Friesen 2005).
- Fourth, support is conditional. Canadians are prepared to accept Multiculturalism if costs are low and demands are reasonable for assisting new Canadians to settle in, removing discriminatory barriers, learning about others, and promoting tolerance (Gwyn 1996). Support is withdrawn when endorsement is seen as eroding Canada's sense of national unity and identity, challenging authority or core values, curbing the integration of cultural communities, criticizing the mainstream, or acquiescing in the seemingly un-Canadian demands of particular groups in utilizing multiculturalism as a smokescreen for illiberal practices.

Critiquing multiculturalism

Official Multiculturalism is unevenly supported across Canada (Duncan 2005). At one level, the federal government has slashed funding to Canada's

Multiculturalism programs by one half, according to a press release from Conservative government dated April 13, 2007 – from $34 million in 2005–06 to about $17 million in 2006–07, with none of the money slated for spending on intercultural relations (Beaumier 2007). At another level are sectorial variations. Residents of Ontario and western Canada appear receptive, but the Québécois and Aboriginal peoples are disapproving (Ignace and Ignace 1998; Breton 2000; Kymlicka 2001). For the "nations within" (namely, Quebec and Aboriginal peoples), their concerns go beyond those of disadvantage or inclusion, but focus on the injustices and disempowerment imposed by conquest or colonization (Baubock 2005). Instead of self-defining themselves as immigrants who want "in" by leveraging Multiculturalism to their advantage, both Aboriginal peoples and the Québécois prefer the nationalist language of "getting out" over multicultural discourses of "getting in" (Harty and Murphy 2005; Maaka and Fleras 2005). With its roots in institutional inclusion and reasonable accommodation, an official Multiculturalism cannot possibly mollify the demands of fundamentally autonomous political communities who claim they are sovereign in their own right yet share in the sovereignty of Canada by way of shared jurisdictions. In short, a consensus-and-control, inclusive multiculturalism is poorly equipped to handle the highly politicized discourses of challenge and transformation (McRoberts 2001).

Political observers and social critics are no less critical (see Fleras 2002 for review). Some dismiss Multiculturalism as a bad idea that is doing badly as predicted: Multiculturalism originated to pander to ethnic interests or electoral politics, and remains a divisive force in Canadian society because it remains hostage to partisan politics and election results rather than sound public policy. Others are no less dismissive of Multiculturalism as a good idea gone bad: noble intentions aside, Multiculturalism continues to undermine Canadian identity and unity, in some cases because of minority leaders who have hijacked it for ulterior purposes. Multiculturalism is seen as divisive because of its tendency to tolerate practices incompatible with Canada's central core, yet also as hypocritical in offering the illusion of tolerance while punishing behavior at odds with core values (Stoffman 2002). None other than the current Governor-General of Canada Michaëlle Jean (2005; also Duceppe 2007), in a speech prior to her installation as Canada's viceroy, chided multiculturalism for ghettoizing Canada:

> Citizenship means living together . . . But does "multiculturalism" really propose us living together? We are even given money so that we will stay in our own separate enclosures. There's a kind of proposition of ghettoization that is there, and that is financed.

Even the much-touted mosaic metaphor comes in for criticism. References to Canada's multicultural mosaic remains an emotionally charged yet potentially misleading metaphor: On the one hand, each tile is distinct and important, and contributes to the overall design. On the other hand, each paint-by-number tile is cemented into place by a mainstream grout that defines what differences count, what counts as difference (Johnston 1994). Not surprisingly, Canada's multicultural discourses continue to be anchored in an almost essentialized reading of ethnicity and difference as primordial, determinative, and immutable rather than flexible, dynamic, and relational. Membership and participation in this sticky mosaic tends to slot individuals into hermetically sealed groups from which choice or escape are difficult. The end result? A virtuous multicultural ideology that glosses over and leaves unchanged the levers of power in Canada (Dupont and Lemarchand 2001; Thobani 2007).

Forty Years of Multiculturalism

Forty years ago Canada blazed a trail in the art of multicultural governance. A commitment to the inclusive principles of Multiculturalism resulted in the establishment of a national agenda for engaging difference in ways consistent with Canada's liberal-democratic framework. A social framework has evolved that to date has managed to balance difference with unity— even if that balancing act is a bit wobbly at times. Such an endorsement may not sound glowing to those with unrealistically high expectations. Nevertheless, the contributions of multiculturalism should not be diminished by unfair comparison with utopian standards.

A sense of proportion is required: Compared to a utopia of perfect harmony, Canada's multiculturalism falls short of the mark; in contrast with the grisliness of monocultural realities elsewhere, it stands as a paragon of virtue. But compared to the ideals enshrined in multiculturalism, Canadians could be doing better in the governance of living together with differences. A sense of perspective is also required: Just as multiculturalism cannot be blamed for shortcomings in Canada, so too should excessive praise be avoided. The nature of its impact and implications falls somewhere between the poles of unblemished good and absolute evil. Multiculturalism is neither the root of all Canada's social evils nor the all-encompassing solution to problems that rightfully originated elsewhere. It is but one component—however imperfect—for improving the integration of migrants and minorities by balancing the tension between difference and equality on the one side and unity and identity on the other side.

Multiculturalism, in short, remains a governance of necessity for a changing and differenced Canada. As a skilful blend of compromises in a country constructed around compromises, multiculturalism is an innovative if imperfect social experiment for living together differently and equitably. It has excelled in extricating Canada from its colonialist past by elevating it to its much-ballyhooed status as a trailblazer in multicultural governance. In building bridges rather than erecting walls, multicultural policies encourage minority women and men to participate in their communities, build productive lives, and make a contribution to society (see also McGauran 2005). Under the circumstances, it is not a question of whether Canada can afford multiculturalism. More to the point, Canada *cannot not* afford to embrace multiculturalism in its constant quest for political unity, social coherence, economic prosperity, and cultural enrichment. That is not to say that Canadians can uncork the bubbly in celebration of "been there, done that." There is much to do before principles align with practices to the satisfaction of all Canadians. Perhaps what passes for multiculturalism is a fear of causing an affront, so that Canadians will do anything to avoid appearing insensitive to any issue involving diversity or difference for fear it will reflect badly on themselves (Fulford 2009). Still, there is much of significance in the entrenchment of multiculturalism as a political project for bonding Canadians by building bridges across differences. It has elevated Canada to the front ranks of countries in endorsing a multicultural governance—not a perfect governance model by any stretch of the imagination, but perhaps one of the less imperfect.

4

Multiculturalisms in the United States: Multicultural Governances, American Style

Introduction: Contesting the "E Pluribus Unum"

The emergence of multiculturalism as a governance blueprint has attracted unprecedented attention in a society whose ideological moorings pivoted around the metaphorical equivalent of a melting pot (Buenker and Ratner 1992; Bak 1993; Kymlicka 2000; Bass 2008). Unlike Canada with its espousal of a multicultural mosaic narrative, national discourses portray the United States as an amalgam that melts all differences into a homogeneous mass (Reitz and Breton 1994). Historically, migrants and minorities were expected to melt (assimilate)into the mainstream pot without much in the way of federal assistance. Even today, no national policies exist for specifically integrating newcomers, so that all immigrants (except refugees) are left largely on their own to navigate entry into the labor market, although some immigrant-specific social and welfare benefits are available (Waters and Vang 2007; also Hero and Preuhs 2006). Admittedly, references to the melting pot as governance model concealed as much as they revealed: European minorities continued to maintain their cultural distinctiveness in private domains beyond jurisdictional control. And racialized minorities, namely African Americans, proved to be largely unmeltable because they were consigned to the margins of society. Nevertheless, the symbolism of the melting pot exerted a powerful hold on the American imagination. The fact that it continues to do so, despite multicultural inroads in advancing an alternative governance framework, speaks volumes about the power of national narratives to move or maintain.

That the United States is experiencing something of a multicultural transformation is widely acknowledged. In acknowledging the presence of well-established public norms affirming American diversity, Nathan Glazer's famous lament, "We are all multiculturalists now," appears to have captured the zeitgeist in the nation. The United States may not possess a formal national multicultural policy, however, despite criticism and backlash (Clausen 2001), a de facto multiculturalism predominates. Even critics acknowledge the pervasiveness of multiculturalism as a core American value in domains from educational and media institutions to politics and business (Auster 2004). Multicultural initiatives are numerous at local and regional levels; they have proven successful and popular in renegotiating the terms of minority and migrant integration into society; and they have shown considerable staying power by taking hold of American politics (Bass 2008). Consider the following examples of this multicultural drift: the designation of Martin Luther King's birthday as a national holiday, observance of Hispanic Heritage Month, hate crime legislation, multicultural education, bilingual service delivery, affirmative action programs, and racially balanced congressional districts (Bass 2008).

But commemoration is one thing; commitment is quite another, especially when multicultural discourses invariably chafe against the monocultural narrative of the melting pot. A mixed reaction to this transformative shift is inevitable: multiculturalism has been applauded by some for reasserting people's control over lives, detested by others as political correctness gone mad, deplored by monoculturalists for "fetishising" difference at the expense of national vision and collective goals, and tut-tutted by still others as a humanizing ideal that is blindly prone to excessive zeal (see Higham 1993). For some, it constitutes a bedrock for constructing an equal and inclusive society; for others a clear and present danger of balkanizing the United States; for yet others, a dynamic in constant competition for dominance with assimilationist forces; and for others still, little more than a fancy new label (multiculturalism) for the same old brew (cultural plurality) (Parrillo 2009). Finally, critics dismiss American multiculturalism as an illusion. The impressive integrative power of American society seems to generate a kind of oblivious indifference to the world, resulting in a tolerant and flexible society that has absorbed the entirety of the earth, yet has difficulty comprehending realities beyond its borders (Schneider 2004). On a planet where America remains a political and military colossus, such an assessment should be cause for concern.

Of course, not all multicultural discourses are shaped by the same American cookie cutter. Vincent Parrillo (2009) distinguishes inclusionist multiculturalism from separatist multiculturalism, with an integrative pluralism lying somewhere in between. Henry Giroux (1994) classifies multiculturalism into demagogic multiculturalism ("reverence for cultural differences"), critical multiculturalism (interrogating the racist foundations of society), and insurgent multiculturalism (action to bring about progressive change). Diane Ravitch (1990) makes a distinction between particularistic multiculturalism (preserving ethnic groups) and pluralistic multiculturalism (melting pot). Patrick West (2005) compares a soft multiculturalism that focuses on removing intolerance and discriminatory barriers to ensure full and equal participation versus a hard multiculturalism that embraces the legitimacy and distinctiveness of minority cultures as equally good and valid. Finally Shana Bass (2008) argues that multicultural politics can be sorted into four classes, based on the promotion of diverse principles and goals—*Celebration*, (fostering respect) *Harmony* (increasing tolerance/less prejudice), *Facilitation* (improving race relations), and *Parity* (advancing equality and political participation). Obvious differences in form and function notwithstanding, each of these multicultural models tends to reflect the fundamental ethos of many multiculturalisms—rejection of a straight-line assimilation norm, promotion of ethnocultural and racial equality, respect for and tolerance of cultural difference and diversity, and assertion of certain rights for particular groups. Taken together, Bass concludes, these policies have produced a multiculturalism whose underlying logic seeks to renegotiate the terms of minority integration and migrant entry into American society.

A four-fold pattern captures the range of multiculturalisms in the United States. To one side are inoffensive styles of "happy-face" or celebratory multiculturalism that are commonly displayed in American schools. Under this milquetoast multiculturalism, multicultural diversity is defined as something to enjoy rather than to act upon (Eisenstein 1996; Hesse 1997; Kundnani 2007). This a commitment to celebrating diversity is normally devoid of critical content, historical context, or patterns of power—in effect reinforcing the status quo rather than contesting it. To the other side is a communitarian style of multiculturalism. With its emphasis on diversity-within-unity (compared to the Canadian slogan of unity-within-diversity), a multicultural governance for living together is promoted, but one with relatively explicit curbs on what is acceptable (one may identify as a Latina, but one is always a Latina within the confines of the United States). To yet another side is laissez-faire multiculturalism that best describes the governance of difference and diversity at federal and state levels, often by consequence or default, in the process confirming America's status as a defiantly multicultural society without a definitive multiculturalism policy. Last is critical multiculturalism. Inasmuch as diverse interests are openly contesting the power to shape the (re)production of knowledge within core institutions, critical multiculturalism complements the cultural wars in contesting the much vaunted "e pluribus unum."

It is clear that the cumulative impact of multicultural discourses is challenging the descriptive prescription of the United States as a melting pot society. Admittedly, reference to the melting pot as an emotionally charged symbol and prescriptive ideal remains solidly entrenched; nevertheless, it does so in the face of demographic upheavals, mounting criticism, and ideological transformations. But problems persist despite growing perception of America as a multicultural society that increasingly abides by the principles of a de facto multiculturalism. No one is quite sure what is meant by multiculturalism, whether the term provides an adequate description or explanation of contemporary intergroup relations, or if multiculturalism represents a worthwhile goal whose long term impacts and implications have yet to be worked out (Kivisto and Rundblad 2000). Because controversy mars its definitional, descriptive, and prescriptive utility, the politics of multiculturalism remains contested in America's evolving governance landscape, with few signs of subsiding from a lingering post-9/11 malaise.

In an effort to make sense of what is going on, and why, this chapter addresses the emergence and entrenchment of multiculturalisms as de facto governance in the United States. The chapter begins by looking at assimilationist (melting pot) governance patterns that preceded the shift toward multicultural governance at state and institutional levels. It then explores the evolution of multicultural discourses as governance narratives in the United States, their impact on national identity and unity, and implications for governing difference and diversity. Also discussed are the different multicultural discourses and models of multiculturalism—celebratory, communitarian, laissez-faire, and critical—as they compete for space in establishing a made-in-the-USA style of multicultural governance. The chapter concludes by comparing the concept of critical multiculturalism with Canada's consensus-oriented equivalent—in the process exposing the oppositional rationales that contrast a state (official or top-down) multiculturalism with a bottom-up peoples' multiculturalism. A note of caution before beginning: Multicultural discourses in the United States tend to incorporate the identities and divisions of gender, ability, and sexual orientation, alongside those of race, ethnicity, and Indigeneity (Hollinger 1995). The content of this chapter is restricted to the politics of multiculturally managing race and ethnic difference.

Diversity and Difference in America

For a country that many see as synonymous with a melting pot metaphor, the United States exhibits an astonishing range of diversity and difference that is projected to accelerate as the twenty-first century unfolds. In 2006, the population of the United States stood at an estimated 298,448,000, with the foreign born accounting for 12.4 percent of the total population. According to Jack Martin, Director of Special Projects for FAIR (Federation for American Immigration Reform), one in every eight residents in the United States (or 37.4 million) was foreign born – the largest immigrant share in this country since 1920. Of the foreign born, 53.5 percent were from Latin America (30.7 percent of those from Mexico alone), including South America, Central America, and the Caribbean; 26.7 percent from Asia; 13.6 percent from Europe; and 3.5 percent from Africa. About 28 percent of the foreign born, or 10.3 million in 2004, were unauthorized (or undocumented or irregular) migrants, with 57 percent of them from Mexico.

Contemporary immigration patterns reflect in part the passage of the 1965 Immigration and Nationality Act. In liberalizing a once highly restrictive immigration program that favored Western and Northern Europeans, the Act abolished the national origins quota system as the basis for immigration and replaced it with a seven-category preference system in allocating immigrant visas (Kivisto and Ng 2005). The Migration Policy Institute (2007) estimates that just over 1.8 million people (including unauthorized migrants) entered the United States between 2002 and 2006. Put into perspective, the United States boasts a net migration rate of 3.05 migrants per 1000 population (2007 estimate), second only to Canada's rate of 5.79 migrants per 1000 population (Seidle 2007). The principal sending countries include Mexico, China, India, the Philippines, and Cuba (in order of importance based on 2006 data). Family members continue to account for the lion's share of new immigrants, with an annual average intake of 64 percent between 2002 and 2006 (Migration Policy Institute 2007). Those entering the USA on employment-based green cards account for only 16 percent of the annual average during that period.

Patterns of permanent residency are no less interesting. In 2007, over one million (1,052,415) individuals attained lawful permanent resident status, with new arrivals accounting for 431,368 of those and readjustment of status for 621,047 (Migration Policy Institute 2007). By contrast, a total of 1,266,264 foreign nationals obtained lawful permanent resident status in 2006, according to the Department of Homeland Security's *Yearbook of Immigration Statistics* (cited in Terrazas et al. 2007), representing an increase of 12.8 percent over 2005 and a 50.6 percent increase from the 841,000 in 2000. The difference between the figures for 2007 and 2006 reflected readjustments of status. Family-sponsored immigrants accounted for 65.5 percent of the new admissions in 2007; 15.4 percent entered through an employment-based preference, 12.9 percent had refugee status, and 4 percent were winners in the diversity lottery. Of the one million who received lawful permanent residence status in 2007, the leading regions of birth were Asia (36 percent) and North America (33 percent). By country, 14 percent came from Mexico, followed by China (7.3 percent), the Philippines (6.9 percent), India (6.2 percent), and Colombia (3.2 percent), accounting for about 37 percent of all such persons. The following is a breakdown of the U.S. population by race for 2000 and projections for 2050 (based on current birth rates, life expectancies, and immigration patterns) (U.S. Bureau of the Census, cited in Parrillo 2009):

	2000	2050
Non Hispanic Whites	70%	50.1%
Hispanic Americans	12.5%	24.4%
African Americans	12.5%	14.6%
Asian Americans	4%	8 %
Native Americans	1%	1%
Other		1.9%

On the basis of revised projections, a demographic revolution is looming. By 2042, those who self-identify as whites will be a demographic minority (46 percent), while the Latino/Latina population will account for 30 percent of the nation's total (Aizenman 2008). In that no other country appears to have experienced such rapid racial and ethnic change (see DiversityInc 2008), this demographic revolution has prompted demographers to call the transformation "unprecedented," with politically explosive repercussions.

Despite impressive intake numbers, integration policies and programs for immigrants have proven ad hoc at best, greatly underfunded at worst (Fix et al. 2008). Not surprisingly, perhaps, significant socioeconomic gaps also exist between the foreign born and American born. According to the 2005 American Community Survey (cited in Seidle 2007), nearly 17 percent of the foreign born lived below the poverty threshold, compared to 12.8 percent of the American born; 3.4 percent of the foreign born earned less than $15,000 per year compared to nearly 7 percent of the American born. However, employment revenue based on full-time, full-year work varied among the foreign born, with median annual income for males from Latin America at about $25,000 per year, while Asian males earned about $51,000. In short, the verdict is uneven: some minorities are doing well, others are not, and no one is quite sure if a commitment to multiculturalism has made (or can make) an appreciable difference (Jimenez 2009).

References to diversity and difference in the United States go beyond the level of immigrant or culture. No less important are those faith-based groups whose religious and cultural differences complicate multicultural governance. This is not surprising, because the United States is a deeply religious society, with religiosity occupying a more important space in private and public life than in many other advanced democracies (Seidle 2007). To be sure, the numbers on religious diversity at present are relatively modest, with approximately 80 percent claiming to be Christian, but significant increases are projected for Islam by 2050. While Americans expect the assimilation of newcomers across varying dimensions, they are more tolerant of religious differences—as might be expected in a country that separates church from state. In that America's concept of secularism seeks to protect religion from the state (versus the European model that seeks to protect the state from religion), the public expression of religion is allowed, thus guaranteeing not only individual rights and autonomy for religious communities, but also freedom from excessive state interference (Blond and Pabst 2008). In other words, although Americans take religion seriously and are a highly religious people, including 92 percent who believe in God or a transcendental spirit, there is an element of openness and lack of dogmatism in their religiosity and approach to other people's faith, according to the Pew Forum on Religion and Public Life (2007). In addition, different religious organizations may be granted special local, national, and state tax exemptions. The following table demonstrates U.S. religious membership by denomination for 2000 and estimates for 2050 (cited in Parrillo 2009; figures for 2007 cited in Pew Forum 2007).

	2000	2007	2050
Protestant	56%	55%	49%
Catholic	25%	24%	30%
Jewish	1.3%	1.7%	1%
Muslim	0.5%	0.6%	3%
Others	4%	2.6%	5%
No religion	13%	16%	12%

Born in the USA: From Americanization to Multiculturalism

The United States has long endorsed the virtue of fostering both diversity and uniformity—aptly captured by the insignia on the American eagle bearing Benjamin Franklin's exhortation, "e pluribus unum" (out of many, one) (Parillo 2009). Immigrant communities have enjoyed the freedom to maintain their own communities, and the emergence of hyphenated citizens attests to the retention of roots. But with continuous mass migration since the latter half the nineteenth century, the absorption of newcomers into the mainstream underscored a key American project: to foster a monocultural America as a measure of success and predictor of greatness. Known as Americanization, an aggressively assimilationist program emerged at federal levels before and after the First World War. Both federal and private effort combined to hasten the assimilation of immigrants into American society (Schain 2008)—primarily by eradicating all vestiges of the immigrant's culture via indoctrination into the American Dream.

Under assimilation, all minorities were expected to absorb the cultural values and social practices of the ruling majority, if only to secure the grounds for centralized control and smooth governance. An obsession with moral and cultural unity stemmed from mindsets that equated moral and cultural differences with deviance and disorder (Parekh 2005). Through assimilation, the mainstream sought to (1) undermine the cultural basis of indigenous societies, (2) expose minorities to dominant norms as normal and acceptable, (3) convert immigrants into patriotic, productive, and God-fearing citizens, and (4) facilitate their entry and transition into the mainstream. Dominant values, beliefs, and social patterns were valorized as inevitable or desirable; conversely, differences were demonized as inferior or irrelevant. Such Eurocentrism proved both paternalistic and patronizing. Those singled out for assimilationist treatment were often portrayed as children in need of discipline under the ever-vigilant eye of a judicious father figure.

The melting pot as governance

A federal commitment to Americanization began to ebb after the initial immigration wave. A melting pot model of governance gradually displaced it, although references to the melting pot continued to justify the Americanization campaigns of the early twentieth century. Under a melting pot paradigm for living together, all immigrants can be transformed into new Americans—a cultural alloy forged in the crucible of democracy, freedom, and civic responsibility (Booth 1998). As widely noted, a commitment to a melting pot envisaged a blending of the best European traditions into a dynamic unity (called America) that would differ from any of the original groups yet reflect a combination of them all. The benefits of such a cultural convergence were widely acclaimed: as Woodrow Wilson said in the 1913, "The great melting pot of America, the place where we are all made Americans of, is the public school, where men of every race, and of every origin and of every station in life send their children, or ought to send their children, and where, being mixed together, they are all infused with the American spirit and developed into the American man and American woman." That the melting pot metaphor continues to be employed as the preferred idiom to describe minority-majority relations—the mixture and assimilation of minorities without state intervention and at their own pace—reveals a lot about the tenacity of national symbols.

But melting pot clichés are one thing and clarification is quite another. What exactly is meant by the melting pot? Does it mean to absorb? To assimilate at a particular pace? To amalgamate ("fuse") like paints in a bucket, resulting in a mix that is homogeneous (Swerdlow 2001)? Are references to the melting pot intended to describe what is happening or to prescribe what ought to happen for best governance results? Are immigrants alone changed by the melting, or will their presence irrevocably transform the pot (Kivisto 2002)? Other difficulties are no less problematic: however popular and useful, metaphors such as "melting pot" may prove inadequate shorthand, especially when oversimplifying complex matters to the point of being simplistic—in the process concealing and confusing more than revealing and clarifying (Kivisto and Ng 2005). Finally, reality does not always match rhetoric. Although immigrants to the United States are expected to forge a new alloy by melting into the American pot, this cauldron remains irrefutably "pale male" in composition and control. Any restructuring of American society is recast along the lines and priorities of the prevailing monocultural framework, while the multicultural sector sprinkles a "dash of spice" into an otherwise monocultural stew.

Toward multicultural governances: Principles as practice

Diversity and difference were historically framed along the assimilationist lines of a melting pot metaphor. But the metaphorical idiom of cultural pluralism and multicultural mosaic challenged the melting pot as a normative governance ideal. Instead of focusing on melting down differences into uniform American citizenship, emphasis shifted to reinforcing minority cultural differences at individual and group levels while retaining an indisputably American outlook and attitude. This commitment to a multicultural governance originated for a variety of reasons, including the civil rights struggles of the 1960s, the relatively open immigration policies after 1965 (Schain 2008), 1960s identity politics (including women's liberation), and government programs (like affirmative action) that effectively consolidated the salience and status of diversity and difference. The ensuing cultural wars and corresponding social movements that emphasized difference and diversity not only undermined the melting pot image of a homogeneous United States. Challenged as well were patterns of power and authority, including the institutional structures that legitimized them (Bass 2008).

Legislation proved pivotal in ushering in a de facto multiculturalism, especially the Civil Rights Act of 1964, followed by the Voting Rights Act and establishment of the Equal Employment Opportunity Commission in 1965. These initiatives not only abolished the formal second-class status of blacks; they also prohibited racial discrimination by upholding the multicultural ideal that individuals should be treated equally regardless of race or ethnicity (Guibernau 2007). In reality, despite seemingly progressive integrationist legislation, a paradox of unintended consequences appeared. It became increasingly apparent that African Americans as a group were unlikely to achieve both equality or acceptance. Having failed in the integrationist project (largely because white America would not allow them to assimilate), blacks proposed the principle of cultural distinctiveness as grounds for living together, while simultaneously critiquing those exclusionary Eurocentric assumptions about the value of cultural pluralism (Stratton 1999). A commitment to a de facto multiculturalism subsequently emerged that legitimized the claims of blacks and other minority groups to their cultural differences. Other fronts proved equally pivotal in advancing the multicultural project, including passage of the 1967 Bilingual Education Act (Banting and Kymlicka 2006). As well, the 1990 Immigration Act created a category of diversity visas to include up to 55,000 immigrants per year by lottery from underrepresented countries.

That the United States embraces a multicultural governance without a formal multiculturalism is neither unique nor inconsequential. With the exception of Canada and Australia, few countries can claim an official multiculturalism, despite commitments and practices that incorporate the multicultural as principle and practice. In general, multiculturalism as governance in the United States addresses issues of identity, diversity, race relations, political participation, and racial inequality. More specifically, programs based on the principles of multiculturalism are numerous and varied, including equal opportunity and participation, voice and representation, respect and tolerance toward cultural diversity and difference, removal of discriminatory barriers, creating racial harmony through hate crimes and diversity training programs, provision of language translation services or multilingual services in fundamental social service environments, bilingual education programs in schools, attainment of equality through affirmative action programs, preservation of ethnic cultures, introduction of ethnic studies programs at universities, and recognition of minority groups with respect to their history and difficulties in adjusting to American society (Bass 2008).

Clearly, then, a multicultural commitment to diversity and difference has evolved into an accepted feature of American life with a

corresponding set of values and priorities that transcends the assimilationism of a melting pot discourse (see Ley 2007:15 for evidence of a
return of assimilation). But reactions to multiculturalism vary. For some,
multiculturalism constitutes the definitive statement in fulfilling America's
quest for universal equality; for others, it represents the antithesis of what
America stands for while subverting its unifying values (Schlesinger 1992).
Some like Kymlicka (2000) defend an emergent consensus and dominant
paradigm of multiculturalism in the United States. The principles and
practice of multiculturalism are here to stay; consequently, debates must
transcend the 'yes' or 'no' and focus, instead, on what kind of multicultural
governance people want.

Critics of multiculturalism are legion, including those who lament the
privileging of culture at the expense of more fundamental categories of
social analysis, including class, gender, and race (Glazer 1997). A multiculturalism restricted to culture alone may well end up bolstering the
advantage of relatively affluent groups, while glossing over the economic
and social difficulties of groups for whom cultural recognition is not
a central priority (Martiniello 1998; Wieviorka 1998). Critics fixate on
the divisiveness of multiculturalism (Huntington 2004; Schlesinger 1992),
fearing that a multicultural cult of ethnicity could endanger national unity
and identity, in part by inflating differences rather than promoting commonalities, in part by reviving ancient prejudices, thus retribalizing and
fragmenting America to the detriment of national unity and democratic
governance. Finally, others like Dinesh D'Souza (1996) have attacked multiculturalism for subverting the universal values of the Enlightenment in
exchange for the relativistic embrace of inferior cultural values on the
somewhat dubious assumption that all cultures are of equal value. In
contrast to liberalism, which extols the primacy individual freedom, multiculturalism is accused of promoting those tribalisms and collective group
rights that impinge on people's freedoms and choices. In other words,
multiculturalism is believed to be incompatible with liberalism because
it compromises people's rights to be treated as individuals, subordinates
the interests of individuals to group interests, and classifies and identifies
people on the basis of ascriptive identities (Baber 2008).

Models of Multiculturalisms: An Abundance of Niches

Notwithstanding these ideological rifts and legislative shifts, there is no
official multiculturalism policy at federal levels. Yes, there is a de facto multiculturalism by consequences or default, including a broad array of civil
rights for leveling the playing field for migrants and minorities. Government policies and state laws do promote tolerance, support equal dignity

and recognition, and guarantee equal rights for minorities (Guibernau 2007). Proactive multiculturalism at state levels is associated with English-Spanish bilingualism, including initiatives by California that allow driver's tests in several languages (although 26 states have also passed English-only legislation). But without an explicit (de jure) policy statement on multiculturalism, multiple multicultural models have emerged, including laissez-faire (or de facto) multiculturalism, celebratory ("multicultural-ism lite") multiculturalism, communitarian multiculturalism, and critical (counterhegemonic) multiculturalism.

Laissez-faire multiculturalism

Laissez-faire multiculturalism is constructed around the principle of indi-vidual choice within a context of civil rights (Barry 2001; Bloemraad 2007). Minorities are accorded equal rights, without having to sacrifice their dis-tinctiveness, although an expectation of conformity to key values prevails. With a laissez-faire multiculturalism, federal authorities do not actively support the principle of ethnic diversity in advancing social justice. The value of difference and diversity may be legitimate topics of debate in the public realm, yet public funds should neither promote the survival of spe-cific cultural groups nor accommodate the cultural concerns of historically disadvantaged minorities. Immigrants are ultimately responsible for utiliz-ing their own resources either to create ethnic associations or to mobilize for political ends as a way of getting things done.

In many ways, the dynamics of laissez-faire multiculturalism tend to mirror the principles of America's immigration program. Immigration policy in the United States revolves almost exclusively around regulating admissions and monitoring unauthorized entries. Issues pertaining to inte-gration and settlement of immigrants rarely receive federal attention; as a result, they are left to fend for themselves by taking advantage of oppor-tunities created by market forces, mainstream and immigrant voluntary organizations, and self-initiatives on the part of the immigrants them-selves. Compare this with Canada's commitment to an immigration-driven multiculturalism. While Canada's immigration program acknowledges the centrality of multiculturalism in promoting naturalization and fostering the settlement of new Canadians, only a small number of newcomers to the United States receive federal assistance or encouragement, with the result that multicultural practices are expressed through initiatives at local, regional, and state levels, although some national measures toward a multicultural integration are known to exist (such as federally mandated affirmative action) (Bloemraad 2006).

Celebratory multiculturalism as multicultural education

The status and value of multiculturalism continue to attract lively debate no more so than at educational levels where the centrality of different cultures puts pressure on dislodging the once-unquestioned canon of traditional American culture and history. The impetus for multicultural education constitutes a departure from conventional ways of doing things. Its introduction has not only challenged how schools should relate to difference but also raised questions about the dynamics of formal education in a changing and diverse society. In striving to be inclusive by ensuring that differences do not disadvantage students, multicultural education encompasses a variety of policies, programs, and practices for engaging difference within the school setting. The National Association for Multicultural Education (2003) provides a definition of multiculturalism that reveals its many dimensions—from empowering to enriching and enlightening.

> Multicultural education is a philosophical concept built on the ideals of freedom, justice, equality, equity, and human dignity...It recognizes the role schools can play in developing the attitudes and values necessary for a democratic society. It values cultural differences and affirms the pluralism that students, their communities, and teachers reflect. It challenges all forms of discrimination in schools and society through the promotion of democratic principles of social justice. Multicultural education is a process that permeates all aspects of school practices, policies, and organization...Thus, school curriculum must directly address issues of racism, sexism, classism, linguicism, ablism, ageism, heterosexism, religious intolerance, and xenophobia. Multicultural education advocates the belief that students and their life histories and experiences should be placed at the centre of the teaching and learning process and that pedagogy should occur in a context that is familiar to students and that addresses multiple ways of thinking. In addition, teachers and students must critically analyze oppression and power relations in their communities, societies, and the world...offer students an equitable educational opportunity, while at the same time, encouraging students to critique society in the name of social justice.

Notwithstanding this range of initiatives under a multicultural education umbrella, celebratory models tend to dominate. They flourish at different levels of education, from primary to universities, with changes primarily to the culture content of textbooks and curriculum (Bass 2008). Under a celebratory multicultural education, students are exposed to a variety of different cultures in the hopes of enhancing an appreciation for cultural diversity. Each of the four major ethnicities (Native American, Latino/a, African American, and Asian American) has a month dedicated to the observance of its history and culture. The curriculum is enriched with various multicultural add-ons: special days are set aside for multicultural awareness, projects are assigned that reflect multicultural themes, and specific cultures are singled out for intensive classroom study. For example, colleges and universities throughout the USA organize "international days" to celebrate diversity by celebrating diverse cultures through food, dance, and information displays (Boli and Elliott 2008). Additional perspectives under celebratory multiculturalism may incorporate insights into healthy identity formation, cultural preservation, intercultural sensitivity, stereotyping awareness, and cross-cultural communication. The goals of these initiatives are to foster greater tolerance, enhanced sensitivity, a more positive sense of ethnic identity, and more harmonious intercultural relations by honoring the pasts of all (Bass 2008).

A celebratory model is widely accepted because of its nonthreatening nature. Yet, the very innocuousness of a samosas-saris-steel bands style of multicultural education makes it vulnerable to criticism. Celebratory styles have been criticized as too static and restrictive in scope. They tend to focus on *diversity* (rather than *difference*), that is, on the exotic components of a culture that everyone can relate to, rather than more substantive issues pertaining to patterns of inequality within contexts of power. Diverse cultures are studied at the level of material culture, stripped of their historical context and existing power relations, and discussed from an outsider's point of view (Mukherjee 1992). A focus on the costumes, cuisine, and customs of culture reinforces the dangers of overromanticizing minorities as remote or removed. Alternatively, in cases where cultural differences are perceived as un-American, minorities are framed as troublesome constituents who have problems or create social problems that cost or create inconvenience. Failure to initiate sweeping institutional changes, much less to challenge the racism within institutional settings, has also besmirched celebratory models. A celebratory discourse is criticized as little more than a hegemonic distraction that does nothing to challenge structural inequalities. Worse still, it conveys the impression that fundamental issues of inequality are addressed, even if nothing is done to disturb the racialized distribution of power and privilege (see Thobani 2007).

Communitarian multiculturalism: Diversity within unity as governance

A commitment to liberal universalism exposes a governance paradox. To one side is a belief in the fundamental unity of humanity—that what we share as free-wheeling and morally autonomous individuals is more important for purposes of entitlement and engagement than what divides us because of membership in some group. Racial and ethnic differences are only skin deep, hence, they really don't matter or count; or, alternatively, they pose a threat that needs to be defused. To the other side is an equally powerful belief that denying the relevance of difference may violate a person's (or group's) equality rights. For an equitable governance, it may be necessary to treat people similarly (equally), but also differently (as equals) by taking context into account. Yet another governance paradox is exposed: on the one hand, a commitment to recognize difference and diversity by incorporating it into a multicultural governance; on the other hand, the need to acknowledge the centrality of unity, if only to secure the conditions for diversity and difference to flourish without erupting into conflict. Ideally this unity should not be imposed by government or decree. For maximum effect it should reflect the outcome of civic education, commitment to the common good, a society's shared values and common experiences, and robust institutions (Communitarian Network 2002).

The emergence of a communitarian movement provides a compromise governance model. By engaging difference and diversity without forsaking unity and order, communitarianism is based on the belief that a just and fair society reflects a carefully crafted balance between the conflicting principles of unity versus difference as played out in the debate between individual rights versus community responsibilities. With its focus on the theme of Diversity Within Unity (DWU) (Communitarian Network 2002), the communitarian network proposes a middle-ground governance. According to a communitarian governance model, members of distinct cultural groups are entitled to identify and practice their cultural customs without having to forfeit their right to democratic citizenship. But the recognition of diversity swings both ways: Just as people's cultural differences should not bar them from full and equal participation in society, so should their differences be deemed irrelevant in terms of allocating who gets what. Yes, difference and diversity, but secondary to national unity and core societal values.

In other words, a communitarian commitment to DWU comes with strings attached. First, while individuals are free to preserve their cultural distinctiveness, they can do so only as long as these cultural practices do not clash with those basic values and core institutions that secure a cohesive societal governance. This shared framework incorporates the protection of fundamental human rights, including gender equality, rule of law, compelling public interest, freedom of movement and expression, and respect for democratic processes. Second, individuals may identify with the cultural tradition of their choice provided that, in situations of conflicting loyalties, their culture of origin does not supersede or compromise their loyalty to the country of permanent residence. Third, minorities have the right to challenge the first and second conditions, but not through violence. They must utilize the democratic processes that are available for such purposes. In the words of the Communitarian Network (2002:2):

> *The basis approach we favor is diversity within unity.* It presumes that all members of a given society will fully respect and adhere to those basic values and institutions that are considered part of the basic shared framework of the society. At the same time every group in society is free to maintain its distinctive subculture—those policies, habits, and institutions that do not conflict with the shared core—and a strong measure of loyalty to its country of origins, as long as this does not trump loyalty to the society in which it lives if these loyalties come into conflict. *Respect for the whole and respect for all is at the essence of our position.* (Emphasis in the original)

The message is clear. A DWU governance not only subordinates difference and diversity to the primacy of national unity as the basis for governance; it also rejects the extremes of either assimilation or separation/segregation as grounds for living together differently. A commitment to assimilation is discredited as unnecessarily homogenizing, morally unjustified, and sociologically implausible. Mainstream institutions like schooling cannot be used to suppress cultural differences or to reinforce minority segregation and ghettoization. By the same token, a DWU governance disallows the notion of minority rights to uphold practices that contradict UN human rights codes or the prevailing laws of the United States. Also rejected is the assertion that minorities are entitled to more rights and entitlements than those of the mainstream population. Special measures may be provided to overcome historical disadvantage in isolated cases, but these concessions must be based on need and discarded when no longer needed. And DWU most certainly rejects the plural notion of minorities establishing separate communities that not only are segregated from society at large, but also legitimize practices and laws at odds with societal standards.

On the surface a communitarian governance model provides an appealing compromise between unbounded multiculturalism and stifling assimilation. In advocating an integrative model within a shared framework, a multicultural governance proposes an overarching vision, laws, and values that simultaneously (and paradoxically) transcend racial and ethnic differences, yet within limits acknowledge their value and importance. To achieve equal citizenship and full democratic rights under this mosaic governance model, minorities only need to depoliticize their differences, that is, privatize and personalize their differences rather than manipulate them in public to secure advantage. But this you-can-be-different-but-not-too-different mentality creates problems when disallowing differences that make a difference. To the extent that a communitarian governance is incapable of taking differences seriously, its status as a compromise in deeply divided societies is jeopardized (Maaka and Fleras 2005).

Multiculturalism as critical discourse

The surge of critically informed "subversive" multiculturalisms is interrogating the culture of whiteness that historically formulated public perception and democratic governance (D'Souza 1996; Eller 1997). A critical multiculturalism transcends the simple construction of identities or celebration of tolerance. Instead it embraces an "insurgent" discourse that challenges (a) the authority and legitimacy of white supremacy, (b) the Eurocentric canon at the core of American cultural life, and (c) the melting pot ideology that infuses government policies and programs. Differences do not just exist under critical multiculturalism; to the contrary, they are part of the struggle to redefine public culture by politicizing the "isms" within American society (Giroux 1994). With media and educational institutions spearheading this counterhegemonic insurgency, who, then, can be surprised when conservative critics equate multiculturalism with a thinly disguised Marxist assault on traditional American culture and values (Schmidt 1997)?

In an effort to unsettle the dominant monocultural conception of history, culture, and society, a critical multiculturalism originated in the 1980s within the context of school reform. In criticizing the Eurocentric bias and exclusion of minorities from a curriculum and pedagogy that privileged a Western canon, critical multicultural models became synonymous with challenge, resistance, and transformation—rather than consensus, conformity, and control as was the case with happy-face multiculturalism. The politics of power and privilege associated with these critically discursive frameworks not only questioned the authority and legitimacy of the status quo; they also contested the prevailing distribution of power and privilege while challenging entrenched patterns of inequality (Thobani 2007; also Hall 2000; Pieterse 2007). As well, a normative critique was directed at those institutional arrangements within the public domain that deprived minorities of their rights (Tiryakian 2004).

Equally contested is the core tenet of liberal universalism, namely, what people have in common as rights-bearing individuals and what they accomplish as equality-seeking rationalists are more important—at least for purposes of recognition and reward—than ascribed membership in racial groups. Critically oriented multiculturalism instead advocates the distinctly un-American axiom that personal patterns of engagement and entitlement should reflect (1) disadvantage or birthright in addition to merit, (2) creativity rather than conformity, (3) identity instead of acomplishment, (4) difference rather than universality, (5) group rights versus individual rights, (6) ethnic cultures versus common cultures, and (7) pluralism versus assimilation (McLaren 1994). Four major themes anchored a critical multicultural discourse: postmodernism, cultural relativism, identity politics, and collective rights.

Postmodernism As an intellectual force, postmodernism challenges the conventional wisdom of order, rationality, and hierarchy associated with modernity. More specifically it disrupts those triumphalist narratives about America—a uniquely bestowed nation that has a date with destiny in the progress toward perfection—by uncovering the histories, perspectives, and voices of the marginalized (Kim 2004). It also takes to task the canons of positivism and universalism on the grounds that imposing homogeneity and hierarchy does a disservice to a fragmented and contradictory reality (Li 1999). In rejecting a concept of reality that is coherent, objective, and amenable to rational analysis by dispassionate language, postmodernism espouses a multiperspective view of reality with no center or authority. In a mind-dependent world of postmodernists, there is no such thing as truth (objectivity, laws, absolutes), only discourses about truth, whose truthfulness reflects social context and power relations. Acceptance of reality as perspectival and provisional as well as socially constructed and culturally constrained not only transforms society into a multiplicity of pluralisms (Adam and Allan 1995); it can also capture the centrality of relativism that underpins a critical multiculturalism (Vertovec 1996).

Cultural Relativism A critical multiculturalism is animated by two related assumptions: First, that in a relativist world, all cultures are of equal validity and worth; as a result no one has any right to criticize or condemn, even if cultural values clash with mainstream values or are manipulated to justify actions at odds with human rights codes. Second, that nothing is neutral or impartial because everything/ everyone is located in time and space. Only different standpoints are espoused; that is, everything is relative and everything could be true or equal since nothing is absolutely knowable, given the inseparability of theoriser and theorised. The patterns of power that traditionally secured societal definitions of truth are contested by this "radical relativism, as are the rules of normalcy and standards of legitimacy" (Harris 1995). This discourse of resistance repudiates the authority and legitimacy of white supremacy by contesting the racism, sexism, and patriarchy embedded in American society—much of which conflicted with the lived experiences of minority women and men (Giroux 1994).

Identity Politics In challenging the cultural hegemony in an advanced capitalist society, minorities have capitalized on their identities for mobilizing in defense of social, political, and cultural interests (Turner 1994; Henry and Tator 1999). Identity politics reflects the tendency to define one's political interests and social identity in terms of some group category like race or gender rather than social class. A 1960s critique of American culture as exclusive or oppressive resulted in the framing of social justice and domination along identity grounds, thus transforming the idea of equality as sameness into the idea of equality as difference. Historically disadvantaged minorities began to identify with these subjugated groups and mobilize into action by pooling resources to defend interests and express values. Challenging the "dominant silencing of diversity" (Eisenstein 1996) fosters a framework by which new identities are (re)formulated, new communities are constructed, knowledge and power are contested, and Eurocentric universalisms are exposed for what they are—discourses in defense of dominant ideology. Both the politics of difference (Young 1990) and demand for recognition (Taylor 1992) transcend the universalism of liberal pluralism: by challenging white privilege and a Eurocentric moral order in defining what differences count and what counts as difference, each also demands nothing less than a commitment to politicize, recover, preserve, or promote the differences of a threatened collective identity.

Collective Rights Equally important is the primacy of collective rights. Just as earlier social movements contested the values and structures that once justified oppression, the new identity politics concedes the oppressiveness of moves to eliminate group differences in favor of individual rights—in consequence if not necessarily by intent (Eller 1997). This commitment to the primacy of ethnic group membership challenges the individualism of liberal universalism. Instead of privileging the liberal-universalist idea that differences are simply skin-deep since everybody is equal before the law, an oppositional reading prevails: because differences are real and fundamental, they must serve as the basis for respect, recognition, and reward. To be sure, the inward-looking dynamic of a critical multiculturalism may be problematic. The insulating and isolating of groups may marginalize minorities by robbing the disprivileged of community or initiative. As bell hooks (1995:201) writes in critique of a multiculturalism that erects walls rather than builds bridges:

> As more people of color raise our consciousness and refuse to be pitted against one another, the forces of neo-colonial white supremacist domination must work harder to divide and conquer. The most recent effort to undermine progressive bonding between people of color is the institutionalization of "multiculturalism." Positively, multiculturalism is presented as a corrective to a Eurocentric vision of model citizenship wherein white middle-class ideals are presented as the norm. Yet this positive intervention is then undermined by visions of multiculturalism that suggest everyone should live with and identify with their own self-contained cultural group. If white supremacist capitalist patriarchy is unchanged then multiculturalism within that context can only become a breeding ground for narrow nationalism, fundamentalism, identity politics, and cultural, racial, and ethnic separatism.

Even within critical multiculturalism, internal disputes prevail. A critical multiculturalism may reject a unified and static concept of identity as a fixed inventory of experiences, meanings, and practices, in lieu of identities that are dynamic, provisional, fluid, and hybridized (Henry and Tator 2006). Descent-based communities may embody positive values and demand recognition in public policy making; nevertheless, this identity politics rarely reflects the dynamics of diversity while rigidifying into a framework that restricts free choice (Hollinger 1995; Gleason 1996). A mosaic multicultural model is rejected in favor of a kaleidoscope model—one that is open (belonging to a community does not exclude belonging/identification to society at large, since people's lives should not be defined or compartmentalized by race or color); fluid (with open boundaries, multiple affiliations, socially constructed entities, and hybrid identities); and voluntary (reflecting deep values of individual freedom and choice) (Hollinger 1995). The presidential politics of 2008 clearly demonstrated this shift toward a postmulticulturality. By transcending notions of race and crossing color lines, the election of Barack Obama as president of the United States not only challenges notions of identity politics but reinforces the trend toward a postethnic America (Hollinger 2008).

Duelling Multicultural Discourses: "Unum" versus "Pluribus"

Many have playfully said that Canadians and Americans use the same words but speak a different language. Nowhere is this pithy aphorism more evident than in the multiplicity of references to multiculturalism. Mosaic versus the melting pot? Tossed salad or kaleidoscope? "Unity in diversity" versus "diversity in unity"? "out of many, one" or "from one, many"? Canada may claim to be a multicultural mosaic but its *pluribus* appears to be more attuned to integrating ethnic Canadians into the *unum*. Or as Sneja Gunew (1993:207) observes in castigating Canada's multiculturalism, "[M]ulticulturalism is a rhetoric of inclusion which can't deal with the politics of exclusion." Conservative and liberal models of multiculturalism in the United States appears consistent with the *unum* in *e pluribus unum*. But a critically informed insurgent multiculturalism has precipitated cultural wars whose *pluribus* threatens to fragment the *unum* of a national vision. Consider the polarities at play:

- Canada's multiculturalism is largely about managing diversity by depoliticizing difference, whereas critical multiculturalisms in the United States are about politicizing difference for managing the mainstream. One is criticized for emphasizing commonality over difference; the other for overemphasizing difference at the expense of commonality.
- One multiculturalism (that of Canada) is directed at modifying the mainstream without straining the social fabric; the other is focused on transforming the monocultural firmament upon which society is grounded.
- One is officially political, yet seeks to depoliticize diversity for society-building purposes; the other falls outside the policy domain, but politicizes differences as a catalyst for minority empowerment.
- One is based on law and rooted in the state; the other consists of practices that challenge the national mythology upon which the legal and constitutional framework of society are constructed.
- One seeks to eliminate the relevance of difference as a basis for entitlement or engagement (depoliticizes); the other privileges and politicizes the salience of differences in allocating who gets what.
- One is riveted to the modernist quest for unity and universality as the basis for multicultural governance; the other embraces a postmodernist zeal for differences as grounds for living together differently.
- One acknowledges respect for diversity and difference without taking differences seriously (pretend pluralism), while the other focuses on empowerment through cultural politics as people of color strive to recover, preserve, or promote their distinct cultural identities (Garcia 1995; Parrillo 2009).
- Canada's official multiculturalism transforms cultural differences into a discourse about *social inequality (redistribution)*; critical

multiculturalism reformulates social inequalities into a discursive framework of cultural differences and *public culture (recognition)*.
- A liberal multiculturalism allows the dominant group to establish the terms of the agenda for minority participation; a critical multiculturalism addresses the removal of barriers to the legitimacy of different ways of being and knowing (Parekh 2000).

Clearly, then, references to Canada's official multiculturalism embrace a commitment to consensus by way of "conformity" and "accommodation" (Fleras 1998). Canadians for the most part have preferred to deploy multiculturalism in a "society-building" sense by endorsing it as a "discourse" for "managing" difference within an existing status quo (Fleras 2002). Canada's consensus multiculturalism endorses a citizenship in which social equality is contingent on everyone being different in the same kind of way (conformity). Opposed to this is the thrust of popular multiculturalisms in the United States, which are critical of the Eurocentric cultural agenda that historically has denied or excluded. America's critical multiculturalists tend to emphasize its "counterhegemonic" dimensions by framing multiculturalism as a subversive discourse that challenges and resists.

How, then, do we account for this discursive divide? Multiculturalism in Canada is primarily a top-down political program for integrating migrants and minorities by balancing the national with the social and the cultural. A state-based multiculturalism is concerned with *managing* cultural differences to ensure that people don't act upon their differences to disrupt the status quo (also Kundnani 2007). This hegemonic discourse in defense of dominant ideology endorses those policies and initiatives that subordinate minority needs to the greater good of national interests. The disruptiveness of diversity is dispelled by homogenizing differences around a singular commonality so that everyone is similarly different, not differently similar (Eisenstein 1996). In other words, the objective is not to celebrate or challenge, but to construct consensus by depoliticizing and institutionalizing difference for governance purposes. In taking the difference out of diversities, Canada's consensus multiculturalism strives to do the improbable: to embrace differences without making a difference.

By contrast the postmodernist discourses that animate America's critical multiculturalism subvert as they resist. Critical multiculturalism is largely driven from the bottom-up, including various forms of identity politics involving any group marginalized from the mainstream. It transcends the constraints of official policy initiatives; therefore, it is not compromised by the demands of political engineering or electoral pandering. Advocated instead is a discourse of resistance that challenges Eurocentricity by relativizing the white capitalist patriarchy with its exclusionary designs on the "Other" (Giroux 1994; Eisenstein 1996). Unlike a consensus multiculturalism with its liberal universalist propensity for treating everyone the same for purposes of reward or recognition, a critical multiculturalism addresses the issue of group differences and ethnic exceptionalism. Unlike consensus multiculturalism that connotes a pluralism devoid of historical context and power relations, a critical multiculturalism signifies a site of struggle around the reformation of historical memory, national identity, self- and social representation, and the politics of difference (Giroux 1994:336). In challenging the traditional hegemony of the dominant group, a critical multiculturalism proposes a fundamental reconceptualization of the power relations between different cultural communities. Such a counterhegemonic challenge could not be further from its consensus-seeking counterpart.

Let's put it into perspective: Many accuse Canada's official multiculturalism of securing the *unum* at the expense of the *pluribus* (Thobani 2007). Critical multiculturalisms in the United States are thought to have privileged the *pluribus* at the expense of the *unum*. Not surprisingly, there is an element of truth behind this fractured howler: Multiculturalism in Canada is essentially a society-building exercise that seeks to depoliticize differences through institutional accommodation. Compare this with American critical multiculturalisms where group differences and identity claims are politicized by challenging the prevailing distribution of cultural power. In other words, for Canada's consensus multiculturalism, the objective is to make society safe *from* difference, in addition to making Canada safe *for* difference. By contrast, the underlying logic of critical multiculturalism seeks to make **difference** safe *from* society, while making **difference** safe *for* society. Time may tell which multiculturalism discourses will prevail in the crucible of a new world order that is pulled by globalization, polarized by ethnic fragmentation, pushed by human rights as trumps, and imperiled by the threat of global terrorism.

5

Multiculturalisms "Down Under": Multicultural Governances across Australia

Introduction: Multiculturalisms in the Antipodes

Society building is a difficult and elusive challenge at the best of times, no more so than in settler societies like Canada and the United States, New Zealand, and Australia (Pearson 2001). Consider the conflict of interests arising from the interplay of three distinct yet interrelated dynamics. First, the process of colonization with its dispossession of indigenous peoples; second, the process of settlement in establishing the colonizer's agenda; third, the process of immigration involving a mix of benefits and costs. The fractured allegiances of each of these dynamics—indigenous, colonizer, immigrant—poses a challenge in constructing a coherent society of commitment, consensus, community, and citizenship. Responses to this multidimensional challenge were varied. Invariably, however, they focused on an assimilationist model that not only privileged a white supremacist governance but also insisted on a universal (homogeneous) and centralized notion of the nation-state that extolled the virtues of one people, one culture, one polity, and one territory (Guibernau 2007).

But yesterday's truths are today's disputes. Narratives in nation-state building have shifted in response to immigrant demographics, identity politics, the politics of indigeneity, and increasingly assertive minorities. In the hope of doing what is workable, necessary and fair, governments in the Antipodes turned to more pluralistic models of governance as grounds for living together differently. For example, in contrast to its assimilationist past, Australia has realigned the accommodation of differences along multicultural lines at both federal and state levels. By contrast, given the demographics and political clout of its indigenous Maori peoples, New Zealand opted for biculturalism as a preferred governance model. In both countries, multiculturalism and biculturalism constitute patterns of governance that have proven useful in controlling troublesome constituents without making governments look bad in the process. Both of the "isms" also foster the appearance (or illusion) of inclusiveness without posing a threat to prevailing patterns of power and privilege. Finally, each ism has come under criticism for failing to deliver a promised governance, resulting in a corresponding decline in profile or popularity.

Australia clearly falls into the multicultural camp. In that official multiculturalism was most likely to originate in those settler societies without homegrown founding myths, Australia's commitment should come as no surprise. Unlike the so-called complete societies of Europe, nation-states like Australia had little choice except to reinvent themselves as reimagined communities because of mass immigration. References to Australian multiculturalism first appeared in Labour government documents in 1972, thereby formally severing a link with Australia's historical status as a white man's country. By 1983, the Labour government established a bold initiative that projected a multicultural Australia whose orientation was toward globalization and economic rationalism, closer economic ties with Asia, and extension of citizenship and equity for previously marginalized groups like Asian Australians (Bulbeck 2004). It was not until 1989, however, that multiculturalism was articulated around an explicit policy framework within which a range of programs and activities could be implemented. Public perceptions and political reactions to multiculturalism have evolved since then. The trajectory stretches from mainstream acceptance of minorities and difference, to acknowledging minority rights to culture and equality, to the notion that multiple minority identities may have to be reined in for the common good. Current trends suggest newer directions: first, a commitment to the corporatization of Australian multiculturalism as an asset for commercial and business success; second, political waffling over multiculturalism because of its implied divided loyalties and separate development; third, a move toward more civic-oriented integration models of governance for living together; fourth, an emphasis on a conservative model of multiculturalism with its neo-monocultural hierarchy of attachments, loyalties, and rights and duties; and fifth, emergence of relatively robust multicultural policies among the commonwealth states.

To deconstruct the how and why behind these dynamics for multiculturally managing difference, the next two chapters address the politics of multicultural governance in the Antipodes. The first of these chapters looks at the evolving fortunes of multiculturalism in Australia, whereas the second chapter explores debates over the status of multiculturalism within the context of a foundationally bicultural (or, more accurately, "binational") New Zealand. Chapter 5 begins by looking at diversity and difference in Australia, in the process demonstrating how a muscular immigration program has transformed a monocultural colony into a cosmopolitan society. Australia's multiculturalism is exposed as a pragmatic exercise for converting a predominantly white Australia narrative into a governance discourse based on the principles of liberal multiculturalism. The chapter explores the emergence of an official multiculturalism, discusses the relative demise in its profile under the stewardship of the Howard government, and demonstrates how . a commitment to the principles of multicultural governance persists at the state level where its expression in Queensland and Victoria provides a counterpoint to developments at federal (or commonwealth) levels. The chapter contends that, despite criticism and deteriorating profile, Australia remains a multicultural governance that continues to abide by multicultural principles—proving yet again the theoretical possibility and practice of a multicultural governance without multiculturalism.

Diversity and Difference in Australia

Until the late 1940s Australia discouraged immigration from non-English-speaking countries. Although exceptions were made for Nordic and Germanic populations, this selective prejudice was justified on the grounds of a white Australia policy that excluded immigrants on the basis of race until 1973. Since then, Australia's immigration policy framework has shifted from a focus on exclusion and nativism, to one designed primarily to cater to domestic labor market needs by bolstering Australia's capacity to compete in the global economy (Teicher et al. 2000). And yet the challenge remains the same—to maintain high levels of immigration for society building, yet minimize the adverse effects of difference and division, including perceptions of lower trust levels because of cultural heterogeneity (see Davidson and Yan 2007; also Putnam 2007). Inasmuch as Australians favor large-scale immigration to offset a declining and aging population, but expect it to serve economic interests while expecting migrants to fit in, neither the formidability of this challenge nor the politics of multiculturalism should be discounted.

Like Canada, Australia constitutes an immigration society. Sociologically speaking, immigrants are seen as assets, they are entitled to citizenship, initiatives exist to facilitate settlement and integration, and policies and programs regulate the intake of immigrants. With respect to immigration intake, 2005–2006 saw the arrival of 142,930 migrants (settler arrivals only and excluding New Zealanders). This figure grew slightly to 147,723 in 2006–2007 (Migration News 2007). Family class accounted for 45,290 arrivals, the skilled class for 97,340 or 68.1 percent of the total, and special eligibility class for 310 (Australian Government 2007). With 23 percent of its permanent population now foreign born, Australia is the world leader in this regard, with both New Zealand and Canada following at 19 percent. Another 40 percent of Australia's population is composed of persons with at least one immigrant parent, with Asia increasingly a significant source of new immigrants. Immigration figures continue to swell: consider the following update based on a more expanded definition of immigrant (Australian Government 2008):

- *Permanent Additions*: In the six months from July to December 2007, the number of permanent additions was 98,233, an increase of 8.8 percent over the previous period. This consisted of 69,597 settler arrivals (those who arrive from overseas and are entitled to permanent residence) and 28,636 onshore grants (those in Australia on a temporary basis but granted permanent residence status). Permanent departures for that period totalled 36,323, giving Australia a net permanent gain of 61,910 persons.
- *Permanent Additions by Birthplace*: On a regional basis, Europe at 21.9 percent was the largest contributor of permanent additions, followed by Southeast Asia at 15 percent, Oceania at 14.7 percent, and Northeast Asia at 14.1 percent. On a country basis, the UK at 16.1 percent was the largest birthplace group. New Zealand at 12 percent was next followed by India at 10.4 percent, and China (excluding Taiwan and Hong Kong) at 9.8 percent. It should be noted that both settler arrivals and onshore grants reflected comparable origin patterns.
- *Permanent Additions by Eligibility*: Of the 76,865 permanent additions under the Migration Program, the Skill Stream accounted for 50,903, the Family Stream for 25,878, and Special Eligibility for 84. Another 6088 were eligible under the Humanitarian Stream (primarily refugees).
- *Permanent Additions by State of Intended Residence*: New South Wales remains the most popular destination and populous state with 32 percent of permanent additions, followed by Victoria at 24.7 percent and Queensland at 18.4 percent.

Sources of immigration also continue to diversify, with Asian countries dramatically increasing their percentage of the ethnic population in

Australia. At present, 85 percent of Australia's 21 million population is of European origin (the majority from UK), 9 percent is Asian, 3 percent is Aboriginal and Torres Strait Islander, and 3 percent is other. Projections suggest that by 2025, those of European origin could decline to about 77 percent of the population; conversely, those of Asian origins could swell to about 18 percent (Price 1999).

A 'Fair Go' Multiculturalism: Unsettling a White Man's Monoculture

The two poster children for multiculturalism—Canada and Australia—have much in common, despite their positioning at opposite curves of the globe (Fleras 2008b). Both countries originated as British-driven white settler colonies, confronted indigenous peoples who were divested of land and authority to facilitate the colonization project, perceived themselves as resolutely "white" societies with a civilizing and Christianizing mission, embarked on vast immigration programs for society-building purposes, and are now compelled to rethink the challenges of coexistence in a globally interconnected world. The politics of immigration also reveals powerful parallels: Australia flung open its doors to immigration from so-called nonconventional sources, that is, those of Non-English-Speaking Backgrounds (NESB) or Culturally and Linguistically Diverse Communities (CALD). Emphasis on immigrants from Asia reflected a move that sharply contrasted with a historical past when an openly racist immigration policy blocked entry to most nonwhites. The postwar increase of immigrants has escalated to the point where the commonwealth (central or federal) government has had little option except to intervene in pursuing the goals of social cohesion, economic benefits, and national identity (Jayasuriya 1989).

From what your multicultural country can do for you . . .

A commitment to multiculturalism originated in response to several post-World War II trends. Most notable of these was the termination of the White Australia policy, largely because of large-scale and diverse immigration to fuel the postwar economic boom. By the late 1960s, evidence indicated that assimilationist policies had failed to dislodge the disadvantages of culturally and linguistically diverse minorities (Inglis 2004). In the hope of making virtue of necessity, the main political parties formally adopted the principles of multiculturalism as basis for the "appreciation of cultural diversity and [to] maintain the languages and cultural traditions of minority groups." A commitment to Multiculturalism was further bolstered when Australia signed the International Convention on the Elimination of all Forms of Racial Discrimination, followed by the passage of its own Racial Discrimination Act in 1975. The Act made it "unlawful for a person to do any act involving a distinction, exclusion, restriction, or preference based on race, colour, descent, or national or ethnic origin which has the purpose or effect of nullifying or impairing the recognition, enjoyment, or exercise, on an equal footing, of any human right or fundamental freedom in the political, economic, social, cultural or any other field of public life" (Racial Discrimination Act, 1975 in Hudson 1987:97).

Multiculturalism as a policy framework sought to define and promote a fresh national image and identity abroad. It was intended to demonstrate how Australia had overcome its racist past, thus sending a strong welcoming signal to those Asian neighbors and trading partners who had become a critical part of a national economic policy (Jupp 1986; Stratton and Ang 1998; Fleras 2008b). Multiculturalism also sought to improve the social, economic, and political integration of new Australians from different cultural backgrounds. This commitment to multiculturalism was predicated on the principle of the state as a neutral arbiter of the interests of different yet equal cultures – in part to make Australia a more equitable place for all citizens, in part to whitewash the racist past of a White Australia narrative, in part to assert control over what differences could be tolerated (Hage 1998; Elder 2007).

However well intentioned if ultimately misguided, an initial emphasis on protecting minority cultural rights was discarded because of mounting criticism (Kerkyasharian 2005). Excessive emphasis on specific considerations for minorities posed a governance danger. Too much diversity not only eroded the legitimacy of multiculturalism in the eyes of the general public; it also created the conditions for social isolation and political fragmentation. The focus of Australia's multicultural policy shifted accordingly—to facilitating the settlement of immigrants through racial tolerance, equal opportunity, and full participation (Kerkyasharian 2005) without disregarding the value of ethnic diversity as part of the national identity (Inglis 2006). In response to the 1978 Report on the Review of Post-Arrival Programs and Services for Migrants (the Galbally Report), the Australian Institute of Multicultural Affairs was established, with the following objectives:

- ensuring that every person has the right to maintain their culture without penalty while accepting the responsibilities of common citizenship;

- enhancing public awareness of Australia's diverse cultures and an appreciation for their contribution to the enrichment of Australian society;
- promoting intercultural harmony and sharing between the various ethnic groups in Australia;
- fostering societal cohesion through understanding and tolerance of diversity;
- facilitating an environment that encourages full and equal participation for all minorities while enhancing opportunities for minority women and men to achieve their own potential;
- creating special programs and services if necessary to ensure equality of access;
- consulting with clients to ensure culturally responsive services;
- encouraging self sufficiency as quickly as possible;
- assuming a responsibility to support Australian values, political institutions, and rule of law (Inglis 2003).

In addition to the creation of this institute, the government accepted the recommendations of a report for improving ethnic broadcasting on multicultural television. A Special Broadcasting Services established a government-funded, nationwide network of radio and TV to procure a variety of foreign language programs. A review panel had also recommended the teaching of languages and cultures in schools and universities. These objectives were consistent with the National Language Policy of 1987, with its advocacy of secondlanguage learning as critical for cultural and intellectual enrichment, economics (foreign trade and tourism), equality (social justice and equity), and external affairs (foreign policy) (Foster and Seitz 1989).

The profile of multiculturalism in Australia was firmly anchored in July of 1989 with the establishment of a National Agenda for Multicultural Australia. In continuing the drift from an ethnic group model of multiculturalism toward a citizenship model (Babacan 2006), three objectives prevailed that clearly sought to balance the social and the cultural without losing sight of the economic, including the following:

- Cultural identity—the right of all Australians to express (within limits) their language and culture
- Social justice—the right of all Australians to equal treatment and opportunity through removal of all discriminatory barriers
- Economic efficiency—the need to capitalize on the skills and resources of all Australians as a marketing asset to meet the global challenge of trade, investment, and financial linkages

Eight basic goals were articulated in advancing these objectives: (1) freedom from discrimination, (2) equality of life-chances, (3) equality of access and resources, (4) equal participation in society, (5) development of potential for all, (6) sharing of cultural heritage, (7) institutional responsiveness, and (8) acquisition of English and community languages (Foster and Seitz 1989). The National Agenda also articulated a set of limits to Australian Multiculturalism—an overriding commitment to Australian society prevailed by prioritizing national interests over parochial concerns. A commitment to respecting difference was acceptable; however, it was secondary to an overarching commitment to Australia, with a corresponding endorsement of basic institutions, principles, and core values (Ferguson 2007). In other words, difference and diversity are valued under a National Agenda, but not to the point of "anything goes." If multiculturalism is to mean anything, it was argued, it must acknowledge the primacy of core values such as mutual respect, tolerance and harmony, the rule of law, and protection of individual rights.

... To what your multiculturalism can do for Australia

Under the Howard government (1996–2007), the fortunes of multiculturalism fluctuated. Fears of catering to special interest groups such as Asian migrants or Muslim radicals reinforced perceptions of multiculturalism as a failure not only in assimilating minorities but also for undermining Australian culture and identity (Pearson 2001; Babacan 2006). In keeping with its move toward pragmatism and national interests that tended to dismiss difference as divisive or detrimental (Robbins 2007; Hawthorne 2008), the government adopted a more assimilationist approach to governance, including a reduction in government financial support for programs in multicultural service delivery (Inglis 2003). Priorities shifted in advancing a new nationalism that secured legitimacy to an Anglo Celtic heritage as the basis for national identity and social cohesion (Babacan 2006). Emphasis focused on improving immigrant integration by way of shared values, common identity, and core values despite corresponding moves to raise the bar for citizenship acquisition (Aly 2008). In an effort to replace the divisiveness of a rights mentality with a responsibility mindset that emphasizes duty and commonality, Australia introduced citizenship tests in October 2007 for all new citizens between the ages of 18 and 60. Last, the term itself was gradually phased out, including its removal from the immigration portfolio in 2007 (Department of Immigration and Multicultural Affairs) and replaced with citizenship (Department of Immigration and Citizenship), on the grounds that immigration should lead to citizenship, not ethnicity (Daily Telegraph 23 January 2007).

But the picture is more ambivalent than one of either hostility or rejection (see Ang et al. 2006). The diminishment of multiculturalism as a national narrative is unmistakable, with the ideal of integration (or even assimilation) as the preferred model of the nation-state (Pearson 2004; Healey 2007; Tate 2009). The political profile of multiculturalism continues to shrink as governments look for ways to pare costs while pandering to international capital and investment. Nevertheless, a commitment to multiculturalism continues to play a pivotal governance role, as articulated in the New Agenda for a Multicultural Australia (originally 2000 but updated in 2003), namely, to build on Australia's success as a culturally diverse society that is united in diversity and a shared community and commitment. Four principles underpin Australia's multiculturalism policy:

a) *Civic Duty (responsibilities of all)*: All Australians must support those basic structures, values, and principles of freedom and equality of Australian society.
b) *Cultural Respect (respect for each person)*: All Australians have the right to religion and cultural expression as long as this expression does not break the law or deny the right for others to do the same.
c) *Social Equity (fairness for each person)*: All Australians are entitled to equality of treatment and equal opportunity in enhancing Australia's social, political, and economic life.
d) *Productive Diversity (benefits for all)*: All Australians benefit from the social and economic dividends of a productive diversity.

These principles are consistent with the position paper on Multiculturalism by the Acting Race Discrimination Commissioner (2007), namely, (a) the freedom for all Australians to practice their culture and religion, (b) equal access and opportunity for all Australian to participate in the political and economic life of Australia, (c) responsibility of all Australians to respect the rights of others and to commit to this country's institutions and democratic principles, and (d) maximisation of economic benefits from multiculturalism.

Two conclusion follow: First, Australia appears unapologetic about linking multiculturalism with business (also see Abu-Laban and Gabriel 2002). The marketing of multicultural differences and an orderly multicultural governance are touted as core assets to enhance Australia's economic advantage in a global market economy. Second, multiculturalism in Australia is not shy about establishing limits for living together differently. In seeking to balance unity with diversity and responsibilities with rights, all Australians are free to pursue their cultural heritage. But this right is secondary to the priorities of mutual civic obligations, including an overriding loyalty to Australia, its people, and the basic structures and principles informing its democratic governance, namely, the Constitution, parliamentary democracy, freedom of speech and religion, English as the national language, the rule of law, acceptance, and equality (Commonwealth of Australia, 1989, 1999, 2003). Strategies and programs are thus designed to (1) make institutions and values more respectful of, more reflective of, and more responsive to diversity; (2) promote intergroup harmony and harmonious community relations; and (3) optimize benefits of cultural diversity for all Australians (New Agenda 2003).

In other words, appearances can be deceiving. The collapse in profile and political popularity notwithstanding, Australia remains multicultural in principle, programs, and practice. According to the then minister of Immigration and Multicultural Affairs, Peter McGauran (2005), a commitment to multiculturalism prevails, but one that disavows celebrating diversity for diversity's sake or promoting special privileges to minorities and migrants. Instead a conservative multicultural model endorses policies and services that enable all Australians to reach their full potential in contributing to Australia's development, while respecting Australian values (freedom of speech, rule of law, equal opportunities). Or as then prime minister John Howard wrote in the introduction to the New Agenda, "All Australians, regardless of their ethnic, cultural, or religious background are encouraged to participate fully in the wider Australian community to show a commitment to our nation, its democratic institutions and its laws."

In short, Australia possesses an active if increasingly muted multicultural policy, together with a comprehensive range of cultural and language programs that bear some resemblance to comparable initiatives in Canada. As in Canada, an official multicultural policy is directed at managing difference by putting it to work on behalf of all Australians. The focus is on disadvantage rather than difference, through removal of discriminatory barriers to bolster institutional inclusiveness and immigrant integration (see Annual Report 2006/2007). Furthermore, multiculturalism is normally touted as central to national narratives involving national identity and nation building. The Acting Race Discrimination Commissioner (Australia Human Rights Commission 2007) put it best when projecting how the positive effect of multiculturalism will continue to play a central role in providing a rational antidote to extremism, protecting human rights for all, securing the ideals of democratic society, and responding to the realities of Australia's ethnocultural diversities.

But differences too can be discerned: Multiculturalism in Australia exists as policy rather than entrenched in law or the constitution. Its status as policy subjects multiculturalism to prevailing ideologies or whims of the government in power. Moreover, Australia has no intention of formally enshrining multiculturalism in legislation (unlike the states of Queensland and Victoria), preferring instead to contend that multicultural principles are arguably safeguarded in existing legislation, like the 1975 Racial Discrimination Act. Australia's commitment to multiculturalism also appears to be more explicit in defining what is acceptable or not. Immigrants must express an overriding and unifying commitment to Australia (yes, you can have multiple loyalties, but loyalty to Australia must prevail in situations involving a conflict of interest); they must also work within basic structures and values of Australia, while accepting obligations as well as rights, including a reciprocal responsibility to respect others. Additional restrictions apply: all adult applicants, when applying for and receiving selected visas from late 2007 on, are required to sign a values document to confirm a commitment to Australian values. In reinforcing the slogan that migrants will be accepted provided they do things "our" way, a conservative multiculturalism model promotes diversities for advancing Australian interests rather than what Australia can do for migrants and minorities.

Multiculturalism in Queensland: "Productive Diversity"

Australia is proving a paradox in its endorsement of multiculturalism. On the one hand, the commonwealth government appears to be retreating from an explicit commitment to multiculturalism as governance. On the other side, most Australian states appear to be strengthening their commitment to multiculturalism as principle, policy, and practice. For example, there is the West Australian Charter of Multiculturalism, the Communitiy Relations Commission and Principles of Multiculturalism Act in New South Wales, Tasmania's Multicultural Policy, and Northern Territories Multicultural Policy (see Acting Race Discrimination Commissioner 2007). More specifically, the state of Victoria introduced a government policy statement in 2002 (Valuing Cultural Diversity) that articulated four themes for managing cultural diversity, including valuing diversity, reducing inequality, encouraging participation, and promoting the economic and cultural benefits of diversity to all Victorians. The Multicultural Victoria Act in 2004 acknowledged Victoria's cultural diversity by endorsing a vision of Victoria as a united community with shared laws, values, responsibilities, and rights, while preserving a people's freedom to express their cultural heritage. In recent years, there has been a move toward a whole-government approach for achieving policy goals (multicultural objectives integrated into mainstream ideas and institutions), in addition to a single-agency approach with specific legislation and programs

(Victoria Multicultural Commission 2008). The Victorian Multicultural Commission constitutes a statutory authority whose commissioners are appointed by the Cabinet—in addition to an advisory body of community advocacy groups—to enhance the contributions of minorities to Australia while ensuring the accountability of government departments in advancing the inclusion of difference (Annual Report, Victoria Multicultural Commission, 2006/2007).

The Queensland government has also bolstered its multicultural profile. By strengthening its predecessor, the 1998 Queensland Multicultural Policy (Queensland Government 2004), the affirmation of the 2004 multicultural policy coincided with parallel developments in advancing Queensland's multicultural governance. Passage of the Queensland Government Language Services Policy reflected an across-the-board government commitment to develop communication strategies for informing eligible clients of services and entitlements, to enable clients to access these services fairly and equitably, and to ensure a service delivery that is respectful of and responsive to diversity and difference. In addition, the formulation of a Charter of Public Service in a Culturally Diverse Society secured yet another multicultural commitment. A framework now exists for the planning and delivery of quality services and programs that are available, accessible, and culturally appropriate.

Launched in 2005 and entitled "Multicultural Queensland—Making a World of Difference," the policy not only confirms the whole-of-government commitment to multiculturalism, that is, to promote equal rights, responsibilities, opportunities, and contributions of all Queenslanders regardless of race or ethnicity. The policy also provides a blueprint *for managing and maximizing Queeenland's diversity* (18 percent of its population is foreign born) *for the economic and social well-being of all Queenslanders.* According to government documents,

> As a policy, multiculturalism promotes social justice and equity for disadvantaged non English speaking communities, women and young people of culturally and linguistically diverse backgrounds, and newly arrived refugees and migrants. It also fosters economic development and participation by supporting skilled migrants, people with multilingual skills, and people with overseas connections and by nurturing cultural capital. Multiculturalism also underpins community cohesion by raising awareness of the benefits of diversity and promoting respect for difference.

In seeking to create an inclusive, cohesive, and harmonious society—one in which all Queenslanders feel valued and welcomed (Queensland

Government, Multicultural Highlights 2006–2007), the policy made provisions for five objectives:

- Capitalize on skills and talents of a diverse workforce
- Maximize economic benefits of cultural diversity
- Increase employment opportunities for new Australians
- Improve responsiveness of government services to cultural differences
- Foster a greater awareness and understanding of multiculturalism

Like its commonwealth equivalent, the policy articulated the limits of a multicultural governance. That is, all Australians are expected to display an overriding and unifying commitment to Australia and its interests and future; to enjoy freedom to express, share, and respect other cultural heritages; to have equality of opportunity to benefit from and contribute to society without fear of prejudice and discrimination; and to uphold universal ideals such as those pertaining to human rights. Of particular salience in advancing a multicultural governance is the need for all Australians to embrace core values, including (1) promoting economic and cultural benefits of diversity for all Australians, (2) ensuring access to services and programs regardless of ethnicity and background, (3) assisting community development and full and equal participation across all aspects of Queensland's life, and (4) ensuring that all Queenslanders share in the responsibility for creating a cohesive and fair Queensland. Four strategies are in place to implement this governance:

- Productive Diversity Economic Strategy
- Supporting Communities
- Strengthening Multiculturalism in the Public Sector
- Community Relations and Anti Racism.

All government departments are required to report annually on their performance in creating more inclusive institutions. They must participate in developing, implementing, and evaluating initiatives that are consistent with the principles and provisions of the Multicultural Action Plan. Each must also commit to strategies for outlining key priorities and outcomes, together with the actions that will be taken to progressively embed multicultural principles and practices throughout its core business. Finally, action teams will be formed to develop, assist, and oversee the implementation of departments' multicultural action plans for achieving outcomes and ensuring sustainable best practice initiatives (Queensland Government, Multicultural Highlights 2006–2007).

These commitments and strategies make the position abundantly clear. First, the fundamental theme underlying Queensland's multicultural governance is about national interests and state building. To put a not-too-fine spin on it: Not what multiculturalism can do for minorities, but what minorities can do for Australia in advancing the benefits of diversity and difference. Second, differences come with limits. You can be different, but this difference is secondary to being a Queenslander Australian. That is, you can be Vietnamese, but always a Vietnamese in Australia. Third, a pragmatic and commercial narrative informs and justifies multiculturalism. This commitment to "multiculturalism means business" should come as no surprise. Responsibility for the implementation of the policy was assigned to the Department of Tourism, Regional Development, and Industry, whose core mission is to advance business growth in Queensland. Admittedly, there remains a celebratory component as demonstrated by the $723,000 allocated for funding 80 multicultural festivals and projects celebrating Queensland's cultural diversity (Lindy 2008:4). Nevertheless, a multicultural commitment for improving the economy through "productive diversity" is unmistakable, and it is pursued accordingly, along the following lines:

- Enhance productivity and competitive advantage for Queensland business through private-public partnerships
- Facilitate international investment
- Attract skilled migrants
- Assist businesses to improve foreign market exports

Time will tell if these ideas and ideals can be implemented in ways both sustainable and productive. The fact that they resemble the multicultural principles of the commonwealth New Agenda suggest the fortunes of both governances will vary in tandem.

Reaction to Multiculturalism: Fair Go for Some, Go Home for Others

'Has multiculturalism failed Australia?' or 'Has Australia failed multiculturalism? (Babacan 2006)

Multiculturalism continues to elicit strong reactions from all sides of the political spectrum (Longley 1999). To one side are those who reject its relevance. First Australians have positioned themselves outside a discursive multicultural framework, despite government's efforts to depoliticize aboriginality as a political movement. As far as the First Australians are concerned, their interests as (descendants of) original occupants are fundamentally different from immigrants and multiculturalism. Similarly in Canada: Instead of self-defining themselves as disadvantaged immigrants in need of integration, accommodation, and equality, both Aboriginal peoples and the Québécois prefer the language of nationalism over multicultural discourses for justifying claims to self-determining autonomy over jurisdictions of land, identity, and political voice (Murphy 2004; Maaka and Fleras 2005). With its roots in consensus, conformity, and control, an official multiculturalism is poorly equipped to handle the highly politicized discourses of challenge, resistance, and transformation associated with the politics of indigeneity (Fleras 2002). In other words, Multiculturalism cannot possibly address the demands of fundamentally autonomous political communities who claim they are sovereign in their own right yet sharing in the sovereignty of Canada by way of shared jurisdictions.

To the other side are those supportive of multiculturalism as governance whose time is now. Praise for multiculturalism reflects its status as one of Australia's great success stories (Kerkyasharian 2005). Supporters acknowledge the challenges in popularizing multiculturalism, given Australia's image as a white man's country, history of exclusionary immigration programs, and commitment to assimilation. Still, its role in improving the quality of Australian life should not be discounted. But even endorsement tends to be conditional. While Australians may embrace the concept of multiculturalism in principle, they also express concerns about its impact in undermining social unity and national identity (Sykes 2008). In acknowledging Ghassan Hage (2003), who argues that official multiculturalism has met its match in the encounter with politicized Islam, the Muslim presence exposes many of the contradictions of multiculturalism, namely, whether it should be tolerant of those who are intolerant of tolerance (Dunn 2003).

To yet another side are the critics and cynics. Multiculturalism is attacked for everything—from selective amnesia over Australia's racist past in confirming a national monoculture (Povinelli 1998), to little more than a "pork barrel" for buying ethnic loyalties (Hughes 2000). Those on the left have been disillusioned by the failure of this hegemonic discourse to eradicate racism; those on the right fear it as a threat to the coherence of a white settler identity; those in the middle are unsure of who to believe or what to think. The multicultural project has also been accused of being (a) too contradictory an ideology to gain wide and enduring support, (b) too limiting because of its cultural approach to structural problems of racism and inequality, (c) too hegemonic in logic and agenda to be anything more than exercises in impression management or conflict resolution, and (d) too reductionist in fossilizing cultural differences into an ethnic cage that amount to a neocolonial strategy of divide and rule (Vasta and Castles 1996; Hage 1998). Finally, the Muslim presence in Australia and in those nearby countries (Bali) where terrorist bombs have killed Australians continues to drive the antimulticultural agenda (Hage 2006). As a result, the politics of multiculturalism remain sharply contested because of government moves to defuse insecurities and anxieties. It remains to be seen if the new Labour Government under Kevin Rudd will reverse the (mis)fortunes of a multiculturalism program that once was the envy of the world. Evidence to date is not promising (Jakubowicz 2008).

6

Contesting Governances in Aotearoa New Zealand: Monoculturalism, Biculturalism, Multiculturalism, and Binationalism

Introduction: The Politics of Isms

Aotearoa New Zealand has long enjoyed an international reputation for its harmonious management of "race" relations (Crothers 2007). This assessment is accurate to some extent, even if the outcome has been tarnished in recent years and attained largely by accident rather than by design. But the challenge of crafting an inclusive governance that recognizes diversity and rewards differences has proven increasingly elusive and daunting. The politics of "isms" is partly to blame. Biculturalism narratives clearly dominate; nevertheless, the politics of both monoculturalism and multiculturalism continue to jockey for status (see Spoonley and Trlin, 2004; Liu 2005; O'Sullivan 2006; Sibley and Liu 2007). To the extent that many Pakeha (non-Maori) New Zealanders waffle over an openly monocultural framework, yet recoil from any proposed constitutional changes lest they lose control of the national agenda, they endorse a preference for multiculturalism as the lesser of evils. In that government policy embraces a bicultural commitment as a basis for cooperative governance, indigenous Maori leaders concur, even if a state-imposed biculturalism may compromise their constitutional status as the "nations within" (Fleras and Spoonley 1999). But critics propose a more politicized biculturalism, one that acknowledges New Zealand's binationality as a

two-nation state (Johnson 2008; Maaka and Fleras 2008). Insofar as neither the concept of indigenous peoples' rights nor the complex notions
of a binational constitutional order have attracted much serious national
debate to date (Barclay 2005), the challenge is unmistakable: a balance between New Zealand's mostly unwritten bicultural constitution
that acknowledges Maori as indigenous peoples and the accommodation
demands of an immigration driven multiculturalism (Friesen 2008).

To say that the politics of isms is sharply contesting a preferred
New Zealand governance is beyond debate (Bromell 2008). A commitment
to multiculturalism is criticized for ostensibly compromising the rights and
primacy of Maori as tangata whenua (peoples of the land) (Huijser 2004;
Sibley and Liu 2004; Clarke 2006). Conversely, a bicultural ideology rooted
in the principles of the Treaty of Waitangi (with its governance principles of partnership, protection, participation, and autonomy) is criticized
for its indifference to immigrant cultures (see DeSouza 2007). Migrants
and minorities are increasingly resentful of absorption into a monocultural framework, yet are equally disdainful of exclusion under a bicultural
governance. Mainstream responses are no less ambiguous. They may prefer a commitment to multiculturalism over biculturalism—not necessarily
out of principle but from fear that excessive bicultural demands could
topple a Eurocentric status quo (Pearson 2001; May 2004). And yet a symbolic biculturalism is proving appealing in advancing a Maori-based New
Zealand culture and national identity (Sibley and Liu 2007). Finally, the
indigenous Maori tribes are equally conflicted over the appropriate ism—
a state-sponsored biculturalism with its focus on addressing Maori needs
and redressing historical wrongs or, alternatively, a robust binationalism with its promise of transformative change along constitutional lines
(O'Sullivan 2006; Humpage 2008).

In short, the politics of isms is posing a governance conundrum (Fleras
2008b). To one side are growing demands for recognition of multiculturalism as the preferred framework for cooperative governance (Liu
2005). The reemergence of multiculturalism as governance design is not
surprising: The influx of Asian immigrants and Pacific Islanders super-
imposes new ethnic fault lines upon increasingly politicized dualities,
resulting in mounting pressure for a governance that is inclusive of all
(Spoonley 2005). To the other side is a politicized Maori assertiveness that
dismisses as grounds for governance both a nascent multiculturalism and
state-sponsored biculturalism. In embracing a binational blueprint that
endorses a dualistic vision of Aotearoa plus New Zealand as foundationally a two-nation state, each partnered in power sharing and constructive engagement, the implications are nothing short of transformative.
The politics of Maori indigeneity calls for a rethinking of Maori-Crown

relations by privileging tribal models of self-determining autonomy over those proposed by the state (Maaka and Fleras 2008; O'Sullivan 2006). Yet another layer of complexity and confusion is the drift toward monoculturalism as national identity—at least judging by enthusiastic political and public acceptance of "we are one people" discourses (Seuffert 2006). The government response? A review of all policies and programs to ensure they address individual needs of all New Zealanders rather than focus on racial entitlement or Maori indigenous rights.

Monoculturalism? Multiculturalism? Biculturalism? Binationalism? Some would argue that the differences among the "isms" are minor and inconsequential. For example, with its inclusionary focus within an institutional status quo, a state-defined biculturalism has proven little more than a "multiculturalism for Maori" (Fleras 1998). Others disagree, and acknowledge fundamental differences in scope, objectives, underlying rationale, strategies, and proposed outcomes. Whereas biculturalism establishes a constitutional imperative, multiculturalism operates at the level of a social objective, with the result that migrants and minorities align their needs along multicultural lines rather than in the language of nationhood and self-determination (Sibley and Liu 2007). Still others concede major differences between the two isms; however, repeated and often imprecise use has rendered biculturalism virtually indistinguishable from its multicultural counterpart. Still others contend that neither multiculturalism nor biculturalism adequately captures the logic underlying indigenous Maori politics in New Zealand. A binational governance arrangement is proposed that embraces the foundational principle of Maori tribes as nations within, with corresponding rights and powers that flow from this recognition (Maaka and Fleras 2005, 2008).

This chapter addresses the complex and evolving politics of isms in Aotearoa New Zealand. In seeking to sort out the logic behind these politics, the chapter explores controversies over core governance issues, including: (a) the relationship of multiculturalism to the other isms, (b) the political primacy of biculturalism over multiculturalism, (c) the tension between binationalism and bi/multiculturalism, and (d) the prospects of a multiculturalism within a binational governance. It also demonstrates the challenge that animates any compromise between the constitutional rights of the tangata whenua with the emergent rights of the tangata tauiwi (immigrants) (Sibley and Liu 2007). Debates over how to balance these competing rights have prompted a former Race Relations conciliator, Dr. Rajen Prasad (1997:A-9), to plead for "... another way of thinking about ourselves as a multi-ethnic society with an indigenous culture, and with a founding document that regulates the relationship between Maori and Crown." Time will tell if a commitment to a multiculturalism within a bicultural (or binational) framework can flourish amid this bewildering welter of isms.

Diversity and Difference in Aotearoa New Zealand

New Zealand as a treaty-based Pacific nation has proven a site of contestation. The politics of isms continues to scramble for position: in shifting from monoculturalism as a tacitly assumed governance, to debates over multiculturalism and biculturalism as governance models, with neo-monoculturalism and binationalism appearing on the government's radar (Fleras and Spoonley 1999; Pearson 2001; Seuffert 2006), the once unfathomable is now the inescapable. New Zealand has evolved from a monocultural British enclave to one that acknowledges the bicultural legitimacy of Maori as a founding peoples and power-sharing partners. But while initial interest in multiculturalism quickly dissipated because it compromised the biculturality of New Zealand (Fleras 1984; May 2004), a new and increasingly politicized demographic has emerged because of immigrant trends, with a corresponding support for multiculturalism.

New Zealand's current immigration policy is designed to produce tangible economic and social benefits. Earlier immigration policies clearly focused on preferred source countries, but current criteria pinpoint individual characteristics, especially skills, education levels, age, and amount of investment capital. Key components in advancing a "productive diversity" include (1) contributing to New Zealand's human resource base (selecting migrants whose expertise matches those in demand), (2) fostering strong international linkages (selecting migrants with economic connections in their homeland), (3) developing a culture of enterprise and innovation (selecting immigrants with entrepreneurial skills and experience), (4) complementing skills training and employment strategies through temporary work permits to fill short-term labor shortages, (5) reuniting families and responding to humanitarian needs by meeting New Zealand's international obligations toward refugees, and (6) maintaining high levels of social cohesion in a bicultural New Zealand that is increasingly diverse in its ethnic composition (Bedford 2003). Still, an air of ambivalence lingers. Notwithstanding a growing unease and ambivalence over immigration as a net contributor to New Zealand society and economy (see Young 2008), many believe that, properly managed, immigration can produce positive outcomes for society (Bedford 2003).

The immigration program involves three residence streams, with each stream allocated a percentage of the total input. In 2007–2008 the Skilled/Business stream will account for 60 percent of the spaces, Family

Sponsored for 30 percent, and Humanitarian/International for 10 percent (Human Rights Commission 2007). With respect to numbers, migration trends are proving impressive for a country with a population of just over 4 million: a total of 46,964 migrants were approved for residence in 2006–2007. The largest group (26 percent) arrived from the United Kingdom, followed by China (12 percent) and India (9 percent). The total number of long-term arrivals in 2007, including 23,500 returning New Zealand citizens, was 82,700. Permanent long-term departures totalled 72,600, including 51,800 New Zealand citizens, resulting in a net permanent long-term migration gain of 10,100 (Human Rights Commission 2007).

In light of these immigration patterns and flows, New Zealand's demography is rapidly changing. In 2006, 67 percent of New Zealanders identified their ethnicity as European, 14.6 percent as Maori, 11.1 percent as New Zealander, 9.2 percent as Asian (including the Peoples Republic of China, Hong Kong, Taiwan, Korea, the Philippines, and Japan), 6.9 percent as Pacific, and 1 percent as other. Compare this ethnic composition with figures from 1976 when 86 percent identified as European, 9.2 percent as Maori, and less than 2 percent as Pacific and Other (Human Rights Commission 2006). There is much of significance in this shift in immigration flows and sources. Proportionately speaking, the percentage of overseas-born people who live in New Zealand is greater than in any other country except Australia and Canada. Auckland, in turn, is home to more foreign born than any other Australasian city (Spoonley 2007).

Such a formidable demographic shift is not without import. First, the fact that New Zealand is demographically multicultural reinforces the rationale for explicitly supporting multiculturalism as governance. But the government is not budging. In response to a question in Parliament ("Is the Government considering introducing a multiculturalism bill?"), the response by the minister of Social Development and Employment on behalf of the minister for Ethnic Affairs was a resounding "No." According to the Hon. Ruth Dyson, such a bill would be redundant; after all,

> New Zealand already has a strong human rights and race relations legislative framework, including the Human Rights Act . . . Everyone enjoys equal treatment and protection under the law, while it respects and values their diversity. (New Zealand Parliament, 7 August 2008)

Second, despite the reluctance of the state to officially recognize multiculturalism, New Zealand remains fully committed to the principles of a multicultural governance. Since 1999, the government has implemented a series of multicultural initiatives, ranging from the establishment of an Ethnic Affairs portfolio within the Internal Affairs Department, to the creation of the Office of Ethnic Affairs, to celebration of important ethnic events at Parliament (including Islamic Awareness Week), and to programs like Connecting Diverse Communities and Building Bridges project (New Zealand Parliament, 7 August 2008). Inasmuch as New Zealand remains a multicultural governance without a official multiculturalism, it joins other countries around the world that are multicultural in all but name.

De Facto Multiculturalism

New Zealand has never officially endorsed multiculturalism as policy or program. Unlike its Tasman neighbors to the west, this unwillingness to formally acknowledge and institutionally accommodate its expanding diversity of languages and cultures is drawing concern and criticism (May 2004). Nevertheless, a de facto multiculturalism is in place for accommodating migrants and minorities by way of institutional inclusion. Government initiatives in responding to increased ethnic diversity include ratification of international human rights conventions and domestic legislation to ensure equal opportunity and reduce disparities (Singham 2006). In addition to a laissez-faire tolerance, specific legal instruments underlying New Zealand's multicultural ethos allow minorities to live as minorities by respecting their cultural and religious differences (Kolig 2006). A Ministry of Pacific Affairs also exists to bolster Pacific Islander capacity building at individual and community levels. Admittedly, much of what passes for New Zealand multiculturalism does not involve major public resources, does little to make Pakeha uncomfortable, and puts the onus on minority communities to preserve their identity and culture (Spoonley 2005). Still, the reemergence of multiculturalism as a complementary national narrative has complicated an already complex balancing act for living together with differences (Race Relations Conciliator 2000).

Proof abounds of New Zealand as a multicultural governance without the multiculturalism. Consider multicultural developments during the past decade: The launch in 2003 of the Ethnic Perspectives in Policy program assisted government agencies to identify gaps in services to ethnic communities (Department of Internal Affairs 2005). In 2004, a revised New Zealand Settlement Strategy, Our Future Together, was launched with the goal of responding to settlement needs and outcomes of migrants and refugees. Its governance vision read as follows:

New Zealand's prosperity is underpinned by an inclusive society, in which the local and national integration of newcomers is supported by responsive services, a welcoming environment, and a shared respect for diversity. (Human Rights Commission 2007:37)

Numerous multicultural centres across urban New Zealand attest to the dynamics of addressing accommodation. For example, Christchurch opened a multicultural centre *"Te Whare O Nga Whetu"* in 2001 (Christchurch City Council Community Plan 2002). The centre's mission statement focused on responding to local needs, securing a safe and friendly meeting ground for a sharing of cultures and knowledge, and providing services, programmes and linkages between ethnocultural groups and the local community.

No less important was the establishment of a Ten Point New Zealand Diversity Action Programme by Parliament in August 2004 for improving race relations (available at www.hrc.co.nz), including

1) Develop a network of people and organizations for advancing the harmonious relationships in a diverse and inclusive New Zealand
2) Establish an internet site with information about New Zealand's diverse communities
3) Create a centre for the study and promotion of cultural diversity
4) Encourage public debate for protecting human rights, including diversity
5) Review school curriculum to ensure the inclusion of cultural diversity
6) Foster diversity in the media to ensure they reflect cultural diversity
7) Support successful settlement programs for immigrations and refugees
8) Celebrate diversity through arts and festivals
9) Provide fora for sharing cultural diverse stories
10) Promote dialogue and exchange among different cultural groups

Other initiatives include the 2007 Connecting Diverse Communities project. As a whole-of-government approach toward inclusiveness, this project promised to better coordinate diversity initiatives across government agencies, promote social cohesion, recognize and respect cultural differences as a positive, and improve intercultural relations between diverse ethnic and religious groups (Ministry of Social Development 2007). Finally, the launch of a new educational curriculum in November 2007 confirmed New Zealand's multicultural commitments. Several core principles underpin the curriculum, including (1) acknowledging the principles of the Treaty of Waitangi and the bicultural foundations of New Zealand society, (2) recognizing and valuing New Zealand's cultural diversity, and (3) embracing inclusiveness by ensuring that no one is excluded because of prejudice and discrimination (Human Rights Commission 2007). Besides promoting cultural diversity, the new curriculum insists on the principles of equity (fairness and justice), community and participation, and respect for others and human rights.

To the extent that multiculturalism is formalized, it resides within government circles. Establishment of the Ethnic Affairs portfolio within the Department of Internal Affairs in 1999 secured a say for ethnic communities within the government. It also provided the government with a handle in addressing major issues confronting ethnic communities, including (1) effective participation in society, (2) fair and equal access to social services, (3) information for the general population of the benefits of ethnic diversity and the contributions of ethnic New Zealanders, and (4) expectations of a more responsive host society, greater economic opportunities, opportunities to build community capacity, and support to maintain heritage language and cultures (Department of Internal Affairs 2006). The subsequent creation of the Office of Ethnic Affairs in 2001 as a stand-alone unit within Internal Affairs advanced its predecessor's goals. With its vision of "strength in ethnic diversity," the Office sought to "contribute to a strong self-directed ethnic sector able to set its own priorities, and to promote the advantages of ethnic diversity for New Zealand" (Department of Internal Affairs 2005). More specifically, the Office sought to address ethnic issues that (a) apply across government, (b) provide information about or for ethnic communities, (c) secure a point of contact between ethnic communities and the government, (d) support settlement processes, (e) raise awareness of the value of ethnic and cultural diversity, and (f) furnish referrals to appropriate agencies.

Reactions to New Zealand's growing multicultural commitment vary. The relevance of multiculturalism is attracting growing support among new New Zealanders, as well as among state elites, minority leaders, and non-Maori academics (Pearson 2005). Advocates of multiculturalism not only criticize the government's bicultural commitment for failing to recognize New Zealand's emergent multicultural reality (Ip and Pang 2005:186; also Eaton 2007). They also believe it is both unfair and unjust to encourage immigration without a corresponding endorsement of multiculturalism to facilitate settlement and integration. Not any kind of multiculturalism, critics contend, but one that goes beyond a set of instructions imposed on minorities by emphasizing a dialogue between different communities (Jakubowicz 2007), while focusing on inequities rather than identities

(Bader 2007b; Biles and Spoonley 2007). But what should be is not the same as what is, owing to definitional slippages, as Clarke (2006:27) ruefully notes:

> The terms "multicultural" and "multiculturalism" litter government documentation and official policy, although little or no attempt is made precisely to define the nature or limits of this multiculturalism [author's note: there is little evidence to support this; the M word is rarely or never used in government documents, including the briefing notes for the incoming Minister of Ethnic Affairs (DIA 2005)]. The term is used in general public discourse in a broadly positive manner, sometimes contrasted but more often juxtaposed, with "biculturalism," as meaning the tolerance and acceptance of a certain form and degree of cultural difference. This "difference" is clearly perceived as a deviation from the majority, Anglo Celtic cultural norm, though it is never explicitly defined as such.

A lack of formal policy and related government legislation is consequential. The ambiguity, lack of reflexivity, and relative weakness of multiculturalism means that, unless enshrined in law, the scope of its effectiveness is curtailed. Consequently, as Clarke (2006) argues, minority rights can be exercised not by assertions of entitlement but by appeals to tolerance within the context of a liberal universal governance. Compare this restrictiveness with Maori who, under a quasi-official biculturalism, possess explicit indigenous and agenda-setting rights that can be addressed and advanced through the legal mechanism of the state.

Clearly, then, not everyone concurs with a commitment to or benefits of multiculturalism (Bromell 2008). Personal attacks are not uncommon. The maverick politician Winston Peters has long railed against the evils of multiculturalism—both imagined and real. Peters warns of the dangers in seeing the world through the prism of multicultural spectacles, while denouncing multiculturalism as a catalyst for inciting crime waves, encouraging welfare/citizenship abuse, and actively promoting the equal worth every culture (thus sowing the seeds of ethnic strife) (Young 2008). Maori attitudes toward immigration and multiculturalism appear to have hardened in recent years, according to a Massey University study. Resistance to immigration-driven multiculturalism reflects fears that New Zealand biculture is undermined by newcomers, that immigration adversely affects Maori in terms of employment and access to services, and that immigrants may compromise Maori indigenous rights under the Treaty of Waitangi (Eaton 2007; also Massey News 2007).

In short, many disagree with any privileging of multiculturalism, especially when promoted at the expense of New Zealand's bicultural heritage

(Greif 1995). They point to the irrevocability of Aotearoa New Zealand as a bicultural partnership between Treaty signatories, with its guarantee of collective Maori rights that supersede the individual rights of recent immigrants. To formalize multiculturalism by extending official recognition to minority rights poses a constitutional threat by delegitimizing the bicultural partnership between Maori and the Crown (Clarke 2006). Accordingly, Maori bicultural rights as original occupants must take precedence over the multicultural rights of immigrants. Otherwise there is a danger of conflating Maori aspirations with those of migrants and minorities, resulting in a corresponding diminuation of Maori foundational status as *tangata whenua* (original occupants). Such reductionism is widely dismissed as irresponsible, colonizing, and contrary to the spirit of Treaty partnership (Walker 1995; Ip and Pang 2005). Only when biculturalism is securely entrenched as the ruling paradigm, it is argued, can multiculturalism begin to negotiate its rightful status as an alternative governance (Stuart 2007).

De Jure Biculturalism

New Zealand has traversed a long and sometimes tricky governance path. From an imagined community based on Anglo settler ideals that prevailed into the 1970s, a commitment to biculturalism as governance has emerged that formally acknowledges Maori and Pakeha as distinct but equal partners who share stewardship of New Zealand's resources and contribute equally to national culture and identity (Sibley and Liu 2007). And yet biculturalism possesses long roots in New Zealand history. The signing of the Treaty of Waitangi in 1840 between the Crown and Maori tribes symbolically expressed and reinforced a fundamental bicultural reality: that is, Maori tribes as sovereign nations with inherent rights to self-determining autonomy in partnership with the Crown (Maaka and Fleras 2008). An explicit commitment to biculturalism was endorsed by the visionary Maori leader Apirana Ngata who encouraged Maori to be bicultural—to adapt to the West while staying true to their language and culture. In 1968, the Canadian scholar Erik Schwimmer published a book on biculturalism in New Zealand that acknowledged both the existence and desirability of a bicultural New Zealand.

However relevant these antecedents, reference to biculturalism as governance is of recent origin. The bicultural principle of Maori-Crown partnership was inaugurated in 1975 with the establishment of the Waitangi Tribunal (an independent commission of inquiry to look into Maori grievances, usually involving dispute land claims and confiscations, with corresponding suggestions for resolution). Biculturalism assumed the status of de facto government policy in 1986 following passage of the State Owned Enterprises Bill, which read: "Nothing in the Act shall permit the Crown to act in a manner that is inconsistent with the principles of the Treaty of Waitangi." (The Treaty of Waitangi, signed in 1840 between the British Crown and many Maori chiefs, is widely regarded as New Zealand's foundational constitutional document.) The 1987 Court of Appeal ruling reaffirmed the bicultural partnership between the Crown and Maori, with each partner expected to act reasonably and in good faith toward the other. Passage of the State Services Act in 1988 confirmed the shift to the biculturality of Aotearoa by instructing state institutions to incorporate the Treaty's obligations of partnership, participation, and protection into the delivery of service (Seuffert 2006).

Popularity and support notwithstanding, there is no consensus over the meaning of biculturalism. Just as multiculturalism can represent a blank screen for for projecting a diverse range of political positions, so too can biculturalism mean different things to different people in different contexts. References to biculturalism span the spectrum from reformist to transformist, from government-sponsored to Maori-determined, and from the collective and political to the personal and the cultural (Humpage and Fleras 2001). On the one hand is the commitment to reform mainstream institutions by reflecting, respecting, and responding to Maori without necessarily any sharing of power. On the other hand, a transformative approach involves fundamental constitutional changes, including the creation of parallel or separate Maori institutions based on the principle of Maori indigenous rights (Doerr 2008). The establishment of Maori-owned and -controlled schools – from language immersion preschools (*te kohanga reo*) to Maori-driven primary-secondary-tertiary institutions (*kura kaupapa Maori*) – attests to the reality of a transformative model of biculturalism.

In conveying the range of biculturalisms from "soft" to "hard", Mason Durie (2001) concedes as much: Since the mid 1970s, New Zealand has been engaged in the politics of biculturalism. Though unsure about its parameters, and often at cross purposes, institutions, government departments and community organizations have been expected to apply biculturalism and the principles of the Treaty of Waitangi to their operations. There has not been agreement about the purpose or practice of biculturalism and the diversity of responses has prompted the construction of a bicultural continuum as a way of defining the parameters of particular bicultural initiatives. At one level, biculturalism could imply a separate Maori way of doing things, at another it means the celebration of culture (though not necessarily any changes to core business), and in some instances its about ensuring a workforce composition to reflect the cultural makeup of the community. Biculturalism has also often been taken to mean partnership between Maori and non Maori, though this can sometimes lead to exploitation, the Maori partner being used as the cultural guide, without incurring any benefits from the process.

"Tukutuku" biculturalism: A multiculturalism for Maori

To what extent are multiculturalism and biculturalism competing frameworks for governance discourse? In theory, they differ: Multiculturalism as governance is generally concerned with balancing unity with difference by integrating migrants and minorities through institutional accommodation. Its underlying logic is hegemonic: that is, to preserve the status quo by modifying people's attitudes without their awareness that attitudes are changing. By contrast, biculturalism ideally is transformative. It acknowledges the centrality of two peoples (or nations) sharing co-sovereignty by way of partnership and power sharing (Stuart 2007). Under a meaningful biculturalism, the indigenous Maori tribes are constitutionally positioned as *tangata whenua* whose inherent self-determining rights (as recognized in common law and confirmed by the Treaty of Waitangi) constitute the cornerstone of New Zealand governance.

In reality, however, the politics of biculturalism in New Zealand falls short of the transformational. To be sure, different models can be discerned, including "soft" (celebrating Maoritanga), "moderate" (improving race relations), "inclusive" (partnership), "strong" (separate but equal), and "hard" (challenging the system) (Johnson 2008). But biculturalism as currently employed barely addresses the possibility of power sharing by way of Maori models of self-determination (O'Sullivan 2006). Emphasis instead under a *tukutuku* (decorative panels) biculturalism focuses on institutional accommodation in two ways (May 2004): first by incorporating a Maori *dimension* into state practices and national symbols, including the adoption of Maori names for government departments, increased use of Maori language in public broadcasts, application of Maori protocols for ceremonial occasions, inscription of official reports in the official languages of Maori and English, and references to Maori as part of "brand New Zealand" (Spoonley 1993; Durie 1995; Poata-Smith 1996; Bromell 2008); second by creating specific Maori institutions and initiatives to address distinctive Maori needs without necessarily departing from a statist agenda. For example, the establishment by Te Puni Kokiri (2008) of a Maori Potential Approach as public policy framework focuses on better positioning Maori to build upon and leverage off their collective resources and skills in the hope of achieving an exceptional life quality through development program rather than politics.

Clearly, then, biculturalism defines Maori as people (not *peoples*) with problems that require solutions. In skirting a commitment to Maori as peoples with rights, biculturalism constitutes an accommodative exercise in state-determination (Humpage 2002; Maaka and Fleras 2008). As Dominic O'Sullivan (2006) explains when contrasting state-determination (state biculturalism) with Maori self-determining biculturalism:

> [B]iculturalism cannot realize greater autonomy because its primary concern is with relationships among people in institutional settings, and within and among bureaucratic institutions. Self-determination is in contrast concerned with creating, to the greatest extent possible, independence and autonomy for groups, not necessarily in isolation from wider society, but certainly apart from the controls and regulations imposed from outside (p. 4)...Biculturalism offers colonial dependence. Self-determination at least legitimises and to some extent offers autonomy, not as an act of government benevolence, but as an inherent right of indigeneity...Biculturalism is a state strategy to manage resistance and a limited concession seeking strategy for Maori. It modifies assimilation, while protecting the nation's state assumed exclusive jurisdiction. It offers cultural space, while self-determination is more concerned with wider issues of citizenship, language, and political participation. Biculturalism misses the point of overlapping and interdependent Maori/Pakeha relationships and ignores the possibility of non colonial relationships beyond Pakeha, which makes it inevitably limiting. (p. 209)

The conclusion seems inescapable: insofar as the objective is to make institutions more respectful of Maori diversity, more reflective of this diversity, and more responsive to it, what passes for biculturalism is really a multiculturalism for Maori—one that reduces Maori to the status of minorities with problem. What should prevail in advancing a postcolonial social contract is a binational governance based on the foundational principle of Maori as *peoples with rights*.

Binational Governance: Truth to Power

A paradox informs the policy basis of Maori-Crown relations. To one side is a continuing commitment to the principles and practices of a state-defined biculturalism. To the other side is a growing commitment to a Maori-determined biculturalism in advancing the status of the original occupants as "nations within" with inherent and sovereign rights (Fleras and Elliott

1992; Humpage 2008). According to a binational narrative, the relational status of Maori goes beyond that of minority groups or ethnic communities. Instead Maori claim they are fundamentally political communities with inherent rights to self-determining autonomy in their own right, yet jointly sharing co-sovereignty in domains of mutual concern.

The implications are far reaching. A binational-grounded biculturalism is not simply an exercise in accommodating indigenous Maori demands by way of institutional inclusiveness. Nor is it about discharging Crown obligations by righting historical wrongs through grievance settlements (Maaka and Fleras 2000). What prevails instead is the recrafting of a constitutional governance around a postcolonial political contract rooted in the foundational principles of partnership, power sharing, and self-determining autonomy. With its notion of resistance and counter-hegemonic change around the politicization of differences, a binational biculturalism challenges the structural and ideological foundations of New Zealand's constitutional order. In light of its potential for perplexity and provocation, no one should be surprised by the reluctance to incorporate binational discourse as a basis for living together (Melbourne 1995; Bargh 2006).

The isms are clearly in opposition. To the extent that Maori-Crown relations should be articulated around a binational partnership of two founding nations within the framework of a single state, the opposition to multiculturalism could not be more forcibly stated. By focusing on institutional accommodation, multiculturalism is primarily about acknowledging Maori as equals. Similarly, state-sponsored biculturalism, because of its depoliticized status and accommodative pretentions, is proving to be little more than a multiculturalism for Maori. But from an indigenous Maori politics perspective, there is no enthusiasm for an exclusively multicultural incorporation into the existing institutional and political framework. To the contrary, the objective is to reconfigure that structure by creating a binational position of power for redefining Maori-Crown relations (Huijser 2004). In contrast to the reformative mindset of multiculturalism ("to change the conventions that are based on the rules"), a transformative agenda is espoused by binationalism ("to change the rules upon which conventions are based").

In that the political claims of Maori involve a fundamentally different order of political magnitude than those of immigrant minorities, binationalism differs from both multiculturalism and biculturalism as governance ideals-demonstrated as follows:

- Multiculturalism and biculturalism (bi/multiculturalism) strive to improve institutional accommodation; binationalism entails creation of constitutional space.

- Bi/multiculturalism are concerned with grafting bits of diversity onto a mainstream core; binationalism endeavors to restructure the foundational principles of settler constitutional order.
- Bi/multiculturalism deal with managing majority-minority relations; binationalism provides a constitutional framework for engaging indigeneity on a people-to-people, nation-to-nation basis.
- Bi/multiculturalism are geared toward placement of immigrants in society by removing discriminatory and prejudicial barriers. A binational agenda is concerned with the sharing of sovereign space between two dominant cultures in complementary coexistence.
- For bi/multiculturalism, the objective is to ensure an ordered social hierarchy in which minorities are nested into a prearranged system of shared goals and common means. By contrast, binationalism focuses on a dualistic constitutional order involving a compact ("covenant") between fundamentally different peoples.
- Bi/multiculturalism are rooted in the principle of universality and liberal pluralism, namely, that what we share in common is more important than any inherited differences that divide or provoke. The rationale behind binationalism differs, reflecting a politicized spin on difference as the basis for recognition, relationship, and rewards.
- Bi/multiculturalism endorse a commitment to working together by building bridges; binationalism acknowledges the necessity to stand apart before the possibility of living together. In other words, if bi/multiculturalism represents a governance for living together with differences, binationalism endorses a governance for living together separately.
- Bi/multiculturalism in Aotearoa are essentially accommodative exercises that bolster the status quo by depoliticizing differences through institutional inclusion, thus *making New Zealand safe from diversity, safe for diversity*. Compare this with the ideal of binationalism (Johnson 2008): With its notion of challenge and change though the politicization of differences, binationalism is about redefining the relationship between colonizer and colonized by making Maori indigeneity *safe from New Zealand as well as safe for society*.

Clearly, then, neither multicultural nor bicultural discourses can possibly address the politicized claims of indigenous peoples. The inclusion of bicultural symbols and practices may be an improvement over a monocultural past. No one should underestimate the symbolic importance of expanding Maori language and protocols at official levels, including Maori in drafting local legislation that is protective of Maori interests, or even the discharging of Crown obligations by righting historical wrongs through grievance settlements. But the incorporation of a state biculturalism hardly alters the balance of power over who gets what. Nor does it challenge the foundational principles that govern New Zealand's constitutional order. Moreover, for as long as the state continues to define what differences count, and what counts as difference, no amount of tweaking will transform biculturalism into a governance strategy involving recognition of two nations who share power through a constitutional partnership. As Russell Bishop (1996) explains, neither multiculturalism nor biculturalism is likely to work unless the dominant group stops dominating.

Reformulating Governance: Multiculturalism within a Binational Framework

It's been said that New Zealand is demographically multicultural, formally bicultural, and, with few exceptions, institutionally monocultural (Sibley and Liu 2007). Trends point to yet another wrinkle in the governance equation: New Zealand constitutes a binational society composed of two founding peoples with agenda tabling capacities. But while the binationality of New Zealand as sociological fact is slowly gaining traction (O'Sullivan 2006; Johnson 2008), its acceptance should not be invoked to diminish the rights of multicultural minorities or recognition of ethnic diversity. Binationalism and multiculturalism need not be mutually exclusive of each other. To the contrary, by sorting out what is "mine", what is "yours" and what is "ours", jurisdictionally speaking, they can work in tandem to sustain a political climate and social partnership consistent with Treaty principles and multicultural realities (Ip and Pang 2005; Ward and Lin 2005). In the words of Connecting Diverse Communities project (Ministry of Social Development 2007: "A cohesive society does not think in an either/or way about these issues. A multicultural nation built on a bicultural past can benefit from incorporating both world views."

Not surprisingly, the isms tend to talk past each other. Inasmuch as governments are largely content with institutional accommodation and grievance settlement rather than overhauling the constitutional basis of society, they will continue to misread the binationality of Maori indigeneity as governance. As long as the Crown insists on defining indigenous peoples as multicultural minorities rather than autonomous and self-determining political communities, inappropriate solutions will be misapplied to incorrectly defined problems (Fleras 2008b). A monocultural governance will continue to prevail for as long as the constitutional order is riveted in Eurocentric values as the normative standard by which policies are formulated, actions are judged, prevailing patterns of power and privilege are perpetuated, and priorities are assigned. The miscalculation is understandable: because a binational agenda constantly interrogates the colonial structures and Eurocentric mindset that organize relations between indigenous peoples and the Crown, its potential for disrupting the status quo is potent. Small wonder, then, that narratives of binational governance have attracted little political sympathy.

In the 1982 booklet *Race against Time*, the Race Relations conciliator proposed a New Zealand identity based on a firm foundation of biculturalism from which a multicultural society could emerge. For a country that is no stranger to the art of remaking itself (Spoonley and Trlin 2004), this challenge should pose few problems in defining who controls what and what belongs to whom. But missing in action is the political will to implement a democratic and inclusive governance that acknowledges a commitment to multiculturalism within a binational framework. Missing as well is the collective mindset for building a truly inclusive society involving recognition and respect for migrants and minorities without undermining prior and preeminent commitments to Maori as *tangata whenua* (May 2004). Time will tell if a political governance that properly captures the duality of a binational society without forsaking multicultural realities—a multiculturalism within a binational framework—can generate the political traction for balancing the politics of isms in New Zealand.

7

Dutch Multiculturalism: Unsettling Multicultural Governance in the Netherlands

Introduction: Multicultural Governance in Turmoil

European countries are retreating from governance paradigms that extolled the multicultural principle of minority rights to social equality and cultural retention (Joppke and Morawska 2003). Seemingly unmulticultural initiatives are promoted instead, involving integration programs and citizenship tests to ensure immigrant absorption and community cohesion—in some cases relying on near-coercive measures to advance national interests. Few should be startled by this rollback of multicultural policies alongside a reframing of questions about immigrant accommodation and national identity (Koopmans et al. 2006). Deeply essentialized notions of nation or culture still prevail in much of Europe,—resulting in societies that remain highly normative, assimilationist, and Eurocentric. With the specter of alien otherness continuing to haunt debates about national identity, historical memory, and social unity, increasingly bitter conflicts over identity, integration, and governance have intensified because of rapidly changing demographics, ranging from the movement northward of Middle Eastern and African Muslims, to the westward flow of Eastern Europeans (Moore 2008). The accelerated spread of integration courses and citizenship tests across Europe attests to these mounting public anxieties (Jacobs and Rea 2007). The end result, as Audrey Kobayashi (2008) points out, is yet another multicultural paradox: normative visions of multiculturalism that make it mandatory for 'them' to become part of 'us', but render it nearly impossible to access the ethnocentric 'we'—a case of Double Dutch in action (a rope-skipping routine involving two ropes twirling in opposite directions). The Netherlands represents one of these countries in the throes of a governance upheaval (Vasta 2007a). The Netherlands has enjoyed a tradition of tolerance going back to the seventeenth century when it offered both freedom of thought and asylum for political and religious refugees (Sniderman and Hagendoorn 2007). It may have once garnered kudos for its multicultural successes (although the term *multiculturalism* was rarely employed within policy circles until the late 1980s) by combining respect for cultural differences with egalitarian goals involving equal access to institutions (Arends-Toth and van de Vijver 2003). Times have changed, however, with a neo-monocultural commitment to integration and citizenship emerging as a preferred framework for living together differently (Bruquetas-Callejo et al. 2007). Like many other European countries, the Netherlands is struggling with its national identity and common vision as a diverse society, culminating in highly polarized debates over immigration and integration (Nana 2007). A laissez-faire plural multiculturalism that conjured up a governance of ethnic communities sharing the same space but leading parallel lives was relatively shortlived. A failed experiment that avoided taking a principled stand on prickly issues or reflected Netherland's guilt over its brush with Fascism (Blond and Pabst 2008), this uncritical live-and-let-live indifference exposed the soft underbelly of its "anything goes" tolerance, as Bruce Bawer (2002) writes in the *Partisan Review*:

> The Dutch, perhaps the most liberal people on the planet, have finally faced a critically important fact: that there is nothing at all liberal about allowing one's reluctance to criticize another's religion to trump one's dedication to individual liberty, human dignity, and equal rights. Tolerance for intolerance is no tolerance at all.

In the face of mounting criticism that immigrants have reneged on their responsibility to integrate, then stung by allegations of excessive Dutch indifference toward their own liberal democratic values in favor of indulging diverse cultural identities, new-style policies of neo-monoculturalism took hold, albeit under the moniker of civic integration. The assassinations of popular politician Pym Fortuyn and filmmaker Theo van Gogh further fueled perceptions of a multiculturalism spinning out of control because of a values schism between Muslims and the mainstream (A Malik 2007; Parekh 2008; also Hage 2006).

To be sure, these high-profile assassinations did not inaugurate post-9/11 debates over the viability of multiculturalism as governance

(Vink 2007). Public and political perception of a country in a downward spiral contributed to the radicalization of an antimulticultural (and anti-Muslim) discourse that ripped the scab (i.e., "political fiction") off the elite consensus masquerading as public support (Arends-Toth and van der Vijver 2003; Breugelmans et al. 2008; Prins and Saharso 2008). Criticism of the Ethnic Minorities Policies of the 1980s further sowed the seeds of dissensus, together with growing politicization of issues related to immigration and integration because of terrorist threats and border insecurities, persistent socioeconomic gaps between immigrants and Dutch citizens, and mounting anxieties over an indulgent multicultural governance. Admittedly, there is no substantive proof that the neo-assimilationism of a robust civic integration paradigm has eclipsed a "soft" multiculturalism agenda (Jacobs and Rea 2007). Nevertheless, as the multiculturalism approach to immigrant integration gave way to increasingly tougher civic integration models, with an insistence on acculturation through courses and tests (Favell 2001), Holland's integration program has evolved into one of Europe's most restrictive and punitive (Jacobs and Rea 2007).

This chapter sets out to explore and explain the politics of multiculturalism with respect to multicultural governance in the Netherlands. Conflicting perspectives over the status of Dutch multiculturalism are shown to have evolved over time and across space. A sequence of largely ad hoc multicultural policy responses prevailed: from pillarization in the 1970s, to the welfarism of the Ethnic Minorities (EM) policy in the 1980s, to the increasingly more intense integration policies of the 1990s to the present (Penninx 2005). Reactions to the status of multiculturalism have varied: For some, Holland was a reluctant multiculturalism at best. In reflecting an elite consensus that papered over public anxieties, it was never committed to the principles of multiculturalism except by default or as expediency. For others, by supporting the distinctiveness and coexistence of racial and ethnic minorities, it symbolized a classic multicultural governance. Paradoxically, however, with the dismantling of these multicultural props for living together differently, Holland is now regarded as the prodigal son of multiculturalism (Joppke 2004; Vink 2007). The question naturally arises: How and why did the Netherlands redefine itself along seemingly unmulticultural lines, despite a glowing reputation for minority accommodation, cross-cultural tolerance, and the institutionalization of difference?

The politics and paths from a multicultural governance to a neo-monocultural agenda constitutes the major theme of this chapter. The chapter argues that a contradictory dynamic may account for this governance "drift" from a laissez-faire plural multiculturalism (or, perhaps, more accurately, a plural monoculturalism) to a neo-monoculturalism of conformity, compulsory citizenship tests, imposed indoctrination, and harsh sanctions against immigrants. According to Vasta (2007a), while models of immigrant incorporation during the postwar years seemingly reflected a degree of open tolerance, in many cases endorsing a benign indifference toward difference on the part of the public and political authorities, the impact was perversely unmulticultural. Not only did the very policies that promoted a tolerance of difference end up intensifying intolerance on both sides, but immigrants also found themselves marginalized and excluded from full involvement in society. Concerns mounted over a permanently marginalized underclass, combined with growing anxieties over homegrown terrorism and border security—in the process unmasking the social fictions that propped up and papered over the contradictions of an evolving Netherlands. The chapter also argues that Holland's governance paradigm remains tentatively multicultural, albeit one that embraces a neo-monocultural agenda along the lines of universal integration and shared citizenship. It concludes by exploring recent developments in patching together a governance framework for cooperative coexistence.

Diversity and Difference in the Netherlands

Historically the Netherlands represented a country of migration. Between the late eighteenth century and the middle of the twentieth century, it was a site of emigration, with Dutch settlers seeking fortunes elsewhere (Penninx et al. 2005). A demographic reversal began after the Second World War, resulting in net immigration. The Netherlands evolved from a monocultural and homogeneous society to one with a relatively high degree of ethnic diversity (Sniderman and Hagendoorn 2007; Vasta 2007a). Several immigrant inflows during this era can be detected: Initially those from the Dutch East Indies (Indonesia) between 1945 and the early 1960s; then labor migration (guestworkers) recruited from Southern Europe, Turkey, and Morocco; followed by Surinamese after the former Dutch colony became independent in 1975; and since the late 1980s, refugees and asylum seekers from the former Yugoslavia and North Africa. Recent intakes are no less robust. In 2007, according to the Dutch Central Bureau for Statistics, a total of 116,819 immigrants arrived, including 74,644 from Europe, 18,261 from Asia, 13,584 from America, and 9,088 from Africa. With a net migration rate of 2.63 migrants per 1000 population in 2007 (by comparison, Canada's rate stood at 5.79 migrants per 1000 population), the foreign-born population of the Netherlands stood at 3.15 million out of a total population of 16.3 million (nearly one in five) (see Dutch Central Bureau for Statistics).

Equally significant is the demographic diversity. The visible ("racialized") minority population numbered 1.7 million or just under 11 percent of the total. With nearly one million Muslims (mostly from Morocco or Turkey) or 6 percent of the population, the Netherlands now has one of the largest concentrations, second only to France, with the vast majority living in major cities like Amsterdam and Rotterdam where residential concentration (or segregation) remains high (Emling 2008). Despite improvements, socioeconomic gaps persist between the native Dutch and the Turkish and Moroccan minorities: in 2006, 27 percent of Moroccans and 21 percent of Turks were unemployed, compared to 9 percent of native Dutch; school dropout rates in 1998 for Moroccan and Turkish immigrant children stood at 39 percent and 35 percent respectively. Finally, religious diversity prevails as well. Islam accounts for 5.5 percent of religious adherents, well behind those who express no religious affiliation at 41 percent; Roman Catholic, 31 percent; Dutch Reform, 13 percent; and Calvinism, 7 percent (Seidle 2007).

In response to these demographic dynamics, the Dutch were poised to reimage the nation by redefining the cultural basis of national identity (Lechner 2006). But while immigrant patterns were one thing, perception of their relational status has been quite another. Continuous net immigration figures by the late 1960s may have transformed the Netherlands into a factually diverse society. Nevertheless, indicators involving labor, family, and asylum did not match public perceptions or translate into political norms (Penninx et al. 2005). As was true of many European societies, a powerful norm of denial resisted attempts to imagine the Netherlands as an immigration society. Insofar as the Netherlands regarded itself as overpopulated vis-à-vis its shrinking territorial space, immigrants were perceived primarily in (short) terms of repatriates, temporary migrants, or "guest workers."

In rejecting this notion of the Netherlands as an immigrant society, patterns of migration were minimally regulated, notwithstanding a requirement for residence and labor permits (Bruquetas-Callejo et al. 2007). This slippage between ideals and reality created powerful tensions: To one side, the norm of denying the Netherlands' status as a country of immigration; to another side, the factual existence of increased immigration and permanent immigrant residence; and to yet another side, a seeming indifference bordering on thinly veiled hostility toward immigrants, especially those of Muslim and Middle Eastern origins. Not surprisingly, perhaps, two-thirds of the Dutch-born population reported having little or no contact with immigrants (Seidle 2007), while a 2005 Pew Global Attitudes survey found that the Netherlands was the only Western country of the 17 surveyed in which the majority (51 percent) of the population viewed Muslims unfavorably (cited in Seidle 2007). Failure to resolve these tensions eventually generated an anti-multiculturalism backlash, prompting some observers to ask whether the Netherlands proved to be the "canary in the coal mine" of multicultural governance.

Evolving Models of Multicultural Governance

To cope with the challenges of this demographic-ideological paradox, models of multiculturalism emerged and evolved in hopes of crafting an appropriate multicultural governance. Three evolving and overlapping phases prevailed—Pillarization, Ethnic Minorities, and (Super) Integration.

Pillarization policy

The Dutch tradition of tolerance originated in the nineteenth century as an accommodative strategy of tolerance. The segmentation of the Netherlands along religious and cultural lines eventually evolved into a structural "silo" system called pillarization. Under pillarization, a working consensus among the elites of these pillars was cobbled together, while their constituents remained largely segregated from each other (Bruquetas-Callejo et al. 2007). Religious groups such as Protestants and Catholics, in addition to Socialists (to a lesser extent), were allowed to maintain their own institutions, with people living and worshipping within their own institutionally complete and state-funded "silos" (Vink 2007). The modern version of accommodating pluralism through pillarization encouraged immigrants to rely on state-sponsored institutions as a means of preserving their own culture and group integrity (Vasta 2007a). The ethnic differences of Muslim groups, including those of Turkish or Moroccan descent, were institutionalized along parallel (or pillarized) lines, from separate radio and TV stations to labor unions, health care services, educational facilities, and sports clubs (Sniderman and Hagendoorn 2007).

Pillarization influenced immigration and integration patterns in two ways (Bruquetas-Callejo et al. 2007): First, the institutional completeness associated with pillarization provided minorities with opportunities to protect and promote their own cultural traditions and practices. Under this approach, the state provided support for such institutional arrangements because of an obligation to treat all communities in the same way (Seidle 2007). Second, ethnocultural groups were framed as cultural minorities (rather than as race or class), thereby legitimating the incorporation of minorities as another special interest pillar instead of a problem for the public agenda. Nevertheless, the logic behind minority pillarization was unmistakable: to equip migrants to leave rather than stay (Phillips 2007; Sniderman and Hagendoorn 2007). Many assumed that immigrants were temporary (guest) workers who would return to their homelands, thus making cultural retention and language preservation of critical importance in facilitating the transition and readjustment from "here" to "there." Relatively strict regulations involving family reunification were put into place, on the assumption that labor migration was temporary and nothing should be done to encourage a perception of permanence (Bruquetas-Callejo et al. 2007). Despite the embargo, domestic arrangements proliferated, with children of migrant families learning Turkish or Berber in primary schools, while many lived in ethnic enclaves that encouraged an inward-looking isolation rather than creative encounters. Clearly, then, a plural expression of multiculturalism had evolved into a consensus ideology that emphasized retention of language and culture without a corresponding commitment to social integration.

Ethnic minorities policy: An accidental multiculturalism

The 1983 Ethnic Minorities (EM) Policy acknowledged the inescapable: Immigrants and minorities were here to stay; as a consequence, policies had to be adjusted accordingly to ensure integration and equal opportunity rather than simply the promotion of cultural differences (Vink 2007; Sykes 2008). The Netherlands became one of the first Western European countries (preceded by Sweden in the mid-1970s) to formulate a minority (preferred over the term *multiculturalism*) policy predicated on the premise of permanent residency of immigrants. True, the postwar influx of immigrant groups was dismissed as a historically unique event, with the result that additional restrictions on immigration were imposed. Moreover, the economic recession following the oil crisis of 1973 aborted the flow of labor migration, although measures to deport migrant workers were never implemented, especially with persistent labor shortages in specific economic sectors (Bruquetas-Callejo et al. 2007). Eventually, however, this assumption of migration as one-off could no longer be sustained. The reality of continuous and permanent immigration proved a wake-up call (Penninx et al. 2005).

A broad multiparty consensus of political elites endorsed the Ethnic Minorities Policy. So too did those ethnic leaders who were co-opted into special advisory bodies—in a manner described elsewhere by Liphardt as consociationalism—to ensure a broad consensus over the prevailing status quo (Penninx et al. 2005). In hopes of depoliticizing immigration and immigrant issues, the Ethnic Minorities Policy promoted a welfarist commitment to stimulate equality and equity for those culturally and religiously vulnerable groups who risked becoming permanently marginalized (Penninx 2005; Bruquetas-Callejo et al. 2007). According to Minorities Memorandum, Ministerie van BiZa 1983 (cited in Penninx et al. 2005), the policy focused on ethnocultural minorities as collectives, promoted socioeconomic participation and removal of discriminatory barriers, and supported group emancipation and cultural identities through subsidies and consultation councils (Phillips 2007).

With time, a commitment to the principles of multiculturalism became more explicit. But this commitment did not necessarily arise from principle; more accurately, it may have originated to avoid the the tarnish of racism and xenophobia. People were increasingly reluctant to criticize minorities and their values; after all, to oppose a multicultural embrace of difference was tantamount to revealing an utter lack of humanity and compassion, while exposing oneself to charges of racism (Sniderman and Hagendoorn 2007). This politically correct refusal to criticize minorities for fear of drawing negative attention to oneself proved double edged. It contributed to the depoliticization of minority issues by way of an elite consensus that papered over awkward topics for fear of drawing attention to the proverbial elephant in the room that no one wants to talk about.

Under EM Policy, multiculturalism was endorsed as the ideal middle ground: Rather than a formal policy, Dutch multiculturalism proved to be a product of developments related to social welfare programs (a combination of guest worker mentality and the principles of an uncritical cultural relativism)(Sykes 2008). Multiculturally oriented welfare programs were introduced for historically segregated groups like Turks, Moroccans, Southern Europeans, Moluccans, Surinamese, refugees, Roma, and Sintis. Because these groups had become permanent residents and the Netherlands had assumed a multicultural character (at least in demographic terms if not in normative standards), minorities insisted on maintaining their cultural identities In keeping with the EM Policy, it was theoretically the responsibility of minorities to protect and preserve their cultures and religion (Bruquetas-Callejo et al. 2007). Admittedly, a symmetrical relation between majority and minority cultures was neither assumed nor allocated the same equivalence and autonomy as the old denominational groups (Vink 2007). But minorities did enjoy the same rights as identity (pillarized) groups in obtaining public subsidies for a host of activities from broadcasting to welfare. Furthermore, the multicultural consensus among elites regarded the presence of immigrants as nonproblematic, immigration was not subject to limits on cultural grounds or family reunification, and incorporation tended to emphasize a commitment to cultural retention and communal survival rather absorption into Dutch society.

With its endorsement of diversity, the EM policy could be interpreted as an extension of pillarization governance (Vasta 2007a). It reflected the principle (or pretext) that immigrant minorities, like other national cultures, deserved respect and had to be seen within their cultural context; their cultural practices should not be condemned or criticized, and it was a government responsibility to preserve and promote them. A place in society had to be secured to preserve these cultures, in part by acknowledging group difference as a basis for integrating into Dutch society, with state funding of parallel institutions related to religion, language and culture, and media (Entzinger 2006). Rather than adapting to Dutch society and culture, migrants and minorities kept to themselves, apart from their jobs. This isolation did not always reflect neglect or hostility but with what passed for contemporary social policy (Kramer 2006). The pillarization framework served as a template for incorporating minorities along EM policy lines, although religious pillarization had been eclipsed by Holland's urban and secular society (Pieterse 2007). Antidiscrimination legislation ensured that all Dutch would be treated equally regardless of race and ethnicity, while facilitating the naturalization process and improving minority representation at local government levels. Initiatives in labor market programs, special training courses, and educational improvements were also established.

Others disagree with this assessment. Maarten Vink (2007) argues that the historical tradition of pillarization, which combined group autonomy with elite cooperation, did not apply to minorities in the same way as to old religious groups. Confronted with the challenge of immigrant incorporation, Dutch policy maker resorted to traditional ways of dealing with diversity by way of pillarization ('pillarisation reflex' as Vink puts it). But there was no reason to believe that a system devised to reduce conflicts between national minorities of a religious or political nature could possibly work as an instrument for immigrant integration (Duyvendak and Scholten 2008). As a result, no explicit government policy existed to address the legal status of migrants or the integration of minorities, in part because of a laissez-faire approach to managing difference under a multicultural umbrella. Ad hoc procedures prevailed instead, since the meaning of multiculturalism under the Ethnic Minorities Policy was never fully explained or accepted (Vink 2007).

Integration policy: Embracing neo-monoculturalism

By the early 1990s, fissures in the Ethnic Minorities Policy could no longer be ignored (Bruquetas-Callejo et al. 2007). The Netherlands as Europe's foremost exponent of multiculturalism policy may have envisaged emancipation for ethnic minorities, albeit within their own state-supported ethnic organizations and infrastructures, from schools to media (Joppke 2007). But what was labeled as Dutch tolerance and commitment to multiculturalism was indifference—that immigrants should be treated as de facto guest workers and separated from the rest of society to facilitate their return home (Legrain 2006). The net result proved a disaster, including higher unemployment and lower employment rates for ethnic minorities than in other EU countries; higher rates of welfare dependency and social benefits (especially since most migrants were asylum seekers or family members); higher school dropout rates and higher levels of incarceration; and more intense forms of residential segregation.

In seeking a multicultural governance pattern that promoted integration without denying difference, the Dutch struggled with various issues, ranging from the challenge of difference (where to draw the line) to the integration of immigrant minorities (how to incorporate). In an effort to consolidate their image and identity as a tolerant and liberal people, the Dutch promoted difference among ethnic groups, in effect not only transforming minorities into targets of resentment and rejection but also reinforcing a clash of competing loyalties (Sniderman and Hagendoorn 2007). As a result, the Netherlands was poorly equipped to cope with evolving realities in the post-9/11 era, largely because multiculturalism proved a default option without a coherent and justifiable policy foundation (Sykes 2008). Instead of inclusion and engagement, a commitment to multiculturalism had the effect of fostering division and exclusion. Yes to participation in society, but not integration, with the result that migrants and minorities were poorly integrated into the labor market; educational attainment was lagging; and residential patterns were increasingly segregated. The relatively high number of children of immigrants who dropped out of school, together with high crime rates among second-generation Moroccan youth, reinforced perceptions of failure . Any lingering commitment to multiculturalism took a further hit with the 9/11 attacks, bombings in Madrid and London, and the politically motivated assassinations of high-profile public figures. In short, something had to be done—in part to avoid further security breaches, in part to diminish the threat of homegrown terrorism, in part to ensure control of the political agenda and social order (Sniderman and Hagendoorn 2007).

Prompted by growing racism and resurgence of the right, a new integration policy was formally introduced in 1994 (Seidle 2007). The new reality differed from previous eras of conflict avoidance, in which both political and ethnic elites ignored publicly debating immigrant issues for fear of blowing the cover off of inconvenient truths (including widespread aversion to immigrants and widespread support for a traditional Dutch national identity). The new policy politicized immigration and integration issues as a top political priority, resulting in a governance shift from respecting cultural differences to promoting socioeconomic participation (Bruquetas-Callejo et al. 2007). Admittedly, multiculturalism as a guiding policy principle was already in a downward spiral, resulting in the collapse of the consensus, especially with the politicization of immigration and integration as issues for public debate. Nor is there any conclusive proof that multiculturalism was to blame for the lack of minority success and migrant integration, given the argument that Dutch multiculturalism never really amounted to much except in the educational sphere, while socioeconomic integration was left to the labor market (Engelen 2008). The new policy sought to distance the government from the policies and the normative ideals of multiculturalism, culminating in moves toward a more restrictive immigration program and a focus on individual integration, including a rethinking of the welfare mentality that characterized government minority relations (Vink 2007).

A new style of governance emerged in response to a civic-oriented Integration Policy focused on promoting the "good citizenship of individual immigrants" (Contours Memorandum, Ministerie van BiZa 1994, cited in Penninx et al. 2005). In shifting from the ethno-specific cultural and religious provisions associated with the EM policy, the new governance model did not dwell on cultural group differences, but on the participatory inclusion of migrants and minorities into the mainstream, while facilitating their integration and settlement through civic integration classes (Bruquetas-Callejo et al. 2007). Newcomers from outside the EU were obligated to take a 12-month integration course that included Dutch language instruction, civic education, and labor market preparation (Seidle 2007). This national policy was intended to be implemented from the top down; that is, while cities and local authorities played important roles in promoting decentralized initiatives sometimes at odds with national strategies and agendas (Bruquetas-Callejo et al. 2007), a centrally coordinated and unitary integration policy was parlayed into a national priority—a situation at variance with other European countries where local authorities are often at the vanguard of proactive integration programs (Penninx et al. 2005).

By the turn of the new century, a further shift intensified a commitment to an integrative governance paradigm. Intellectual debates about multiculturalism as well as those around immigration, integration, Muslims, and national identity contributed to concerns over (a) the cultural relativism (by rejecting a belief that all cultural practices are equally valid but insisting instead that some are anachronistic or barbaric compared to Enlightenment ideals); (b) the required degree of homogeneity and integration for society to survive (the Netherlands had exceeded its absorptive capacity); and (c) the incompatibility of multiculturalism with democracy (especially with the so-called Islamification of the Netherlands as part of the so-called "Eurabia" thesis; [Yo'er 2005]). Ensuing political changes not only interred the last vestiges of Dutch multiculturalism by virtue of what some called the revolt of the masses against the elites. It also ripped the scab off long-standing taboos, including open racism and xenophobia, in addition to the elite consensus that had masqueraded as national unity and identity while sidestepping reference to corresponding problems and public unease—thus engendering the potential for backlash (Lovell 2003). By seemingly coming to the defense of female victims of violence or inequality, politicians could easily criticize minorities and cultural differences without being criticized for doing so, while managing to look progressive in the process.

Passage of the Civic Integration of Newcomers Act in 1998 had already heralded things to come. In hopes of familiarizing immigrants with Dutch culture, language, and society, sanctions and fines were introduced to foster migrant participation in language, social orientation, and civic courses. New immigrants were obligated to take 600 hours of state-funded language classes and civic courses on Dutch culture. The remaking of citizenship shifted accordingly: the formulation of Integration Policy New Style (Ministerie van Justitie 2003 cited in Penninx et al. 2005) shifted from "good citizenship" to the promotion of "common citizenship" based on greater adaptation to Dutch norms and common values. A commitment to multicultural governance now embraced neo-assimilationist principles of a seemingly monocultural Netherlands (Bruquetas-Callejo et al. 2007). A series of measures were introduced to ensure greater selectivity of immigrants and to significantly curb immigration (since 2003, there has been a negative net immigration) (Bruquetas-Callejo et al. 2007). Integration policies were subsequently linked with immigration policies, in particular for those applying for asylum, family reunion, and marriage migration. Programs were now intended to function as filters to screen out new immigration; for example, family reunification was possible but only if the incoming partner passed a language and citizenship test (at his or her personal cost) in the country of origin (Jacobs and Rea 2007).

In 2005, a bill for a new Integration Act promised to further enforce immigrant obligations and responsibilities through the provision of compulsory programs and enforcement of sanctions. Current legislation introduced mandatory forms of civic integration for newcomers and old-comers alike, including threats to withhold citizenship status from those who fail to pass the tests or achieve adequate civic and language standards (Jacobs and Rea 2007). By March 2006 prospective permanent migrants from non-EU countries had to pass a Dutch language and social orientation test at one of the country's 138 embassies before receiving a visa (MRI 2006). The Civic Integration Act, which came into effect in January 2007, compelled both spiritual leaders and "aliens" to complete an "introductory program" ("an integration exam") as a prerequisite for naturalization, including mandatory attendance at naturalization ceremonies to foster a sense of pride in acquiring Dutch citizenship while reminding newcomers of the duties and obligations of a citizen (Nana 2007; Seidle 2007). In shifting integrative responsibility to individual minorities, Bruquetas-Callejo and colleagues (2007) conclude, newcomers are expected to find and finance civic integration courses, with a 70 percent refund if they pass. The offloading of financial responsibilities to newcomers conveyed a whole new spin to the expression "Dutch treat."

The seemingly draconian measures under the Civic Integration Policy raise a number of awkward questions. How can a society that saw itself as liberal and tolerant do the seemingly antimulticultural, that is, blame immigrants for not integrating; define some religions and cultures as backward; tolerate high levels of structural marginalization; and invoke measures of conformity, using coercive means to achieve this goal? Chapter 9 will explore the how and why behind the multicultural backlash in Europe in general and the Netherlands in particular. At this point it suffices to state what must appear obvious: Holland's commitment to the principles of multiculturalism was relatively superficial; its logic tended to exclude rather than include; diversity and isolation discourses prevailed over those of integration and equality; and its survival was unsustainable without a corresponding commitment to multiculturalism as society building. As it was nicely put by Professor Boris Slijper at Amsterdam's Institute for Migration and Ethnic Studies (2004), Holland never endorsed a multiculturalism as part of a new national identity—that is, a nation composed of different but generally equal cultures—but continued to embrace a core Dutch culture that admittedly placed a strong emphasis on tolerance toward dissenting views. Moreover, an ill-conceived multiculturalism disregarded widespread public unease over a seemingly out-of-control immigration program and a radical cultural relativism that played havoc with a still pervasive if largely suppressed ethnic national identity. Not surprisingly, the politicization of immigration and multiculturalism in the 1990s contributed to the collapse of the consensus, in the process creating what might be called a Dutch Dilemma—can one be tolerant of those who are intolerant of tolerance? In a cleverly titled article, "Going Un-Dutch: Can You Really Riot for Tolerance," Doug Saunders (2004) writes of this dilemma:

> You consider yourself a champion of tolerance, social justice, and equality, so you create a completely free and open society. Then you realize this society has tolerated and even encouraged the presence of some very dangerous people who are fighting for a closed and restrictive society. So you hit the streets and take action to stop those people, and in the process find yourself championing intolerance, exclusion, social ostracism, and racial discrimination.

To be sure, the Netherlands is not alone in rejecting multiculturalism. Most Western European countries since the mid to late 1990s have adopted a restrictive integration agenda—learn our language, culture, values, and norms—in effect shifting away from minority rights to a focus on the language of integration, cohesive communities, and citizenship (Phillips 2007). In many ways, however, the Netherlands has taken the hardest line.

And yet the politics of backlash cannot be casually dismissed. An aggressive commitment against multiculturalism could easily backfire and create a catch-22. As immigrants and minorities continue to be defined as racialized and inferiorized "others" who lie outside the imagined national community, it becomes increasingly difficult for them to integrate and become part of a new national identity. A revised and more draconian civic integration law reflects a key paradox: the Dutch state is simultaneously withdrawing from yet increasing its presence in the integration process (Joppke 2007). To one side is the extension of integration tests before granting permanent residence permits; to the other side, immigrants are expected to defray the cost of courses and testing. And there is another paradox involving immigrant integration. Whereas it was previously assumed that securing legal status would enhance integration into society, now lack of integration provides grounds for refusal of legal status. A surer recipe for antimulticulturalism is difficult to imagine.

To sum up: The Netherlands is site to several major policy changes with respect to the governance of immigrant integration (Duyvendak and Scholten 2008). Policy paradigms have evolved that differently conceptualize the nature and magnitude of the problem as well as causes and solutions involving the relational status of migrants and minorities.

- The guest worker era (1950s to 1970s) reflected a lack of official policy since migrants were seen as temporary, with the result that ad hoc measures to improve socioeconomic participation and cultural identity were aimed at facilitating the return home.

- The Ethnic Minorities Policy (1980s) reframed guest workers as disadvantaged minorities in need of laws and programs to enhance their integration into society by combating discrimination, enhancing their socioeconomic rewards, and supporting culturally responsive services and separate ethnic communities.
- Integration Policy (1990s) emphasized the social and economic participation of immigrants as individuals and active citizens rather than as minority groups in need of emancipation. This policy reversed the direction of the Ethnic Minorities Policy which was predicated on enhancing culture to improve integration and economic success
- Integration Policy New Style (2000s) focuses on the principle of securing common citizenship by emphasizing the unity and identity of Dutch society based on shared commonalities aroundlanguage, values, and norms.

Clearly, as Duyvendak and Scholten argue, there is no consistent governance model of immigration integration. While continuities in problem definition and solution can be discerned, resulting in overlap, no less evident are very different ways of conceptualizing immigrant integration, resulting in inconsistencies and conflicts within prevailing policy models in addition to challenges by alternative models and advocates (also Entzinger 2006).

Rethinking the Multiculturalism in Dutch Governance: Paradigm Muddle?

The Netherlands was widely regarded as the quintessential multicultural society. In the words of Sniderman and Hagendoorn (2007), as much was accomplished under Dutch multiculturalism as could be done, including, instruction in minority languages, separate radio and television programs, government subsidies for a range of social and religious organizations, consultation prerogatives for community leaders, and special publicly financed housing to meet Muslim needs. Yet the concept of Dutch multiculturalism as a coherent and consistent model of immigration integration is problematic. According to Duyvendak and Scholten (2008), Holland's commitment to abide by the principles of multiculturalism is exaggerated, while references to a Dutch multicultural model are mistakenly based on a misleading linear idea of continuity and coherence in government policies. More recently, the Dutch approach has been sharply contested because of a new realism that has encouraged a breaking of taboos and speaking frankly about truths once suppressed by dominant discourse and political correctness (Prins and Saharso 2008).

Evidence suggests the Netherlands has abandoned a commitment to multiculturalism principles as a paradigm for multicultural governance. The rise of civic integration programs and citizenship tests is but one indicator of a more general shift toward the logic of assimilation as a replacement agenda (Joppke and Morawska 2003). There is a renewed commitment to a monocultural nationalism and neo-assimilationist fundamentalism, with its attendant notion of drawing immigrants and minorities into the Dutch conception of nation. Instead of a civic identity based on support for diversity, justice, and belonging, the focus has shifted toward a more restrictive shared citizenship anchored in Dutch values, beliefs, and norms, in part to discipline newcomers by weaning them off dependency on the state welfare system while reinforcing the goal of acculturation (Vasta 2007a; Jacobs and Rea 2007).

Others disagree with this assessment, arguing that a shift toward assimilation models of multicultural governance does not necessarily jettison multicultural principles (Jacobs and Rea 2007). Put bluntly, multicultural principles do not have to be explicitly articulated as formal policies or programs to have practical effect, but may prevail in name, commitment, or practice. Nor is there any solid proof that a paradigm shift has taken place, with an attendant demise of multiculturalism as a model for immigrant integration. How, then, does the Netherlands continue to embrace multiculturalism, albeit one that is modified to affix the label "neo"? To one side is the glaring absence of consistency regarding integration policy. With the politicization of immigration and integration issues, both principles and policies have become increasingly incoherent rather than expressing a single overarching policy paradigm—reflecting a combination of political party power relationships with ad hoc policy compromises for electoral advantage (Jacobs and Rea 2007).

To the other side, there remains a commitment to selective dimensions of multiculturalism. If official multiculturalism is defined by Jacobs and Rea (2007) as a policy recognition and endorsement of racial and ethnic diversity, the Netherlands remains a multicultural governance because (a) ethnicity remains a variable in policymaking; (b) policymaking is adjusted for specific ethnic groups; (c) minorities are allowed to maintain their cultural specificities; (d) institutions are sensitive to cultural differences and are expected to reasonably accommodate by modifying procedures and practices, including allowing minorities the right to refuse work on holy days for religious reasons; and (e) ethnic groups are encouraged to organize themselves in pursuit of specific interests—there is an extensive network of Islamic educational institutions in the country's largest city, from primary to university level, all of which receive public funding at the same level as other religious schools (Seidle 2007). Furthermore, in the period following the assassination of Theo van Gogh in 2004, the government has reemphasized institutional dialogue with ethnic minority associations. A government coalition agreement in 2007 entitled "Living Together, Working Together," focuses on cooperation and consultation among social partners in formulating policy on socioeconomic integration and amelioration of social welfare challenges (Nana 2007). Finally, to the extent that both European Council agreement on common basic principles of immigrant integration and those of the Netherlands are formulated in a general way rather than the doctrinaire expression of specific nationalism (Jacobs and Rea 2007), a commitment to a neo-multicultural discourse remains intact.

To sum up, it might be premature to argue that an assimilationist (or integrationist) policy model has unequivocally superseded a multicultural model of multicultural governance. What appears instead is perhaps more accurately called a paradigm muddle—an acknowledgment that Holland's governance paradigm is sharply contested, in the throes of upheaval and change, and riddled with a confusing and conflicting amalgam of new and old. As Jacobs and Rea (2007) concede, the multiculturalism in Holland's multicultural governance paradigm has been under criticism in the post-Fortuyn and post – Van Gogh period. Conventional notions of multiculturalism in the EM Policy period have been downgraded and even withdrawn in some cases. Subsidies to ethnic associations come with more strings attached by stressing the importance of integration and intergroup interaction. But for the time being, multiculturalism is not completely dead (Jacobs and Rea 2007). Yes, it is in a deep coma and hanging on through life support, yet alive and continuing to animate Dutch governance politics albeit in the more euphemistic and less politicized language of integration, citizenship, and cohesion.

8

Multiculturalism in Britain: Contesting Multiculturalisms, Evolving Governances

Introduction: Politics of Difference, Silos of Indifference

European countries are confronting a governance paradox: how to democratically and inclusively govern multiethnic, multiracial, and multireligious polities—and the identity politics generated by these differences—without collapsing into chaos or regressing into rigidity (also Saunders 2004; Panossian et al. 2007). Of those European countries in the forefront of multicultural governance, Britain ranks high in grappling with the paradoxes of governing diversities and difference—primarily generated by Commonwealth immigration of predominantly male labor from the 1950s onward, followed by family reunification in the 1970s, and the 1980s flow of both professionals and refugees (Modood 2006). It is true that initial legislation for managing difference proved restrictive rather than facilitative; for example, under the Commonwealth Immigration Act, entry into the United Kingdom was restricted to citizens from the "Empire". But the growing presence of "blacks", together with the proliferation of racism, exerted pressure for measures to address racial discrimination (Mac Einri 2007). Passage of the Race Relations Acts in 1965 and 1976 proved critical in advancing a racial equality paradigm (Meer and Modood 2008), although nearly a quarter century passed before further progress with the Human Rights Act (1999) and the Race Relations Amendment Act (2000), which imposed a statutory duty on all public institutions to promote racial equality (Ahmed 2007). Over time, however, Britain has constructed a unique mix of legislation and policies for managing difference, regulating immigration, and fostering inclusion (Giddens 2006; Vasta 2007; Mac Einri 2007).

Initial discourses, policies, and programs related to multiculturalism were framed around the experiences of migrants from the Caribbean and South Asia. In the post—World War II period, most immigrants came from colonies or Commonwealth countries (Caribbean and South Asian), with the majority of newcomers arriving as dependents of newly settled migrants because of restrictive entry regulations. A commitment to multicultural principles sought to promote tolerance and respect for collective identities in establishing well-organized communities—in part by supporting community associations, places of worship, and cultural activities, in part by advocating a more accommodative British society that was respectful and reflective of difference, and responsive to it through institutional accommodation (Vertovec 2006). To be sure, Britain's approach to diversity may be more accurately described as multicultural by drift or by default (Phillips 2007), that is, an emergent multicultural governance based on the principle of passive coexistence, but neither codified in official documents nor expressed as formal nationwide policy (Joppke 2004; Phillips 2005;Conference 2006). As well, many of the ideas and practices associated with multiculturalism were pursued by proxy through race relations initiatives (Kymlicka 2004/2007).

Nevertheless, a commitment to multiculturalism as governance has proven awkward. Peak periods of mass migration (1958–1962; 1967–1975; 1997–2002) invariably generate public hostility, press hysteria, and political expediencies. Newcomers are perceived as competing for jobs, housing, and social services; threatening the character of existing communities; undermining social solidarity; and, in refusing to integrate, eroding Britain's capacity for social cohesion (Hansen 2007; Joseph Rountree Foundation 2008). Compounding the unease is growing concern over the institutionalization of tolerance toward difference, ranging from financial subsidies for minority schools, to accommodation of diet and dress codes, to exemption from mainstream practices at odds with religious and cultural dictates. The consequences of such concessions have proved disarming. Instead of an integrated society based on interaction and inclusiveness, silos of (in)difference emerged instead under Britain's de facto multiculturalisms, with a corresponding erosion of identity and unity (Grillo 2007).

With the emergence of Muslim political agency contributing to both policy reversals and growth of an increasingly intolerant nationalism, multiculturalism is now the new scapegoat for integration failures (Modood 2007). Once immune to criticism because of a crippling political correctness that equated it with curry and carnivals, the concept of multiculturalism is increasingly reviled as a political blasphemy, with main political parties united in their denunciation of yesterday's "ism" (*Economist* June 14, 2007; Jimenez 2007). Arguments against multiculturalism are legion—especially with events since the mid-1990s undermining public confidence in the ability and efficacy of the government's multicultural policies to integrate migrants and minorities (Hansen 2007). Criticisms include: multiculturalism leads to segregation, prevents immigrant integration into the dominant sector, undermines Britishness and core British values, focuses too much on group rights rather rights of individuals, emphasizes culture over cohesion, and dwells on attitudinal barriers instead of structural impediments to integration and cohesion (Vasta 2007b; Sykes 2008). Or as smartly conveyed by Nick Pearce, Director of the Institute for Public Policy Research, (2007:50):

> Multiculturalism is a classic floating signifier, attached to different sets of ideological baggage by its critics and defenders. For the right, it is a politically correct assault on British nationhood and cultural history, a vessel for the dangerous platitudes of limp-wristed lefties and human rights lawyers. For the radical left, its an abdication of egalitarian truths, a fatal compromise with pre-Enlightenment obscurantism and a diversion from solid class politics.

But criticism is no match for evolving demographic realities. With hundreds of thousands of migrants arriving annually in the UK—numbers that are expected to remain steady for the foreseeable future because of the Labour government's proactive strategic approach to managing immigration for economic benefit (Somerville 2007)—debates over multicultural governance are unlikely to dissipate soon (see Secretary of State 2002). In light of growing criticism and a pending backlash, Britain's plural governance paradigm is experiencing yet another identity crisis of confidence. Pressure is mounting for a more civic-oriented integrationist model to replace the multiculturalism in a multicultural governance governance. The rationale seems relatively straightforward: the greater the diversity, the greater the need to spell out what people have in common (Ash 2008). And without commonalities and a sense of sharedness, critics argue, the notion of Britain for the British is compromised.

Britain is now in the forefront of evaluating the benefits and drawbacks of its long-standing multiculturalism policy (Meer and Modood 2008). In acknowledging the shift from emphasizing cultural distinctiveness to a focus on Britishness and corresponding values (Sykes 2008), this chapter addresses the politics, paradoxes, and policies of Britain's multicultural governance project. The chapter explores the origins, growth, and entrenchment of multiculturalism in Britain as well intentioned but ill conceived, with unforeseen but damaging consequences. A series of multicultural goverance paradigms can be discerned: (a) antiracist models of multicultural governance that were eventually usurped by predominantly ethnocultural discourses (Lentin and Titley 2008); (b) a plural monocultural governance with its laissez faire notion of passively existing minority communities; (c) a neo-monoculturalism model whose objectives are explicitly integrationist in outlook and tone, yet arguably multicultural in process and outcome; and (d) and the possibility of a neo multicultural governance based on new demographic patterns and politics (Vertovec 2006; Rutter et al. 2008).

To the extent that an argument is proposed, this chapter contends that a multicultural agenda involving a Britain of many cultures was possible by establishing a mosaic of culturally autonomous and institutionally complete communities. But Britain's commitment to the principle of a plural multiculturalism (or more accurately, plural monoculturalism) proved to be shortsighted and misdirected (Dustin and Phillips 2008). Not only did it foster passive pockets of social and cultural isolation, but a political and public backlash was also unleashed when the costs of multicultural governance proved unsustainable. The chapter concludes by pointing out how the crisis in multicultural governance exposes what critics have long said: that a tacked-on multiculturalism or a multiculturalism by drift or default rather than 'mainstreamed' generates the potential for divisiveness and danger (Norton-Taylor 2008; Munck 2008). It should be noted that the chapter is primarily concerned with multicultural politics and programs in Britain at large (the United Kingdom). Space limitations preclude a look at specific developments in Wales, the Irelands, and Scotland, however groundbreaking and progressive.

Diversity and Difference in Britain

Britain has long enjoyed a history of emigration and immigration (Sriskandarajah et al. 2007). But it took until the mid-1980s for Britain to become a country of net immigration, with a peak of 222,600 people in 2004, according to Home Office statistics, before falling back to 185,000 in 2005 when the entry of 292,000 foreign nationals was offset by the departure of 107,000 British nationals. (This figure is disputed by the Commission on Integration and Cohesion [2008:31], which asserts a total of 565,000 migrants in 2005 who resided for at least one year.) In 2006 the number of immigrants increased to 591,000, followed by a slight decline to 577,000 in 2007. However, the difference between those coming in and going out in 2007 stood at 237,000, an increase of 46,000 from 2006 (*Guardian Weekly*, 2008).

This surge in net immigration reflects a variety of factors, including an increased number of (1) work permits for the highly skilled, (2) asylum applications, (3) foreign students studying in Britain, (4) migrants reuniting with families, and (5) citizens from new EU member states. Nearly 10 percent (9.7 percent) of Britain's population is now foreign born, according to OECD data for 2005, up from 4.2 percent in 1951, with the largest numbers from India and the Republic of Ireland (cited in Sriskandarajah et al. 2007). With passage of at least four migration-related parliamentary acts in favor of migrants who study or work, the former prime minister Tony Blair leaves behind a fundamentally reshaped immigration system (Somerville 2007). Britain has reinvented its approach to immigration, emphasizing the economic value of immigrants, a more restrictive approach to asylum seekers and security, and a new set of settlement and integration tools (Papademetriou 2007).

The scale and nature of recent immigration is transforming British demographics (Commission for Racial Equality 2007). Britain possesses a significantly diverse population, reflecting migratory patterns of those who (a) fled to escape religious and political persecution, (b) want reunification with family and kin, or (c) covet better economic opportunities. Approximately 430,000 or 0.7 percent of the population consisted of irregular (or illegal or undocumented) immigrants in 2005, thus exerting additional pressure for securing borders (Somerville 2007). In the year 2001–2002, a Labour Force Survey estimated that those who described themselves as other than white numbered approximately 4.5 million people in Britain (or 8 percent of the population—this figure had increased to 4.9 million or 8.3 percent of the population by 2004 according to Home Office statistics; but see Seidle 2007). South Asians including Pakistani, Indian, and Bangladeshi composed 4 percent of the total population or 2.3 million. Blacks including Caribbean and African were 2.1 percent of the population or 1.2 million persons. The combination of Chinese, mixed, and "other" composed 1.7 percent of the population or 1 million persons. With respect to spatial concentration, about 600,000 of the 1.6 million British Muslims live in and around London, another 140,000 in Birmingham, and 75,000 in Bradford. Overall, ethnic minorities are geographically concentrated in the Greater London area; they are less inclined than their white counterparts to live in Wales, Scotland, or Northeast and Southwest England (Sriskandarajah and Road 2005).

Glaring gaps in the socioeconomic performance of different ethnic groups are unmistakable. Recent arrivals and especially those who arrive as asylum seekers often confront immense challenges in integrating into

British society, particularly in terms of English language acquisition and recognition of overseas qualifications (Sriskandarajah and Road 2005). Muslims, for example, are more likely to live in the most deprived districts, in effect reinforcing the socioeconomic gaps between Muslims and non-Muslims. According to Leslie Seidle (2007), 60 percent of Muslim households have a breadwinner with low income, while Bangladeshis (most of whom are Muslim) were unemployed at the rate of 38 percent in 2000–2001, more than nine times the national average. By the early 2000s, Muslims in Britain had three times the unemployment rate of the population as a whole, including 16 percent who have never worked or are among the long-term unemployed. Performance indicators among other ethno-cultural groups are mixed. Among second-generation immigrants, Chinese and Indians often outperform whites in schools and labor markets; by contrast, children of Pakistani, Bangladeshi, and black Caribbean parents tend to experience higher unemployment and lower earnings compared to whites (Sriskandarajah and Road 2005; Giddens 2006).

In general, two conclusions prevail. First, immigrant diversity has increased dramatically since the 1990s. Britain has attracted a diverse range of immigrants—including Afghans, Congolese, Filipinos, Poles, Slovaks, and Somalis—many of whom are less familiar with the country, language, and cultural practices than previous cohorts from colonies or the Commonwealth (Rutter et al. 2008). Nevertheless, certain patterns can be discerned. Ethnic minority populations tend to be younger than the age profile of the general population, are overwhelmingly drawn to urban areas, and are more prone to economic disadvantage in terms of employment and income (Kundnani 2007). Second, the increased diversity of backgrounds and experiences of Britain's population exerts pressure on the prevailing governance paradigm. As noted in a 13-country survey by the Pew Centre in 2006, public attitudes toward Muslims in Britain are less hostile than in many parts of Europe (cited in Seidle 2007). Despite this reservoir of relative goodwill, anxieties and tensions mount when surveys by think tanks like Policy Exchange publish information that – however inadvertently – erodes race relations and undermines goodwill. Consider public reaction when hearing that many British Muslims value their religion as the most important reality in their lives, while younger Muslims insist on a stronger connection to their religion than to community or country (Mirza et al. 2007). The impact of such conclusions, may prove highly destabilizing, especially when taken out of context and fuelled by media "stereohype." Such negativity not only feed into public prejudices about Arabs and Muslims but also exaggerate the problem of Islamophobia (Mirza et al. 2007) By instilling a sense of victimhood, Muslim resentment is inevitable in a country where "... many Britons are indeed more interested in assessing Muslim's potential for violence than in anything else about them" (The Economist 2009:60). In a move to "cool out" these potentially troublesome constituents, an integrative governance paradigm has emerged to foster community cohesiveness and a commitment to Britishness as core identity (Commission for Racial Equality 2007).

Trajectories of British Multiculturalism: Rise, Growth, Crisis, and Decline

The need to sustain a post – World War II economic boom exerted pressure for migrant labor. Britain's (former) colonies were viewed as a logical source. But the postwar arrival of "black" immigrants from India, Pakistan, and the Caribbean generated conflicting pressures on policy makers. (In Britain, reference to blacks originally included South Asians.) To one side, the influx of new labor would bolster the economy; to the other side, worries mounted over its impact on national identity. The traditional concept of Britishness was highly racialized; that is, British self-identity was informed by the concept of race, including the tacit assumption of white superiority. But this notion of Britishness as a racial concept was inexorably hollowed out by large-scale migration from the colonies. Moreover, an assimilationist model that prevailed from the 1950s to 1970s tended to underestimate the resilience of ethnic identities, especially in contexts where the minority community is marginalized and confronts hostility (Abbas 2007). Despite efforts by nativists to turn back the clock (Enoch Powell's infamous "rivers of blood" speech in 1968 was but one of many), it was increasingly apparent that black immigrants composed part of an evolving national identity. With immigration, in brief, Britain's national identity was gradually deracialized; as a result, no one had to be white or Christian to qualify as British (Parekh 2005).

From combating racism to accommodating diversity

Policy makers embraced a two-track governance strategy in response to the challenges of migration and difference (Malik 2001). Restrictive immigration controls were imposed, as was a legislative framework for removing discriminatory barriers to facilitate immigrant integration into British society (Somerville 2007). The Race Relations Act of 1965 reflected a belief that the welfare state had a responsibility to eradicate discrimination and promote equality (Vasta 2007b). The logic behind this interweaving of restrictive immigration with progressive race relations as governance was cryptically captured by Labour MP Roy Hattersley's comment (cited in Malik 2001): "without limitation [of immigration], integration is impossible, without integration, limitation is inexcusable." Under the Conservatives (1979–1997), an explicit commitment to the principles of multiculturalism declined to the point where multicultural practices were generally restricted to Left-leaning local councils. The election of Labour in 1997 realigned the narrative. Government policies and rhetoric acknowledged the reality of multiculturalism in advancing a progressive governance, despite debate over what it really meant, whether Britain was truly a multicultural society, and if multiculturalism contributed to the inclusion of immigrant communities (Abbas 2007).

The coupling of immigration with multiculturalism proved double edged. On the one hand, it reinforced the idea of Britain as a tolerant and pluralistic society that combined cultural difference with equal access to British citizenship rights (Vertovec and Wessendorf 2004; Bertossi 2007). Public and political discourse that highlighted notions of group/cultural/minority rights—including the right to self-segregate as an antiracism intiative—were subsumed under the broader rubric of multiculturalism (Vertovec and Wessendorf 2004). On the other hand, this multicultural strategy reinforced a blaming-the-victim mindset. In that Britain didn't self-define as an immigrant society, newcomers were seen as isolated aberrations, legacies of empire, and regrettable consequences of misguided government policies. Without any overarching rationale to avert the drift into relatively self contained ethnic communities , migrants and minorities assumed a right to practice their culture and religion – often with state subsidies to underwrite the costs of doing so (Legrain 2006). Predictably, fingers were pointed at Britain's minority communities as the as the architects of their own misfortune. Rather than pointing blame at racism and structural discrimination, the crisis in coexistence was attributed to minority cultural differences and those self-segregating practices that precluded minority integration. The multicultural malaise was further intensified by the perceived failure of ethnic leaders to encourage greater interaction and integration (Malik 2001).

Divisions within minority communities also proved a problem. For much of the 1960s until the early 1980s, black Britains were divided over strategies pertaining to integration and settlement (Malik 2001). Some preferred to withdraw into their institutional shells (such as mosques) as a buffer from the racism and discriminatory barriers of an unwelcoming society. For others, the focus was on challenging political inequality by mobilizing the masses into a united front along multiple fronts. These localized struggles politicized a new generation of black activists whose militancy culminated in the inner-city riots of the late 1970s and early 1980s. Issues related to discriminatory immigration controls, racist attacks, vulnerability to discrimination, exclusion from the mainstream, and police brutality served to radicalize black politics—especially of those born or raised in Britain—by proposing to remake British society along fundamentally different lines instead of simply tinkering with cosmetic reform.

Central authorities conceded the importance of depoliticizing this activism. Unless blacks were given a political stake in the system by improving access and outcomes, many believed their frustration could erupt and disrupt Britain's political stability and social order. Local authorities struggled in an effort to soften the sharp edges of black politics, in the hopes of suppressing its radical political element or by preventing one group's militancy from infecting the others (Kundnani 2007). Pacts were negotiated with black leaders who were instructed to dampen community resistance in exchange for funding of pet projects or a free rein in preserving their authority and/or patriarchy (Kundnani 2002). Initiatives and programs focused on redirecting black (African, Caribbean, and Asian) activism into conventional institutional channels where its potential could be depoliticized. Or to put the co-optation more bluntly, to ensure a celebrating of culture instead of an acting upon it, as Kundnani (2007) eloquently claims:

> ... the policies that were implemented in the 1980s in the name of multiculturalism were a mode of control rather than a line of defence. Multiculturalism in this sense referred to a set of policies directed at taking African-Caribbean and Asian cultures off the street – where they had been politicized and turned into rebellions against the state – and putting them in the council chamber, in the classroom and on television, where they could be institutionalized, managed and commodified. Black culture was turned from a living movement into an object of passive contemplation, something to be 'celebrated' rather than acted upon. The method of achieving this was the separation of different ethnic groups into distinct cultural blocs, to be managed by a new cadre of 'ethnically defined' community leaders, and the rethinking of race relations in terms of a view of cultural identity that was rigid, closed, and almost biological.

Paradoxically, then, segregation did not arise from state pandering to cultural diversity or a refusal to mix. To the contrary, Kundnani writes, it reflected years of conscious racist manipulation and deliberate community exclusion for short term political gain. Nor did commitment to multiculturalism originate as a response to minority concerns and migrant demands. More accurately, it represented a political act primarily for political goals—namely, for "cooling out" troublesome constituents by institutionalizing differences A commitment to multiculturalism emerged as an opportunistic strategy of social contral to defuse crisis of legitimacy by accentuating identities and redirecting energies along religious or cultural outlets (Fitzpatrick 2005). A new cadre of opportunistic community leaders,colluded in fostering the "culturalization" of race relations, with local governments doling out funding for promotion of minority cultures but generally ignoring ways for improving minority access to the labour markets (Lentin and Titley 2008). This intergroup competition had the effect of not only isolating (ghettoizing) communities from each other, but also encouraging passivity in the face of oppression (Alibhai-Brown 2000; Sykes 2008). The allocation of resources between communities, followed by the recruiting of community leaders to organize this process, reinforced a corporate (or plural) multiculturalism, with its tendency to freeze intergroup relations while creating incentives to look inwards (Phillips 2007).

The result proved all too familiar for those acquainted with the British Empire: a colonial project of divide and rule by way of an elite consensus—albeit under a more benign multicultural umbrella that proved more of a straightjacket in hindering rather than helping the struggle against racism (Vasta 2007b). Parallel societies flourished under the managerial auspices of an internal class leadership that could be counted on to stay silent and maintain community order. Not only were black communities fragmented horizontally by ethnicity (including competition for ethnic grants) and vertically by class. With the emergence of culturism and ethnic enclaves, the problem of racism was reformulated around cultural protectionism while political energies were diverted into promoting cultural rights and specific ethnic agendas (Kundnani 2002; Sivananadan 2006). In the competitive struggle for prestige and resources, minority leaders were forced into justifying their claims for funding by exaggerating their suffering, grievances, and sense of victimhood (Fitzpatrick 2005). A strategy of distraction and diversion could not be more artfully constructed.

Definitions of racism shifted with the privileging of diversity as governance. Instead of defining racism as something that was done to deny equal rights, it now focused on the right to be different. According to this line of relativist thinking, rather than forcing minorities to accept British values and identity, they should have the right to protect and promote their culture, language, and identities. Those who dared criticize minorities or government initiatives were themselves criticized as racist by advocates of a politically correct multiculturalism. But transforming the discourse of equality from the social to the cultural was not without consequences. However unintended, the effects of shifting from an antiracism stance on equality to promoting different group-specific rights were threefold:

First, those stereotypical assumptions that historically underpinned the debate over race relations were reinforced—namely, that blacks are fundamentally different. As a result, the governance challenge (or race relations problem) had to focus not only on accommodating these differences, but also on defusing negative stereotypes.

Second, the political struggles that had characterized the fight against racism were transformed into battles over cultural issues. But while these struggles over racism attracted alliances across ethnocultural divisions, cultural contestations invariably divide. Unlike the struggles that constructed bridges across difference divides, the politics of multiculturalism thwarted intercultural interaction by asserting the primacy of differences in the competition for scarce state resources over the embracing of commonalities in challenging state hegemony (Lentin and Titley 2008). With state funding increasingly tied to cultural and religious identities, particular groups articulated their specific identities to the exclusion of others, in the process not only reinforcing old divisions while creating new ones but also strengthening conservative elements in every community while defusing the more militant voices on the street.

Third, the politics of promoting identity can generate a vicious circle (Mirza et al. 2007). Minorities like Muslims may be encouraged to be different and have their cultures respected. Yet the more different the treatment, the greater the disconnect from society at large. To feel more included, demands expand for more recognition and respect, in the process reinforcing their consciousness of vulnerability as the "other". The end result of this double bind? A multiculturalism that equates multicultural governance with diversity funding, segregated communities, and parallel institutions; People are channelled into compartments that are separated from each other and society at large, in effect encouraging the perpetuation of ethnic enclaves that can imprison or isolate in the name of culture (Alibhai-Brown 2000). The compartmentalization of cultural communities into self-segregated silos not only erodes any sense of commonality. It also draws people inward toward religion as one way of creating meaning and identity in a Britain that once boasted of a secure sense of national identity with deep historical and cultural roots but is now increasingly fragmented because of narrower identity politics.

In responding uncritically to the repercussion of a passive pluralism, successive governments sowed the seeds of dissension and division (Mirza et al. 2007). The paradox of multiculturalism unleashed a divisiveness whose consequences few anticipated, namely, residential segregation. As Malik (2001) notes, residential segregation between blacks and whites had always existed. But as Asian communities fought each other for greater allocation of council funding, ethnic fault lines proliferated. Muslims, Sikhs, and Hindi began to live in different areas, attend different schools, and organize through different institutions. Instead of directly tackling the problems of racism and exclusion of disaffected communities, both local and national authorities encouraged black and Asian communities to passively coexist by pursuing "parallel lives" under the umbrella of multiculturalism.

Contesting the Multiculturalism in a Plural Monocultural Governance

Governance structures changed appropriately in response to the politics of multiculturalism. British governments may have embraced a commitment to a multicultural ideal, but its conceptualization and implementation was often a matter for local government and various state departments (Brighton 2007). Conservative governments strongly opposed the intro-duction of antiracism measures and multicultural education, while repudi-ating any structural or institutional cause of racial discrimination or need for special measures (Hewitt 2005). Multicultural discourses and programs were pursued through inner city local councils and municipal authorities who pioneered strategies for managing diversity and integrating minorities into areas of immigrant settlement, including the creation of consulta-tion committees, establishment of race relations units, and disbursement of funds to minority organizations (Malik 2001; Meer and Modood 2008). For example, the multicultural agenda of Ken Livingstone, the mayor of London, included antiracism initiatives and celebrating diversity, in addi-tion to promoting cross-cultural understanding through promotion of eth-nic projects such as the Notting Hill carnival and Chinese new year (Butt 2008). As well, multiculturalism was expressed in debates over schooling and education, most notably in the broadening of the curriculim to respect, reflect, and respond to diversity and difference (Bhattacharyya 1998). The introduction of multicultural initiatives into schools secured a culturally relevant curriculum for migrant and minority children; local governments, in turn, introduced labor market training programs for ethnic minorities (Vasta 2007b).

By the late 1990s the multiculturalism within multicultural gover-nance proved increasingly untenable. From a tool for defanging militant antiracism, multiculturalism evolved into a general prescription for British society. According to Kenan Malik (2001), British identity no longer revolved around racialized lines, but increasingly re-identified itself as tol-erant of different identities. People began to retreat into their communities or religion as an affirmation of identity; after all, if there was no compelling reason to embrace an increasingly relativistic definition of Britishness, why bother to commit? In rejecting openness for inwardness, dialogue for muteness, and integration for separation, minorities forfeited the opportunity to engage in collective political action. A commitment to a default multiculturalism exerted a paralyzing effect by suppressing open debate and constructive dialogue in exchange for deference to anything-goes tolerance and a don't-rock-the-boat political correctness. Instead of improving sensitivity to cultural difference, multiculturalism fostered an indifference to other people's lives, thereby reinforcing a mosaic of parallel societies, with each tile firmly grouted into place without an overarching vision of shared values to conceal the cracks. Of particular note were concerns over the politics of redistribution. Would an excessively diverse Britain be capable of sustaining the mutual obligations that secure the rationale behind and legitimacy of the welfare state (Goodhart 2004; Banting and Kymlicka 2006)?

In short, emergence of laissez-faire plural multiculturalism generated a more splintered Britain whose fragmentation fostered fears over religious militancy and anxieties over homegrown terrorism (Malik 2001). Despite concerted efforts to include and protect Muslims in British society, an opposite effect prevailed. Muslims, especially the younger generation, continue to experience vulnerability, isolation, and racism as well as alienation and disengagement (Mirza et al. 2007). The summer of 2001 proved a wake-up call. Riots in Oldham, Burnley, and Bradford demonstrated how the interplay of industrial decline with institutional discrimination in employment and the alienation of segregated communities could prove an incendiary mix. For example, according to a survey for the Commission for Racial Equality, less than 10 percent of whites have friends from different racial groups (BBC News 2004). Paradoxically, however, this segregation was blamed on excessive cultural differences, with particular animus directed at Britain's Muslim community for refusing to move beyond a "parallel lives" mentality (Kundnani 2007).

Pundits and politicians pounced on multiculturalism as the problem source: those on the Right criticized multiculturalism as threat to unity, identity, and security, including a failure to foster Western values in appeasing an Islamist extremism (see Uberoi 2008), while Those on the Left (and liberals) took multiculturalism to task for dividing and distracting. Not surprisingly, the 2002 white paper *Secure Borders, Safe Haven: Integration with Diversity in Modern Britain* rejected the existing governance model—one based on zero migration, antidiscrimination initiatives, and parallel lives within segregated communities—and proposed instead a managed migration in conjunction with improved community cohesion.

An aggressive integrationist governance model was predicated on the premise that security and solidarity must embody the confidence and trust associated with a strong sense of belonging and identity, common purpose, and equal opportunities. Or as Home Secretary David Blunkett (2002) dryly put it, "migrants and minorities need to become more British."

The 7/7 terrorist attacks were equally instrumental in rethinking the governance agenda. Perhaps what was most disconcerting about the London bombings was a chilling realization that Britain couldn't trust their own. Young British-born men appeared willing to annihilate their own compatriots in pursuit of an ulterior cause—as if they sensed no connection to each other or felt a common cause with British citizens (Mirza et al. 2007). The attacks exposed the flaws of Britain's plural mono-cultural governance; it also bolstered demands for fortifying integration into a more identifiable British society. Multiculturalism came under yet more criticism as a political correctness gone wild. The cover of multiculturalism spawned the proliferation of alienated Muslim ghettos whose young men committed mass murder against British citizens, in part by privileging religious-cultural priorities over civic duties related to loyalty, tolerance, rule of law, and respect for democracy (Kundnani 2007). Or consider the outrage over the forced marriages (marriages without consent) between British Muslims and Muslim partners overseas that sometimes culminated in domestic violence, suicide, and honor killings, in effect more proof of Britain's multicultural failure to successfully integrate immigrant communities.

Reaction was blunt: Trevor Phillips, the then chair of the Commission for Racial Equality, spoke of Britain as "sleepwalking into segregation." For Phillips (2005), an uncritical tolerance for multiculturalism proved an incubator not only for hatching terrorist plots but also for breeding unhealthy unBritish values. The passive coexistence model conveyed by a laissez faire and corporate ('plural') multiculturalism insisted that every institution had to understand, respect, and respond to ethnic and religious differences even if their practices compromised core values and beliefs. Critics like Munira Mirza et al. (2007), too, warned of the dangers of institutionalizng difference over commonality and connection as grounds for multicultural governance. The emergence of a strong Muslim identity in Britain under multiculturalism emphasized difference over shared national identity. It also gave rise to Islamist groups who acquired influence at local and national levels by playing identity politics and demanding a Muslim right to be different – as noted by Mirza et al (2007):

> The inability to feel a connection with other people is a damning indictment of the multicultural approach in Britain. For over twenty years, successive

governments have uncritically ... pushed an agenda which has effectively undermined the possibility of shared communal experience. Stressing difference has pushed some people apart to the degree that they feel no empathy for the suffering of others who are "not their own." In the name of multiculturalism, immigrants have been taught that belonging to Britain is something to be ashamed of, and that, as "outsiders," they have a special, superior status as a result of being untainted. Instead of helping immigrants to learn English and acculturate to the mainstream, the multicultural approach has aimed to preserve distinct ethnic identities and groups.

And without clear guidelines regarding limits or content, the potential for disconnection and disarray escalated. A commitment to multiculturalism created unrealistic expectations about limits within minority communities. It also reinforced a belief that Britain would accept and adjust to whatever traditions and cultures endorsed by ethnic minority groups (see also Collacott 2007). The line of reasoning was simple enough: Since culture defines a person in terms of who she is, it is important to protect, preserve, and promote both culture and minority communities.

To be sure, a conventional multicultural governance paradigm was justified on well-intentioned grounds of making migrants feel welcome. Supporters of the new Labour government believed they were promoting an integration without assimilation, that is, protecting the rights of minorities to preserve their culture while encouraging their participation as citizens. Nevertheless, the unintended effect of this disconnect exposed the politics of paradox: To one side, the state insists on immigrant integration, yet is increasingly restricted in doing so because of human rights norms; to the other side, the state acknowledges the need to socialize migrants and minorities but is hardpressed to isolate any values and beliefs that are specifically British except in a universalistic sense of a commitment to the rule of law or democracy (Joppke 2008). Without an explicit sense of Britishness to draw on for inspiration or guidance in advancing an in integration agenda, a rethinking of multiculturalism governance could no longer be ignored. A series of speeches in 2006, including Tony Blair's clarion call for the immigrant's duty to embrace Britain's essential values did not explicitly reject multiculturalism but it certainly recommended a more nuanced repositioning of its role in Britain's future (Joppke 2008). Blair's last speech on the topic is worth quoting at length (cited in Meer and Modood 2008:12):

> ... [W]hen it comes to our essential values – belief in democracy, the rule of law, tolerance, equal treatment for all, respect for this country and its shared heritage – then that is where we come together, it is what we hold in common; it is what gives us the right to call ourselves British ..... The

whole point is that multicultural Britain was never supposed to be a celebration of division; but of diversity. The purpose was to allow people to live harmoniously together, despite their difference; not to make their difference an encouragement to discord. The values that nurtured it were those of solidarity, of coming together, of peaceful co-existence. The right to be in a multicultural society was always, always implicitly balanced by a duty to integrate, to be part of Britain . . . . So it is not that we need to dispense with multicultural Britain. On the contrary, we should continue celebrating it.

Nevertheless, the turn toward civic integration reflected a rethinking of multiculturalism—from a prescription for public policy to a primarily descriptive term to describe a diverse society—in the process breaking many of the taboos that had shielded Britain's etiquette-conscious ("PC") race relations from honest and open debate (Joppke 2004). A change of leadership did little to avert the slide. Like his predecessor who also argued for defining the limits of multiculturalism and tolerance in Britain, Gordon Brown in February of 2008 reinforced a commitment to British values, earned citizenship, and the pairing of rights with responsibilities (in Sykes 2008). An early speech appears to capture his multicultural sensibilities:

> While we have always been a country of different national, and thus of plural identities - . . . . Muslim, Pakistani, or Afro-Caribbean, Cornish, British, and English – there is always a risk, that when people are insecure, they retreat into more exclusive identities rooted in 19th century conceptions of blood, race, and territory – when instead, we the British people should be able to gain great strength from celebrating a British identity which is bigger than the sum of its parts, and a union that is strong because of the values we share and because of the way these values are expressed through our history and our institutions. Gordon Brown, Labour Prime Minister and then Chancellor of the Exchequer 2006 (quoted in Schain 2008:152)

It remains to be seen if moves to tighten up integration and cohesion—in part by compelling migrants to enroll in citizenship classes, to acquire English competence, and to declare their allegiance to core British values as proof of loyalty—will paper over the fissures of an ill-conceived governance.

Depoliticizing Difference, Repoliticizing Britishness

The multiculturalism in Britain's governance model originated in response to an evolving demographic reality. The inability of central authorities to create a more inclusive sense of belonging and national identity resulted in the emergence of a multicultural model best described as plural mono-culturalism (Sen 2006; Fleras 2007). A governance framework not alto-gether different from those plural societies described by J. S. Furnival and M. G. Smith envisioned Britain as a series of relatively isolated ethnocul-tural and religious communities with little in common. This emphasis on plural monocultural silos as the basis for governance (Muir 2007) was predicated on the belief that blacks and Asians should not be forced to accept British values or adopt a British identity. To the contrary, minorities had a multicultural right to establish their own communities, express their identities, explore their own histories and language, formulate their own values, and pursue their own lifestyles. As the Cantle Report into the 2001 disturbances concluded (cited in Muir 2007):

> Separate educational arrangements, community and voluntary bodies, employment, place of worship, language, and social and cultural networks, means that many communities operate on a basis of parallel lives. These lives often do not seem to touch at any point, let alone overlap and promote any meaningful interchanges. (p. 9)

The result proved divisive: a residential, educational, and workplace segre-gation that reflected, reinforced, and advanced the parallel lives implicit in a plural monoculturalism.

By the turn of this century, an embrace of a passively plural monocul-turalism was no longer sustainable. In its place a neo-monocultural model of governance emerged, foundationally anchored around the principles of cohesion and integration with primary goals fixated on community, Britishness, and shared values. The tilt toward integration and commu-nity cohesion models of governance transformed the politics of managing diversity and difference in fundamentally different ways. Admittedly, refer-ences to integration were no stranger to the governance scene: In 1967, Roy Jenkins had declared (cited in Grillo 2007:983): "I define integration, there-fore, not as a flattening process of assimilation but as equal opportunity, coupled with cultural diversity, in an atmosphere of mutual tolerance." But a more explicit commitment to integration has taken a more assimilation-ist turn, with civic Britishness displacing multiculturalism as the preferred governance discourse (Squires 2007). Not that the specifics of Britishness were easy to define, although the Home Office (2004), cited in Jacobs and Rea (2007), did declare:

> To be British seems to us to mean that we respect the laws, the elected Par-liamentary and democratic political structures, traditional values of mutual tolerance, respect for equal rights and mutual concern; and that we give our

allegiance to the state (as commonly symbolised in the Crown) in return for its protection. To be British is to respect those overarching specific institutions, values, beliefs, and traditions that bind us all, the different nations and cultures, together in peace and in a legal order.

In rejecting multiculturalism for promoting differences rather than commonalities, the Commission on Integration and Cohesion (2008) espouses a commitment to the principles of an integrated (mutual adjustment) and cohesive (getting along) community agenda. Key principles include (a) a shared sense of a visionary future by articulating what binds rather than divides, (b) duties related to responsibilities and rights of citizenship, (c) civility and mutual respect as the basis for an ethic of hospitality, and (d) models of social justice to foster mutual trust in local institutions. In hopes of creating the inclusion necessary for a cohesive Britain, the Commission advocates the value of interaction between different racial and ethnic groups at local levels. The focus is in getting people to relate to one another in their everyday lives: "different people getting along well" (cohesion) with "new and existing residents adapting to each other" (integration) because they feel they have something in common by sharing communal space (Muir 2007; Phillips 2007).

Political response to the Commission's final report reinforced a commitment to cohesion and integration at local levels. Six principles prevailed: a shift away from a one-size-fits-all approach, mainstreaming of cohesion into broader policy areas, a national framework for support and guidance (the central government sets the national framework, local authorities and partners implement improvements to cohesion), integration of new migrants and existing communities, building positive relationships, and a stronger focus on what works (Department for Communities and Local Government 2008). A new definition of integrated and cohesive community embraced three foundational principles: everyone possesses similar life opportunities; people are aware of obligations and rights; and people trust each other and local institutions to act fairly. Finally, three keys for living together were promulgated: a vision of a shared future and sense of belonging; a focus on what community members have in common without discrediting the value of diversity; and positive relations between people with different backgrounds.

How is this shift toward cohesion, citizenship, and integration a move toward a neo-monoculturalism? In contrast to assimilation with its connotation of absorption into a single homogeneous culture (Vasta 2007b), a neo-monoculturalism endorses the principles of integration as a two-part process of adjustment with responsibilities on both migrants and the maintream to improve community cohesion and reduce inequality. Unlike a laissez faire multiculturalism with its emphasis on silos of differences as grounds for plural monocultural governance, a neo-monoculturalism espouses a belief in a Britain of many cultures provided people's differences do not preclude attainment of community, cohesion, and common values. A conservative multicultural model does not necessarily eschew difference per se, but subordinates it to the principles of integration and cohesion as the basis for governance. Or as noted by the Report on Secure Borders, Safe Havens (Secretary of State 2002), the challenge in sustaining a cooperative coexistence is conditional upon properly managing diversity upon the firm foundation of integration.

Consider passage of the Nationality, Immigration, and Asylum Act of 2002 as a neo-monocultural prototype. The Act may have introduced a seemingly draconian citizenship test based on sufficient knowledge of English (or Welsh or Gaelic) and life in Britain (insufficient knowledge translating into user-paying English or citizenship classes). But the Act did not openly advocate assimilation with a corresponding loss of distinctive identities. Instead, it proposed an integration within a wider British identity, according to the Home Office (2004, cited in Jacobs and Rea 2007). Even one of Britain's most vociferous critics of multiculturalism, Chief Rabbi Sir Jonathan Sacks (2007) envisions a Britain as home to shared values in which difference is balanced with an overarching commitment and common identity. Such a sentiment was similarly expressed by the government document *Improving Opportunity, Strengthening Society* (Home Office 2005:45, cited in Vasta 2007b) in espousing the principle that you can be different, but you are different in a British society with a corresponding set of responsibilities, commitments, and expectations:

> For those settling in Britain, the Government has clear expectation that they will integrate into our society and economy because all the evidence indicates that this benefits them and the country as a whole . . . we consider that it is important for all citizens to have a sense of inclusive British identity. This does not mean that people have to choose between Britishness and other cultural identities, nor should they sacrifice their particular lifestyles, customs, and beliefs. They should be proud of both.

To be sure, the emphasis on integration marks a shift away from an overt multiculturalism. But to suggest as some have that this position has embraced assimilation misses the mark as well. Multiculturalism is too deeply entrenched in an overarching infrastructure of policies, funding streams, services, voluntary and semigovernmental organizations, and professionals who are deployed to manage difference and ensure its incorporation (Mirza 2006). By making these institutions more respectful, reflective, and responsive to difference, institutions from housing and health care, to public broadcasting, policing, and education have been "multiculturalized" to the point where they cannot escape a commitment to inclusiveness. by. In reflecting a rebalancing rather than an erasure or retreat (Meer and Modood 2008), a commitment to multicultural principles persists, including: (a) Britain is a society of diverse cultures, (b) diversity when properly managed is bonus (c) no one should have to abandon their culture to become British, (d) all migrants and minorities achieve full socioeconomic integration, (e) no ethnic penalty applies, and (f) attachment to culture does not conflict with commitment to Britain or liberal democratic values (Hansen 2007). Clearly, then, responses to the question that currently confronts British multiculturalism – the extent to which multiculturalism and citizenship can be mutually constitutive in ways inclusive of Muslims -confirm the governance equivalent of a continuity in change (Meer and Modood 2008). What is less clear is where a new multiculturalism is heading (Somerville 2007)

Super Diversity/Super Mobility: Toward a Neo-Multicultural Goverance?

Contemporary Britain is experiencing a crisis of governance. To one side is an unmistakable shift toward the integrative principles of community, commonality, and cohesion as a preferred governance discourse. To the other side, concerns are mounting over the relevance of this governance model in light of evolving realities and contested demands. Put bluntly, Britain's diversity has become increasingly differenced and politicized (Vertovec 2006), with the result that difference and diversity are not what they used to be. Since the 1990s, migrants are much more heterogeneous in terms of experiences, opportunities, constraints, economic relations, and a wider set of social contexts – thus exerting pressure for an anti-essentialist multiculturalism to replace the reification of British plural monoculturalism (see Meer and Modood 2008). Factors that are promoting this super diversity include variations in (a) countries of origin, including EU migrants, (b) migration channels, (c) legal status associated with migration patterns, (d) migrants' human capital, (e) locality of destination, (f) transnational links without homeland communities, and (g) host country response from local authorities, service providers, and residents.

No less evident are new patterns of temporal and circular migration. Together with greater residential mobility, these patterns have created what Jill Rutter and colleagues (2008) call "super mobility." The dynamic interplay of super diversity with super mobility is not without repercussion, given the increase of recently arrived migrants who are geographically dispersed, of multiple origins and plurality of affiliations, transnationally connected, socioeconomically differentiated, and legally stratified. This interpretation—poses formidable challenges not only for naturalization into citizenship, but for helping migrants also to identify with or establish roots within local communities, encouraging active participation , and achieving cohesion and integration (Rutter et al. 2008).

These emerging trends are challenging orthodox notions of governance about what the government can or should do in promoting integration(Vertovec 2006; Rutter et al. 2008). Public discourses, policy debates, and intergroup relations developed in the past—for example, addressing newcomers solely in terms of some presumably fixed ethnic identity—may have only limited applications at present. In need of rethinking are governance frameworks that dwelt on ethnicity as the prevailing or exclusive criterion that ostensibly locked individuals into compartmentalized enclaves of existence. The universality implicit in the commitment, cohesion, and integration under a neo-monoculturalism may prove inconsistent with the politics of super diversity/mobility.

Clearly, then, policy makers, local authorities, and social service providers must learn to embrace the profound implications of super diversity/mobility in realigning multiculturalism with patterns of a new inclusive governance at both national and local levels. Minority realities no longer revolve around the modernist notion of a mosaic (fixed, foundational, or deterministic), but about the postmodernist metaphor of a kaleidoscope, with its dynamics of fluidity, hybridity, and multiplicity (Waters 2007). Fresh and innovative ways are required for understanding and responding to complex interplays in which ethnicity intersects with race, class, gender, age, sexuality, and location to create overlapping and interlocking patterns of identity and entitlement, membership, and belonging.

In rethinking a governance for the 21st century, two multicultural drivers are at play. To one side is a neo-monocultural commitment to integration with a difference. With a neo-monocultural governance, the crisis in multiculturalism is defused by emphasizing commonality over difference, social cohesion over ethnic particularity, and shared liberal/national values over a default relativism (see Lentin and Titley 2009). To the other side is a neo multicultural narrative that challenges conventional notions of diversity and difference. For neo-multiculturalism, a mosaic metaphor of identity and belonging (with its connotation of static and uniform communities) is rejected in favour of a kaleidoscope model of multicultural diversity, with its anti-essentialist connotation of internally diverse and highly contested communities (Waters 2007; Fleras and McClinchey 2009) It remains to be seen if Britain can rise to the challenge of balancing a neo-monocultural governance with the principles of neo-multiculturalism. As the slogan says, perhaps a new social contract based on reconciling these conflicting principles represents a governance paradigm whose time is prime.

9

The Politics of Multicultural Politics: Transatlantic Divides, Intercontinental Discourses

Introduction: This (Mis)Adventure Called Multiculturalism

One of the more vexing shibboleths of the twenty-first century is the much-trumpeted death knell of multiculturalism. In the security-conscious era following 9/11 and 7/7, the politics over multiculturalism have leapt into prominence, with some saying "yes," others insisting on "no," and still others, a "maybe" (reflecting a combination of ignorance, confusion, or indifference). Pundits of varying political stripes have declared that, in outlasting its usefulness, multiculturalism is dying or in retreat, in part because of the encounter with the Islamic "other" (Hage 2006; IMISCOE 2006; Modood 2008). And good riddance too, according to critics. To one side of the dismissive divide are the perceived excesses associated with campus speech codes, compulsory sensitivity training, the expunging of dead white male authors from course curricula, and ruined careers because of frivolous "ism" charges (Bernstein 1994). To the other side are those who criticize multiculturalism as a thinly veiled hegemony for consolidating prevailing patterns of power and privilege (Bannerji 2000; Thobani 2007). To yet another side are the risks associated with careless multicultural policies, including the proliferation of tribally inspired identity politics and unbounded collective rights, whose cumulative impact results in a splintered society of monocultural ghettos ("cultural apartheid") (Alibhai-Brown 2000; Malik 2008). Thankfully, critics conclude, a yearning for national solidarity and a singularity of citizenship has discredited this misadventure called multiculturalism, while reviving a more monocultural normalcy (Wirten 2008).

But there is a major exception to this anti-multiculturalism movement: Canada. While some Canadians contend that multiculturalism isn't working because it demands too much or expects too little (Gregg 2006; Kay 2007, 2008), there are few signs of backlash or backpedalling. To the contrary, multiculturalism has evolved into such a staunch national icon that few political leaders dare challenge it—even during election years when playing the multiculturalism card could reap electoral dividends if deftly deployed among the dissaffected. For example, during the 2008 federal election, none of the five major political parties even raised the issue of multiculturalism as a point of debate. Or consider the muted political and public reaction in June 2006 to the capture of 18 Toronto-based terrorists. According to an Ipsos poll (Dale 2007), the Toronto Terror "crisis" appears to have had a galvanizing effect in consolidating Canada's commitment to multiculturalism, with the majority of respondents endorsing multiculturalism as protection against such extremism, including this display of support by Prime Minister Harper:

> It [the arrests] has led some to some commentary to the effect of Canada's open and culturally diverse society makes us a more vulnerable target for terrorist activity. I believe that exactly the opposite is true. Canada's diversity, properly nurtured, is our great strength. (Third World Urban Forum, Vancouver, June 2006)

Additional surveys for CRIC (the Centre for Research and Information on Canada) and ASC (Association for Canadian Studies), in addition to a poll of 1000 respondents by the Strategic Counsel for the *Globe and Mail* and CTV (Canadian Television Network), further confirmed what many had suspected: Canadians cherish multiculturalism as a defining and definitive characteristic of Canada's national identity, with a host of positive economic benefits and cultural advantages (Jedwab 2006, 2007).

Let's put it into perspective: Europe's love affair with multiculturalism as a preferred governance model may be dissipating. National narratives in New Zealand and the United States seem to be waffling as well in their support for multiculturalism as a governance blueprint. Even federal Australia appears to have fallen off the multicultural bandwagon, although some of the states continue to be multiculturally gung ho. But Canada remains relatively impervious to criticism or backlash, with a continued groundswell of support and commitment that shows no signs of diminishing. How do we account for these differences? Why is Canada seemingly immune to calls for retrenchment, whereas European jurisdictions have circled the proverbial wagons against what they see as excessive (read, Muslim) immigration and politically correct (read, anything goes) multiculturalism? Should Canada be worried as well since its much-ballyhooed multicultural fabric may be fraying at the edges because of a so-called Islamic peril (Karim 2002; Cohen 2007; Hurst 2007)? Is there something about Canada's culture, values, mindset, history, or geography that transforms a commitment to multiculturalism into a low-risk option for living together differently (Kymlicka 2005)? Does the institutionalization of an inclusive multiculturalism make it less susceptible to critique or backlash? Or is Canada just plain lucky because of geographical when it comes to the politics of multiculturalism because of distances that buffer it from threat or risks t?

This chapter on the politics of multicultural politics analyzes the transatlantic divide between Canada and Europe involving intercontinential discourses over the viability of multiculturalism as governance. The chapter argues that Canada's official multiculturalism is designed (although not always by design) for advancing the principles and practices of an inclusive multicultural governance. That is, Multiculturalism is institutionally embedded in policy, statute, and constitution; inextricably linked with Canada's status as an immigration society; central to national narratives; supportive of a culture of minority and human rights; commited to social justice and antiracism; and focused on inclusiveness by improving migrant settlement and minority integration. In other words, multiculturalism equals Canada-building. By contrast, both Dutch and British models of multiculturalism tend to be driven by a combination of expediency, default, or (mis)calculation in the hope of defusing troublesome situations or assuaging white guilt. The fact that neither Britain nor the Netherlands saw themselves immigrant societies made it doubly difficult to justify multiculturalism when pressure mounted to discard.

The conclusion follows accordingly: the multiculturalism in a multicultural governance is likely to thrive when the appropriate institutional and ideological architecture is in place. Conversely, failure or hostility are more likely when multiculturalism (a) is rendered an option or add-on to the system, only to be discarded when deemed irrelevant or counterproductive, (b) puts the onus on minorities to adopt the values and institutions of society, and (c) is incapable of addressing institutional inequality or fostering group interaction (Munck 2008). In looking at the expressions of multiculturalism in Canada and in Europe, this chapter focuses on what appears to have worked in securing a multicultural governance, and what doesn't.

Canadian Perspectives: Multiculturalism as Canada-building

There is little mystery to Canada's success as a multicultural society. Its multicultural success story is inseparably linked to Canada's sociological status as an official immigrant society. Unlike the so called complete (or civilizational) nations of Europe—as sites of language, culture, and historical memory (Castles and Miller 2003)—an immigrant society like Canada embraces immigration as a key resource for society building (Beach et al. 2003). To qualify as an immigrant society (normatively speaking), the following criteria are critical: principled and proactive policies to regulate the intake (both quality and quantity) of immigrants; programs for improving migrant settlement and facilitating their integration into society; and a framework that strongly encourages the attainment of citizenship status (Ucarer 1997). As well, immigrants are seen as assets rather than burdens, as crucial contributors to Canada-building rather than a national liability, and as fully fledged members rather than outsiders in need of control or return (Joppke 2007). In that a commitment to multiculturalism reflects and reinforces Canada's status as an immigration society, while contributing to the creation of a national identity and social cohesion (Clarke 2006), its legitimacy is all but assured (Dale 2007; McDonald and Quell 2008).

The link between immigration and multiculturalism is mutually enhancing. A robust immigration program not only creates a need for multicultural governance; it also depends on multiculturalism for success. Conversely, Canada's Multiculturalism program could hardly flourish outside the context of a proactive and comprehensive immigration program. As pointed out by Queen's University political philosopher Will Kymlicka (2005), Canada's Multiculturalism program represents a safe governance alternative because of an immigration program that (a) attracts legal, skilled, and unthreatening migrants; (b) is reasonably well managed; (c) reflects Canada's liberal values; (d) discourages and deters the entry of those 'incapable'of adjusting to Canada; (e) ensures bona fide permanent residents with access to citizenship rights; and (f) contributes to Canada-building. Its popularity and success is secured by the fact that Canada outperforms other countries when measured on grounds of immigrant participation, citizenship, pride of country, and levels of trust (Bloemraad 2006). Not surprisingly, both immigration and multiculturalism tend to garner public support when perceived to be under control, a low-risk option, and of benefit to Canada and Canadians.

Geographical location also plays into its multicultural strength. Canada is so geographically isolated from the mass migration centers of the world (for example, North Africa, the Middle East, and Central America) that it can afford to be multiculturally magnanimous (but see Hier and Greenberg 2002). The luxury of distance makes it a lot easier for Canada to to cherry-pick its new residents, while disbarring those whose differences are unwelcome or pose a threat. The politics of timing is no less relevant. The emergence and entrenchment of multiculturalism reflected an era when most immigrants were from Europe, with a willingness to comply with

Canada's liberal values and rights-based framework (Granastein 2007). The absence of a state-endorsed model of identity, citizenship, and culture (in 1947 the Citizenship Act no longer defined Canadians as British subjects, but failed to articulate what they now were) encouraged a collective mindset where culture could diversify and embrace change with minimal tension. As a result, when immigration shifted toward more culturally contentious non-European sources, Canadians had already internalized a familiarity and fondness for multiculturalism discourses as a template for cooperative coexistence (Kymlicka 2004/2007).

Support for multiculturalism is further bolstered by Canada's response in drawing the multicultural line. Unlike the perceived anything-goes excesses of some multicultural regimes, multiculturalism in Canada is about limits and boundaries. Difference may be tolerated under an inclusive multiculturalism, but this tolerance is conditional and principled: that is, cultural differences must be freely chosen, cannot break the law, violate individual rights, preclude individuals from full and equal involvement, or contravene core constitutional values. Furthermore, differences should not be expressed through inward-looking ethnic enclaves or politicized for public power grabs, but depoliticized as a basis for dialogue, interaction, and understanding. Even passage of the 1988 Multiculturalism Act sought to integrate new Canadians into the mainstream through their ethnic identity rather than offer unqualified preservation of their differences. Clearly, then, reference to the Multiculturalism in Canada's multicultural governance is not what it appears to be. Instead of many equating it with a mosaic of cultural tiles in unconnected isolation, a commitment to Multiculturalism transforms differences into discourses about social equality and institutional inclusion . Displacing culture with the social as the primary lens for engaging with diversities and difference renders Multiculturalism an indispensable component in advancing Canada's inclusiveness agenda as stipulated by the Charter of Rights and Freedoms (Khan 2008).

Of course, this bucolic image of multiculturalism does not always align with reality. How else to explain the multicultural paradox that is Canada: to one side, one of the most diverse yet tolerant and open societies in the world; to the other side, continuing patterns of racism, injustice, and exclusion (Key 2007; Fleras 2009; Hier et al. 2009). On the one hand, a pacesetter in the arts of managing difference; on the other hand, the site of numerous human rights violations (from racial profiling to aboriginal poverty to migrant worker exploitation). Even concepts like inclusion are multiculturally problematic. As currently framed in Canada, inclusiveness implies a power imbalance that privileges some Canadians—those doing the accommodating—over those being accommodated. By contrast, true inclusion embodies the assumption that all Canadians are Canadian with a corresponding right to contribute and converse (Berns-McGown 2007).

In light of such inconsistencies, what works in Canada may not be applicable elsewhere. A host of varying political, historical, and geographical circumstances may prove insurmountable in making the multicultural leap from here to there. This caveat raises questions: How situation-specific is Canada's multiculturalism model for managing difference? To what extent is the Canadian model a product of a unique history and fortuitous geography? Can this multicultural governance as a source of best practices be duplicated elsewhere (Ibbitson 2007)? For some, the principles and practices of Canada's Multiculturalism is exportable but only when combined with a principled approach to immigration (Fleras 2007). For others, the combination of favorable conditions, historical factors, and timely developments that propelled Multiculturalism to Canada's governance ranks may make it difficult to duplicate in the European theatre (Helly 2005; Kymlicka 2007a).

European Perspectives: Multicultural on the Outside, Xenophobic on the Inside

When multiculturalism is unhinged from equality, it tends to career off in unpleasant directions. (Pearl Eliadis 2007)

European societies have evolved through three phases in the governance of difference and diversity (Grillo 2007). A commitment to the principles and ideology of assimilation (i.e., conformity to national norms) prevailed until the 1960s. The economic reconstruction and development of Europe required and attracted both skilled and unskilled people from culturally diverse and less-developed sources (Modood and Werbner 1997). But this entry of "strangers" to address labour shortages proved disruptive. It complicated the balancing act between unity and diversity in those countries whose sense of national identity was anything but inclusive and whose boundaries were largely impermeable (Citrin and Sides 2008). Not surprisingly, Europe's post – World War II response to this flow of immigration was framed around the principles of assimilation (Hickman 2007). Two strategies were employed to ensure a monocultural governance: actively suppress difference and diversity or, alternatively, prevent it from gaining a foothold through "guest worker" programs.

Over time, a drift toward the tolerance of diversity and difference was inevitable. European countries in the aftermath of the Second World War ratified a range of statutes addressing the elimination of hate crime, racial and religious discrimination, and fascist ideologies (which included declaring 1997 as the European Year Against Racism) (Goodey 2007). A commitment to multiculturalism gradually emerged as a preferred governance framework—corresponding with a concomitant shift in Western thought from a reductive focus on race to a more relativistic emphasis on culture (Stratton 1999; Lentin 2004). In looking for ways to display its liberalism while disassociating itself from oppressive ideologies like Nazism or colonialism (Singh 2007), national narratives shifted accordingly. The combination of demographic shifts, intellectual trends, and political expediencies consolidated a commitment to multiculturalism as a blueprint for living together differently yet equitably. Under multiculturalism, national norms were reframed in increasingly heterogeneous terms in order to accommodate and legitimize diverse immigrant identities and values. With its embrace of tolerance and promotion of ethnic minority distinctiveness, identity, and community, multiculturalism was extolled as a necessary compromise that occupied the governance space between assimilation and separation/segregation. To think otherwise was tantamount to betrayal by racism.

The multicultural politics of diversity and difference have fallen on hard times. As noted by Jasmeet Singh (2007), the unmasking of multiculturalism in Britain and the Netherlands has blown the cover off a massive façade, in effect exposing the hypocrisies of multiculturalism on the outside and the persistence of xenophobia on the inside. A commitment to multiculturalism is rapidly eroding as a preferred framework for democratic governance, resulting in both a moral panic and public backlash. Events in Europe during the mid-1990s have shaken public confidence in politically-driven moves to integrate migrants under a multicultural governance, resulting in an atmosphere of unease, a fundamental sense of dislocation, and periodic crisis over failure (Hansen 2007; Ley 2007). The interplay of national trends and global developments also contributed to a crisis in multicultural governance, namely, (Vasta 2007b): the absorption of eastern European states in the EU, the labor markets of an ageing society, increasingly porous borders, the politics of fear over the politicization of Islam, the playing of the security card to avert terrorism, the suppression of minority rights, and the futility of curbing undocumented asylum seekers. Nor is there much doubt that criticism of multiculturalism constitutes a thinly veiled gripe about the place and value of Muslims in society (Allen 2007; Parekh 2007). Finally, Europe has had to rethink its status as an a people-moving society. If Europe was once an exporter of people to Canada, the United States, and Australia, the status is now reversed. But in shifting from an emigrant source to an immigrant destination, there is growing pressure to keep immigration under control and immigrant differences under wraps—resulting in conditions for backlash and polarization (Ley 2007).

Accounting for the backlash: Multiculturalism and its discontents

With the hardening of European arteries toward immigration and the Islamic "other," the politics of multicultural politics has catapulted to the forefront of twenty-first-century challenges (Saunders and Haljan 2003; Goodspeed 2006; Morphet 2007). Multiculturalism may have reigned supreme in Europe as a blueprint for eradicating xenophobia and intolerance, but no more, with the result that a multicultural consensus has proven much more fragile than many would have imagined. Multiculturalism appears to have abdicated its legitimacy and public saliency as governance, in part because multicultural discourses rarely dovetailed with the empirical reality behind these normative expectations (Koopmans et al. 2006). European liberals found themselves hoisted with their own multicultural petard, not because of excessive tolerance or uber-inclusiveness, but by endorsing a multiculturalism agenda grounded in indifference and expediency rather than commitment or conviction (Siddiqui 2002).

To be sure, reaction to the crisis in multiculturalism may have been exaggerated. In the aftermath of 9/11, the Madrid and London bombings, and the grisly slaying of Dutch filmmaker Theo van Gogh, multiculturalism is widely blamed (scapegoated) for everything, from terrorist attacks to social ghettoization, and demonized accordingly (Lentin and Titley 2009). A sense of perspective is helpful: As Christian Joppke (2007) warns, no amount of multiculturalism or inclusiveness could possibly have averted these terrorist tragedies. Moreover, in that the multicultural backlash against migrants and minorities may be more symbolic than substantive, references to multiculturalisms death are grossly inflated (Kymlicka 2008). What is dying are specific expressions of multiculturalism that no longer work in the twenty-first century.

Generally speaking, the prophets of multicultural doom fall into three camps: *anti-multiculturalism as anti-immigration; anti-multiculturalism as anti-Muslim; and anti-multiculturalism as anti-multicultural governance.* First, the backlash against multiculturalism functions as a code (or proxy) for expressing hostility toward unwanted immigrants and unsustainable immigration patterns (Joppke 2007). While Europe has transformed into a multicultural continent of new immigrants (Zick et al. 2008), much of what passes for European immigration constitutes an ill-conceived and mismanaged guest worker program, the patriation of former colonial subjects, or flows of asylum seekers from largely North African and Middle

Eastern sources. Many migrants into Europe continue to be largely unskilled, unversed in the local or national culture, lacking competence in the language of the home country (France excepted), and prone to dependency on social assistance. Because immigrants were rarely seen as potential permanent residents, but rather as temporary laborers who would eventually return upon completion of their work, most European countries tended to define migrants as a "necessary encumbrance." Too often, the relationship between immigration and national identity is cast along win-lose lines, whereby the gains of one side contribute to losses on the other. If immigrants are accommodated, the host country loses something; if the host culture is unaccommodative, immigrants are lost (Hansen 2007). In other words, national ideologies about multiculturalism may have reinforced myths about the virtues of tolerance; unfortunately, they also glossed over the harsh realities of poverty, segregation, and disempowerment (Koopmans et al. 2006). As a result, public resentment toward immigrants and immigration mounts, even as elite consensus dismiss these concerns as baseless or xenophobic, as Ian Buruma (2008:A-15) observes:

> ... When the offspring of manual workers imported from countries like Turkey or Morocco in the 1960s began to form large Muslim communities in European cities, tensions arose in working class neighbourhoods. Complaints about crime or unfamiliar customs were dismissed by liberal elites as "racism." People simply had to learn to be tolerant. None of this was necessarily wrong. Tolerance, European unity, distrust of nationalism, and vigilance against racism are laudable goals. But promoting these aims without discussion, let alone criticism, resulted in a backlash.

Last, a commitment to multiculturalism suffers from location. The relatively easy movement of individuals across borders exerts additional pressure to play the security card against perceived threats to national identity and social cohesion. These insecurities tend to erode support for multiculturalism; after all, before the state can begin to negotiate multicultural rights, it must first secure its existence (Kymlicka 2008).

In contrast to Canada's evolving and migrant-driven national identity, long-standing European populations embrace a singular and well-defined identity that often excludes immigrants. Immigrants are perceived as lacking less conviction and commitment than in Canada because of the prevalence of guest worker schemes, family reunification practices, and asylum systems. Migrants are rarely preselected, often poorly schooled and unskilled, and largely unfamiliar with the language and culture of the host society (Joppke 2007). The ethnic seclusion, particularly of Moroccan and Turkish communities in the Netherlands because of endogamous marriage practices perpetuates the problem of ill-adapted minorities, including even second- and third-generation offspring. The end result? Far too many immigrants find themselves marginalized as an underclass because of a de facto cultural apartheid. In short, the governance status of multiculturalism within Europe differs from Canada. Most European societies rarely see themselves as immigrant societies, with everything that entails in terms of entry, acceptance, settlement, and citizenship (Koopmans et al. 2005). Even the commitment to an inclusive society in Europe is somewhat compromised by exclusionary practices that tend to isolate or deny, either through intent or by default. Insofar as immigration and difference appear to be spiraling out of control to the detriment of safety and security, multiculturalism is unhinged from society building. The multicultural recipe for a societal disaster is further exacerbated by a commitment to a plural monoculturalism that pigeonholes minorities into separate enclaves, discourages people from interacting with others, and disavows any criticism of the cultural "other" as racist or disrespectful (Alibhai-Brown 2000; Buruma 2007). A lose-lose reaction prevails. To one side, resentment mounts when migrants and minorities recoil at being reduced to the status of a tile within an all-encompassing multicultural mosaic (Hage 2006). To the other side, the superiority of a white European culture is defiantly asserted when immigrants are dismissed as incompatible, illegal, and ill-equipped (Kymlicka 2005). Under these circumstances of confusion and collapse it is doubtful if even the most robust of multiculturalisms could preempt the worst excesses of the twenty-first century.

Second, the presence of an increasingly politicized Islam has unsettled the multiculturalism in European governances. As Abdul-Rehman Malik (2008:1) writes:

> Long gone are the halcyon days when emboldened intellectuals declared the "end of history" and the decisive destruction of wars over ideology. They seem like the good old days—too bad they were so short-lived. Islam has crashed the party, sideswiped the cake, and stolen the champagne. The same thinkers now spend their time asking, "What went wrong?"

A fundamental incompatibility between contemporary multiculturalism and the Islamic tenets of Muslim people is widely perceived (Parekh 2005). Insofar as Muslims are failing to integrate and assimilate into European societies, as critics contend, they (rather than Islamophobic prejudice and discrimination) are primarily responsible for undoing the multiculturalism in a multicultural governance. But as others have noted, this perception may reflect a narrow view of integration based on seeing society as a nation-state with a shared national culture that is crucial for national unity. Many believe an integrationist façade must be maintained at all costs—at least in the public domain—since political unity is impossible without cultural unity. Under this totalist interpretation of integration governance, Muslims are expected to assimilate into national culture—at all levels including the economic, political, social, and cultural (Parekh 2008). In that many Muslims have integrated politically and economically, but not socially and culturally, they are perceived as reflecting the failure of multiculturalism.

Multiculturalism is seen as a contributing factor in radicalizing Muslims (Siapara 2007). To growing dismay, many young European Muslims express greater alienation from the country they live in than do/did their parents (Ash 2006). Rootless and restive, alienated from their communities and shunned by society, young Muslims (an October 3, 2005, issue of *Time* magazine referred to them as Generation Jihad) increasingly embrace religious extremism—further reinforcing public fears that a bankrupt multiculturalism spawned radical spaces for dismantling Europe's liberal-democratic project. Another study by the Pew Research Centre found that one in four younger Muslims in the United States believe suicide bombings are justified, although nearly 80 percent of American Muslims—mainstream, moderate, and middle class—reject the legitimacy of such actions (Trounsen 2007). Not surprisingly, many interpret the backlash against immigration/multiculturalism as a coded subtext for Islamophobia, prompted by fears of jihadist terrorism, hatred of Islamicized Muslims, unease over a clash of cultural values, or resentment over the "influx" of Muslim migrants from the poor, unstable countries of North Africa or the Middle East, whose young inhabitants are anxious for opportunities whether as legal migrants, illegal workers, guest workers, or asylum seekers (Parekh 2006).

In this Huntingtonian clash of cultures and intolerance, white European culture is increasingly portrayed as besieged, beleaguered, and devalued. As Ghassan Hage (2006) comments, failure to integrate a growing, devout, and alienated Muslim minority into a relativistic and aggressive secular culture has prompted hostility toward minorities with conflicting loyalties (Blond and Pabst 2008). Differences are no longer couched in the discourse of the cultural "other," with their connotation of tolerance and acceptance. They are framed instead around the discursive framework of the "enemy within" because of the "Islamification of Europe," with its connotation of insecurity, loss of identity, and failure to connect and cohere.

The politics of religion is key. First, European Muslims are unwilling to divest themselves of their religious identities, since religion encompasses an inextricable component of who they are and how they act (A-R Malik 2008). They are expected to fulfill their religious obligations in ways that many Christians would regard as excessive (Meer and Modood 2008), involving a pattern of behavior that in itself constitutes a culture. To deny Muslims the right to follow their practice is thus tantamount to denying the rites of their religion. Second, European Muslims continue to believe in the moral superiority of their religion, in the process making it difficult to participate in the creative tension of a give-and-take multiculturalism (Parekh 2008). Multiculturalism supports tolerance of Muslims and Islamic religion, but this very multicultural tolerance puts Islam on a par with other inferior religions. This challenge of integrating Islam into a secular democracy has generated a crisis over "whose rules rule" as Ghassan Hage (2006) explains:

> For multiculturalism was always about finding a space for the culture of the other, in so far as that culture does not claim a sovereignty over itself that clashes with the laws of the nation . . . Multiculturalism has always had capacity to find a space for such minor laws within an all encompassing national law. This is part of what defines it. However, for people who take their religion seriously, this situation is reversed. The laws of God are all encompassing, and the national laws of the host nation are minor. For a seriously religious Muslim migrant, to integrate into the host nation becomes a matter of finding space for these national laws within the all encompassing laws of God. We then see how the very relationship between encompassing and encompassed cultures, on which multiculturalism is based, is here inverted

A conflict of interest is inevitable (Blond and Pabst 2008). The Islamicist presence poses a governance threat when challenging conventional foundational principles that enshrine the primacy of secular law and the legitimacy of the secular state to assert control over all spheres of life. The taken-for-granted secularism of European societies is exposed, as is the so called value neutrality of the state and its institutions, with ominous consequences for state-religion relations. This European commitment to protect the state from religion (rather than religion from the state as is the case in America (Blond and Pabst 2008) comes with a cost. It fosters the creation of a compartmentalized universe in which different groups inhabit ghettoized existences in isolation from others (Parekh 2008).

Third, the politics of multicultural governance in European societies is prone to divisiveness. On too many occasions what passes for European multiculturalism is best envisaged as a plural monoculturalism—a situation in which segregation is preferred over community because people didn't know how to live together differently or feared that any compromise would dilute their cultural or national authenticity (Sen 2006). The stifling of criticism of cultures and religions did not generate acceptance as much as feelings of resentment and estrangement over parallel communities that disregarded mainstream norms and values (Vinocur 2008). With different ethnic groups passively coexisting alongside each other without having to interact, communicate, or exchange, a plural monoculturalism is prone to an uncritical relativism. As Melanie Phillips writes in her book *Londonistan*, this doctrine holds that all minority cultures are of equal status and worth so that any criticism of diversities – much less an imposition of majority standards – is by definition racist. In inviting migrants to maintain their own ethnocultural/religious traditions, Europeans abdicated the right to demand immigrant adaptation to the mainstream as the price of entry into society (Moens and Collacott 2008). A plural-based monoculturalism emerges that explicitly recognizes and financially supports migrants as distinct and segregated ethnic groups with parallel lives under the benign gaze of their adopted country (Koopmans et al. 2006). Paradoxically, Western cultures are rarely accorded relativistic equivalence but usually are denounced as imperialistic or offensive (Minogue 2005; West 2005). However well-intentioned and intellectually laudable, the dangers of this plural monoculturalism were captured by Trevor Phillips, then chair of Britain's Commission for Racial Equality, when he complained, "We focused far too much on the 'multi' and not enough on the common culture"—thereby solidifying a drift into isolation rather than shared values.

In other words, Europe's embrace of multiculturalism was predicated on a separatist governance known as a plural society. According to the plural principle, society can consist of ethnically different and self-contained groups, often reflecting a national division of labor, with interaction restricted largely to the marketplace (Furnival 1948; Smith 1965). But as Naomi Klein writes in the summer 2005 issue of the *Nation*, equating pluralism with multiculturalism is a misnomer. European-style pluralism has little to do with inclusion or equality, but everything to do with an elite arrangement between politicians and community leaders for funnelling potentially troublesome constituents into state funded enclaves. Lip service to multicultural ideals is dutifully deployed, yet the privileged position of the dominant sector is rarely abandonned, while centers of public life remain blissfully oblivious to the changes around them. But context is critical when gauging the consequences. When applied to those who are seen as temporary or unwelcome, a multicultural governance creates the potential for segregation by excluding foreign elements from the mainstream (Bloemraad 2007). And when cultural differences are promoted at the expense of social equality and justice, disunity eventually ensues.

The consequences of this miscalculation have proven costly. A commitment to multiculturalism emerged as a default governance option once

Europeans were reconciled to the fact that guest workers would be staying (Neill and Schwedler 2007). The segregation of ethnic communities into urban enclaves not only disengaged immigrants from full and equal citizenship rights (Joppke 2007). Under a plural monocultural model, governance was reduced to the level of a visionless coexistence, one in which dominant and subdominant groups retreated into relative isolation from each other except for interaction in the marketplace. Without an overarching vision for living together differently, the social and economic integration of migrants and minorities stalled, then collapsed. The benign neglect of immigrant communities was readily justified: European countries did not see themselves as immigrant societies; accordingly, as primarily emigrant countries, they had minimal responsibility to multiculturally accommodate immigrants (guest workers) into the social and political fabric.

Contrasting Realities, Comparative Perspectives

> For many of us in Europe, Canada is seen (even envied) as a society that is more at ease with its increasing diversity. To be a Canadian is to be a friend, a spouse, partner, colleague, or a neighbour with someone who is from a different background to your own, in an unthreatening atmosphere. There is little appetite to change the way anyone thinks or behaves.

A sense of perspective is crucial in putting multiculturalism to the governance test. Multiculturalism appears to be atrophying in those societies that do not see themselves as immigration societies, feel defensive because of security anxieties, tend to emphasize respecting diversity or removing disadvantage, or have badly miscalculated the politics of migration resulting in an alienated and marginal underclass. In time, neither the politicians nor the public could Condone what a politically correct plural monoculturalism was doing. Insofar as multiculturalism was seen as dividing, destabilizing, or destroying, resistance on both sides stiffened accordingly, especially with the revival of an ethnicized national identity and retrieval of historical memory. In rejecting a commitment to 'carte blanche' multiculturalism, what appears instead is an embrace of neo-monoculturalism. With their insistence on compulsory language courses, mandatory classes on national history and cultural values, and culture-specific citizenship tests to ensure the right kind of immigrants and citizens, European societies are moving toward a more conservative model of multicultural governance. But references to the death of multiculturalism as governance are premature (Nye 2007). A retreat from multiculturalism is not the same as an abandonment of multicultural principles and practices as much as a retrenchment along integrative lines and patterns of mutual adjustment. Admittedly, with the collapse of an elite consensus, multiculturalism is losing some of its lustre as a governance model; nevertheless its reincarnation under an integrative label speaks volumes about its enduring quality as a framework for living together with differernces. Countries looking for multicultural solutions to governance challenges are inclined to mimic models that work. Consider Canada's inclusive Multiculturalism model with its unwavering commitment to a liberal multicultural governance (Adams 2007). Multiculturalism provides a workable recourse for uniting Canadians—at times by rejecting differences, at times by insisting that differences should not preclude full and equal participation, at times by taking differences into account to provide more culturally responsive services. Paradoxically, it is precisely this principled two-way balancing act—treating people the same as a matter of course, but treating them differently when needed—that holds the possibility of a new paradigm for constructive engagement, one that goes beyond the polarized discourse of "us" versus "them" but benefits from the presence of the "we" in enhancing social solidarity and national identity (see Ahmed 2006).

It's tempting to theorize the Canadian model as a universal and normative standard for living together with differences. But the political, social, demographic, and economic circumstances that secured Multiculturalism in Canada may preclude its expression elsewhere (Kymlicka 2008; Baubock 2008a). Whereas Multiculturalism in Canada is inextricably linked to national identity and society building, this connection is rarely the case in Europe. To the extent that immigration in Europe existed, it was seen as a necessary evil (temporary labor, family reunification, asylum seekers, and former colonial subjects), hence less deeply rooted and commanding less commitment. Collective experiences are no less divergent. Immigrant societies like Canada are based on a belief that everything is possible because everything can be reinvented, including the transformation of immigrants from over there to over here (Chhatwal 2007). By contrast, the weight of tradition, religion, history, and stratification in European societies exerts limits rather than possibilities, generating fears that society is increasingly fragmented along racial and religious lines with the possible consequence of disorder or destruction (O'Donnell 2007). As a result, the politics of multiculturalism in Europe differs from its North American counterpart, reflecting an array of distinctive dynamics (Triandafyllidou et al. 2006):

1) the emergence of populist and anti-immigration political parties
2) the proliferation of transnational citizenships because of Europe's geographical proximity to migrant source societies

3) a conflict of interest between Europe's increasingly aggressive secularism versus the religiosity of European Muslims, including those
extremists who invoke Islam to justify resistance and action
4) Muslim values/practices at odds with Western values (Bousetta and
Jacobs 2006; Modood 2006)
5) a colonial past that influences debates over who enters and how to
facilitate the settlement process
6) persistence of hard-core racists and xenophobic sympathies with
strong regional appeal

In summary: Immigration and integration issues are attracting political attention. Debates over migration policies and the integration of
minorities and migrants have captured the political agenda in many
OECD countries (OECD 2008). Fears are mounting that a multicultural response to immigration and immigrant integration will disrupt
the social fabric, dilute national identities, imperil borders and security,
and balkanize society into isolated and warring fragments (Collett 2008).
In acknowledging that policies designed to protect distinctiveness and
promote tolerance are paradoxically breeding intolerance on both sides
(Sniderman and Hagendoorn 2007), European countries are adopting
integrative/assimilative approaches to governance in hopes of counteract-
ing what many perceive as the failure of former multicultural policies to
(a) to ensure the safety, security, and solidarity of society at large and
(b) to successfully incorporate and enhance the participation of migrants
and minorities, many of whom are seen as making unacceptable political, cultural, and religious demands upon allegedly secular and democratic
European societies (Modood 2006; Parekh 2006; Triandafyllidou et al.
2006). But for any democratic governance to work in ethnically different
contexts, migrants and minorities must be viewed as integral members
of society, not as temporary sojourners. As aptly articulated by Tariq
Modood: "Ultimately, we must rethink 'Europe' and its changing nations
so that Muslims are not a 'Them' but part of plural 'Us,' not merely
sojourners but partners into the future" (Modood 2006:53).

10

Reconstitutionalizing Multiculturalism: Governance Pathways for the Twenty-first Century

Introduction: Review, Overview, Preview

This book has addressed a singular challenge: to explore, analyze, and compare the politics of multiculturalism as a complex of ideologies, policies, and programs in advancing an inclusive multicultural governance. All of the countries under this cross-national study—Canada, the United States, the Netherlands, Britain, Australia, and New Zealand—have demonstrated a propensity toward the principles and practices of multiculturalism. Each has also committed to actively depoliticizing the politics of difference by utilizing the principles of multiculturalism for securing governance goals in a politically acceptable manner. In some cases, multiculturalism is formally expressed at national or state levels. In other cases, for example in Europe where no country has adopted multiculturalism as an official policy (Phillips and Saharso 2008), multicultural responses are unofficial and indirect, manifest at local and regional levels, and reflected in initiatives that are multicultural in everything but name. Whether named or not, formal or informal, direct or indirect, the conclusion is inescapable: multiculturalism as a set of governance ideals—and policies and programs for transforming these ideals into practices (from antiracism to employment equity)—rarely wavers from its central mission. That is to make society safe from difference, yet safe for difference by improving the process of minority integration while neutralizing the salience of ethnocultural differences as sources of disadvantage or divisiveness (Eisenberg 2002).

Of particular relevance in advancing the book's argument is the evolving status of diversity and difference. Until recently, Western democracies dismissed the legitimacy of difference and diversity except as a threat to political stability, national unity, and cultural identity (Guibernau 2007). Migrants and minorities were subject to a host of policies and programs that sought to assimilate or marginalize (Banting and Kymlicka 2006). These monocultural governances have now been shelved in favor of those more accommodative alternatives, including a commitment to multiculturalism as principle and practice managing diversity and difference in hopes of maximizing benefits while minimizing costs and conflict (Giddens 2006). Multicultural responses to the governance challenge are understandably varied, spanning the spectrum from (a) promoting a degree of order, stability, and cohesiveness in advancing national interests to (b) ensuring both cultural protection and social equality for migrants and minorities to (c) bolstering the benefits of diversity and difference for society at large or instead (d) cooling out potentially unruly constituents by co-opting them into the system.

This study has made it abundantly clear that multiculturalism as governance constitutes a moving target, assumes diverse forms in different national settings (its use in robustly multicultural societies like Canada is far from universal), and reveals a capacity to evolve and remake itself according to local circumstances and international trends. For example, the Multiculturalism program in Canada may have emerged to address intolerance and discrimination, but it currently focuses on social justice, civic participation, institutional accommodation, and national identity. With such an array of functions and consequences (both in Canada and abroad), the folly of collapsing multiculturalism into a one-size-fits-all model cannot be underestimated:

- For countries like Canada and Australia, there is no mistaking the centrality of an official multiculturalism in formally advancing a national narrative for society building. Both countries are multicultural societies that abide by the principles of multiculturalism as governance for living together differently.
- For other countries, the assessment is more mixed. A commitment to multiculturalism in many European countries may have initially secured a multicultural governance. For example, by accentuating discrimination rather than recognition of minority cultures, Britain initially embraced a multicultural governance that extolled the principle of racial equality (Bousetta and Jacobs 2006). Eventually, however, multiculturalism became synonymous with the culturalization of race relations. But with multiculturalism in retreat in both Britain

and the Netherlands (but see Eckardt 2007), the national discourse has shifted toward a multiculturally grounded civic integration along the lines of common good and shared moral order (Sacks 2007).

- The situation in the United States is complicated by jarring disconnects among different multiculturalisms, namely, celebratory, laissez-faire, communitarian, and critical. Not surprisingly, the role of multiculturalism has proven both elusive and enigmatic—no more so than at official levels where the assimilationism implicit in the melting pot metaphor continues to hold sway in reaction to the menace of post-9/11 politics and the surge of undocumented immigration of Mexicans and Latin Americans (Ley 2007:15).

- Finally, New Zealand remains a multicultural outlier. The status and role of multiculturalism is secondary to that of a semi-official biculturalism, especially when the politics of indigeneity reflect and reinforce the binationality between the Crown and the indigenous Maori tribes (Maaka and Fleras 2005). Nevertheless, with trade and immigration from Asia accelerating in profile and importance, a commitment to multiculturalism (within a bicultural framework) is gathering momemtum—in practice if not always in principle.

The status of multiculturalism is equally prone to contestation. While all the countries under study are committed to a multicultural governance (at least in practice or by default, if not officially or by intent), no single model can capture the richness of multiculturalism in its entirety. As Parekh (2000) has rightly argued, each country must and did customize its own multicultural governance to reflect not only its commitment to multiculturalism but also its history and culture. To one side are official multiculturalism models, with formal policies and programs at national levels to ensure an inclusive society (Australia and Canada). Even here, fissures in the multicultural façade are apparent. Australia remains officially multicultural, yet its moves toward an integrationist agenda are unmistakable, most notably at federal levels. Only Canada remains defiantly multicultural, with no retreat or apologies, despite tentative forays into rethinking its rationale (Freeze 2008; Annual Report 2009). To the other side are countries that are multicultural in all but name, with programs and initiatives that are multicultural in intent, nominally multicultural in expression, and consequently multicultural in impact. New Zealand and the United States are still grappling with the status of multiculturalism in light of competing agendas (biculturalism) or national discourses (melting pot). In between are those countries whose expressions of multiculturalism are capitalizing on nationhood discourses that are aggressively integrationist or neo-assimilationist. Both Britain and the Netherlands are recoiling from multiculturalism as a preferred national discourse and model for inclusive governance, primarily because of security concerns, changing demographics, socioeconomic disparities, and perceived Muslim threats.

Reactions to multiculturalism and multicultural governances are no less splintered. To one side are the yeas. People who invoke multiculturalism in a positive manner tend to project the ideals of tolerance, including minority rights to maintain language and culture, right to collective expression, equal access, and full participation in society. To the other side are the nays. Those who negatively dismiss multiculturalism tend to criticize it as disruptive, divisive, distracting, and destructive, citing threats to core values, national identity, and social cohesion; a balkanization ("tribalization") of society leading to a breakdown in social order; essentialization of culture by mechanically applying it to all members in a determinative way; and a form of divide-and-rule neo-colonialism that co-opts ethnic leaders into promoting elite interests (Vertovec and Wessendorf 2004). To yet another side are the in-betweens. Endorsement of the multiculturalism in multicultural governance is conditional upon fostering the goals of democracy and development (Baubock 2008b). But when costs outstrip perceived benefits, fears mount over the unintended consequences of multiculturalism in eroding the interpersonal trust and social solidarity that (1) sustains the welfare state (by generating resentment over the distribution of resources), (2) enhances the likelihood of cooperation (by encouraging a focus on differences rather than similarities), and (3) promotes the ideal of social justice and equality (Barry 2001; Eisenberg 2002; Banting and Kymlicka 2006; Putnam 2007). Clearly, then, in a world of change and uncertainty, older models of multiculturalism may no longer address the realities of the emergent world, with the result that traditional concepts must be recast and move beyond understandings and frameworks conceived during an earlier era.

It is within this mix of disarray and dismay that this final chapter addresses the politics of rethinking the multiculturalism in multicultural governances. The chapter demonstrates that multiculturalism is not dead as many pundits believe. Only those forms that never took differences and disadvantage seriously as a basis for society building are dying off. To the extent that multiculturalism is neither dead nor dying, it may be more accurate to think of it as being reincarnated to meet the emergent realities and evolving challenges of the twenty-first century. Of these realities, few pose as much challenge as the emergence of highly politicized faith-based groups who increasingly demand a place in the public domain, despite beliefs and practices that may be at odds with constitutional values. Only time can tell if a renewed multiculturalism—based on the principles of shared community and common belonging—will prove a governance success. In that the right architecture needs to be in place for living together by managing difference to eliminate conflict and bias, the reconstitutionalizing of multiculturalism as a governance pathway remains a key twenty-first-century priority.

Death or Rebirth? Repriming Multiculturalism

Nearly 25 years ago, Nathan Glazer (1997) published a book, *We Are All Multiculturalists Now*, that captured the zeitgeist of an era. For Glazer, America was in the throes of a cultural revolution that pivoted around a vision and embrace of multiculturalism (Rubinstein 2006). With multiculturalism cresting the wave of a provocative future, a new social and political order was in ascendancy, one seemingly married to the promotion of diversity (cultural) and equality (social) without forsaking the prospect of national unity, including the following:

1. a commitment to respect, protect, or promote ethnocultural differences at individual or group levels
2. a commitment to social justice to ensure equality for migrants and minorities by leveling the playing field, including the introduction of preferential measures to foster full and equal participation
3. A commitment to secure national interests (identity, unity, and prosperity) by ensuring the integration of migrants and minorities into a coherent package
4. a commitment to acknowledge the legitimacy of minority rights, ranging in scope from group community rights to individual identity rights

The shifts have proven consequential. For Glazer (1997) and others (Modood 2005), a commitment to multiculturalism profoundly transformed the society-building process by (a) extending the concept of equality from the sphere of the individual to cultural minorities, (b) signifying the end of white patronage and hegemony, (c) representing a revolt against colonialism in the old world and racial discrimination in the new world, and (d) securing a respect for cultural "others" by treating different cultures on an equal footing. Even criticism of minorities became increasingly untenable under multiculturalism. In the absence of absolute standards because of an imposed relativism, who would dare criticize or condemn without incurring the risk of moral opprobrium or social sanctions?

That was then, this is now. Today the more common refrain veers toward eulogizing the death of multiculturalism—or at least the end of multiculturalism as we know it (Lloyd 2002; Rubinstein 2006; Harrison 2008). The sacred cows that once underpinned multiculturalism have been toppled—in the process exposing an elite consensus that mistook public silence for political support (see Bissoondath 1994). The concept of a society of passively coexisting but isolated cultures no longer resonates with authority or legitimacy. With multiculturalism in crisis as a seemingly failed experiment that emphasized difference over disadvantage, dismay mounts over moves to create a multicultural society that respects cultural differences without corresponding efforts to promote equality and integration. (Foote 2006; Cameron 2007; Ibbitson 2007; Stein 2007; Lentin and Titley 2009). Nor is there as much traction to be gained from the seemingly quaint multicultural notion that anything goes because all cultures are defined as equally valid and of equal worth (Minogue 2005; West 2005). Finally, with difference having gone global because of communication and transportation technologies, the scope of multiculturalism has altered appreciably (Pieterse 2007; Karim 2007). The state can no longer regulate multicultural governance as exclusively as it once did because of a growing disjuncture between the transnational/diasporic identities of migrants/minorities and the national policy options of the host country.

Even the possibility of living together differently under a multicultural governance is imploding as countries (like individuals) hunker down by circling the wagons (see Putnam 2007). This is particularly evident in European countries where a commitment to multiculturalism is largely on life support following the collapse of consensus over multiculturalism, coupled with the introduction of integration agendas that seemingly endorse the assimilationism of a de facto monocultural governance. In contrast to Canada (and until recently Australia), where multiculturalism is equated with inclusiveness rather than diversity enhancement, the European model has not worked out according to plan. A misplaced respect for cultural relativism to offset imperial guilt culminated in privileging minority cultural rights as grounds for an almost anything-goes governance. Both political support and public legitimacy have been squandered because of a politically correct and laissez-faire multiculturalism that conferred excessive authority on cultural communities at the expense of national interests and public good—a sentiment captured by Sir Jonathan Sacks (2007:3), who writes:

> Multiculturalism has run its course, and now it's time to move on. It was a fine, even noble idea in its time. It was designed to make ethnic and religious minorities feel more at home in society, more appreciated and respected, better equipped with self esteem and therefore better able to mesh with the larger society as a whole. It affirmed their culture. It gave dignity to

difference. And in many ways it achieved its aims. Britain, for example, is a more open, diverse, multicoloured, energizing, cosmopolitan environment than it was... But there has been a price to pay and it grows year by year. Multiculturalism has not led to integration but to segregation. It has allowed groups to live separately, with no incentive to integrate and every incentive not to. It was intended to promote tolerance. Instead, the result has been, in countries where it has been tried, societies more abrasive, fractured, and intolerant than they once were.

But is multiculturalism really dead or, more accurately, undergoing rebirth? Is it disappearing or downsizing? Is multiculturalism disappearing because it doesn't work, or are certain forms of multiculturalism unworkable? And who is to say it hasn't worked or isn't working? On what grounds can such an assertion be made and justified? Consider the legacy of multiculturalism that informs the present—in effect proving that it worked and works—including the following truisms: (a) compared to the past, there is increased tolerance and acceptance (within limits) of cultural others; (b) an open hegemony in defense of white Eurocentric traditions has been rejected; (c) racism is no longer socially or legally acceptable; (d) institutions are under pressure to move over and make social and cultural space; and (e) minorities have made significant strides into mainstream institutions and the middle class (Modood 2005; Rubinstein 2006). Even national narratives increasingly recognize dimensions of difference as integral and legitimate components of public discourses (Kymlicka 2007a). Finally, a commitment to multiculturalism as governance appears unavoidable in a globalized world where the dynamics of cultural hybridity and diasporic transnationalism challenge the modernist notion of individual affiliation with a single and unchanging culture (Keith 2005; Pieterse 2007). In other words, multiculturalism may well continue to inspire and motivate as the driving force behind urban growth and prosperity, the lifeblood of innovation, and the engine of economic growth. It will also challenge conventional notions, familiar hierarchies, and binary oppositions such as black versus white, mainstream versus sidestream, and majority versus minority (Sardar 2005). Needless to say, a new conceptual language for coping with these shifts will need to be articulated.

Clearly, then, caution should prevail before burying multiculturalism as a good idea gone bad. Abrasiveness and discord do not necessarily suggest a failure of multiculturalism—at least no more so than public silence and political acquiescence are reflective of political appeal or popular support (Kymlicka 2004/2007). Nor should the growing clamor over the politics and politicization of difference be indicative of a backsliding. Contrary to popular and political belief—that the success of multiculturalism should measured by its ability to control minority politics or eliminate interethnic strife—the opposite is more true. Rather than diminishing ethnic political mobilization, the inception of a multicultural governance is likely to intensify competition for valued resources. A commitment to multiculturalism may institutionalize these competitive dynamics by (a) building a people's capacity to mobilize, (b) securing increased access to state resources, and (c) legitimizing ethnic claims as part of the public domain. In other words, the multiculturalism in a multicultural governance should not be about dampening protest and politics in the pursuit of some politically tranquil utopia. More accurately, multicultural governance and politicized diversities are inseparable from each other, mainly because the former sustains and is sustained by the latter.

In short, multiculturalism is neither dead nor dying. What appear to be dead are the seemingly antiquated forms of multiculturalism, including those that (1) tended to encourage division rather than unity, (2) privileged diversity over inclusiveness as a formula for living together, (3) accepted or promoted ethnic communities as grounds for governance, (4) tolerated ethnocultural differences and practices at odds with mainstream values, (5) refused to criticize minorities or government minority policies because of cowardice rather than conviction, (6) insisted on imposing what Kenneth Minogue (2005) calls a "dictatorship of virtue" by modifying any aspect of mainstream culture that minorities might find offensive, (7) reflected ad hoc arrangements rather than a principled response, and (8) divorced multicultural governance from society building at large, thereby enhancing its perceived status as costly irrelevance or unacceptable risk factor. Equally antiquated are multiculturalisms that uncritically embraced relativism as a principle of governance, on the somewhat dubious and politically correct assumption that no culture is better or worse than others (only different), that all cultures are equally different and differently equal, and that each is entitled to equal treatment or preferential promotion (Rubinstein 2006; Harrison 2008). Interred as well are the multicultural notions that migrants and minorities (especially those historically disadvantaged and/or oppressed) enjoyed the right—or even the duty—to promote their separate cultures, and that mainstream culture dared not criticize or intervene out of political correctness or from fear of causing affront to minorities.

The Multiculturalism Challenge, A Governance Paradox

A central challenge for the twenty-first century is gradually taking shape; namely, to improve the society-building prospect of living together with difference under an inclusive governance—with or without an explicit reference to multiculturalism (Governing Diversity 2007). As Michael Ignatieff (2001) reminds us, the major problems of the world are not climate change or the clash of civilizations but, more accurately, the creation of a stable governance order among diverse peoples. As long as people can cohere as viable political communities, all problems can be managed; without inclusion or cohesion, nothing can be solved. In rejecting a laissez-faire and politically correct multiculturalism as divisive, what is required is o a neo-multicultural governance, with its espousal of inclusiveness at social and cultural levels, treatment of individuals equally and as equals, and critically informed limits to tolerance, especially when beliefs and practices clash with mainstream laws and culture (Lloyd 2002).

But this challenge is interpreted differently by different sectors of society. From a state point of view, diversity and difference are ultimately problems of social order and social control. Any long-term prospects for living together under a state governance must invoke the hegemony of multiculturalism to make *society safe from difference, safe for difference.* Opposing tensions prevail within this governance framework: On one side, Western societies perceive themselves to be besieged from within by migrants and minorities who refuse to integrate into society or openly despise Western values (Guibernau 2007). (There is little evidence that minorities threaten social cohesion in terms of claiming political autonomy or formalizing their culture in opposition to the mainstream (Baubock 2002). On the other side are a host of centrifugal dynamics—from globalization to security/terrorism concerns to transnational citizenships—all of which conspire to compromise the principles of a coherent multicultural governance (Pieterse 2007). From a minority perspective, however, the rejection of multiculturalism may intensify a backlash toward more exclusionary notions of national identity (Phillips 2007). A different national narrative is proposed: how to craft an inclusive multicultural governance that ensures *differences are safe from society, safe for society without sacrificing a commitment to distinctiveness or equity.* Clearly, then, the interplay of these tensions – the balancing of mainstream interests with minority rights to equality, inclusion, and difference – generates the politics that drives contemporary governance debates.

To say that the challenge of multiculturalism is proving a governance paradox is surely an understatement. The politics of multicultural governance is likely to intensify as minorities become increasingly politicized in demanding a redistribution of power and privilege, while the mainstream, in turn, retrenches and resists in hopes of consolidating its core against the margins. For centralized authorities, different options are available for addressing the politicized presence of migrant and minorities, including (a) exclusion and expulsion, (b) tolerant indifference, (c) (non) recognition as citizens, and (d) institutional inclusion under the multiculturalism banner. Conversely, racialized migrants and minorities are no less equipped with options in advancing their interests, ranging from retreat and isolation (thus withdrawing their consent to be ruled) to politicizing their difference through disobedience or protest. And yet the politics of multicultural governance can swing both ways because multiculturalism, paradoxically, may easily be victimized by its own success. To one side, entitlement, participation, and representation based on a respect for culture can perversely stigmatize difference as the "other," while reinforcing patterns of exclusion. To the other side, ignoring culture when difference needs to be taken into account can neglect legitimate concerns by perpetuating patterns of exclusion (Vertovec and Wessendorf 2004).

At the crux of this governance conundrum is the politics of difference. How much difference can a society tolerate without unraveling at the seams? How much unity do societies require before imploding from within? Is there an appropriate amount of difference that should be tolerated, who will decide, and on what grounds? Can a balancing act be operationalized? Is respect for cultural differences viable when Western societies are unsure about the viability of their own beleaguered values and weak collective identities—thus defaulting ideological space to minorities with a stronger sense of who they are (Fukuyama 2007)? The more successful multicultural governances have responded to these questions by embracing a principled framework for balancing unity with difference. A respect for difference is endorsed without trampling on those shared rules and common vision that unequivocally assert the primacy of core values, rules, and priorities. Australia's revised multiculturalism program demonstrates a commitment to setting limits by accentuating the priority of integration and settlement over difference and division (McGauran 2005). Quebec's interculturalism model is similar in that it explicitly articulates limits by privileging the primacy of French language and culture, democratic rights, and respect for others, while striking a balance between individual rights and social cohesion (Garcea 2006; Nugent 2006; McAndrew 2007; Salee 2007; Bouchard-Taylor Commission 2008).

But even the most ambitious and inclusive models of multiculturalism confront a dilemma when addressing multireligiosity: how to make society safe from religion yet safe for religion when religions want to be taken seriously. The dilemma is particularly acute when multiculturalism must reconcile secularism with the accommodation of religious minorities whose claims challenge the legitimacy of the state by seemingly violating the principle of separating politics from religion (Modood 2007; Laegaard 2008). The politicization of religious extremism, together with politicized orthodox and ethnocultural faith groups, promises to be one of the more vexing twenty-first-century challenges in the arts of multicultural governance.

Is Multiculturalism Bad for Religion? Is Religion Bad for Multiculturalism?

Those who thought that religion could be separated from politics understand neither religion nor politics. (Gandhi, cited in Hashemi 2008)

The post-9/11 epoch has confirmed what many had suspected: religion—whether of a transcendental nature or corrupted for economic or political purpose or as an expression of human need—is now a force to contend with in the public domain (Stein et al. 2007). Neither religiosity nor faith commitments from extremism to orthodoxy are likely to drift into irrelevance or vanish into the private domain as widely predicted. Many had believed that with advances in science and reason, religion would retreat; after all, was it not conflated with ignorance and superstition or a reaction to poverty and oppression (Gray 2007)? But rather than retreating or disappearing, religion remains a powerful and pivotal force in human affairs (*Economist*, November 3, 2007). Religion is rapidly replacing ideology as a meaning system as more people increasingly crave stability and order in a borderless and unpredictable world. Even diversity discourses about social cohesion and national identity are beginning to shift their focus, from on emphasis on race/ethnicity to the realities of religion and religious diversity as challenges in their own right (Koenig 2005; Bramadat and Seljak 2005; 2008; DeSouza 2007).

Particularly virulent are debates involving the relation of religious claims to the multicultural governance of secular states (Taylor 2009; Levey and Modood 2009). Secular states everywhere are in crisis because of their aversion to deep religious diversity as grounds for governance (Bhargava 2007)—no more so than in those societies that embraced the historical ideal of separating state from religion, and vice versa, at least in theory if not always in practice. According to the doctrine of separation of church from state, a secular state (one that does not explicitly endorse an official religion) does not normally interfere in religious matters, but uses its powers to limit the role of religion in the public domain, thus protecting constitutional rights to freedom of religion. In turn, religion does not meddle in state functions. Religiosity is restricted to the personal and the private, thereby negating public displays of religion in the workplace or community. The exclusion of religion from the public domain because of the private/public divide is thought to consolidate the principle of state neutrality.

Not surprisingly, aggressively secular and increasingly diverse societies confront a a series of governance paradoxes (Gray 2007). First, in an age defined by identity in which people assert faith as one of their primary forms of self identification, what is the place of faith based communities in a secular and democratic society (Cooper and Lodge 2008)? Second, the growing challenges of a multiple inequalities agenda makes it doubly important to acknowledge not only racial and ethnic differences, but also the more complex field of intersecting inequities related to groups and identities, including religion (as well as gender, dis/ability, age, and sexuality) (Squires 2008). Third, is it possible to accommodate religious differences yet respect individual rights while reducing injustice between groups without sacrificing justice within ethno-religious communites (Shachar 2007)? Without a template to work from, even democratic governments are compromising the freedom of religious expression of those whose faiths are viewed as incompatible by European standards (including the banning of conspicuous religions symbols such as the burqa in the Netherlands and head scarves in France) (Singh 2007). And yet just as multicultural countries withdraw from formal religiosity, religious minorities are increasingly asserting religious rights, including the right to go public. In a democratic society that aspires to the principle of an inclusive multiculturalism, they ask, why should minority religions and cultural identities be privatized whereas those of the dominant group are normalized in public places (Modood 2003)? Because this politicization of religiosity increases the potential for intergroup strife, especially when religious identification clashes with mainstream values and patterns of loyalty,there is growing pressure to rethink the politics of reasonable accommodation (Cahill et al. 2006). Consider the issues:

- A belief in the separation of church (religion) from state by creating as neutral a public domain as possible, thereby eliminating the risk of a state religion
- An adherence to the privatization of religion (i.e., a separation between the private realm of religion and the public domain of neutrality) (Modood 2007; Orwin 2007) if only to reduce the risks of ethnic/religious entanglements by politicized ethnicities
- The paradoxical tension in the relationship of religion to society— whether to keep religion safe from the state, or keep the state safe from religion
- The contradiction that while secular societies are predicated on the premise that religions are neither public nor social but private and

personal—yes, you can be doctrinaire and passionate about religion in private, but tolerance and dialogue must prevail in the public domain—such a dichotomy may be unacceptable to the devout or dogmatic.

Sorting through this dilemma may be relatively easy when people are willing to disconnect their private lives from the public domain (a kind of symbolic religiosity). But the prospect of an inclusive multicultural governance becomes a lot more convoluted when people take religion seriously, resent any external intrusion into their religious domain, are reluctant to separate private from public, demand the incorporation of their religion into the public sphere, and are unwilling to compromise their religious beliefs to accommodate a relativistic live-and-let-live situation. In other words, there is a world of difference between religious groups that compartmentalize their religiosity from daily life and those groups whose religion is a lived and everyday experience (for example, the Muslim requirement to pray five times daily). In other words, Tariq Modood (2003) argues, a healthy and inclusive multicultural governance must accommodate religion as a valid social category to ensure the religious "other" becomes part of the secular "us". And yet there are growing fears that too much inclusiveness of faith based communities may prove a problem.

Is religiosity and multiculturalism biased against women?

An official multiculturalism is widely regarded as a principled framework for constructively engaging diversity. With multiculturalism, individuals are allowed to affiliate with the cultural tradition of their choice (within limits), without having to forfeit their right to full and equal participation in society. Yet, not all individuals are equal beneficiaries of an official multiculturalism. In the name of tolerance and respect for diversity, a commitment to multiculturalism may serve as a smokescreen in condoning cultural practices that systemically exclude women from the full and equal exercise of their rights (Okin 1999; Song 2007). Multiculturalism is thought to be bad for women in those contexts where the principle of gender equality clashes with the collective claims of racialized groups to preserve culture and identity (Reitman 2005). The "badness" of multiculturalism is particularly acute in cases where faith-based groups insist on beliefs that compromise a woman's equality rights. In that protection of cultural diversity trumps gender equality rights under such a multiculturalism, a commitment to tolerance may supersede women's claims for equality—a situation that is clearly unacceptable to those who denounce multiculturalism for privileging diversity at the expense of equality (Kuper 2007).

These competing claims and conflicting equalities pose a governance dilemma: Under what Shachar (2007) calls the paradox of multicultural vulnerability, even well meaning accommodation of religious difference may leave minorities within minorities vulnerable to injustice by reinforcing traditional patterns of inequality and exclusion. Responses to this paradox in multicultural governance raises questions over limits to religious diversity (Stein et al. 2007). Is it possible to live together with religious pluralism without allowing disagreements to erupt into conflict that can "rent asunder"? How can multicultural policies of tolerance and inclusiveness be balanced with a commitment to gender equality? How to reconcile the tension between respect for both religious rights and women's rights when these rights collide? Can the state balance a commitment to shared values with a multicultural commitment to difference without penalizing either women's rights or the rights ethnically based religious differences? Where does a commitment to both minority difference and gender equality stand in relationship to practices like female genital mutilation, forced marriages, or honor killings?Such challenges are sharply pronounced in countries where debates over inclusiveness are inextricably linked with an official multiculturalism, constitutional protection of individual rights, and a commitment to equality before the law.

The politics of "drawing the line" has taken on new resonance with respect to faith-based cultural groups whose beliefs and practices clash with constitutional guarantees of gender equality. Put bluntly, faith-based groups from Christian fundamentalists to Muslims to Jews endorse religious and scriptural beliefs that tend to diminish the status of women or erase their presence. John Ibbitson (2006) writes in reinforcing the paradox between tolerance and equality while assuming that separation automatically equates to inequality: "Whether you are Jewish or Christian or Muslim or Hindu or whatever, if you hold on to a strict interpretation of the tenets of your faith, you will not accept the full equality of women in society, or of homosexuals . . ." Consider, for example, debates over the politics of religious accommodation: Should universities allocate prayer space to faith-based student groups who segregate women in worship? Should places of worship be given tax privileges when they discriminate against women, for example, when women are not counted as part of the ten people who must be present for Jewish prayers to begin (Stein 2007)? Can the Catholic Church continue to receive special state entitlements and charitable tax status when it refuses to ordain women as priests? The paradox is palpable: some want gender equality within a faith; for others the dictates of their faith outweigh gender equity rights (Siddiqui 2006). But while recognizing the dilemma is a start, doing something about it is trickier. Consider the situation in Canada: Neither the courts nor the legal system have been much help in sorting out the impasse. Both tend to work on the assumption that religious bodies are largely private voluntary associations. As such, central authorities exert less control over these bodies unless there are coercive restrictions on exiting, unacceptable levels of abuse, and public outrage over rules. As long as members are free to join and equally free to leave if they so choose, the government is reluctant to interfere. If women find their equality rights compromised by a particular religion, according to this line of reasoning, they are under no obligation to stay but can vote with their feet. In theory, this is true; in reality, however, how plausible is leaving a congregation after a lifetime of religious involvement in that faith? Or is leaving an alternative for those minority women who find themselves literally ostracized not only by the congregation, but also by circles of friends and support?

In short, while certain forms of multiculturalism may be biased against women (i.e., multiculturalism is used to legitimize appeals to cultural practices that justify the subordination of women), perhaps the anti-multiculturalism backlash has prematurely thrown the diversity baby out with the multicultural bathwater (Phillips 2007; Song 2007). In seeking to create a female-friendly multiculturalism, one solution lies in rejecting a reified concept of culture in a primordial and essentialist sense of real, fixed, uniform, uncontested, and determining. Rather than seeing cultures as singular and uniform entities with intrinsic worth and in need of protection, a socially constructed model of culture is proposed instead. That is, culture per se doesn't exist except in its material manifestations; more accurately, it represents a logical fiction that is employed to account for relatively consistent patterns of thought and behavior at individual and group levels. (According to this line of thinking, culture may not be real, but people believe its real and (re)act accordingly. In that reified notions of cultures are widely deployed by group members who often lead their lives through this reification, fiction is not the same as fabrication, with the result that references to culture or groups must be taken seriously [Squires 2008]). Thus culture as construct is continually evolving, constantly contested and internally diverse, and aspirational rather than determinative. Individuals, including women, should be considered autonomous persons who choose the extent of their involvement in cultural forms, with the result that cultures assume significance only to the extent they are important to individuals. With a more fluid notion of culture as a logical fiction, collective interests can no longer call on something that doesn't really exist to justify the denial or exclusion of women—hence the expression "Multiculturalism without Culture" (Phillips 2007).

Another helpful solution in unblocking this impasse is a rejection of group-based multiculturalism. As long as there are multicultural narratives that explicitly condone group rights, tension will prevail between women's individual rights to equality and the collective rights of the group for survival—even if this means compromising women's rights in the process. An inclusive multiculturalism provides a working alternative: according to such a governance model, a society of many cultures is possible provided that no one is excluded from full and equal participation because of their culture. Yes, individuals have the right to identify, affiliate, and practice their culture, but only if these cultural practices do not violate people's rights, break the law, or contravene core constitutional values like gender equity. These limitations in drawing the line suggest- the possibility of a different spin than that endorsed by critics. Instead of being bad for women, an inclusive and liberal multiculturalism may prove a protective ally for racialized and immigrant women within those religious traditions that deny or exclude in the name of god or holy books.

Rethinking the sacred-profane relationship

Is there room for reasonable accommodation within the public square whereby both religious and nonreligious persons claim a public and social identity that allows each to freely mingle in public, make policy proposals, and have their ethical values influence public policy? Can a governance be created that allows people to live together peacefully despite differences by finding those domains we share in common yet holding in creative tension those differences that we disagree about without resorting to confict? Can societies uphold core values yet accommodate new citizens from different religious backgrounds by marrying equality with diversity and difference (Ramadan 2008)? Responses vary, but a commitment to compromise would appear critical. As Chris Baker, director of the faith-based research body the William Temple Foundation concludes, a two-way accommodation is critical, with all sides striving for common ground while respecting each other's differences. Faith-based groups must do more to allay secularists' concerns over imposing a "sacred" agenda; conversely, secularists must acknowledge an emergent new reality without making religions apologize for contesting the public. A new religious cosmopolitanism is advocated that incorporates religiosity with a foundation but without fundamentalism; a religious identity without exclusivity; and a certainty of truth without fanaticism. In the words of Cahill and colleagues (2006):

Society's needs to define the social and political space for faith communities to practice their faith with due regard to their civic and multi-faith contexts is a delicate art. The task requires faith communities to accomplish their task in building up cultural, social, and spiritual capital that contributes to the broader nation-building and world citizenship agenda. But it also requires a civil society to allow religion to be counter-cultural in critiquing society for its corruption and for its social and spiritual ills.

In crafting the basis for reasonable accommodation in a secular society, a repositioning of the relationship between state and religion is necessary. According to Janice Stein at the 2007 Ethnicity and Democratic Governance Conference at Montreal, secularists may have to examine core beliefs by redefining secularity not as a society without religion but one with an openness to diverse religious experiences. A meeting ground is proposed where religion and the secular state reach an accommodation that empowers both, but threatens neither, contends Hans Kung, one of the architects behind the Parliament of World Religions (see Jakubowicz 2007). A principled code in defense of religious diversity is a promising start, including the following tenets (see National Statement 2006):

- In that the diversity of religions plays an important role in people's lives, the implications for living together differently are threefold: separation of faith and state cannot mean strict state neutrality or the exclusion of religion from public affairs; the state cannot avoid creating a policy toward religion and religious organizations; and the state must devise a secularism consistent with religious diversity (Panossian et al. 2007). In other words, injecting religion into the public domain may be the best way of dealing with intolerant attitudes between faiths.
- Secularism cannot be either servile or hostile to religion. Nor should it reflect an attitude of blind deference or indifference, but demonstrate a commitment to respect and equality (Panossian et al. 2007).
- Both the secular state and religious communities have a responsibility to extend the freedom of religion to all religions and diversities within faith groups.
- In that there should be room within the Canadian project for all differences, those religious and cultural practices that are contrary to the principles of a liberal society must be altered or reinterpreted in ways that are not conflictual (Berns-McGown 2007).
- All religious communities have a right to safety and security as part of the multicultural governance contract.

- Religious diversity should be respected in the public domain in the same way that cultural differences are. By the same token, it is important not to "religionise" (Ramadan 2008) social problems. Religious dimensions may be contributing factors but not the main determinants of socioeconomic inequality or social marginalization.
- Disagreement and debate are inevitable because of religious diversity, but must be conducted in an atmosphere of mutual respect.
- Government and faith groups need to build and sustain working relationships within the context of democratic processes, the rule of law, and human rights legislation.
- Countries that are signatories to international conventions are obligated to respect religious freedom and dissent at individual and communal levels.
- All citizens have a right to be free of discrimination on religious grounds.
- Religious diversity needs to be recognized and accommodated in the workplace.
- Different branches of government and state need to develop religious diversity policies to put these principles into practice.

To conclude: the public-private divide between state and religion may have to be rethought in light of emergent realities (Koenig 2005). Religion can no longer be marginalized to the peripheries or the private but must be taken seriously and must be taken into account in defining who gets what in the public domain. Even the continued exclusion of religion from the public domain does not necessarily preclude a place for accommodating religious diversity. A compromise through reasonable accommodation—one that balances the principles of secularity with the realities of the sacred without straying from the inclusiveness principle of mutual accommodation (you adjust, we adapt; we adjust, you adapt)—may well provide the framework for living together with religious differences in a secular-humanistic society.

Toward an Inclusive Multicultural Governance: Common Belonging, Shared Community, Overarching Vision

"At the Commission for Racial Equality, we now frequently say that there are two major challenges for mankind in the 21st century. One is how to live with our planet. The other is how to live with each other. (Stevenson 2007)

Governments throughout the world have embarked on formal strategies of multicultural governance, including controlling immigration, managing ethnic relations, accommodating differences, and integrating ethnocultural minorities into the mainstream (Hudson 1987; Bleich 2008). Those governance frameworks such as assimilation or segregation that may have worked in the past no longer do; rather they come across as antiquated and inadequate when addressing contemporary difference demands. By contrast, multiculturalism as governance represents an innovative and inclusive blueprint for living together equitably and with differences. A new symbolic order addresses the integration of migrants and minorities through respect for cultural differences and removal of discriminatory barriers (Banting et al. 2007). To be sure, a normative framework for transforming multicultural ideals into governance programs and practice may not be openly articulated. Nevertheless, even an implicit commitment to multiculturalism secures the underlying agenda that legitimizes a multicultural governance. That these aspirational goals are not always realized to everyone's satisfaction is not necessarily a flaw in multiculturalism, although there are multicultural models more prone to provoke and partition than to unite and commit. The combination of implementation woes and lax enforcement are often the stumbling blocks.

What now? A commitment to the principles of separation or assimilation are deeply problematic (Parekh 2005). Even reference to integration as governance is no panacea if dictatorially imposed, loosely bandied about as a proxy for assimilation, and focused on a one-way pattern of adaptation. Instead of governance models that deny or exclude, a more workable alternative in the art of living together with difference is required, including a commitment to the principles of shared community, overarching vision, and common belonging. The key challenge in securing an inclusive governance is not about integrating migrants and minorities, but about ensuring they become equal citizens who are emotionally bonded to society and to other members of society through ties of mutual commitment, engagement, and attachment. To ensure the ideal of community and connections across differences, a two-pronged approach is proposed. To one side of this inclusionary dynamic are the responsibilities of immigrants. They must commit to the society they have chosen and express their commitment by accepting those responsibilities, involvement, and obligations that citizenship entails (Parekh 2005). To the other side are societal obligations. Society must commit to inclusiveness through removal of all discriminatory barriers, assurances of settlement assistance from housing to language, and provision of services, including health and education, at local levels (Reitz 2009). A reciprocating inclusiveness is critical; after all, immigrants cannot belong to a society that doesn't welcome them, respect the terms of the relationship, and discharge its obligations. Conversely, society cannot accept migrants and minorities as members unless they are prepared to belong, with everything that entails in assuming responsibilities and commitments. Alternatively phrased, we are all in this together as part of a grander ongoing national project, and everybody needs to make adjustments and concessions that go beyond self-interest but foster the vision of a common good.

In short, a multicultural governance of many cultures is possible if the appropriate architecture is in place. For a successful multicultural governance, a shared framework seems indispensable, one in which everyone abides by agreed-upon rules, embraces a common blueprint for living together with differences, agrees to the principle of agreeing to disagree, and partakes of the principles and practices of a shared citizenship (see Hansen, cited in Hurst 2007). A perspective is required that emphasizes the importance of both national identity and national laws in addition to a sensitivity to cultural differences since individuals experiences continue to be grounded in group identities. No less pivotal is the centrality of connections between diversities and difference—about social solidarity not separateness (Giddens 2006; Modood 2007; Phillips 2007).

Still, formidable hurdles hinder the prospects for doing what is workable, necessary, and equitable under a multicultural governance. Potential tensions prevail in accommodating the need to share common values with the notion of society as a nation that welcomes diversity and difference—even if multicultural governances are not shy about what they expect of minorities and migrants (and vice versa) (Stevenson 2007). Particularly urgent is the issue of formulating a set of principled norms for responding to minority realities without sacrificing national unity and liberal-democratic values in the process. Some governance models appear better suited for addressing this challenge. Neither assimilation nor isolation can survive in these politicized times. Pulling up the drawbridge and retreating behind a fortress Europe is no less defeatist or reactionary. A much-touted return to traditional values for integrating minorities into a coherent whole sounds good in theory; nevertheless, it may prove impractical in this postmodernist era. Whether by default or necessity, the path ahead seems unavoidable. The multiculturalism in an inclusive governance offers the most viable option for addressing the interrelated dynamics of defiant diversities, surging immigration flows, politicized agendas, and competing (transnational) citizenships.

Under the circumstances, it is not a question of multiculturalism as blueprint for inclusive governance. More to the point, the issue is what kind of multiculturalism can cope with the contested realities of the twenty-first century. With or without multiculturalism as a governance blueprint, the inescapable challenge cannot be averted: how to share political, social, and cultural space for belonging together under an inclusive and democratic governance without conflict or incoherence (Modood

2005)? In an increasingly interconnected yet uncertain world of difference and change, societies *cannot* afford not to embrace multiculturalism in their constant quest for political unity, social coherence, economic prosperity, and cultural enrichment. But for multiculturalism to work, two preconditions appear necessary.

First is the need to challenge the misconceptions that distort people's understanding of the multiculturalism in a multicultural governance. Few fields of governance are more littered with myths, half-truths, spin, and an unwillingness to speak truth to power. Of note is a reluctance to appreciate a fundamental contradiction: rhetoric versus reality. As this book clearly and repeatedly demonstrates, multiculturalism is ultimately a political act to achieve political goals in a politically acceptable manner. Even the seemingly innocuous slogan "unity within diversity" conceals an unwritten code: unity = control, containment, and co-optation (hegemony); diversity = paint-by-number tiles in a sticky mosaic. As a result, what multiculturalism says it does (respecting differences, removing disadvantage) is not necessarily what it really does (cooling out troublesome constituents who pose a threat to national and vested interests). Also in need of a debunking is the belief that multiculturalism can't work. As countries like Canada have shown, a commitment to multiculturalism is neither a hindrance to immigrant citizenship nor a barrier to social equality and political incorporation (Bloemraad 2007). Properly managed with clearly articulated instructions on limits, expectations, and responsibilities, even a state-based multiculturalism can prove pivotal in managing difference in ways workable, necessary, and fair.

Second, the appropriate infrastructure must be in place for multiculturalism to advance an inclusive governance. In constructing an inclusive multicultural governance, three foundational principles must prevail, namely: (1) the necessity to put multiculturalism at the center of a principled immigration program, and vice versa; (2) acknowledgement of the centrality of multiculturalism as a framework not only for protecting minority and majority rights, but also for building society safe from difference, safe for difference; and (3) a willingness to negotiate the terms of cooperative coexistence by way of shared citizenship, common belonging, and overarching national vision. After all, it stands to reason that if people and communities are not integrated at some level, they are unlikely to see any benefits from multiculturalism, thus intensifying resentment over paying a price for changes they neither understand nor approve (see Tierney 2007).

In that some of the more successful multicultural governances continue to abide by these principles speaks volumes about the importance of compromise and negotiation in constructing rules, priorities, and standards at the heart of living together without drifting apart.

Despite claims of multiculturalism as little more than a passing fad (Barry 2001), reality suggests otherwise. Even the much-ballyhooed retreat from multiculturalism is subject to diverse interpretation. Approve or disapprove, like it or not, evidence suggests multiculturalism is here to stay, albeit recast in a form and function that reflects contemporary realities. Yes, multiculturalism's halcyon days are over. Who can deny the downscaling of multicultural governance as an explicit commitment (although much of the animus toward multiculturalism is often meant for immigration programs and certain categories of immigrants). Yet to announce the death of multiculturalism may be premature. A commitment to multiculturalism is so deeply embedded in the legislation, jurisprudence, institutions, and self-image of Western countries that references to backlash and demise are misleading. Such negativity or denial can blind us to its embeddedness in principle and in taken-for-granted practices (Banting and Kymlicka 2006).

Let's face it: in a world of globalized migrant movements, evolving demographic patterns, and the politicization of difference (as minorities become more vociferous in competing for valued resources), multiculturalism is hardly an option to discard when no longer fashionable (Tierney 2007). Nor should multiculturalism be envisaged as a finalized policy or a settled governance but rather a perpetual and unfinished work in progress (Sandercock 2005). And the debates and disagreements unleashed by a commitment to multiculturalism should not be seen as a problem to solve, but a tension to be creatively played out. In that the forces of difference and the politics of diversity are as unavoidable as the tides of the sea, what must transpire instead are moves to reevaluate the concept of multiculturalism along the lines of an inclusive governance.

The book deserves to finish on an optimistic note. To the extent that multiculturalism is experiencing a crisis of confidence and an identity crisis, the danger is not the result of too much multiculturalism as a blueprint for living together differently. To the contrary, the problem lies in not enough of an inclusive multiculturalism with a corresponding two-way commitment to connect and interact. Or to put a not-too-fine spin on it, it's not so much the death of multiculturalism that should be mourned, but rather the dearth of an inclusive multiculturalism for the contested realities of twenty-first-century governance.

Bibliography

Abbas, Tahir. 2005. Recent Developments to British Multiculturalism. Paper presented to the International Conference on Establishing Evaluation Models for Administrative Reform in the 21 Century: Analytical Tools and Cases. Louvain –la – Neuve, Belgium.

Abbas, Tahir. 2007. "British Muslim Minorities Today: Challenges and Opportunities to Europeanism, Multiculturalism, and Islamism." *Sociology Compass* ½: 720–736.

Abu-Laban, Yasmeen. 2003. "For Export: Multiculturalism and Globalization." In *Profiles of Canada*. K Pryke and W Soderland (eds.), pp. 249–278. Toronto: Canadian Scholars Press.

Abu-Laban, Yasmeen and Christina Gabriel. 2002. *Selling Diversity: Immigration, Multiculturalism, Employment Equity, and Globalization*. Peterborough, ON: Broadview Press.

Abu-Laban, Yasmeen and B. Abu-Laban. 2007. "Reasonable Accommodation in a Global Village." *Policy Options* (September): 28–33.

ACS/Environics. 2002. "Public Opinion Poll." *Canadian Issues* (February): 4–5.

Acting Race Discrimination Commissioner. 2007. *Multiculturalism: A Position Paper*. Canberra: Human Rights and Equal Opportunity Commission.

Adam, Barbara and Stuart Allan (eds.). 1995. *Theorizing Culture: An Interdisciplinary Critique After Postmodernism*. New York: New York University Press.

Adam, Heribert. 1998. "German and Canadian Nationalism and Multiculturalism: A Comparison of Xenophobia, Racism, and Integration." In *Multiculturalism in a World of Leaking Boundaries*. D Haselbach (ed.), pp. 193–210. New Brunswick, NJ: Transaction Publishers.

Adams, Michael. 2007. *Unlikely Utopia: The Surprising Triumph of Canadian Pluralism*. Toronto: Viking.

Adams, Michael. 2008. *Dimensions of Diversity*. Canadian Government Executive, April, pp. 14–14.

Agocs, Carole and Monica Boyd. 1993. "The Canadian Ethnic Mosaic Recast for the 1990s." In *Social Stratification in Canada*. 3rd edition.

J Curtis, E Grab, and N Guppy (eds.), pp. 330–52. Scarborough ON: Prentice-Hall.

Ahmed, Parvez. 2006. "Western Muslim Minorities: Integration and Disenfranchisement." In *Changing Identities and Evolving Values: Is There Still a Transatlantic Community?* E Brimmer (ed.), pp. 53–64. Washington, DC: Centre for Transatlantic Relations, Johns Hopkins University.

Ahmed, Sara. 2000. *Strange Encounters: Embodied Others in Post-Coloniality.* London: Routledge.

Ahmed, Sara. 2007. "You End up Doing the Document Rather Than Doing the Doing: Diversity, Race Equality, and the Politics of Documentation." *Ethnic and Racial Studies* 30(4): 590–609.

Aizenman, NC. 2008. U.S. "To Grow Grayer, More Diverse." *Washington Post.* August 14.

Alba, Richard and Victor Nee. 2003. *Remaking the American Mainstream: Assimilation and Contemporary Immigration.* Cambridge, MA: Harvard University Press.

Alibhai-Brown, Yasmin. 2000. *After Multiculturalism.* London: Foreign Policy Centre.

Allen, Chris. 2007. "Down with Multiculturalism, Book Burning and Fatwas: The Discourse of the Death of Multiculturalism." *Culture and Religion* 8(2): 125–138.

Aly, Waleed. 2008. The End of the Culture Wars. First published in *The Sunday Age.* Reprinted in Australians All. Available online at www.australianall.com.au.

Anderssen, Erin and Michael Valpy. 2003. "Face the Nation. Canada Remade." *The Globe and Mail.* June 6.

Ang, Ien, Greg Noble, Jeff Brand, and Jason Sternberg. 2006. *Connecting Diversity: Paradoxes of Multicultural Australia.* Commissioned by Special Broadcasting Services. March. Available online at www.sbs.com.au.

Ang, Ien and Brett Saint Louis. 2005. "The Predicament of Difference: Guest Editorial." *Ethnicities* 5(3): 291–304.

Angus Reid Group Inc. 1991. *Multiculturalism and Canadians: Attitude Study.* Ottawa: Survey Commissioned by the Department of Multiculturalism and Immigration.

Annual Report. 1997. On the Operation of Canada's Multiculturalism Act. Ottawa: Canadian Heritage. Minister of Public Works and Government Services.

Annual Report. 2005/2006. Annual Report on the Operation of the Canadian Multiculturalism Act. Ottawa.

Annual Report. 2006/2007. Victoria Multicultural Commission. Melbourne.

Annual Report. 2006/2007. Annual Report of the Victorian Multicultural Commission on the Operation of the Multicultural Victoria Act.
Melbourne. Available online at www.multiculturalvictoria.gov.au.

Annual Report. 2008. Promoting Integration. Annual Report on the
Operation of the Canadian Multiculturalism Act 2006–2007. Ottawa:
Canadian Heritage.

Annual Report 2009. Annual Report on the Operation of the Canadian
Multiculturalism Act 2007–2008. Ottawa: Citizenship and Immigration.

Anthias, Floya. 2007. "Boundaries of 'Race' and Ethnicity and Ques-
tions about Cultural Belongings." In Racism in the New World Order.
N Gopalkrishan and H Babacan (eds.), pp. 12–21. Cambridge MA:
Cambridge University Press.

Arends-Toth, J and FJR van der Vijver. 2003. "Multiculturalism and Acculturation: Views of Dutch and Turkish-Dutch." European Journal of Social
Psychology 33: 249–266.

Asari, Eva-Maria, D Halikiopoulou, and S Mock. 2008. "British National
Identity and the Dilemmas of Multiculturalism." Nationalism and Ethnic
Politics 14(1): 1–28.

Asch, Michael. 1997. Aboriginal and Treaty Rights in Canada: Essays on
Law, Equality, and Respect for Differences. Vancouver: University of
British Columbia Press.

Ash, Timothy Garton. 2006. "It's Shocking but True." Guardian Weekly.
August 18–24.

Ash, Timothy Garton. 2008. "I Am Brit, Hear Me Roar." The Globe and
Mail. April 8.

Australian Government. 2007. Migration Program Statistics. Publication
of the Department of Immigration and Citizenship.

Australian Government. 2008. Immigration Update. July to December
2007. Department of Immigration and Citizenship.

Australian Human Rights Commission. 2007. Multiculturalism: A Position
Paper. The Acting Race Discrimination Commissioner. Available online
at http://www.hreoc.gov.au.

Babacan, Hurriyet. 2006. Racism and Multiculturalism. Paper presented
to the Responding to Cronulla: Rethinking Multiculturalism National
Symposium at Griffith University, Nathan Australia. Published by the
University of the Sunshine Coast.

Baber, HE. 2008. The Multicultural Mystique: The Liberal Case Against
Diversity. Amherst, NY: Prometheus Books.

Backhouse, Constance. 1999. Colour-Coded: A Legal History of Racism in
Canada 1900–1950. Toronto: University of Toronto Press.

Bader, Veit. 2007a. "The Governance of Islam in Europe: The Perils of
Modelling." Journal of Ethnic and Migration Studies 33(6): 871–886.

Bader, Veit. 2007b. "Defending Differentiated Policies of Multicultural-ism." *National Identities* 9(3): 197–215.

Bak, Hans. 1993. "Introduction." In *Multiculturalism and the Canon of American Culture*. H Bak (ed.), pp. ix–xviii. Amsterdam: Amerika Instituut.

Bannerji, Himani. 2000. *The Dark Side of the Nation*. Toronto: Canadian Scholars Press.

Bannerji, Himani. 2003. "Multiple Multiculturalisms and Charles Taylor's Politics of Recognition." In *Whither Multiculturalism?* D Saunders and D Haljan (eds.), pp. 35–46. Leuven: Leuven University Press.

Banting, Keith. 2008. "Canada as Counternarrative: Multiculturalism, Recognition, and Redistribution." In *The Comparative Turn in Canadian Political Science*. Linda A White (ed.), pp. 59–76. Vancouver: UBC Press.

Banting, Keith, Thomas J Courchene, and Leslie Seidle (eds.). 2007. *Belonging? Diversity, Recognition, and Shared Citizenship in Canada*. Montreal: Institute for Research on Public Policy (IRPP).

Banting, Keith and Will Kymlicka. 2006. "Introduction: Multiculturalism and the Welfare State: Setting the Context." In *Multiculturalism and the Welfare State: Recognition and Redistribution in Contemporary Democ-racies*. K Banting and W Kymlicka (eds.), pp. 1–48. Toronto: Oxford University Press.

Barclay, Kelly. 2005. "Rethinking Inclusion and Biculturalism: Towards a More Relational Practice of Democratic Justice." In *New Zealand Identi-ties*. James Liu et al. (eds.), pp. 118–139. Wellington: Victoria University Press.

Bargh, Maria. 2006. *Resistance: An Indigenous Response to Globalisation*. Wellington, NZ: Huia Publishers.

Barry, Brian. 2001. *Culture and Equality: An Egalitarian Critique of Multiculturalism*. Cambridge, UK: Polity Press.

Bass, Shana B. 2008. "Multiculturalism, American Style: The Politics of Multiculturalismin the United States." *The International Journal of Diversity in Organizations, Communities, & Nations* 7(6): 133–141.

Baubock, Rainer. 2002. "Farewell to Multiculturalism? Sharing Values and Identities in Societies of Immigration." *Journal of International Migration and Integration* 3(1): 1–16.

Baubock, Rainer. 2005. "If You Say Multiculturalism Is the Wrong Answer, Then What Was the Question You Asked?" *Canadian Diversity* 4(1): 90–94.

Baubock, Rainer. 2008a. "The Global Odysseys of Liberal Multicultural-ism. Review Symposium." *Ethnicities* 8(2): 251–254.

Baubock, Rainer. 2008b. "What Went Wrong with Liberal Multicultural-ism?" *Ethnicities* 8(2): 271–276.

Bawer, Bruce. 2002. "Tolerating Intolerance: The Challenge of Fundamentalist Islam in Western Europe." *Partisan Review* 69(3).

BBC News. 2004. "Few Black Friends" for Whites. July 19. Available at http://news.bbc.co.uk.

Beach, Charles M, Alan G Green and Jeffrey G Reitz (eds.) 2003. *Canadian Immigration Policy for the 21ˢᵗ Century*. Montreal/Kingston: McGill/Queen's University Press.

Beaumier, Colleen. 2007. Press release issued by the Liberal Party, April 16, 2007. Released by the Canadian Ethnic Media Association. Available online at http://canadianethnicmedia.com.

Bedford, Richard. 2003. *New Zealand: The Politicization of Immigration*. Migration Information Source. January. Available at http://www.migrationinformation.org.

Beissinger, Mark R. 2008. "A New Look at Ethnicity and Democratization." *Journal of Democracy* 19(3): 85–97.

Belanger, Yale (ed.), 2008. *Aboriginal Self-Government in Canada*. 3rd edition. Saskatoon: Purich Publishing.

Belkhodja, Chedly. John Biles, Ian Donaldson, and Jennifer Hyndman 2006. "Introduction. Multicultural Futures: Challenges and Solutions?" *Canadian Ethnic Studies* 38(3): ii–v.

Bell, Michael. 2004. "Tripping up on the Dual Citizenship." *The Globe and Mail*. July 29.

Ben-Eliezer, Uri. 2008. "Multicultural Society and Everyday Cultural Racism: A Second Generation of Ethipian Jews in Israel's 'Crisis of Modernization'." *Ethnic and Racial Studies* 31(5): 935–961.

Ben-Rafael, E and Y Peres. 2005. *Is Israel One?* Leiden: Brill.

Bennett, David. 1998. "Introduction." In *Multicultural States: Rethinking Differences and Identity*. D Bennett (ed.), pp. 1–26. New York: Routledge.

Berman, Bruce. 2007. "Ethnic Politics, Democracy and Globalization." In *Governing Diversity*. R Panossian et al. (eds.), pp. 31–38. Kingston: Queen's University Press.

Berliner, Michael S and Gary Hull. 2000. *Multiculturalism and Diversity: The New Racism*. The Ayn Rand Institute. Available online at http://www.aynrand.org.

Berns-McGown, Rima. 2007. What It Means to Belong: Reframing "Accommodation" in a Multicultural Liberal Democracy. Paper presented to the Immigration, Minorities, and Multiculturalism Conference. Montreal, October 24–27.

Bernstein, Richard. 1994. *Dictatorship of Virtue. Multiculturalism and the Battle for America's Future*. New York: Alfred A. Knopf.

Berry, John. 2006. "Mutual Attitudes Among Immigrants and Ethnocultural Groups in Canada." *International Journal of Intercultural Relations* 30: 719–734.

Berry, John and Rudolph Kalin. 1993. Multiculturalism and Ethnic Attitudes in Canada. An Overview of the 1991 National Survey. Paper presented to the Canadian Psychological Association Annual Meeting. Montreal, May.

Berry, John, R Kalin and D M Taylor. 1977. *Multiculturalism and Ethnic Attitudes in Canada*. Ottawa: Minister of Supply and Services.

Bertossi, C. 2007. French and British Models of Integration. Public Philosophies, Policies, and State Institutions. Working Paper no. 46. COMPAS. University of Oxford.

Bhabha, Homi. 1998. *The Location of Culture*. London: Routledge.

Bhargava, Rajeev. 2007. "How Should Secular States Deal with Deep Religious Diversity: The Indian Model." *Policy Options*. September.

Bhattacharyya, Gargi. 1998. "Riding Multiculturalism." In *Multicultural States*. D Bennett (ed.), pp. 252–266. New York: Routledge.

Bibby, Reginald. 1990. *Mosaic Madness*. Toronto: Stoddart.

Biles, John and Paul Spoonley. 2007. "Introduction. National Identity: What Can It Tell Us About Inclusion and Exclusion." *National Identities* 9(3): 191–195.

Biles, John, Errin Tolley, and Humera Ibrahim. 2005. "Does Canada Have a Multicultural Future?" *Canadian Diversity* 4(1): 23–28.

Bissoondath, Neil. 1994. *Selling Illusions: The Cult of Multiculturalism in Canada*. Toronto: Penguin.

Bleich, Erik. 2008. "Immigration and Integration Studies in Western Europe and the United States: The Road Less Traveled and a Path Ahead." *World Politics* 60(3).

Bloemraad, Irene. 2006. *Becoming a Citizen: Incorporating Refugees and Immigrants in the United States and Canada*. Berkeley: University of California Press.

Bloemraad, Irene. 2007. "Unity in Diversity? Bridging Models of Multiculturalism and Immigrant Integration." *DuBois Review* 4(2): 317–336.

Blond, Phillip and Adrian Pabst. 2008. "Integrating Islam into the West." *International Herald Tribune*, February 14.

Bogaards, Matthijs. 2006. "Democracy and Power-Sharing in Multinational States: Thematic Introduction." *International Journal on Multicultural Societies* 8(2): 119–126.

Boli, John and Michael A Elliott. 2008. "Façade Diversity: The Individualization of Cultural Differences." *International Sociology* 23(4): 540–560.

Bottomley, Gill, Marie de Lepervanche, and Jeannie Martin. 1991. *Intersexions: Gender/Race/Culture/Ethnicity*. Sydney: Allen & Unwin.

Bouchard-Taylor Commission. 2008. Building the Future: A Time for Reconciliation. P Bouchard and C Taylor. Report Submitted to the Quebec Government.

Bousetta, Hassan and Dirk Jacobs. 2006. "Multiculturalism, Citizenship, and Islam in Problematic Encounters in Belgium." In *Multiculturalism, Muslims, and Citizenship*. T Modood et al. (eds.), pp. 23–36. New York: Routledge.

Bramadat, Paul and David Seljak. 2005. "Beyond Christian Canada: Religion and Ethnicity in a Multicultural Canada." In *Religion and Ethnicity in Canada*. Paul Bramadat and David Seljak (eds.), pp. 1–18. Toronto: Pearson Longman.

Bramadat, Paul and David Seljak (eds.). 2008. *Ethnicity and Christianity in Canada*. Toronto: University of Toronto Press.

Breton, Raymond. 1998. "Ethnicity and Race in Social Organizations: Recent Developments in Canadian Society." In *The Vertical Mosaic Revisited*. R Helmes-Hayes and J Curtis (eds.), pp. 60–115. Toronto: University of Toronto Press.

Breton, Eric. 2000. "Canadian Federalism, Multiculturalism, and the Twenty-first Century." *International Journal of Canadian Studies* 21(spring): 160–175.

Breugelmans, SM, FJR van de Vijver, and SGS Schalk-Soeker. 2008. "Stability of Majority Attitudes Toward Multiculturalism in the Netherland between 1999 and 2007." *Applied Psychology: An International Review*. 2008.

Brighton, Shane. 2007. "British Muslims, Multiculturalism, and UK Foreign Policy." *International Affairs* 83(1): 1–17.

Bromell, David. 2008. *Ethnicity, Identity, and Public Policy: Critical Perspectives on Multiculturalism*. Wellington NZ: Institute of Policy Studies.

Brubaker, Rogers. 2004. *Ethnicity Without Groups*. Cambridge, MA: Harvard University Press.

Bruquetas-Callejo, Maria, Blanca Garces-Mascarenas, Rinus Penninx, and Peter Scholten. 2007. Policymaking Related to Immigration and Integration. Working Paper no. 15 IMISCOE. International Migration, Integration, Social Cohesion.

Bryden, Joan. 2008. Refugee Claims Backlog Sparks Flurry of Appointments. Canadian Press. Reprinted in *Waterloo Region Record*, June 25.

Buenker, John D, and Lorman A Ratner (eds.). 1992. *Multiculturalism in the United States: A Comparative Guide to Acculturation and Ethnicity*. Westport CT: Greenwood Press.

Buenker, John D, and Lorman A Ratner (eds.). 2005. *Multiculturalism in the United States: A Comparative Guide to Acculturation and Ethnicity*. Revised edition. Westport, CT: Greenwood Press.

Bulbeck, Chilla. 2004. "The 'White Worrier' in South Australia: Attitudes toward Multiculturalism, Immigration, and Reconciliation." *Journal of Sociology* 40(4): 341–361.

Bulmer, Martin and John Solomos. 1998. "Introduction: Rethinking Ethnic and Racial Studies." *Ethnic and Racial Studies* 21(5): 819–838.

Burayidi, Michael A. 1997. *Multiculturalism in a Cross-National Perspective.* New York: University Press of America.

Buruma, Ian. 2007. *The Strange Death of Multiculturalism.* Real Clear Politics. April 30. Available online at http://www.realclearpolitics.com.

Buruma, Ian. 2008. "Fear and Loathing in Europe." *The Globe and Mail.* October 13.

Butcher, Andrew and Leonie Hall. 2007. Immigration and Social Cohesion: From Policy Goal to Reality? Paper presented to the ESOL Home Tutors Conference May 19. Sponsored by the Asia NZ Foundation, Wellington NZ.

Butt, Riazat. 2008. Multicultural Mayor with a Divisive Tongue. February 10. Reprinted in and available online at www. guardian.co.uk.

Cahill, D, Bouma, G, Dellal, H and Leahy M. 2006. *Religion, Cultural Diversity, and Safeguarding Australia.* Canberra: Published by the Department of Immigration and Multicultural and Indigenous Affairs, and the Australian Multicultural Foundation.

Cameron, David Robertson. 2007. "An Evolutionary Story." In *Uneasy Partners.* Janice Stein et al. (eds.), pp. 71–94. Waterloo, ON: Wilfrid Laurier University Press.

Cameron, Elspeth (ed.). 2004. *Multiculturalism and Immigration in Canada: An Introductory Reader.* Toronto: Canadian Scholars Press.

Canadian Heritage. 2001. *Canadian Multiculturalism: An Inclusive Citizenship. Citizenship and Immigration Canada.* Ottawa. Available online at www.cic.gc.ca.

Caplan, Gerald. 2005. "The Genocide Problem: 'Never Again, to All Over Again'." *The Walrus.* May, pp. 68–76.

Cardozo, Andrew. 2005. "Multiculturalism vs Rights." *Toronto Star.* September 15.

Cardozo, Andrew and Luis Musto (eds.). 1997. *Battle over Multiculturalism: Does It Help or Hinder Canadian Unity?* Ottawa: Pearson-Shoyama Institute.

Cardozo, Andrew and Ravi Pendakur. 2008. Canada's Visible Minority Population: 1967–2017. Working Paper Series No 08-05 for the Centre of Excellence for Research on Immigration and Diversity. Vancouver: Metropolis British Columbia.

Castles, Stephen and Mark Miller. 2003. *The Age of Migration.* 3rd edition. New York: Guildford Press.

Caws, Peter. 1994. "Identities: Cultural, Transcultural, Multicultural." In *Multiculturalism: A Critical Reader.* DT Goldberg (ed.). Oxford: Blackwell.

Cheema, GS and DA Rondinelli. 2007. *Decentralization in Government.* Washington, DC: Brookings Institution Press.

Cheng, Hau Ling. 2005. "Constructing a Transnational, Multilocal Sense of Belonging: An Analysis of Min Pao (West Canada edition)." *Journal of Communication Inquiry* 29(2): 141–159.

Chhatwal, Kyle. 2007. "New World Visions Clash with Old World Values." *Waterloo Region Record.* Kitchener Ontario. June 12.

Chhotray, V and G. Stoker 2009 Governance Theory and Practice. A Cross Disciplinary Approach. New York: Palgrave.

Christchurch City Council Community Plan. 2002. Multicultural Centre – Te Whare O Nga Whetu. Available online at http://archived.ccc.govt.nz.

Choudhry, Sujit. 2007. "Does the World Need More Canada? The Politics of the Canadian Model in Constitutional Politics and Political Theory." *International Conference on National Language* 5(4): 606–638.

Choudhry, Sujit (ed.). 2008. *Constitutional Design for Divided Societies: Integration or Accommodation?* Toronto: Oxford University Press.

Choudry, Aziz, Gada Mahrouse, and Eric Shragge. 2007. *Neither Reasonable Nor Accommodating.* Canadian Dimension, pp. 16–21.

Citizenship and Immigration. 2006. *Facts and Figures – Immigration Overview: Permanent and Temporary Residents.* Ottawa.

Citrin, Jack and John Sides. 2008. "Immigration and the Imagined Community in Europe and the United States." *Political Studies* 56: 33–56.

Clarke, Ian. 2006. "Essentialising Islam: Muticulturalism and Islamic Politics in New Zealand." *New Zealand Journal of Asian Studies* 8(2): 69–96.

Clausen, Christopher. 2001. *Faded Mosaic: The Emergence of Post-Cultural America.* Chicago: Ivan R. Dee.

Cobb, Chris. 1995. "Multiculturalism Policy May Be Outdated, Says MPs." *Ottawa Citizen.* July 4.

Collacott, Martin. 2002. Canada's Immigration Policy: The Need for Major Reform. *Public Policy Sources.* A Fraser Institute Occasional Paper. No. 64. Vancouver.

Collacott, Martin. 2006. "Refugee System in Need of Overhaul." *National Post.* March 9.

Collacott, Martin. 2007. *Submission to the Consultation Commission on Accommodation Practices Related to Cultural Differences (Bouchard-Taylor Commission).* Vancouver: Fraser Institute. September 21.

Collett, Elizabeth. 2008. *What Does the EU Do on Integration.* European Policy Centre. Available on line www.epc.eu.

Commission for Racial Equality. 2007. The Reception and Integration of New Migrant Communities. Rachel Pillai, Research Project leader. Published by the Institute for Public Policy Research.

Commission on Integration and Cohesion. 2008. Our Shared Future. Final Report.

Commonwealth of Australia. 1989. *National Agenda for a Multicultural Australia.* Canberra: Australian Government Publishing Service.

Commonwealth of Australia. 2003 *Multicultural Australia United in Diversity.* Canberra: Australian Government Publishing Service.

Commonwealth of Australia. 1999. *New Agenda for a Multicultural Australia.* Canberra: Australian Government Publishing Service.

Communitarian Network. 2002. *Diversity Within Unity: A Position Paper.* Washington, DC: Communitarian Network.

Conference. 2006. Multiculturalism Is Working. Mosaic of Multiculturalism Conference. Goodenough College, London, November 16–17.

Cooke, Martin et al. 2007. "Indigenous Well-Being in Four Countries: An Application of the UNDPs Human Development Index to Indigenous Peoples in Canada, New Zealand, Australia, and the United States." *BMC International Health and Human Rights.* 7(9). Available online at www.biomedcentral.com.

Cooper, Davina. 2004. *Challenging Diversity: Rethinking Equality and the Value of Differences.* New York: Cambridge University Press.

Cooper, Zaki and Guy Lodge. 2008. *Faith in the Nation: Religion, Identity, and the Public Realm in Britain Today.* London, Institute for Public Policy Research.

Cornell, Stephen and Douglas Hartman. 1998. *Ethnicity and Race: Making Identities in a Changing World.* Thousand Oaks, CA: Pine Forge Press.

Cornwell, Grant Hermans and Eva Walsh Stoddart (eds.). 2001. *Global Multiculturalism: Comparative Perspectives on Ethnicity, Race, and Nation.* Lantham, MD: Rowman & Littlefield Publishers.

Coyne, Andrew. 2007. *The Unfinished Canadian.* Toronto: McClelland & Stewart.

Crothers, Charles. 2007. "Review Article: Race and Ethnic Studies in New Zealand." *Ethnic and Racial Studies* 30(1): 165–170.

Crul, Maurice 2008 The Second Generation in Europe. Canadian Diversity 6(2):17–19.

Cryderman, Brian, Chris O'Toole, and Augie Fleras. 1998. *Policing, Race, and Ethnicity: A Guidebook for Police Officers.* 3rd edition. Toronto: Butterworth.

Daily Telegraph. 2007. End of Multiculturalism. January 23.

Dale, Daniel. 2007. "What, Us Worry?" *Toronto Star.* July 7.

Dallago, Bruno. 2007. "Corporate Governance in Transformation Economies: A Comparative Perspective." In *Corporate Restructuring and Governance in Transition Economies.* B Dallago and I Iwasaki (eds.), pp. 15–39. New York: Palgrave Macmillan.

Dalmage, Heather M (ed.) 2004 *The Politics of Multiculturalism: Challenging Racial Thinking*. Albany: State University of New York.

Dasko, Donna. 2005. Public Attitudes Toward Multiculturalism and Bilingualism. Paper presented to the Canadian and French Perspectives on Diversity Conference. Ottawa, October.

David, Blunkett. 2002. Foreword. Secure Borders, Safe Haven. Integration with Diversity in Modern Britain. Home Office, CM 5387. London.

Davidson, Sinclair and Christina Yan. 2007. "... Who Comes to Australia?" *Policy*. The Centre for Independent Studies Autumn.

Day, Richard. 2000. *Multiculturalism and the History of Canadian Diversity*. Toronto: University of Toronto Press.

de Hart, Betty. 2007. "The End of Multiculturalism: The End of Dual Citizenship?" In *Dual Citizenship in Europe*. T Faist (ed.), pp. 77–122. Burlington, VT: Ashgate.

Deak, Istvan. 2002. "The Crime of the Century." *The New York Times*. September 26, pp. 48–50.

Dei, George Sefa. 1996. *Anti-Racism Education. Theory and Practice*. Halifax: Fernwood.

Dei, George Sefa. 2000. "Contesting the Future: Anti Racism and Canadian Diversity." In *21ˢᵗ Century Canadian Diversity*. S Nancoo (ed.), pp. 295–319. Toronto: Canadian Scholars Press.

Dei, George Sefa. 2005. "Anti-Racist Education – Moving Yet Standing Still." *Editorial Commentary: Directions*. 3(1): 6–9.

Delaney, Joan. 2007. "Canada's Role in the World Seen as Positive." *Epoch Times*. March 15–21.

Department of Internal Affairs. 2006. *Briefing for Incoming Minister – Ethnic Affairs*. Wellington. Available online at www.dia.govt.nz.

Department for Communities and Local Government. 2008. The Government's Response to the Commission on Integration and Cohesion Communities and Neighbourhoods. Available online at communities.gov.uk.

DeSouza, Ruth. 2007. *New Zealand Today: Biculturalism and Immigrants*. Available at http://www.wairua.co.nz.

Deveaux, Monique. 2006. *Gender and Justice in Multicultural Liberal States*. New York: Oxford University Press.

DiversityInc. 2008. *Whites Will Comprise Less Than Half of the Population by 2042*. August 15. Available online at www.diversityinc.com.

Doerr, Neriko Musha. 2008. "Global Structures of Common Difference, Cultural Objectification, and Their Subversions: Cultural Politics in an Aotearoan New Zealand School." *Identities* 15(4): 413–436.

Donaldson, Ian. 2004. "Identity, Intersections of Identity, and the Multicultural Program." *Canadian Diversity* 3(1): 14–16.

D'Souza, Dinesh. 1996. *The End of Racism: Principles for a Multiracial Society.* New York: Free Press.

Duceppe, Gilles. 2007. "Deceppe Slams Multiculturalism by Daniel Leblanc." *The Globe and Mail.* October 11.

Duncan, Howard. 2005. "Multiculturalism: Still a Viable Concept for Integration?" *Canadian Diversity* 4(1): 12–14.

Dunn, K. 2003. *Representations of Islam in Australia.* Research Institute for Asia and the Pacific. Diversity of Islam Seminar Series 2. University of Sydney.

Dupont, Louis and Nathalie Lemarchand. 2001. "Official Multiculturalism in Canada: Between Virtue and Politics." In *Global Multiculturalism.* GH Cornwell and EW Stoddard (eds.), pp. 309–336. Lantham, MD: Rowman & Littlefield Publishers.

Durie, Mason. 2001. *Mauri Ora: The Dynamics of Maori Health.* Melbourne: Oxford University Press.

Dustin, Donna. 2007. *The McDonaldization of Social Work.* Aldershot: Ashgate.

Dustin, Moira and Anne Phillips. 2008. Whose Agenda is It? *Ethnicities* 8(3): 405–424.

Duyvendak, JW and P Scholten. 2008. Questioning the Dutch Multicultural Model of Immigrant Integration. Published by the Amsterdam School of Social Sciences Research. Paper available online at www.assr.nl/conferences/documents/Burgerschap.

Early, Gerald. 1993. "American Education and the Postmodernist Impulse." *American Quarterly* 45(2): 220–241.

Eaton, Dan. 2007. "Migrant Study Backs Turia." *Christchurch Press.* Christchurch NZ. February 28.

Eckardt, Frank. 2007. "Multiculturalism in Germany: From Ideology to Pragmatism—and Back?" *National Identities* 9(3): 235–245.

Economist. 2007a. Has British Multiculturalism Really Failed. June 14.

Economist. 2007b. The New Wars of Religion. November 3.

Economist. 2009. How the Government Lost the Plot. February 28.

EDG (Ethnicity and Democratic Governance). 2007. Call for Papers. *Immigration, Minorities, and Multiculturalism in Democracies.* October 25–27. Montreal.

Editorial. 1997. "Multiculturalism South: Cultural Perspectives from Oceania." *Poetica: An International Journal of Linguistic-Literature Study.*

Editorial. 2006. Canadian Diversity. Spring Issue.

Eisenberg, Avigail. 2002. "Equality, Trust, and Multiculturalism." *Social Diversity.* May.

Eisenstein, Zillah. 1996. *Hatreds: Racialized and Sexualized Conflicts in the Twenty-First Century.* New York: Routledge.

Elder, Catriona. 2007. *Being Australian: Narratives of Nationalism*. Sydney: Allen & Unwin.

Eliadis, Pearl. 2007. "Diversity and Inequality: The Vital Connection." In *Belonging?* K Banting et al. (eds.), pp. 547–560. Montreal: IRPP.

Elkins, Zachary and John Sides. 2007. "Can Institutions Build Unity in Multiethnic States." *American Political Science Review* 101(4): 693–707.

Eller, Jack David. 1997. "Anti-Anti-Multiculturalism." *American Anthropologist* 99(2): 249–260.

Emling, Shelley. 2008. European Resentment of Muslims is on the Rise. Cox Newspapers. Published in the *Waterloo Region Record*. January 3.

Engelen, Ewald. 2008. "Through a Looking Glass, Darkly." *Ethnicities* 8(1): 128–143.

Entzinger, H. 2006. "Changing the Rules While the Game is on. From Multiculturalism to Assimilation in the Netherlands." In *Migration, Citizenship, Ethnos: Incorporation Regimes in Germany, Western Europe, and North America.* M Bodemann and G Yurkadul (eds.). New York: Palgrave Macmillan.

Epilepsy Foundation. 2007. Reasonable Accommodation (ADA Title 1). Available online at www.epilepsyfoundation.org.

European Policy Centre. 2008. *Multiculturalism and the Law: Testing the Limits*. Report. Available on line at www.epc.eu.

European Union. 2005. European Union Disability Discrimination Project. Available online at www.euroddlaw.org.

Favell, Adrian. 2001. "Integration Policy and Integration Research in Europe: A Review and Critique." In *Citizenship Today: Global Perspectives and Practices.* TA Aleinikoff and D Klusmeyer (eds.), pp. 349–399. Washington, DC: Brookings Institution/Carnegie Endowment for International Peace.

Fenton, Steve. 2004. "The Sociology of Multiculturalism: Is Culture the Name of the Game?" In *Governance in Multicultural Society.* J Rex and G Singh (eds.), pp. 49–55. Burlington, VT: Ashgate.

Ferguson, Laurie. 2007. Multiculturalism—Rumors of its Demise Greatly Exaggerated. Australian Fabian Society. Available online at www.fabian.org.au.

Fish, Stanley. 1997. "Boutique Multiculturalism, or Why Liberals Are Incapable of Thinking About Hate Speech." *Critical Inquiry*, Winter, pp. 378–394.

Fitzpatrick, Michael. 2005. The Price of Multiculturalism: Spiked Politics. Available online at http://www.spiked-online.com.

Fix, Michael, M McHugh, T Terrazas, and L Laglagaron. 2008. Los Angeles on the Leading Edge: Immigrant Integration Indicators and Their Policy Implications. Migration Policy Institute. Available at http://www.migrationpolicy.org.

Fleras, Augie. 1984. "Monoculturalism, Multiculturalism, or Bicultural-ism: The Politics of Maori Policy in New Zealand." *Plural Societies* 15(1/2): 52–75.

Fleras, Augie. 1994. "Multiculturalism as Society-Building: Blending What Is Workable, Necessary, and Fair." In *Cross-Currents: Contemporary Political Issues*. Mark Charleton and Paul Baker (eds.), pp. 26–42. Scarborough, ON: Nelson.

Fleras, Augie. 1998. " 'Working Through Differences': The Politics of Isms and Posts in New Zealand." *New Zealand Sociology* 13(2): 56–87.

Fleras, Augie. 2002. *Engaging Diversity: Multiculturalism in Canada: Poli-tics, Policies, and Practices*. Scarborough, ON: Nelson.

Fleras, Augie. 2006. "Toward a Cultural Empowerment Model for Men-tal Health Services. Paper presented to the Mental Health Conference by CREHS (Centre for Research in Educational and Health Services), Waterloo ON, Wilfrid Laurier University, December 4.

Fleras, Augie. 2007. Multiculturalisms in Collision: Transatlantic Divides, Intercontinental Discourse. Paper presented to the Universities of Augs-burg and Nuremburg. (Erlangen) Germany, June.

Fleras, Augie. 2008a. The Politics of Re/Naming. Paper commissioned by the Department of Justice and delivered to the Ninth National Metropolis Conference. Halifax, April 6.

Fleras, Augie. 2008b. "Cooling Out Troublesome Constituents: The Politics of Managing the 'Isms' in the Antipodes." *Rebranding Multiculturalism*. R Hasmath (ed.). Vancouver: UBC Press.

Fleras, Augie. 2009. *Unequal Relations: An Introduction to Race, Ethnic, and Aboriginal Dynamics in Canada*. 6th edition. Toronto: Pearson.

Fleras, Augie and Barry McClinchey 2009 Policing the Kaleidoscope. Paper presented to the National Metropolis Conference, Calgary AB. March 22.

Fleras, Augie and Jean Leonard Elliott. 1992a. *Multiculturalism in Canada: The Challenges of Diversity*. Toronto: Nelson.

Fleras, Augie and Jean Leonard Elliott. 1992b. *The Nations Within*. Toronto: Oxford University Press.

Fleras, Augie and Jean Leonard Elliott. 2007. *Unequal Relations: An Intro-duction to Race, Ethnic, and Aboriginal Relations in Canada*. 5th edition. Toronto: Pearson.

Fleras, Augie and Jean Lock Kunz. 2001. *Media and Minorities: Misrepre-senting Minorities in a Multicultural Canada*. Toronto: TEP.

Fleras, Augie and Paul Spoonley. 1999. *Recalling Aotearoa: Indigenous Poli-tics and Ethnic Relations in New Zealand*. Melbourne: Oxford University Press.

Foote David, K. 2006. *Boom, Bust, & Echo: Profiting from the Demographic Shift in the 21ˢᵗ Century*. Toronto: Stoddart.

Forbes, Hugh Donald. 2007. "Trudeau as the First Theorist of Canadian Multiculturalism." In *Multiculturalism and the Canadian Constitution*. S Tierney (ed.), pp. 27–42. Vancouver: UBC Press.

Forbes, Donald 2009. *What is Multiculturalism? A Political Answer*. Online publication available at http://www.utoronto.ca.

Ford, Caylan and Joan Delaney. 2008. Is Official Multiculturalism Failing in Its Own Homeland." *Epoch Times*. February 17.

Ford, Richard Thomson. 2005. *Racial Culture: A Critique*. Princeton: Princeton University Press.

Foster, Cecil. 2005. *Where Race Does Not Matter: The New Spirit of Modernity*. Toronto: Penguin.

Foster, Lois and Anne Seitz. 1999. "The Politicisation of Language Issues in 'Multicultural' Societies: Some Australian and Canadian Comparisons." *Canadian Ethnic Studies* 21(3): 55–73.

Foster, Lorne. 1998. *Turnstile Immigration: Multiculturalism, Social Order, and Social Justice in Canada*. Toronto: Thompson Education.

Fox, Nick J and Katie J Ward. 2008. "What Governs Governance, and How Does It Evolve? The Sociology of Governance-in-Action." *British Journal of Sociology* 59(3): 519–538.

Freeze, Colin. 2008. "Heritage Department Takes Aim at Religious Radicals." *The Globe and Mail*. September 1.

Frederickson, GM. 1999 Mosaics and Melting Pots. *Dissent* (Summer): 36–43.

Frideres, James. 2008. "Creating an Inclusive Society: Promoting Social Integration in Canada." In *Immigration and Integration in Canada in the Twenty-first Century*. J Biles, M Burstein, and J Frideres (eds.), pp. 77–102. School of Policy Studies. Kingston/Montreal: McGill/Queen's University Press.

Frideres, Jim and Rene Gadacz 2008 *Aboriginal Peoples in Canada*. 7th edition. Scarborough, ON: Pearson Education.

Friesen, Joe. 2005. "Blame Canada (for Multiculturalism)." *The Globe and Mail*. August 20.

Friesen, Wardlow. 2008. *Diverse Auckland: The Face of New Zealand in the 21ˢᵗ Century*. Published by the Asia-New Zealand Foundation. Wellington NZ, April.

Fukuyama, Francis. 2007. "Identity and Migration." *Prospect*. February. Issue no. 131. Available at http://www.prospect-magazine.co.uk.

Fulford, Robert. 2009. Taking Tolerance Too Far. *National Post*. May 16.

Furnival, JS. 1948. *Colonial Policy and Practices: A Comparative Study of Burma and Netherlands India*. Cambridge: Cambridge University Press.

Gagnon, Alain-G and Raffaele Iacovino. 2007. *Federalism, Citizenship, and Quebec: Debating Multinationalism*. Toronto: University of Toronto Press.

Gagnon, Lysiane. 2008. "Unmasking the Bloc on Integration." *The Globe and Mail*. May 19.

Galabuzi, Grace-Edward. 2006. *Canada's Economic Apartheid: The Social Exclusion of Racialized Groups in the New Century*. Toronto: Canadian Scholars Press.

Garcea, Joseph. 2006. "Provincial Multiculturalism Policies in Canada: 1974–2004: A Content Analysis." *Canadian Ethnic Studies* 38(3): 1–20.

Garcia, John A. 1995. "A Multicultural America: Living in a Sea of Diversity." In *Multiculturalism From the Margins*. Dean A Harris (ed.), pp. 29–38. Westport, CT: Greenwood Press.

Giddens, Anthony. 2006. *Misunderstanding Multiculturalism*. Available online at guardian co.uk. October 14.

Gillespie, Marie. 1996. *Television, Ethnicity, and Cultural Change*. London: Routledge.

Gilroy, Paul. 2004. *After Empire: Melancholia or Convivial Culture?* London: Routledge.

Giroux, Henry E. 1994. "Insurgent Multiculturalism as the Promise of Pedagogy." In *Multiculturalism: A Critical Reader*. DT Goldberg (ed.), pp. 325–343. Oxford, UK: Blackwell.

Giscombe, Katherine. 2008. Career Advancement in Corporate Canada: A Focus on Visible Minorities—Workplace Fit and Stereotyping. Toronto: Catalyst.

Gitlin, Todd. 1995. *The Twilight of Common Dreams. Why America is Wracked by Culture Wars*. New York: H. Holt.

Givens, Terri E. 2006. "Immigration and Immigrant Integration: Context and Comparisons." In *Changing Identities and Evolving Values: Is There Still a Transatlantic Community?* E Brimmer (ed.), pp. 65–72. Washington, DC: Centre for Transatlantic Relations, Johns Hopkins University.

Glazer, Nathanial. 1997. *We Are All Multiculturalists Now*. Cambridge, MA: Cambridge University Press.

Glazov, Jamie. 2006. "Symposium: the Death of Multiculturalism?" Available online at www. *FrontPageMagazine.com*.

Gleason, Philip. 1997. "Review of Postethnic America (Untitled)." *The Journal of American History* 84(2).

Goar, Carol. 2003. "Immigration Report Masks Truths." *Toronto Star*. November 8.

Goldberg, David Theo. 1994. "Introduction: Multicultural Conditions." In *Multiculturalism: A Critical Reader*. DT Goldberg (ed.), pp. 1–44. Oxford, UK: Blackwell.

Goldberg, David Theo and John Solomos (eds.). 2002. *A Companion to Race and Ethnic Studies*. Malden, MA: Blackwell.

Goren, William. 2007. *Concept of Undue Hardship and Reasonable Accommodation in the Employment Context*. Available online at www.mediate.com.

Goodey, Jo. 2007. " 'Race', Religion and Victimisation: UK and European Responses." In *Handbook of Victims and Victimology*. Sandra Walklate (ed.), pp. 423–445. Cullompton, UK: Willen Publishers.

Goodhart, David. 2004. *Too Diverse*. Available at http://www.geocities.com.

Goodspeed, Peter. 2006. "Death of Multiculturalism." *National Post*. November 25.

Granastein, JL. 2007. *Whose War Is It? How Canada Can Survive in the Post 9/11 World*. Toronto: HarperCollins Publishers.

Gray, John. 2007. *Black Mass. Apocalyptic Religion and the Death of Utopia*. New York: Farrar, Strauss, Giroux.

Gregg, Allan. 2006. "Identity Crisis. Multiculturalism: A Twentieth Century Dream Becomes a Twenty first Century Conundrum." *Walrus*. March, pp. 28–38.

Greif, Stuart (ed.). 1995. *Immigration and National Identity in New Zealand: One People, Two Peoples, Many Peoples*. Palmerston North NZ.: Dunmore Publishing.

Grillo, Ralph. 2007. "An Excess of Alterity? Debating Difference in a Multicultural Society." *Ethnic and Racial Studies* 30(6): 979–998.

Guardian Weekly. 2008. "No Flood but Rhetoric on Immigration Flows." November 28.

Guibernau, Monserrat. 2007. *The Identity of Nations*. Malden, MA: Polity Press.

Gunew, Sneja. 1993. "An Interview." In *Postcolonial Discourse and Changing Cultural Contexts: Theory and Criticism*. G Rajan and R Mohahram (eds.), pp. 205–217. Wesport, CT: Greenwood Press.

Gunew, Sneja. 1999. "Colonial Hauntings: The (Post) Colonialism of Multiculturalism in Australia and Canada." *Australian-Canadian Studies* 17(2): 11–31.

Gunew, Sneja. 2004. *Haunted Nations: The Colonial Dimensions of Multiculturalism*. New York: Routledge.

Gwyn, Richard. 1996. *Nationalism Without Walls: The Unbearable Lightness of Being Canadian*. Toronto: McClelland & Stewart.

Hagan, Jacqueline Maria. 2006. "Negotiating Social Membership in a Contemporary World." *Social Forces* 85(2): 631–642.

Hage, Ghassan. 1998. *White Nation: Fantasies of White Supremacy in a Multicultural Society*. Sydney: Pluto Press.

Hage, Ghassan. 2003. *Against Paranoid Nationalism: Searching for Hope in a Shrinking Society*. Sydney: Pluto Press.

Hage, Ghassan. 2006. "The Doubts Down Under." *Catalyst Magazine*. May 17. Available online http://www.catalystmagazine.org.

Halka, Elizabeth. 1996. "Madam Justice Bertha Wilson: A 'Different' Voice in the Supreme Court." *Alberta Law Review* 35(1): 242–265.

Hall, Stuart. 2000. "Conclusion: The Multicultural Question." *Unsettled Multiculturalisms: Diasporas, Entanglements, Transruptions*. B Hesse (ed.). London: Zed Books.

Hamilton, Graeme. 2008. Quebec Demands Immigrants Sign Off On "Shared Values." *National Post*. October 30.

Hannerz, Ulf. 1992. *Cultural Complexity: Studies in the Social Organization of Meaning*. New York: Columbia University Press.

Hansen, Randall. 2007. "Diversity, Integration, and the Turn from Multiculturalism in the United Kingdom." In *Belonging?* K Banting et al. (eds.), pp. 351–386. Montreal: IRPP.

Harris, Fred. 1995. *Multiculturalism From the Margins*. Westport, CT: Bergin and Harvey.

Harrison, Lawrence E. 2008. "The End of Multiculturalism." *National Interest* 93: 88–96.

Harty, S and M Murphy. 2005. *In Defence of Multinational Citizenship*. Vancouver: UBC Press.

Hashemi, Nader. 2008. "Political Islam Versus Secularism." *Literary Review of Canada* 16(7): 12–13.

Hasselback, D (ed.). 1998. *Multiculturalism in a World of Leaking Boundaries*. New Brunswick: Transaction Publishers.

Hawthorne, Lesleyanne. 2008. "The Impact of Economic Selection Policy on Labour Market Outcomes for Degree Qualified Migrants in Australia and Canada." *Choices* (Institute for Research on Public Policy) 14(5).

Healey, Justin (ed.). 2007. *Immigration and Citizenship*. Sydney: Spinney Press.

Helly, Denise. 1993. "The Political Regulation of Cultural Plurality: Foundations and Principles." *Canadian Ethnic Studies* 25(2): 15–31.

Helly, Denise. 2005. "Canadian Multiculturalism: Lessons for the Management of Cultural Diversity." In *Canadian and French Perspectives on Diversity*. Conference Proceedings, pp. 9–13, October 16. Published by Canadian Heritage.

Henry, Frances and Carol Tator. 1999. "State Policy and Practices as Racialized Discourse: Multiculturalism, the Charter, and Employment Equity." In *Race and Ethnic Relations in Canada*. 2nd edition, PS Li (ed.), pp. 88–115. Toronto: Oxford University Press.

Henry, Frances and Carol Tator. 2006. *The Colour of Democracy: Racism in Canadian Society*. 3rd edition. Toronto: Harcourt Brace/Nelson.

Hero, Rodney and Robert R Preuhs, 2006. "Multiculturalism and Welfare Policies in the USA: A State Level Comparative Analysis." In *Multiculturalism and the Welfare State*. K Banting and W Kymlicka (eds.), pp. 121–151. Toronto: Oxford University Press.

Hesse, Barnor. 1997. "It's Your World: Discrepant M/Multiculturalisms." *Social Identities* 3(3): 375–394.

Hesse, Barnor (ed.). 2000. *Un/Settled Multiculturalism: Diasporas, Entanglements, Transruptions*. New York: St. Martins Press.

Hewitt, Roger. 2005. *White Backlash and the Politics of Multiculturalism*. New York: Cambridge University Press.

Hickman, Mary J. 2007. "Multiculturalism in One Country?" *Economy and Society* 36(2): 318–324.

Hier, Sean and Josh Greenberg. 2002. "News Discourses and the Problematization of Chinese Migration to Canada." In *Discourses of Domination*. F Henry and C Tator (eds.), pp 138–162 Toronto: University of Toronto Press.

Hier, Sean and B. Singh Bolaria (eds.). 2007 Race and Racism. Peterborough ON.: Broadview Press.

Hier, Sean, Daniel Lett, and B. Singh Bolaria (eds). 2009 Racism and Justice. Halifax: Fernwood Books.

Higham, John. 1993. "Multiculturalism and Universalism: A History and Critique." *American Quarterly* 45(3): 195–219.

Hill, Christopher. 2007. "Bringing War Home. Foreign Policy Making in Multicultural Societies." *International Relations* 21(3): 259–283.

Hinze, Annika. 2007. Worlds Colliding? Multiculturalism in Theory and Practice. Paper presented to the Immigration, Minorities, and Multiculturalism in Democracies Conference. Montreal, October 25–27.

Hjort, Mette. 1999. Between Conflict and Consensus: Multiculturalism and the Liberal Arts. Canadian Aesthetics Journal 4 (Summer). Available online at http://www.uqtr.uquebec.ca.

Hollinger, David A. 1995. *Postethnic America Beyond Multiculturalism*. New York: Basis Books.

Hollinger, David A 2008 "Obama, Blackness, and Postethnic America." *The Chronicle of Higher Education* 54(25): B7.

Horton, JO and LE Horton. 2004. *Slavery and the Making of America*. New York: Oxford University Press.

Hudson, Michael. 1987. "Multiculturalism, Government Policy, and Constitutional Entrenchment – A Comparative Study." *Multiculturalism and the Charter: A Legal Perspective*. Canadian Human Rights Foundation (ed.), pp. 59–122. Toronto: Carswell.

Huijser, Henk. 2004. "Representing Multiculturalism in a Bicultural Nation." *International Journal of Diversity in Organisations, Communities, and Nations* 4.: 395–401.

Human Rights Commission. 2006. *Tui Tui Tuituia: Race Relations in 2006*. Wellington, NZ.

Human Rights Commission. 2007. *The Race Relations Report*. Wellington, NZ.

Human Rights Commission. 2008. *Tui Tui Tuituia: Race Relations in 2007*. Wellington, NZ.

Humpage, Louise. 2002. "Closing the Gaps?" The Politics of Maori Affairs Policy. Unpublished Ph.D. Thesis. Albany, NZ: Massey University.

Humpage, Louise. 2008. "Revision Required: Reconciling New Zealand Citizenship with Maori Nationalism." *National Identities* 10(3): 247–261.

Humpage, Louise and Augie Fleras. 2001. "Intersecting Discourses. Closing the Gaps, Social Justice, and the Treaty of Waitaingi." *Social Policy Journal of New Zealand* 16: 37–54.

Huntington, Samuel P. 2004 Who Are We? The Challenges to America's National Identity. New York: Simon & Schuster.

Hurst, Lynda. 2007. "Multiculturalism Policy Falling Behind the Times." *Toronto Star*. May 29.

Hyden, Goran, Julius Court, and Kenneth Mease. 2004. *Making Sense of Governance: Empirical Evidence from Sixteen Developing Countries*. Boulder, CO: Lynne Rienner Publishers.

Ibbitson, John. 2005. *The Polite Revolution: Perfecting the Canadian Dream*. Toronto: McClelland & Stewart.

Ibbitson, John. 2006. "Canada's Tolerance Conundrum." *The Globe and Mail*. September 7.

Ibbitson, John. 2007. "Let Sleeping Dogs Lie." In *Uneasy Partners*. J Stein et al. (eds.), pp. 49–61. Waterloo, ON: WLU Press.

Ignace, MB and RE Ignace. 1998. " 'The Old Wolf in Sheep's Clothing'. ": Canadian Aboriginal Peoples and Multiculturalism." In *Multiculturalism in a World of Leaking Boundaries*. Dieter Haselbach (ed.), pp. 101–132. New Brunswick, NJ: Transaction Publishers.

Ignatieff, Michael. 1995. "Nationalism and the Narcissism of Minor Differences." *Queen's Quarterly* 102(1): 1–25.

Ignatieff, Michael. 2001. "The Attack on Human Rights." *Foreign Affairs*. November/December: 102–114.

Ignatieff. 2001. *The Rights Revolution: Massey Series Lectures*. Toronto: *Anansi* Press.

IMISCOE (International Migration, Integration, Social Cohesion). 2006. Reassessing Multiculturalim in Europe: Critical Debates, Changing

Policies, and Concrete Practices. International Workshop, University of Oxford, June 30–July 1.

Inglis, Christine. 1996. *Multiculturalism: New Policy Response to Diversity.* MOST policy paper no 4. Paris.

Inglis, Christine. 2004. "Australian Education Changes and Challenges in Response to Multiculturalism, Globalization, and Transnationalism." *Migration, Education, and Change.* S Luchtenberg (ed.), pp. 186–205. London: Routledge.

Inglis, Christine. 2003. "Australian Judges Mull Integration, Multiculturalism." *Migration Policy Institute.* October.

Inglis, Christine. 2006. *On the Beach: Racial Confrontation in Australia.* Migration Information Source. February 1 Available online at http://www.migrationinformation.org.

Institute of Governance. 2007a. Aboriginal Governance. Available on line at http://www.iog.ca.

Institute of Governance. 2007b. Principles of Good Governance in the 21st Century. Policy Brief no. 15. Ottawa. Available online at http://www.iog.ca.

Ip, Manying and David Pang. 2005. "New Zealand Chinese Identity: Sojourners, Model Minority, and Multiple Identities." In *New Zealand Identities.* James Liu et al. (eds.), pp. 174–190. Wellington: Victoria University Press.

Isajiw, W (ed.). 1997. *Multiculturalism in North America and Europe: Comparative Perspectives on Interethnic Relations and Social Incorporation.* Toronto: Canadian Scholars Press.

Jackson, Sandra and Jose Solis (eds.). 1995. *Beyond Comfort Zones in Multiculturalism: Confronting the Politics of Privilege.* Westport, CT: Greenwood Press.

Jacobs, Dirk and Andrea Rea. 2007. "The End of National Models? Integration Courses and Citizenship Trajectories in Europe." *International Journal on Multicultural Societies* 9(2): 264–283.

Jacobs, Melinda. 2008. "Multiculturalism and Multicultural Issues in Online Gaming Communities." *Journal for Cultural Research* 14(4).

Jakubowicz, Andrew, H Goodall, J Marin, T Mitchell, L Randall, and K Seneviratne. 1994. *Racism, Ethnicity, and the Media.* Sydney: Allen & Unwin.

Jakubowicz, Andrew. 2005. "Multiculturalism in Australia.Apogee or Nadir?" *Canadian Diversity* 4(1): 15–18.

Jakubowicz, Andrew. 2007. "Political Islam and the Future of Australian Multiculturalism." *National Identities* 9(3): 265–280.

Jakubowicz, Andrew. 2008. *A Stunned Silence: The Slow Death of Multiculturalism.* From Australia Policy Online. Posted November 25, 2008. Available at http://andrewjakubowicz.com.

James, Carl (ed.). 2005. *Possibilities and Limitations: Multicultural Policies and Programs in Canada*. Halifax: Fernwood.

James, Jacquelyn B. 1997. "What are the Social Issues Involved in Focusing on *Difference* in the Study of Gender?" *Journal of Social Issues* 53(2): 213–232.

Jaret, Charles. 1995. *Contemporary Ethnic and Racial Relations*. Scarborough, ON: HarperCollins.

Jaworsky, John. 1979. A Case Study of Canadian Federal Government's Multiculturalism Policy, Unpublished MA Thesis, Department of Political Science, Carleton Universitiy, Ottawa.

Jayasuriya, D L. 1989 Immigration Policies and Ethnic Relations in Australia. IN Canada 2000: Race Relations and Public Policy. O.P. Dwivedi et al (eds.). pp. 103–142. Guelph ON.: University of Guelph Press.

Jean, Michaëlle. 2005. The Government's Policy of Multiculturalism Encourages People to Stay in Their Own Ethnic Ghettos. *NovoPress Info*. September 27. Available on line. http://www.novopress.info.

Jedwab, Jack. 2005. "Neither Finding Nor Losing Our Way: The Debate over Canadian Multiculturalism." *Canadian Diversity* 4(1): 95–102.

Jedwab, Jack. 2006. "Canadian Integration: The Elusive Quest for Models and Measures." *Canadian Diversity* 9(1): 97–103.

Jedwab, Jack. 2007. *Canadian 'Separatists' Value Accommodation of Religious Differences: Exploring the Relationship between Church-State Separation and Reasonable Accommodation*. Montreal: Association for Canadian Studies.

Jenson, Jane and Martin Papillon. 2001."The Canadian Diversity Model: A Repertoire in Search of a Framework." *Canadian Policy Research Network* Paper F/19. Ottawa, Available online at http://www.cprn.org.

Jimenez, Marina. 2007. "When Multi Morphs into Plural." *The Globe and Mail*. December 8.

Jimenez, Marina. 2009. "Blacks, Hispanics at Bottom of Income Ladder." *The Globe and Mail*. March 10.

Jiwani, Yasmin. 2006. *Discourses of Denial: Mediations on Race, Gender, and Violence*. Vancouver: UBC Press.

Johnson, Jay T. 2008. "Indigeneity's Challenge to the White Settler State: Creating a Third Space for Dynamic Citizenship." *Alternatives: Global, Local, Political* 33(1): 29–52.

Johnston, Patricia Maringi. G. 1994. "Examining a State Relationship: 'Legitimation' and Te Kohanga Reo." *Te Pua* 3(2): 22–34.

Joppke, Christian. 1999. "How Immigration Is Changing Citizenship: A Comparative View." *Ethnic and Racial Studies* 22(4): 629–652.

Joppke, Christian. 2004. "The Retreat of Multiculturalism in the Liberal State: Theory and Policy." *British Journal of Sociology* 55(2): 237–257.

Joppke, Christian. 2007. "Beyond National Models: Civic Integration Policies for Immigrants in Western Europe." *Western European Politics* 30(4): 1–22.

Joppke, Christian. 2008. "Immigration and the Identity of Citizenship: The Paradox of Universalism." *Citizenship Studies* 12(6): 533–546.

Joppke, C and E Morawska. 2003. *Toward Assimilation and Citizenship: Immigrants in Liberal Nation-States.* Basingstoke, UK: Palgrave Macmillan.

Jordan, Glenn and Chris Weedon. 1995. "The Celebration of Difference and the Cultural Politics of Racism." In: *Theorizing Culture.* B Adam and S Allan (eds.), pp.149–164. New York: New York University Press.

Joseph Rountree Foundation. 2008. *Immigration and Social Cohesion in the UK.* Ref 2249.

Jupp, James. 1986. Don't Settle for Less: Review of Migrant and Multicultural Programs and Services. Report for the Labour Government. Canberra: Australian Government Publishing Service.

Jupp, James. 1997. "Tacking into the Wind: Immigration and Multicultural Policy in the 1990s." *Journal of Australian Studies* 53: 29–39.

Jupp, James. 2005. "Immigration and Multiculturalism." In *Howard's Second and Third Governments.* C Aulich and R Wettenhaul (eds.), pp. 173–188. Sydney: University of New South Wales Press.

Karim, Karim H. 2002. *Islamic Peril: Media and Global Violence.* Montreal: Black Rose Books.

Karim, Karim H. 2007 "Nation and Diaspora: Rethinking Multiculturalism in a Transnational Context". *International Journal of Media and Cultural Politics* 2(3): 267–282.

Kay, Barbara. 2008. "Turning Self-hatred into a State Creed." *National Post.* April 9.

Kay, Jonathan. 2007. "Multiculturalism, R.I.P. (1982–2007)." *National Post.* April 25.

Keill, Roger and Kurt Hubner. 2005. "Introduction to a Debate on Migration, Diversity, Multiculturalism, Citizenship: Challenges for Cities in Europe and North America." *International Journal of Urban and Regional Research* 29(3): 641–643.

Keith, Michael. 2005. *After the Cosmopolitan? Multicultural Cities and the Future of Racism.* New York: Routledge.

Kelly, Jennifer. 1998. *Under the Gaze: Learning to be Black in White Society.* Halifax: Fernwood Publishing.

Kenney, Jason. 2008. *Address to the Canadian Club, Winnipeg Manitoba.* November 18.

Kerkyasharian, Stepan. 2005. "Multiculturalism in Australia: Finding or Losing Our Way?" *Canadian Diversity* 4(1): 109–112.

Kernerman, Gerald. 2005. *Multicultural Nationalism: Civilizing Differences, Constituting Community.* Vancouver: UBC Press.

Khan, Sheema. 2008. "Lessons of Canada to Heal the Wounds of Mumbai." *The Globe and Mail.* December 1.

Kim, Claire Jean. 2004. "Imagining Race and Nation in Multiculturalist America." *Ethnic and Racial Studies* 27(6): 987–1005.

Kivisto, Peter. 2002. *Multiculturalism in a Global Society.* New York: Blackwell.

Kivisto, Peter and Georganne Rundblad (eds.). 2000. *Multiculturalism in the United States: Current Issues, Contemporary Voices.* Thousand Oaks, CA: Pine Forge.

Kivisto, Peter and Wendy Ng. 2005. *Americans All.* 2nd edition. Los Angeles: Roxbury.

Kobayashi, Audrey. 1999. "Multiculturalism and Making a Difference: Comments on the State of the Multiculturalism Policy in Canada." *Australian-Canadian Studies* 17(2): 33–39.

Kobayashi, Audrey 2008. A Research and Policy Agenda for Second Generation Canadians. Canadian Diversity 6(2): 3–6.

Koenig, Matthias. 1999. Democratic Governance in Multicultural Societies. Discussion Paper No. 30. Management of Social Transformations (MOST). Available at http://www.unesco.org.

Koenig, Matthias. 2003. "Editorial. Pluralism and Multiculturalism in Colonial and Post-Colonial Societies." *International Journal on Multicultural Societies* 5(2): 104–105.

Koenig, Matthias and Paul de Guchteneire. 2004. "Political Governance of Cultural Diversity." In *Democracy and Human Rights in Multicultural Societies.* M Koenig and P de Guchteneire (eds.). UNESCO Publishing/Ashgate.

Koenig, Matthias and Paul de Guchteneire. 2007. Democracy and Human Rights in Multicultural Societies. UNESCO. Available on line http://unesco.org.

Koenigsberg, Richard. 2004. *Dying for One's Country: The Logic of War and Genocide.* Available online http://home.earthlink.net.

Kolig, Erich. 2006. "New Zealand Muslims: The Perimeters of Multiculturalism and its Legal Instruments." *New Zealand Sociology* 20(2).

Koopmans, Ruud. 2005. *Contested Citizenship: Immigration and Cultural Diversity in Europe.* Minneapolis: University of Minnesota Press.

Koopmans, Ruud, Ulf Hedetoft, and Adrian Favell. 2006. Not Easy Being Danish. Integration and Multiculturalism in a Comparative Perspective. Seminar at Danish Institute for International Studies. Copenhagen, November 16.

Kostash, Myrna. 2000. *The Next Canada: In Search of Our Future Nation.* Toronto: McClelland & Stewart.

Kramer, Jane. 2006. "The Dutch Model: Multiculturalism and Muslim Immigrants." *The New Yorker.* April 3: 60–67.

Kruhlak, Orest. 2003. Multiculturalism is About Inclusiveness, Social Justice, and Empowerment Says Former Director of Canada's Multiculturalism Program. Press Release, University of Alberta.

Kundnani, Arun. 2002. *The Death of Multiculturalism.* Available online at http://www.irr.org.uk.

Kundnani, Arun. 2007. *The End of Tolerance: Racism in 21st Century Britain.* Ann Arbor, MI: Pluto Press.

Kunz, Jean Lock and Stuart Sykes. 2008. From Mosaic to Harmony: Multicultural Canada in the 21st Century. Results of Regional Roundtables PRI (Policy Research Initiative) Project Cultural Diversity. Ottawa: Government of Canada.

Kuper, Adam. 2007. "It's Poverty, Stupid." *Catalyst Magazine.* March 20.

Kurien, Prema A. 2006. "Multiculturalism and 'American' Religion: The Case of Hindu Indian Americans." *Social Forces* 85(2): 723–741.

Kurthen, Hermann. 1997. "The Canadian Experience with Multiculturalism and Employment Equity: Lessons for Europe." *New Community* 23(2): 249–270.

Kymlicka, Will. 1995. *Multicultural Citizenship.* London: Oxford University Press.

Kymlicka, Will. 1998. *Finding Our Way: Rethinking Ethnocultural Relations in Canada.* Toronto: Oxford University Press.

Kymlicka, Will. 2000. "American Multiculturalism and the Nations Within." In *Political Theory and the Rights of Indigenous Peoples.* D Ivison et al. (eds.), pp. 216–236. Melbourne: Cambridge University Press.

Kymlicka, Will. 2001. *Politics of the Vernacular.* Don Mills, ON: Oxford University Press.

Kymlicka, Will. 2004/2007. The Global Diffusion of Multiculturalism: Trends, Causes, and Consequences. Paper originally delivered to the International Conference on Leadership, Education, and Multiculturalism in the Armed Forces, La Paz, Bolivia (2004); Reprinted in S. Tierney. (ed.) *Accommodating Cultural Diversity*, pp. 17–34. Aldershot: Ashgate; also in *Governing Diversity* (2007). R Panossian et al (eds.), pp. 11–18. EDG Kingston: Queen's University.

Kymlicka, Will. 2005. "The Uncertain Futures of Multiculturalism." *Canadian Diversity* 4(1): 82–85.

Kymlicka, Will. 2007a. "The Canadian Model of Diversity in Comparative Perspective." In *Multiculturalism and the Canadian Constitution.* S Tierney (ed.), pp. 61–90. Vancouver: UBC Press.

Kymlicka, Will. 2007b. "Disentangling the Debate." In *Uneasy Partners*. J Stein et al. (eds.), pp. 137–151. Waterloo, ON: WLU Press.

Kymlicka, Will. 2007c. "The Global Diffusion of Multiculturalism." In *Governing Diversity*. R Panossian et al. (eds.). Ethnicity and Democratic Governance. Kingston: Queen's University Press.

Kymlicka, Will. 2007d. *Multicultural Odysseys*. Toronto: Oxford University Press.

Kymlicka, Will. 2008. "Reply." *Ethnicities* 8(2): 277–281.

Kymlicka, Will and Bashir Bashir. 2008. *The Politics of Reconciliation in Multicultural Societies*. New York: Oxford University Press.

Kymlicka, Will and Magda Opalski (eds.). 2001. *Can Liberal Pluralism Be Exported? Western Political Theory and Ethnic Relations in Eastern Europe*. New York: Oxford University Press.

Laegaard, Sune. 2008. "Moderate Securalism and Multicultural Equality." *Politics* 28(3): 160–168.

Laviec, Jean Pierre. 2005. "Preface." In *Unity and Diversity in Multicultural Societies*. B Parekh (ed.). Geneva: International Institute for Labour Studies.

Lechner, Frank. 2006. *The Netherlands, Globalization, and National Identity*. Routledge.

Leeuwen, Bart van. 2008. "On the Effective Ambivalence of Living with Cultural Diversity." *Ethnicities* 8(2): 147–156.

Legrain, Philippe. 2006. *Immigrants: Your Country Needs Them*. New York: Little, Brown.

Lentin, Alana and Gavan Titley. 2008. "More Benetton than Barricades?" '*IN The Politics of Diversity in Europe*. A Lentin and G Titley (eds). Pp. 1–19. Strasbourg: Council of Europe.

Lentin, Alana and Gavan Titley. 2009. Questioning the European "Crisis of Multiculturalism' Conference Notes January 13. Available online at http://multiculturality.wordpress.com.

Levey, Geoffrey Brahm and Tariq Modood. 2009. *Secularism, Religion, and Multicultural Citizenship*. New York: Cambridge University Press.

Levine-Rasky, Cynthia. 2006. "Discontinuities of Multiculturalism." *Canadian Ethnic Studies* 38(3): 87–104.

Ley, David. 2005. "Post-Multiculturalism." Working Paper No. 10–17. Research on Immigration and Integration in the Metropolis. Vancouver: Vancouver Centre of Excellence.

Ley, David. 2007. Multiculturalism: A Canadian Defence. Working Paper No. 07–04. Research on Immigration and Integration in the Metropolis. Vancouver: Vancouver Centre of Excellence.

Li, Peter S. 1999. "The Multiculturalism Debate." In *Race and Ethnic Relations in Canada*. 2nd edition. PS Li (ed.), pp. 148–177. Toronto: Oxford University Press.

Li, Peter S. 2003. *Destination Canada: Immigration Debates and Issues.* Toronto: Oxford University Press.

Libin, Kevin. 2009. "This Man Wants to Reinvent Canadian Multiculturalism." *National Post.* March 28.

Lieberman, Robert C. 2006. "The Storm Didn't Discriminate: Katrina and the Politics of Color Blindness." *Du Bois Review* 3(1): 7–22.

Liu, James H. 2005. "History and Identity: A System of Checks and Balances for Aotearoa/New Zealand." In *New Zealand Identities.* James Liu et al. (eds.), pp. 69–87. Wellington: Victoria University Press.

Lloyd, John. 2002. "The End of Multiculturalism." *New Statesman.* May 27.

Longley, K. 1999. "Beyond Multiculturalism: Australia and Canada." *Australian-Canadian Studies* 17(2): 75–83.

Lovell, David W. 2003. *Critical Essays on Contemporary European Culture and Society.* New York: Peter Lang.

Lupul, Manoly. 2005. *The Politics of Multiculturalism: A Canadian-Ukrainian Memoir.* Edmonton: Edmonton Institute of Ukrainian Studies Press.

Maaka, Roger and Augie Fleras. 2005. *The Politics of Indigeneity.* Dunedin, NZ: Otago University Press.

Maaka, Roger and Augie Fleras. 2008. "Contesting Indigenous Peoples Governance." In *Aboriginal Self-Government In Canada.* 3rd edition. Y Belanger (ed.), pp. 69–105. Saskatoon: Purich Publishing.

Mac Einri, Piaris. 2007. "The Challenge of Migrant Migration in Ireland." *International Journal on Multicultural Societies* 9(1): 75–90.

Mackey, Eva. 1998. *The House of Difference: Canadian Politics and National Identity in Canada.* London: Routledge.

Magsino, R. 2000. "The Canadian Multiculturalism Policy: A Pluralist Ideal Revisited." In *21st Century Canadian Diversity.* S Nancoo (ed.), pp. 320–341. Toronto: Canadian Scholars Press.

Mahtani, Minelle. 2002. "Interrogating the Hyphen-Nation: Canadian Multiculturalism Policy and Mixed Race Identities." *Social Identities* 8(1).

Malik, Abdul-Rehman. 2007. "Take Me to Your Leader." *Eurozine.* Available online at http://www.eurozine.com.

Malik, Kenan. 2001. *The Trouble with Multiculturalism.* December 18. Available online http://www.spiked-online.com.

Malik, Kenan. 2008. Mistaken Identity. *Eurozine* (originally in the *New Humanist*). Available online at http://www.eurozine.com.

Manji, Irshad. 2005. Not all Traditions Deserve Respect. NY Times, Reprinted in the National Post, August 11.

Martin, Jack. 2006. The Immigrant Population of the United States in 2006. A Report by the Federation for American Immigration Reform (FAIR). Washington, D.C.

Martiniello, Marco. 1998. "Wieviorka's Views on Multiculturalism: A Critique." *Ethnic and Racial Studies* 21(5): 911–919.

Massey News. 2007. Study Finds Maori Views on Immigration Hardening. Available on line at http://www.masseynews.massey.ac.nz.

May, Harvey. 2004. *Broadcast in Colour: Cultural Diversity and Television Programming in Four Countries.* Available on line.

May, Stephen (ed.). 1999. *Critical Multiculturalism.* Madison: University of Wisconsin Press.

May, Stephen. 2004. "Multiculturalism and Biculturalism: Implications for Language Policy." In *Tangata Tangata.* P Spoonley et al. (eds.), pp. 247–264. Palmerston North NZ: Dunmore.

McAndrew, Marie. 2007. "Quebec's Interculturalism Policy: An Alternative Vision." In *Belonging?* K Banting et al. (eds.), pp. 143–154. Montreal: IRPP.

McDonald, Mark and Carsten Quell. 2008. "Bridging the Common Divide: The Importance of Both 'Cohesion' and 'Inclusion'." *Canadian Diversity* 12: 35–38.

McGarry, John and Brendan O'Leary. 2007. "Integration vs Accommodation." In *Governing Diversity.* R Panossian et al. (eds.), pp. 19–30. Kingston: Queen's University Press.

McGauran, Peter. 2005. "Interview with the Australian Minister for Citizenship and Multicultural Affairs." *Canadian Diversity* 4(1): 6–9.

McKnight, David 2005. Beyond Right and Left. New Politics and the Culture Wars. Sydney: Allen & Unwin.

McLaren, Peter. 1994. "White Terror and Oppositional Agency: Towards a Critical Multiculturalism." In *Multiculturalism: A Critical Reader.* DT Goldberg (ed.), pp. 45–74. Oxford, UK: Blackwell.

McRoberts, Kenneth. 1997. *Misconceiving Canada: The Struggle for National Unity.* Toronto: Oxford University Press.

McRoberts, Kenneth. 2001. "Canada and the Multinational State." *Canadian Journal of Political Science.* 24(4): 683–713.

McRoberts, Kenneth. 2003. "Managing Cultural Differences in Multinational Democracies." In *The Conditions of Diversity in Multinational Democracies.* A-G Gagnon et al. (eds.). pp. 1–14. Montreal: IRRP.

Meer, Nasar and Tariq Modood. 2008. The Multicultural State We're In: Muslims, "Multiculture" and the "Civic Rebalancing" of British Multiculturalism. *Political Studies* September, pp. 1–25.

Mendelsohn, Matthew. 2003. "Birth of a New Ethnicity." In *The New Canadians.* E Anderssen and M Valpy (eds.), pp. 59–66. Toronto: McClelland & Stewart.

Melbourne, Hineana. (ed.) 1995. *Maori Sovereignty, Maori Perspectives.* Auckland: Penguin.

Michaels, Walter Benn. 2007. *The Trouble with Diversity. How We Learned to Love Identity and Ignore Inequality.* New York: Henry Holt.

Migration Information Source. 2005. A New Century: Immigration and the US. Migration Policy Institute.

Migration Information Source. 2006. Top 10 Migration Issues of 2006. Issue #1. Good-bye Multiculturalism—Hello Assimilation? Migration Policy Institute. Available online at http://migrationpolicy.org.

Migration News. 2007. Australia, New Zealand. 14(3): July.

Migration Policy Institute. 2007. United States Historical Immigration Trends. Washington, DC.

Ministry of Social Development. 2007 *Connecting Diverse Communities Project.* Available online at http://www.msd.govt.nz.

Minogue, Kenneth. 2005. "Introduction. Multiculturalism: A Dictatorship of Virtue." In *The Poverty of Multiculturalism.* P West (ed.). London: Civitas.

Mirza, Munira. 2006. "Tribal Thinking." *Catalyst.* July 14.

Mirza, Munira, Abi Senthikumaran, and Zein Ja'far. 2007. *Living Apart Together: British Muslims and the Paradox of Multiculturalism.* London: Policy Exchange.

Mitchell-Powell, Brenda. 1993. "Color Me Multicultural." *Multi-Cultural Review* 1(4): 15–17.

Modood Tariq. 2003. *Muslims and European Multiculturalism.* Available online at http://www.opendemocracy.net.

Modood, Tariq. 2005a. *Multicultural Politics: Racism, Ethnicity, and Muslims in Britain.* Edinburgh: Edinburgh University Press.

Modood, Tariq. 2005b. "Rethinking Multiculturalism after 7/7." *Open Democracy.* September 29. Available online at http://www.opendemocracy.net.

Modood, Tariq. 2006. "British Muslims and the Politics of Multiculturalism." In *Multiculturalism, Muslims and Citizenship.* T Modood et al. (eds.), pp. 37–56. New York: Routledge.

Modood, Tariq. 2007a. *Multiculturalism and National Identity.* May. Available at http://www.australiansall.com.au.

Modood, Tariq. 2007b. Multiculturalism and Nation-Building Go Hand in Hand." *Guardian Unlimited.* May 23. Available on line at http://www.guardian.co.uk.

Modood, Tariq. 2007c. *Multiculturalism: A Civic Idea.* Polity Press.

Modood, Tariq. 2008. "Multiculturalism and Groups." *Social and Legal Studies* 17(4): 549–553.

Modood, Tariq and Fauzia Ahmad. 2007. "British Muslim Perspectives on Multiculturalism." *Theory, Culture, & Society* 24(2): 187–213.

Modood, Tariq and Prina Jane Werbner. 1997. *The Politics of Multiculturalism in the New Europe.* New York: Zed Books.

Moens, Alexander and Martin Collacott. 2008. "Introduction." In *Immigration Policy and the Immigration Threat in Canada and the United States.* Vancouver: Fraser Institute. Available online at www.fraserinstitute.org.

Moghaddam, Fathali M. 2008. *Multiculturalism as Intergroup Relations.* Washington, DC: American Psychological Association.

Monod, Jean Claude. 2006. "The Integration of Islam in European Countries: Models and Developments" *Changing Identities and Evolving Values: Is There Still a Transatlantic Community?* E Brimmer (ed.), pp. 73–84. Washington, DC: Centre for Transatlantic Relations, Johns Hopkins University.

Moore, Molly. 2008. E.U. Moves to Standardize Immigration Policy. Illegal Residents Could be Jailed for as Long as 18 Months Pending Deportation. Washington Post Foreign Service. June 19.

Moosa, Zohra. 2007. "Minding the Multicultural Gap." *Catalyst.* March 16. Available online at http://www.catalystmagazine.com.

Morphet, Janet. 2007. "Embracing Multiculturalism: The Case of London." In *Migration and Cultural Inclusion in the European City,* In Migration and Cultural Inclusion in the European City. W. Neill and H-V Schwedler (eds.). pp. 167–183. New York: Palgrave Macmillan.

Muir, Rick. 2007. The New Identity Politics. Institute for Public Policy Research.

Munck, Ronaldo. 2008. Multiculturalism and the Integration Agenda. Review Essay. Translocation 3(1).

Munshi, D. 1998. "Media, Politics, and the Asianisation of Polarized Immigration Debate in New Zealand." *Australian Journal of Communication* 25(1).

Murray, Ted 2008. "The Media's Delusional Take on Multiculturalism." *Canada Free Press.* Available on line.

Nagle, John. 2008. "Multiculturalism's Double Bind." *Ethnicities* 8(2): 177–198.

Nana, Chavi Keeney. 2007. With Strict Policies in Place, Dutch Discourse on Integration Becomes More Inclusive. Migration Policy Institute. April.

National Association for Multicultural Education 2003 Definition of Multiculturalism. Available online at http://www.nameorg.org.

National Statement on Religious Diversity. 2006. Available online at www.hrc.co.nz.

Neill, William JV and Hanns-Uve Schwedler (eds.). 2007. *Migration and Cultural Inclusion in the European City.* New York: Palgrave.

Nelson-Carr, Lindy. 2008. Editorial. *Diversity Matters (published by the Queensland Government, Brisbane, Australia).* Autumn, p. 4.

Norton-Taylor, Richard. 2008. "Deference to Multiculturalism Undermines Those Fighting Extremism." *The Guardian.* February 15.

New Agenda. 2003. "Multicultural Australia: United in Diversity." *Updating the 1999 New Agenda for Multicultural Australia: Strategic Directions for 2003–2006.* Canberra: Australian Government Publishing Service.

New Zealand Parliament. 2008. "Multiculturalism Bill—Possible Introduction." *Parlimentary Debates* (Hansard) Vol. 649, p. 17 845.

Nugent, Amy. 2006. "Demography, National Myths, and Political Origins: Perceiving Official Multiculturalism in Quebec." *Canadian Ethnic Studies* 38(3): 21–36.

Nye, Malory. 2007. "The Challenges of Multiculturalism." *Culture and Religion* 8(2): 109–123.

O'Donnell, Mike. 2007. "We Need Human Rights, Not Nationalism 'Lite'." *Ethnicities* 7(2): 248–283.

OECD. 2008. A Profile of Immigrant Populations in the 21st Century. Data from OECD Countries. Available online at http://oecd.org.

O'Hare, Noel. 2004. *The Unfriendly Isles.* Carter Centre. Available online at www.cartercentre.org.

Okin, Susan (ed.). 1999. *Is Multiculturalism Bad For Women?* Princeton: Princeton University Press.

Olsen, Johan P. 2005. Unity and Diversity: European Style. Working Paper no. 24. ARENA: Centre for European Studies. Available online www.arena.uio.no.

Orwin, Clifford. 2007. Shallow Diversity—Our National Muddle." *The Globe and Mail.* November 2.

O'Sullivan, Dominic. 2006. *Beyond Biculturalism.* Wellington NZ: Huia Publishers.

Panossian, R, B Berman, and A Linscott. 2007. "The Missing Piece: The Politics of Identity." In *Governing Diversity: Democratic Solutions in Multicultural Societies.* R Panossian et al. (eds.), pp. 7–10. EDG Ethnicity and Democratic Governance. Kingston: Queen's University.

Papademetriou, DM. 2007. "Preface, the Blair Years." In *Immigration Under New Labour.* Will Somerville. Migration Policy Institute. Available online at http://www.migrationpolicy.org.

Parekh, Bhikhu. 1999. *Rethinking Multiculturalism: Cultural Diversity and Political Theory.* Cambridge MA: Harvard University Press.

Parekh, Bhikhu. 2000. "Preface." *The Future of Multi-Ethnic Britain – Report on the Commission on the Future of Multi-Ethnic Britain.* London: Profile Publishers.

Parekh, Bhikhu. 2005. *Unity and Diversity in Multicultural Societies.* Geneva: International Institute for Labour Studies.

Parekh, Bhikhu. 2006. "Europe, Liberalism, and the 'Muslim Question'." In *Multiculturalism, Muslims, and Citizenship*. T Modood et al. (eds.), pp. 179–203. New York: Routledge.

Parekh, Bhikhu. 2008. *A New Politics of Identity: Political Principles for an Interdependent World*. New York: Palgrave Macmillan.

Parrillo, Vincent. 2009. *Diversity in America*. 3rd edition. Thousand Oaks, CA.:Pine Forge Press.

Pearce, Patrick WJ. 2006. Bridging, Bonding, and Trusting: The Influence of Social Capital and Trust on Immigrants' Sense of Belonging to Canada. Atlantic Metropolis Working Paper Series.

Pearce, Nick. 2007. "Not Less Immigration, but More Integration." In *Britishness. Towards a Progressive Citizenship*. Nick Johnson (ed.), London: The Smith Institute.

Pearson, David 1994. "Canada Compared: Multiculturalism and Biculturalism in Settler Societies." ISER Occasional Paper No. 3. Memorial University, Newfoundland.

Pearson, David. 1995. "Multi-Culturalisms and Modernisms: Some Comparative Thoughts." *Sites* 30 (Autumn): 9–30.

Pearson, David 1996. "Crossing Ethnic Thresholds: Multiculturalisms in Comparative Perspective." In *Nga Patai*. P Spoonley et al. (eds.), pp. 247–266. Palmerston North: Dunmore.

Pearson, David. 2001. *The Politics of Ethnicity in Settler Societies*. London: Palgrave.

Pearson, David. 2004. "Rethinking Citizenship in Aotearoa/New Zealand." In *Tangata Tangata: The Changing Ethnic Contours of New Zealand*. P Spoonley et al. (eds.), pp. 291–314. Palmerston North NZ: Dunmore.

Pearson, David. 2005. "Citizenship, Identity, and Belonging: Addressing the Mythologies of the Unitary Nation State in Aotearoa/New Zealand." In *New Zealand Identities*. James Liu et al. (eds.), pp. 21–37. Wellington: Victoria University Press.

Peleg, Ilan. 2007. *Democratizing the Hegemonic State. Political Transformation in the Age of Identity*. Cambridge University Press.

Pendakur, Krishna. 2005. *Visible Minorities in Canada's Workplaces: A Perspective on the 2017 Projection*. Vancouver, BC: Metropolis Project.

Penninx, Rinus. 2005. "The Vicissitudes of Dutch Integration Policies." *Canadian Diversity* 5(1): 57–62.

Penninx, Rinus, Blanca Garces-Mascarenas, and Peter Scholten. 2005. Policymaking Related to Immigration and Integration: A Review of the Literature of the Dutch Case. Country Report on the Netherlands. IMISCOE.

Penslar, Derek. 2005. *Contemporary Anti-semitism: Canada and the World*. Toronto: University of Toronto Press.

Peter, Karl. 1978. Multi-cultural Politics, Money, and the Conduct of the Canadian Ethnic Studies. *Canadian Ethnic Studies Association Bulletin* 5: 2–3.

Pew Forum on Religion and Public Life. 2007. Religious Affiliation. Report No. 1.

Phillips, Anne. 2007. *Multiculturalism Without Culture*. Princeton: Princeton University Press.

Phillips, Anne and Sawitri Saharso. 2008. "Guest Editorial: The Rights of Women and the Crisis of Multiculturalism." *Ethnicities* 8(3): 291–301.

Phillips, Melanie. 2006. *Londonistan*. New York: Encounter Books.

Phillips, Trevor. 2005a. "Multiculturalism Plus. Cited in Editorial of *The Globe and Mail*. October 14.

Phillips, Trevor. 2005b. "After 7/7: Sleepwalking to Segregation." *Commission for Racial Equality*. September 22.

Phillips, Trevor. 2005c. *New Perspectives on Multiculturalism*. Presentation to WOSK Centre for Dialogue. Vancouver, February 15.

Phillips, Trevor. 2007. "Britishness and Integration." *Britishness: Towards a Progressive Citizenship*. Nick Johnson (ed.), pp. 38–47. London: The Smith Institute.

Phillips, Trevor. 2008. "Multiculturalism's Nemesis." Lynda Hurst in the *Toronto Star* March 15.

Pieterse, Jan Nederveen. 2007. *Ethnicities and Global Multiculture*. Lantham, MD: Rowman and Littlefield Publishers.

Pilkington, Andrew. 2007. "In Defence of Both Multiculturalism and Progressive Nationalism." *Ethnicites* 7: 269–278.

Possner, Michael. 1997. "A Battlefield Primer on Multiculturalism. A Review." *Globe and Mail*. July 12.

Povinelli, E A 1998 "The State of Shame: Australian Multiculturalism and the Crisis of Indigenous Citizenship" Critical Inquiry 24: 575–610.

Price, Charles. 1999. "Australia's Population: Ethnic Origins." *People and Place* 7(4): 12–16.

Prins, B and S Saharso. 2008. "In the Spotlight: A Blessing and a Curse for Women in the Netherlands." *Ethnicities* 8(3): 365–384.

Putnam, Robert. 2007. "E Pluribus Unum: Diversity and Community in the 21st Century." *Scandinavian Political Studies* 30(2): 137–174.

Queensland Government. 2004. *Multicultural Queensland – Making a World of Difference*. Queensland Government Multicultural Policy. Brisbane: Queensland Government.

Queensland Government. 2008. *Multicultural Highlights 2006–07*. Brisbane: Queensland Government.

Ramadan, Tariq. 2008. *Europe's Islam Question*. December 4 Available online at http://www.guardian.co.uk.

Ravitch, Diane (ed.) 1990 The American Reader. Words That Moved a Nation. New York: HarperCollins.

Razack, Sherene. 2004. Dark Threats and White Knights: The Somalia Affair, Peacekeeping and the New Imperialism. Toronto: University of Toronto Press.

Reitman, Oonagh. 2005. "Multiculturalism and Feminism." Ethnicities 5(2): 216–247.

Reitz, Jeffrey. 2009. "Assessing Multiculturalism as a Behavioural Theory". In Multiculturalism and Social Cohesion: Potentials and Challenges of Diversity. J G Reitz et al. (eds), pp. 1–43. Springer.

Reitz Jeffrey and Raymond Breton. 1994. "The Illusion of Difference." Realities of Ethnicity in Canada and the United States. Toronto: C.D. Howe Institute.

Reitz, Jeffrey and Rupa Banerjee. 2007. "Racial Inequality, Social Cohesion, and Policy Issues." In Belonging? K Banting et al. (eds.), pp. 489–546. Montreal: IRPP.

Rex, John. 1998. "The Problematics of Multicultural and Multinational Societies." Ethnic and Racial Studies 20(3): 1–15.

Rex, John and Gurharpal Singh (eds.). 2004. "Governance in Multicultural Societies." Research in Migration and Ethnic Relations Series. Ashgate: Aldershot.

Rhodes, RAW. 1996. "The New Governance: Governing without Government." Political Studies 44: 652–667.

Rizvi, Fazal. 1994. "The New Right and the Politics of Multiculturalism in Australia." In Multiculturalism and the State, Vol. 1., collected seminar papers no. 47. University of London: Institute of Commonwealth Studies.

Robbins, Jane. 2007. "The Howard Government and Indigenous Rights: An Imposed National Unity." Australian Journal of Political Science 42(2): 315–328.

Robinson, Andrew M. 2007. Multiculturalism and the Foundations of Meaningful Life: Reconciling History, Identity, and Community. Vancouver: UBC Press.

Royal Commission. 1996. "Looking Forward, Looking Backward." Vol. 1. Report of the Royal Commission on Aboriginal Affairs. Ottawa: Minister of Supply and Services.

Rubinstein, Amnon. 2006. "The End of Multiculturalism." New York Sun. May 1.

Rummell, RJ. 2005. Genocide: Meaning and Definition. Available at www.hawaii.edu/powerkills.

Rutter, Jill, Maria Latorre, and Dhananjayan Sriskandarajah. 2008. Beyond Naturalisation: Citizenship Policy in the Age of Super Mobility. London. Institute for Public Policy Research.

Sacks, Sir Jonathan. 1997. *The Politics of Hope*. London: Jonathan Cape.

Sacks, Sir Jonathan. 2007. *The Home We Build Together: Recreating Society*. New York: Continuum US.

Sajoo, A. 1994. "New Dances with Diversity." *Policy Options*. December 14–19.

Salee, Daniel. 2007. "The Quebec State and the Management of Ethnocultural Diversity: Perspectives on an Ambiguous Record." In *Belonging?* K Banting et al. (eds.), pp. 105–142. Montreal: IRPP.

Salmon, Jacqueline L. 2008. "Believing in a Higher Power." *Hamilton Spectator*. Associated Press. June 28.

Samuel, J and D Schachhuber. 2000. "Perspectives on Canadian Diversity." *21ˢᵗ Century Canadian Diversity*. S Nancoo (ed.), pp. 14–35. Mississauga: Canadian Scholars Press.

Sandercock, Leonie. 2003. Rethinking Multiculturalism for the 21ˢᵗ Century. Working Paper No. 03–14. Research on Immigration and Integration in the Metropolis. Vancouver: Vancouver Centre of Excellence.

Sandercock, Leonie. 2005. "A Lifelong Pregnancy? Immigrants and the Crisis of Multiculturalism." *Dialogue on the Future of Multiculturalism in BC*. WOSK Centre for Dialogue. Vancouver, February 14.

Sardar, Ziauddin. 2005. "Book Review" *New Statesman*. August 1.

Satzewich, Vic and Lloyd Wong (eds.). 2006. *Transnational Identities and Practices in Canada*. Vancouver: UBC Press.

Saul, John Ralston. 2008. *A Fair Country: Telling Truths About Canada*. Toronto: Viking.

Saunders, Barbara and David Haljan (eds.). 2003. *Wither Multiculturalism? A Politics of Dissensus*. Leuven: Leuven University Press.

Saunders, Doug. 2004. "Going Un-Dutch: Can You Really Riot for Tolerance?" *The Globe and Mail*. November 13.

Schain, Martin. 2008. *The Politics of Immigration in France, Britain and the United States*. New York: Palgrave Macmillan.

Schlesinger Jr, Arthur M. 1992. *The Disuniting of America: Reflections on a Multicultural Society*. New York: Norton.

Schmidt, Alvin J. 1997. *The Menace of Multiculturalism: Trojan Horse in America*. New York: Praeger Publishers.

Schneider, Peter. 2004. "Across the Great Divide." *New York Times*. March 13.

Schwimmer, Erik (ed.). 1968. *The Maori People in the 1960s*. Auckland: Longman Paul.

Scott, James C. 1998. *Seeing Like a State: How Certain Schemes to Improve the Human Condition Have Failed*. New Haven: Yale University Press.

Secretary of State. 2002. Secure Borders, Safe Haven: Integration with Diversity in Modern Britain. Presented to Parliament by the Secretary of State for the Home Department by Command of Her Majesty.

Seidle, Leslie. 2007a. Diversity, Recognition, and Shared Citizenship in Canada. Presentation to the Roundtable: The Future of Multiculturalism—A German–Canadian Debate. Berlin. March 29.

Seidle, Leslie. 2007b. United States Country Profile/United Kingdom Country Profile. Commission de Consultation sure les pratiques d'accommodement reliees aux difference culturelles. Available online at http://www.accommodements.qc.ca.

Seidle, Leslie. 2007c. United Kingdom. Country Profile. Commission de Consultation sure les pratiques d'accommodement reliees aux difference culturelles. Available online at http://accommodements.qc.ca.

Seiler, Tamara Palmer. 2002. "Thirty Years Later: Reflections on the Evolution and Future Prospects of Multiculturalism." *Canadian Issues* (February): 6–8.

Sen, Amartya. 2006. "Identity and Violence." *The Illusion of Destiny.* New York: W W Norton.

Seuffert, Nan. 2006. *Jurisprudence of National Identity: Kaleidoscopes of Imperialism and Globalisation from Aotearoa New Zealand.* Burlington, VT: Ashgate Publishing.

Shabani, OP (ed.). 2007. *Multiculturalism and Law: A Critical Debate.* Cardiff: University of Wales Press.

Shachar, Ayelet. 2007. *Multicultural Jurisdictions: Cultural Differences and Women's Rights.*: Cambridge: Cambridge University Press.

Shohat, Ella and Robert Stam. 1994. *Unthinking Ethnocentrism: Multiculturalism and the Media.* New York: Routledge.

Siapera, Eugenia. 2006. "Multiculturalism Online: The Internet and the Dilemmas of Multicultural Politics." *European Journal of Cultural Studies* 9(1): 5–24.

Siapera, Eugenia. 2007. "Multiculturalism, Progressive Politics, and British Islam". *International Journal of Media and Cultural Politics* 2(3): 243–248.

Sibley, CG and JH Liu. 2004. Attitudes toward Biculturalism in New Zealand. *New Zealand Journal of Psychology* 33: 88–99.

Sibley CG and JH Liu. 2007. "New Zealand Bicultural? Implicit and Explicit Associations Between Ethnicity and Nationality in the New Zealand Context." *European Journal of Social Psychology* 37(6): 1222–1243.

Siddiqui, Haroon. 1999. "Wave the Flag for Canadian Mosaic." *Toronto Star.* July 1.

Siddiqui, Haroon. 2002. "European Liberals Failing to Lead Pluralistic Model." *Toronto Star.* February 17.

Siddiqui, Haroon. 2006. "The Muslim Malaise." *Toronto Star.* August 20.

Siddiqui, Haroon. 2007. "Don't Blame Multiculturalism." In *Uneasy Partners.* J Stein et al. (ed.), pp. 23–47. Waterloo, ON: WLU Press.

Simpson, Jeffrey. 2005. "There's a Lesson for All of Us from the Sharia Issue." *The Globe and Mail.* September 14.

Singham, Mervin. 2006. "Multiculturalism in New Zealand—the Need for a New Paradigm." *Aotearoa Ethnic Network Journal* 1(1). Available on line at http://www.aen.org.nz.

Singh, Jasmeet. 2007. "The End of Multicultural Europe." *Mozaik Magazine.* April. Available online at http://www.urbanmozaik.com.

Sivanandan, A. 2006. *Britain's Shame: From Multiculturalism to Nativism.* Available online at http://www.irr.org.uk.

Skidelsky, Robert. 2004. "The Killing Fields." *New Statesman.* January 26.

Slijper, Boris. 2004. "Cited in Going Un-Dutch: Can You Really Riot for Tolerance? By Doug Saunders." *The Globe and Mail.* November 13.

Smith, MG. 1965. *Plural Societies in British West Indies.* Berkeley CA: University of California Press.

Sniderman, Paul M and Louk Hagendoorn. 2007. *When Ways of Life Collide: Multiculturalism and its Discontents in the Netherlands.* Princeton: Princeton University Press.

Somerville, Will. 2007. "The Immigration Legacy of Tony Blair." *Migration Policy Institute.* May.

Song, Sarah. 2007. *Justice, Gender, and the Politics of Multiculturalism.* Berkeley CA: University of California Press.

Soroka, Stuart, Richard Johnston, and Keith Banting. 2006. Ties that Bind? Social Cohesion and Diversity in Canada. Published by the Institute for Research on Public Policy.

Spoonley, Paul. 2005. "Multicultural Challenges in a Bicultural New Zealand." *Canadian Diversity* 4(1): 19–22.

Spoonley, Paul. 2007. "He Iwi Tahi Tatou?" *Massey News.* April. Available on line at http://www.massey.ac.nz.

Spoonley, Paul and Andrew Trlin. 2004. Immigration, Immigrants, and the Media. Making Sense of a Multicultural New Zealand. Massey University. New Settlers Program.

Squires, Judith. 2007. "Negotiating Equality and Diversity in Britain: Towards a Differentiated Citizenship." *Critical Review of International Social and Political Philosophy* 10(4): 531–559.

Squires, Judith. 2008. "Multiculturalism, Multiple Groups, and Inequalities." *Social and Legal Studies* 17(4): 535–542.

Sriskandarajah, D and FH Road. 2005. *United Kingdom: Rising Numbers, Rising Anxieties.* Migration Policy Institute. London, May.

Sriskandarajah, D, L Cooley, and T Kornblatt. 2007. *Britain's Immigrants: An Economic Profile.* London: Institute for Public Policy Research.

St. Lewis, Joanne. 1996. "Identity and Black Consciousness in North America." In *Clash of Identities.* J Littleton (ed.), pp. 21–30. Englewood Cliffs, NJ: Prentice Hall.

Stein, Janice. 2007. "Searching for Equality." In *Uneasy Partners*. J Stein et al. (eds.), pp. 1–22. Waterloo, ON: WLU Press.

Stein, Janice et al. (eds.). 2007. *Uneasy Partners: Multiculturalism and Human Rights in Canada*. Waterloo, ON: WLU Press.

Stevenson, Wilf. 2007. "Preface." *Britishness: Towards a Progressive Citizenship*. Nick Johnson (ed.), pp. 3–4. London: The Smith Institute.

Stoffman, Daniel. 2002. *Who Gets In? What's Wrong with Canada's Immigration Program and How to Fix It?* Toronto: MacFarlane Waller and Ross.

Stratton, Jon. 1999. "Multiculturalism and the Whitening Machine, or How Australia Became White." In *The Future of Australian Multiculturalism*. G Hage and Couch (eds.). Sydney: Allen & Unwin.

Stratton, Jon and Ien Ang. 1998. "Multicultural Imagined Communities: Cultural Differences and National Identity in the USA and Australia." In *Multicultural States*. D Bennett (ed.), pp. 135–162. New York: Routledge.

Stuart, Ian. 2007. Toward a Bicultural and Multicultural Discipline. *He Wero-New Zealand Journal of Medical Studies* 10(2).

Sturgess, Gary. 1998–1999. "Review of *Seeing Like a State* by James C Scott." *Policy*. (December–February).

Sunahara, Anne. 1981. *The Politics of Racism: The Uprooting of Japanese Canadians During the Second World War*. Toronto: James Lorimer and Sons.

Swerdlow, Joel L. 2001. "Changing American." *National Geographic*. September.

Sykes, Stuart. 2008. A Survey of the World's Oceans: International Approaches to Managing Diversity and Implications for Second Generation Acculturation. PRI Project. Government of Canada.

Taras, Raymond and Rajat Ganguly. 2002. *Understanding Ethnic Conflict: The International Dimension*. Montreal: Longman.

Task Force. 2006. Call for Coalition of Municipalities Against Racism and Discrimination. Ontario Human Rights Commission, Toronto.

Tate, John William. 2009. "John Howard's 'Nation': Multiculturalism, Citizenship, and Identity." *Australian Journal of Politics and History* 55(1): 97–120.

Taylor, Charles. 1992. "The Politics of Recognition." In *The Politics of Recognition*. Amy Gutman (ed.), pp. 25–48. Princeton NJ: Princeton University Press.

Taylor, Charles. 2009. "Foreword: What is Secularism." In *Secularism, Religion, and Multicultural Citizenship*. G Levey and T Modood (eds.), pp. iv–xi. Cambridge University Press.

Te Puni Kokiri. 2008. *Maori Potential Approach*. Available online at http://www.tpk.govt.nz.

Teelucksingh, Cheryl and Grace-Edward Galabuzi. 2005. "Working Precariously: The Impact of Race and Immigrants Status on Employment Opportunities and Outcomes in Canada." *Canadian Race Relations Foundation*. Toronto.

Teicher, Julian, Chandra Shah, and Gerrard Griffin. 2000. Australian Immigration: The Triumph of Economics over Prejudice? Centre for Economics of Education and Training. Working Paper No. 33. Monash University, Melbourne.

Temelini, Michael. 2007. "Multicultural Rights, Multicultural Virtues: A History of Multiculturalism in Canada." In *Multiculturalism and the Canadian Constitution*. S Tierney (ed.), pp. 43–60. Vancouver: UBC Press.

Terkessidis, Mark. 2007. "Partners in Humanity. The Limits of Multicultualism: Muslims in Germany." *Common Ground News Service*, August 14. Available online at http://www.commongroundnews.org.

Terrazas, Aaron, Jeanne Batalova, and Velma Fan. 2007. *Frequently Requested Statistics on Immigrants in the United States*. Migration Policy Institute.

Thobani, Sunera 1995. "Multiculturalism: The Politics of Containment." In *Social Problems in Canada Reader*. A Nelson and A Fleras (eds.), pp. 213–216. Scarborough, ON: Prentice Hall.

Thobani, Sunera. 2007. *Exalted Subjects: Studies in the Making of Race and Nation in Canada*. Toronto: University of Toronto Press.

Tierney, Stephen. 2007. "Cultural Diversity: Normative Theory and Constitutional Practice." In *Accommodating Cultural Diversity*. S Tierney (ed.), pp. 1–16 Burlington, VT: Ashgate Publishing.

Tiryakian, Edward A. 2004. "Assessing Multiculturalism Theoretically: E Pluribus Unum, Sic et Non." In *Governance in Multicultural Societies*. J Rex and G Singh (eds.), pp. 1–18. Aldershot: Ashgate.

Tong, Rosemary Putnam. 1998. "Multiculturalism and Global Feminism." In *Feminist Thought*. 2nd edition. Boulder CO.:Westview Press.

Triandafyllidou, Anna, Tariq Modood, and Ricard Zapata-Barrero. 2006. "European Challenges to Multicultural Citizenship." In *Multiculturalism, Muslims, and Citizenship: A European Approach*. T Modood et al. (eds.), pp. 1–22. New York: Routledge.

Trounson, Rebecca. 2007. 1 in 4 Muslims back suicide bombings." *Toronto Star*. March 2.

Tsasis, Peter. 2008. "The Politics of Governance: Government-Voluntary Sector Relationship." *Canadian Public Administration* 51(2): 265–290.

Turner, Bryan S. 2006. "Citizenship and the Crisis of Multiculturalism. Review Article." *Citizenship Studies* 10(5): 607–618.

Turner, Terrance. 1994. "Anthropology and Multiculturalism: What Is Anthropology That Multiculturalists Should Be Mindful of It?" In *Multiculturalism: A Critical Reader*. D Goldberg (ed.), pp. 406–425. Cambridge: Blackwell.

Turton, Anthony R, H. Hattingh, GA Maree, DJ Roux, and M Claassen. (eds.). 2007. Governance as a Trialogue: Government-Society-Science in Transition. Springer.

Uberoi, Varun. 2008. "Do Policies of Multiculturalism Change National Identities?" *The Political Quarterly* 79(3): 404–415.

Ucarer, Emek M. 1997. "Introduction. The Coming of an Era of Human Uprootedness: A Global Challenge." In *Immigration into Western Societies: Problems and Policies*. E Ucarer and DJ Puchala (eds.), pp. 1–16. London: Cassells.

Uitermark, J, U Rossi and H van Houtum. 2005. "Reinventing Multiculturalism: Urban Citizenship and the Negotiation of Ethnic Diversity in Amsterdam." *International Journal of Urban and Regional Research* 29(3): 622–640.

Ujimoto, K Victor. 1999. "Studies of Ethnic Identity, Ethnic Relations, and Citizenship." In *Race and Ethnic Relations in Canada*. 2nd edition. PS Li (ed.), pp. 253–290. Toronto: Oxford University Press.

Ujimoto, K Victor. 2000. "Multiculturalism, Ethnic Identity, and Inequality." In *Social Issues and Contradictions in Canadian Society*. B Singh Bolaria (ed.), pp. 228–247. Toronto: Harcourt Brace.

UNDP. 2004. *Cultural Liberty in Today's Diverse World*. Summary: Human Development Report.

United Nations Report. 2006. *The Concept of Reasonable Accommodation In Selected National Disability Legislation*. Available online at www.un.org/esa/socdev/rights/

Vasta, Ellie. 1996. "Dialectics of Dominion: Racism and Multiculturalism." In *The Teeth Are Smiling*. E Vasta and S Castles (eds.), pp. 46–72. Sydney: Allen & Unwin.

Vasta, Ellie. 2007a. "From Ethnic Minorities to Ethnic Majority Policy: Multiculturalism and the Shift to Assimilationism in the Netherlands." *Ethnic and Racial Studies* 30(5): 713–740.

Vasta, Ellie. 2007b. Accommodating Diversity: Why Current Critiques of Multiculturalism Miss the Point. COMPAS (Centre on Migration, Policy, and Society). Working Paper No. 53. University of Oxford.

Vasta, Ellie and Stephen Castles (eds.) 1996. *The Teeth Are Smiling: The Persistance of Racism in Multicultural Australia*. Sydney: Allen & Unwin.

Vertovec, Steven. 1996. "Multiculturalism, Culturalism, and Public Incorporation." *Ethnic and Racial Studies* 19(1): 49–68.

Vertovec, Steven. 2006. The Emergence of Super-Diversity in Britain. Working Paper No. 25. Centre on Migration, Policy, and Society. University of Oxford.

Vertovec, Steven. 2007. "Super-Diversity and Its Implications." *Ethnic and Racial Studies* 30(6): 1024–1054.

Vertovec, Steven and Susanne Wessendorf. 2004. "Migration and Cultural, Religious, and Linguistic Diversity in Europe." *An Overview of Issues and Trends*. COMPAS. Oxford UK:University of Oxford.

Victoria Multicultural Commission. 2008. Multicultural Affairs in Victoria. A Discussion Paper for a New Policy. Victoria University Institute for Community, Ethnicity, and Policy Alternatives. Melbourne.

Vinocur, John. 2008. From the Left, A Call to End the Current Dutch Notion of Tolerance. International Herald Tribune. December 29.

Vink, Maarten, P. 2007. "Dutch 'Multiculturalism' Beyond the Pillarisation Myth." *Political Studies Review* 5: 337–350.

Walker, James St. G. 1997 '*Race*', *Rights, and the Law in the Supreme Court of Canada*. Waterloo ON: Wilfrid Laurier Press/Osgoode Society for Canadian Legal History.

Walker, Ranginui. 1995. "Immigration Policy and the Political Economy in New Zealand." In *Immigration & National Identity in New Zealand*. SW Greif (ed.), pp. 282–301. Palmerston North: Dunmore.

Wallis, Maria and Augie Fleras. (eds.). 2009 *The Politics of Race in Canada*. Toronto: Oxford University Press.

Ward, Colleen and En -Yi Lin. 2005. "Immigration, Acculturation and National Identity in New Zealand." In *New Zealand Identities*. James Liu et al. (eds.), pp. 155–173. Wellington: Victoria University Press.

Waters Ian. 2007. "Policing, Modernity and Postmodernity." *Policing & Society* 17(3): 257–278.

Waters, Mary and Zoua M Vang. 2007. "The Challenges of Immigration to Race Based Diversity Politics in the United States." In *Belonging?* K Banting et al. (eds.). Montreal: IRRP.

Watt, Philip. 2006. "An Intercultural Approach to Integration." *Translocations* 1(1): 151–160.

Weinfeld, Morton. 2005. "The Changing Dimension of Canadian Anti-Semitism." *Contemporary Anti-Semitism: Canada and the World*. D Penslar (ed.), pp. 35–51. Toronto: University of Toronto Press.

West, Cornell. 1996. *The Affirmative Action Debate*. Reading MA: Addison-Wesley.

West, Patrick. 2005. *The Poverty of Multiculturalism*. London: Civitas, Institute for the Study of Civil Society.

Wieviorka, Michel. 1998. "Is Multiculturalism the Solution?" *Ethnic and Racial Studies* 21(5): 881–910.

Willett, Cynthia. 1998. *Theorizing Multiculturalism: A Guide to the Current Debate*. Malden, MA: Blackwell.

Wilson, V Seymour. 1995. "Canada's Evolving Multicultural Policy." In *Canada's Century: Governance in a Maturing Society*. C E S Franks et al. (eds.), pp. 165–195. Montreal/Kingston: McGill/Queen's University Press.

Wirten, Per. 2008. "Doing the World Differently." *Eurozine*. Available online at http://www.eurozine.com.

Wise, Amanda and Selvaraj (eds.) 2009 Everyday Multiculturalism. New York: Palgrave.

Wood, Patricia and Liette Gilbert. 2005. "Multiculturalism in Canada: Accidental Discourse, Alternative Vision, Urban Practice." *International Journal of Urban and Regional Research* 29(3): 679–691.

Yates, Joshua. 2001. "Debunking Diversity's Discontents." *The Hedgehog Review*: 3(2) 106–116.

Ye'or, Bat. 2005. *Eurabia: The Euro-Arab Axis*. Madison, NJ: Fairleigh Dickinson University Press.

Young, Audrey. 2008. "Peters: We Warned of Racial Crimes." *New Zealand Herald*. July 21.

Young, Iris. 1990. *Justice and the Politics of Difference*. Princeton: Princeton University Press.

Zachariah, Matthew, Alan Sheppard, and Leona Baratt. (eds.). 2004. *Canadian Multiculturalism: Dreams, Realities, Expectations*. Edmonton: Canadian Multicultural Education Foundation.

Zhou, Min. 1997. "Segmented Assimilation: Issues, Controversies, and Recent Research on the New Second Generation." *International Migration Review* 31(4): 975–1008.

Zick, Andreas, TF Pettigrew, and U Wagner. 2008. "Ethnic Prejudice and Discrimination in Europe." *Journal of Social Issues* 64(2): 233–251.

Index

Abbas, T., 2, 24, 170, 172
Abu-Laban, B., 80, 81
Abu Laban, Y., 75, 80, 81, 121
Adams, M., 60, 64, 207
Agocs, C., 65
Ahmed, S., 7, 165, 201
Aizenman, N. C., 94
Alba, R., 42
Alibhai-Brown, Y., 174, 175, 187, 196
Allen, C., 193
Aly, W., 120
Americanization, 95–6
Anderssen, E., 85
Ang, I., 33, 118
Anglo-conformity, 42
    see also assimilation
Anthias, F., 17, 20
anti-multiculturalism, 188, 194–200
Aotearoa, see New Zealand
Arends-Toth, J., 148, 149
Asari, E.-M., viii
Asch, M., 48
Ash, T., 167, 197
assimilation, 41–3
Australia, 113–28, 212
    diversity and difference, 115–17
    Queensland, 124–6
    Victoria, 123–4

Babacan, H. vii, 119, 120, 126
Baber, H. E., 99
Babican, H., vii
Backhouse, C., 44, 60
Bader, V., 7, 20, 51, 137, 195
Bak, H., 89
Banerjee, R., 46

Bannerji, H., 7, 19, 20, 67, 74, 187
Banting, K., xi, 13, 35, 52, 98, 205,
    220, 224
Barclay, K., 130
Bargh, M., 142
Barry, B., 8, 100, 177, 205, 206, 224
Bass, S., 13, 89, 90, 91, 98, 101, 102
Baubock, R., 85, 201, 206, 211
Bawer, B., 148
Bedford, R., 132
Beissinger, M. R., 26, 35
Belanger, Y., 62
Bell, M., 20
Ben-Eliezer, U., 16, 42, 47
Bennett, D., 10
Ben-Rafael, 48
Berliner, M., 57
Berman, B., x
Berns-McGowan, R., 219
Berry, J., 35, 85
Bertossi, C., 172
Bhabha, H., 12
Bhargava, R., 213
Bhattacharyya, G., 176
biculturalism, 48, 129–31, 138–40
    vs. multiculturalism, 140–1, see also
    New Zealand
Biles, J., 2, 137
binationalism, 48, 129–31
    see also biculturalism; New Zealand
Bissoondath, N., 208
black activists, 172
Blair, T., 169, 179
Bleich, E., 220
Bloemraad, I., 8, 38, 42, 48, 100, 190,
    200, 223

Blond, P., 95, 148, 197, 198
Bogaards, 26, 53
Bolaria, B. S., 61
Boli, J., 27, 102
Bouchard-Taylor Commission, 72–3, 81, 212
Bousetta, H., x, 202, 205
Boyd, M., 65
Bramadat, P., 74, 213
Breton, E., 68, 86
Breton, R., 89
Breugelmans, S. M., 149
Brighton, S., 176
Britain, 165–86
    see also Politics of Multiculturalism
Bromwell, D., 130, 137
Brubaker, R., 41, 42
Bruquetas-Callejo, M, 148, 151, 152, 153, 154, 156, 157, 158, 159
Buenker, J., 89
Bulbeck, C., 114
Buruma, I., 195, 196
Butt, R., 76

Cahill, D., 214, 218
Cameron, E., 19, 84, 208
Canada, 55–88, 189–92
    critiquing multiculturalism, 85–7
    diversity and difference, 58–60
    official multiculturalism, 62–73
Cantle Report, 181
Caplan, G., 40, 41
Cardozo, A., 11, 56, 84
Castles, S., xi, 128, 190
Caws, P., 11
celebratory multiculturalism, 101–2
challenges of multiculturalism, 210–213
Charter of Rights and Freedoms, 61, 65, 67, 81, 82
Cheema, G. S., 50
Cheng, H., 42
Chhatwal, K., 201

Chhotray, V., 49
Choudhry, S., ix, x, 29, 35, 47
Christchurch, 135
Citrin, J., 192
Civic Integration of Newcomers Act, 159
civic multiculturalism, 68–9
Clarke, I., 130, 137, 138, 190
Clausen, C., 90
Collacott, M., 85, 179, 199
collective rights, 107
Collett, E., 202
Commission on Integration and Cohesion, 168, 182
Commission for Racial Equality, 169–70
communitarian network, 102–5
Cooke, M., 78
Cooper, D., 32, 214
counterhegemony, 110
critical multiculturalism, 105–8
criticism of multiculturalism, 85–7
Crothers, C., 129
Cryderman, B., 78
cultural relativism, 106–7

Dale, D., 188
Dasko, D., 85
Davidson, S., 115
Day, R., 1
Deake, I., 40
De facto multiculturalism, 134–8
De Guchteneire, P. viii, 25
De Hart, B., 46
Dei, G. S., 20, 32, 33
De jure biculturalism, 138–40
De Souza, R., 130, 213
diversity politics, 27–34
diversity vs. difference, 31–4
    in Aotearoa New Zealand, 132–4
    in Australia, 115–17
    in Canada, 58–60
    in the Netherlands, 150–2
    in the United States, 92–5
Doerr, N., 139

Donaldson, I., 65
D'Souza, D., 99, 105
Duceppe, G., 86
Duncan, H., 85
Dunn, K., 127
Dupont, L., 57, 64, 87
Durie, M., 139, 140
Dustin, M., 3, 30, 168
Duyvendak, J. W., 155, 160, 161
Dyson, R., 133

Eaton, B., 136
Eckhardt, F., 13, 206
EDG, 23
Eisenberg, A., 203, 206
Eisenstein, Z., 107, 110, 111
Elder, C., 118
Eliadis, P., 66
Elkins, Z., 39
Eller, J., 105, 107
Elliott, J. L., 76
Elliott, M., 27, 102
Entzinger, 155, 161
equity multiculturalism, 65–8
ethnicity multiculturalism, 63–5
Ethnic Minority Policy, 149, 153–5
'Eurabia Thesis', 158
Eurocentrism, 110
Europe, 192–202
European Union, 81

Favell, A., 149
Federation for American Immigrant
    Reform, 93
Ferguson, L., 120
Fish, S., 28, 33, 57
Fitzpatrick, M., 174
Fix, M., 45, 94
Foote, D., 64, 208
Forbes, D., 4, 20
Ford, R. T., 20
Foster, L., 119, 120
Fox, 26, 49
Frederickson, G. M., 27
Freeze, C., 70, 205
Frideres, J., 44, 62

Friesen, J., 85, 130
Fukuyama, F., 51, 212
Furnival, J. S., 200

Gabriel, C., 75, 121
Gadacz, R., 62
Gagnon, A.-G., 6, 9, 13, 16, 52, 71, 82
Gagnon, L., 72, 74
Galabuzi, G.-E., 62
Gandhi, M., 213
Ganguly, R., 40
Garcea, J., 212
gender and multiculturalism, 215–18
genocide, 40–1
Giddens, A., 166, 170, 205, 221
Gilbert, L., 57, 74
Gilroy, P., 1
Giroux, H., 90, 107, 111
Glazer, N., 90, 99, 207
Goldberg, D. T., 17
Goodey, J., 56, 193
Goodhart, D., 177
Goodspeed, P., 194
governance, 23–53, 203–24
    conceptualizing, 49–53
    defining, 49
    historical patterns, 38–9
    models of, 39–48
    paradoxes in, 210–213
    paradox of multiculturalism, 26
    rethinking, 203–24
    theorizing, 37
Granastein, J., vii, 191
Gray, J., 213
Greenberg, J., 190
Gregg, A., 11, 188
Greif, S., 138
Grillo, R., 12, 15, 166, 181, 192
Guibernau, M., 25, 29, 51, 98, 100, 113,
    205, 211
Gunew, S., 13, 109
Gwyn, R., 85

Hagan, J., xi
Hage, G., vii, 10, 75, 118, 127, 128, 148,
    187, 197, 198

Hagendoorn, L., 10, 37, 149, 150, 152, 153, 154, 156, 161, 202
Haljan of saunders, 194
Hall, S., 6, 22, 32, 105
Hamilton, G., 71
Hansen, R., 34, 166, 167, 184, 193, 195, 221
Harper, S., 188
Harris, F., 107
Harrison, L, 208, 210
Harty, S., 86
Hashemi, N., 213
Hawthorne, L. A., 120
Healey, J., 121
hegemony, 69, 102
Helly, D., 74, 192
Henry, F., 62, 76
Hero, R., 89
Hesse, B., 11, 12, 83, 91
Hickman, M., 192
Hier, S., 61, 190, 191
Higham, J., 90
Hill, C., 11
historical perspectives on diversity, 29
Hjort, M., 5
Holland, see Netherlands
Hollinger, D., 33, 92, 108
Hooks, B., 108
Horton, J. O., 44
Horton, L. E., 44
Howard, J., 120–1, 220
Huijsers, H., 5, 130, 142
Hull, G., 57
Humpage, L., 130, 139, 141, 142
Huntington, S., 99
Hurst, L., 189, 221
Hyden, G., 49

Iacovino, R., 6, 9, 13, 16, 52, 71, 82
Ibbitson, J., 60, 192, 208, 216
identity politics, 107
Ignatieff, M., 21, 211
inclusive multiculturalism, 220–4
inclusiveness, 62–88, 220–4
Indonesia, 24

Inglis, C., 25, 41, 43, 47, 117, 118, 120
Institute for Public Policy Research, 167
institutional inclusiveness, 76–84
integration, 44–7
Integration policy in the Netherlands, 156–61
integrative multiculturalism, 71
interculturalism, 71–6
Ip, M., 136, 138, 144

Jacobs, D., x, 63, 147, 149, 158, 159, 162, 163, 181, 183, 202, 205
Jakubowicz, A., 2, 74, 128, 136, 218
Jaret, C., 41, 43, 45
Jawani, Y., 61
Jayasuriya, D. L., 117
Jean, M., 60, 86
Jedwab, J., 85, 188
Jimenez, M., 62, 94, 167
Johnson, J., 130, 140, 143, 144
Johnston, P. M., 28
Joppke, C., 28, 46, 147, 149, 156, 160, 162, 166, 178, 180, 190, 194, 198, 200
Joseph Rountree Foundation, 166
Jupp, J., 75, 118

Karim, K., 189
Kay, B., 188
Kay, J., vii, 188
Keith, M., 209
Kenney, J., 70
Kerkyasharian, S., 118
Khan, A., 55
Khan, S., 191
Kim, C. J., 7, 20, 106
Kivisto, P., 92, 97
Klein, N., 200
Kobayashi, A., 147
Koenig, M., viii, 25, 49, 213, 220
Koenigsberg, 41
Kolig, E., 134
Koopmans, R., 147, 195, 196, 199
Kostash, M., 57
Kramer, J., 155
Kruhlak, O., 63

Ku Klux Klan, 44
Kundnani, A., 91, 110, 127, 170, 173, 174, 177
Kung, H., 218
Kunz, J. L., ix, xi, 36, 63, 70, 78
Kuper, A., 216
Kurien, P., 20
Kymlicka, W., vii, x, xi, 1, 6, 7, 11, 13, 16, 23, 24, 25, 28, 38, 47, 51, 52, 55, 56, 60, 63, 75, 82, 83, 86, 89, 98, 166, 177, 189, 190, 191, 192, 194, 195, 201, 205, 206, 209, 224

Labour Party, 172
Laegaard, S., 212
Laissez faire multiculturalism, 100–2, 148
Laviec, J. P., 23, 44
Lechner, F, 151
Leeuwen, B., ix, 36
Legrain, P., 156, 172
Lemarchand, N., 57, 64, 87
Lentin, A., vii, 8, 20, 27, 30, 53, 168, 174, 175, 185, 193, 194, 208
Levey, G., 213
Levine-Rasky, C., 9
Levitt, C., 61
Ley, D., 1, 21, 99, 193, 205
liberalism, 28
Libin, K., xi, 70
Lieberman, R., 76
Lin, E.-Y., 145
Li, P., 60, 106
Liu, J., 129, 130, 131, 138, 144
living together with differences as governance, 34–7
Lloyd, J., 208, 211
Lodge, G., 214
Longley, K., 126
Lovell, D., 158
Lupul, M., 48, 55

Maaka, R., ix, 44, 48, 61, 86, 130, 131, 138, 142, 205
McAndrews, M., 212
McClinchey, B., 186

McDonald, M., 5, 190
Mac Einri, P., 165, 166
McGarry, J., ix, 17, 38
McGauran, P., 88, 122
Mackey, E., 7, 74, 127
McKnight, D., 24
McLaren, P., 32
McRoberts, K., 65, 74, 86
Madrid, A., 30
Malik, A., 148
Malik, K., 16, 51, 171, 172, 174, 176, 177, 187, 197
Manji, I., 19
Maori, 141
    see also New Zealand
Marxism, 29–30
Massey University, 137
May, S., 7, 16, 130, 132, 134, 140
Meer, N., 165, 167, 176, 179, 184
Melbourne, H., 142
melting pot, 45, 96–7
Mendelsohn, M., 215
migration policy institute, 93
Miller, M., xi, 190
Minogue, K., 199, 210
Minority Agenda, 75–6
Mirza, M., 170, 175, 177, 178, 183
Mitchell, B., 75
Modood, T., ix, 3, 9, 10, 12, 13, 15, 16, 165, 166, 167, 176, 179, 184, 192, 202, 207, 209, 212, 213, 214, 221
Moens, A., 199
Moghaddam, F., 1
Monoculturalism, 50–1, 129–31
Moore, M., 147
Moosa, Z., 56
Morphet, J., 194
Muir, R., 181, 184
Mukherjee, A., 102
Mulroney, B., 74
multiculturalism, 1–21
    Canada vs. USA, 108–11
    contested domain, vii–ix, 1–4
    criticism of, 18–21
    demise of, vii

multiculturalism – *continued*
Europe, 192–202
governance, 23–53
models of, 13–18, 34
paradoxicality, 55–8
re-constituting multiculturalism,
203–24
religion, 213–20
society building, 189–92
theorizing of, 4–13
vs. monocultural, 50–1
Multiculturalism Act, 47, 66–7
multinationalism, 48
Munck, R., 189
Murphy, M., 86, 127
Muslims, 151, 166, 170, 188, 197–8
Musto, L., 84

Nagle, J., 21
Nana, C., 148, 159, 163
National Agenda for Multicultural
Australia, 119
Nee, V., 42
Neill, W., 14, 200
neo monoculturalism, 156–61
Netherlands, 147–63
see also Politics of Multiculturalism
New Agenda for Multicultural
Australia, 121
New Zealand, 114, 129–45
Ng, W., 97
Nugent, A., 212
Nye, M., x, 6, 13, 53, 200

O'Donnell, M., 201
Office of Ethnic Affairs, 136
Okin, S., 56, 215
O'Leary, B., ix, 17, 38
Opalska, M., 28
Orwin, C., 17, 214
O'Sullivan, D., 129, 130, 140, 141, 144

Pabst, A., 95, 148, 197, 198
Pang, D., 136, 138, 144
Panossian, R., viii, x, 50, 51, 219
Papademetriou, D. M., 169

paradoxes in governance, 39, 210–213
Parekh, B., vii, 37, 41, 44, 45, 52, 96,
110, 148, 170, 193, 196, 197, 198,
202, 205, 220
Parrillo, V., 90, 94
Pearce, N., 1, 167
Pearson, D., 13, 20, 21, 43, 57, 113, 120,
130, 132, 136
Peleg, 24, 25, 38
Pendakur, 62
Penninx, R., 149, 150, 151, 153, 154,
157, 158
Penslar, D., 60
Peres, Y., 48
Peter, K., 7, 74
Peters, W., 137
Pew Centre, 95, 151, 170
Phillips, A., 13, 168, 174, 203,
217–18, 221
Phillips, M., 153, 154, 199
Phillips, T., 166, 178, 182
Pieterse, J., 21, 155, 208, 209
pillarization, 152–3
pluralism, 47–8
pluralist dilemma, 33
Poata-Smith, E., 140
political agenda, 73–5
politics of difference, 27–34
politics of living together with
difference, 34–7
politics of multiculturalism, 187–201
Possner, M., 1
postmodernism, 30–1, 106
Povinelli, E., 127
Powel, E., 171
Prasad, R., 131
Preuhs, (of hero), 89
Prins, B., 149, 162
public perception, 84–5
Putnam, R., 37, 115, 206

Quebec, 71–3, 212
Quell, C., 5, 190

Race Relations Amendment Act, 165
Race Relations conciliator, 131, 134

Racial Discrimination Act, 118
Ramadan, T., 8, 218, 220
Ravich, D., 91
Razack, S., 61
Rea, A., 147, 149, 158, 162, 163, 181, 183
reasonable accommodation, 72, 79–82
re-constituting multiculturalism, 203–24
Reitman, O., 11, 215
Reitz, J., 46, 89
religion, 213–20
rethinking governance, 203–24
Rex, J., x, 1, 6, 47, 51
Rhodes, R. A. W, 49, 50
Road, F. H., 160, 169
Robbins, J., 20
Robinson, A., xi
Rubinstein, A., 207, 208, 209, 210
Rudd, K., 128
Rummel, R. J., 40, 41
Rundblad, G., 92
Rutter, J., 168, 170, 184, 185

Sacks, J., 51, 183, 206, 208
Saharso, S., 149, 162, 203
Saint Louis, B., 33
Salee, D., 53, 212
Samuel, T., 57
Sandercock, L, x, 9, 35, 224
Sardar, Z., 209
Satzewich, V., 39
Saul, J. R., 55
Saunders, B., 165, 194
Schachuber, D., 57
Schain, 96, 97
Scheider, P., 90
Schlesinger, A., 6, 99
Scholten, P., 155, 160, 161
Schwedler, H.-U., 14, 200
Schwimmer, E., 138
Scott, J., 51
segregation, 43–4
Seidle, L, 94, 95, 151, 152, 157, 159, 163, 169, 170

Seiler, T., 69
Seljak, D., 74, 213
Sen, A., 14, 33, 181, 198
separation, 44
    see also segregation
Seuffert, N., 131, 132, 139
Shabani, O. P., 14, 38
Shachar, A., 23, 25, 214, 216
Shohat, E., 5
Siapara, E., 36
Sibley, C. G., 129, 130, 131, 138, 144
Siddiqui, H., 2, 21, 57, 194, 217
Sides, J., 39, 192
Singham, M., 134
Singh, G., x, 1, 6, 47, 51
Sivananadan, A., 174
Slijper, B., 159
Smith, M. G., 200
Sniderman, P., 10, 37, 149, 150, 152, 153, 154, 156, 161, 202
Somerville, W., 167, 169, 171, 184
Song, S., 215, 217
Soroka, S., 11, 38
Spoonley, P., 2, 13, 48, 129, 130, 132, 133, 134, 137, 140
Squires, J., 10, 181, 214, 217
Sriskandarajah, D., 168, 169, 170
Stam, R, 5
Statistics Canada, 58–60
Stein, J., 11, 16, 53, 208, 213, 216, 221
Stevenson, W., 220, 221
Stoffman, D., 86
Stoker, G., 49
Stratton, J., 98, 118, 193
Stuart, I., 138, 140
Sturgess, G., 51
Sunahara, A., 4, 60
Swerdlow, J., 97
Sykes, S., ix, xi, 36, 63, 70, 127, 153, 154, 156, 167, 174, 180

Taras, R., 40
Tate, J., 121
Tator, C., 62, 76, 107
Taylor, C., 9, 16, 38, 107, 108, 213

Teicher, J., 115
Te Puni Kokiri, 140
Terkessides, M., 12
theorizing governance, 49–53
Thobani, S., 7, 19, 20, 61, 64, 74, 87,
    102, 105, 187
Tierney, S., 24, 223, 224
Tiriyakian, E., 39, 105
Titley, G., vii, 8, 20, 27, 30, 53, 168,
    174, 175, 185, 194, 208
Toronto Terror Crisis, 188
Treaty of Waitangi, 130, 138, 139
Triandafyllidou, A., viii, 201, 202
Trlin, A., 129
Trudeau, P. E., 63
Tsasis, P., 52
Turner, B., 19

Uberoi, V., 177
Ucarer, E., 7, 190
Uitermark, J., 12, 17
United States, 80, 89–111
    see also Critical Multiculturalism
Universal Declaration of Human
    Rights, 53

Valpy, M., 85
van de Vijver, F. J. R., 148, 149
Vang, Z., 89
Vasta, E., 12, 128, 148, 150, 152, 155,
    162, 167, 171, 176, 182, 183, 193
Vertovec, S., 106, 168, 172, 184, 185,
    206, 212

Vertovec, S., 172, 206, 212
Vincour, J., 199
Vink, M., 148, 149, 152, 153, 154,
    155, 157

Waitangi Tribunal, 138–9
Walker, J., 44, 60
Walker, R., 138
Wallis, M., 8, 44, 61
Ward, C., 145
Ward, K., 26, 49
Waters, I., 185, 186
Waters, M., 89
Watt, P., 23
Weinfeld, M., 61
Wente, M., 79
Werbner, P., 9, 192
Wessendorf, S., 172, 206, 212
West, C., 18, 31
West, P., 91
Wieviorka, M., 99
Willett, C., 4, 13
Wirten, P., 187
women and multiculturalism,
    215–18
Wood, P., 57, 74

Yan, C., 115
Yates, J, 33
Yo'er, B., 158
Young, A., 132

Zick, A., 194